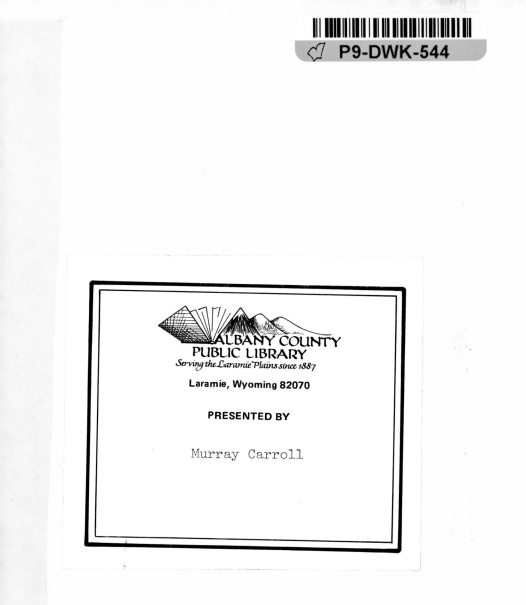

LONE VOYAGERS

LONE VOYAGERS

Academic Women in
Coeducational Universities
1870–1937

Edited by
Geraldine Jonçich Clifford

The Feminist Press
at The City University of New York
New York

Published 1989 by The Feminist Press at The City University of New York, 311 East 94 Street, New York, N.Y. 10128

Distributed by The Talman Company, 150 Fifth Avenue, New York, N.Y. 10011

Printed in the United States of America

92 91 90 89 5 4 3 2 1

Library of Congress Cataloging-in-Publication Data

Lone voyagers: academic women in coeducational universities, 1870–1937 / edited by Geraldine Jonçich Clifford.
    p. cm.
    Includes bibliographies.
    ISBN 0-935312-84-6: $29.95.—ISBN 0-935312-85-4 (pbk.): $12.95
    1. Women college teachers—United States—Biography. 2. Women college teachers—Canada—Biography. 3. Coeducation—United States—History—19th century. 4. Coeducation—United States—History—20th century. I. Clifford, Geraldine Jonçich.
LA2311.L66   1989
378.1′2′082—dc20   89–31878
                                                                            CIP

Cover photos: top, Lucy Diggs Slowe, courtesy of the Moorland-Springarn Research Center, Howard University; bottom, Grace Raymond Hebard with a student, courtesy of the Archives of the American Heritage Center, University of Wyoming.

Text design: Melodie Wertelet

This publication is made possible, in part, by funds from the New York State Council on the Arts. The Feminist Press at CUNY also gratefully acknowledges the gifts of Barbara Sicherman and of an anonymous woman donor toward the publication of this book. The anonymous contribution is made in honor of Ursula Schwerin, president of New York City Technical College, 1978–1988, "a woman who moves mountains."

For Katie

"She was sensible and clever, but eager in everything; her sorrows, her joys, could have no moderation. She was generous, amiable, interesting: she was everything . . ."

JANE AUSTEN
Sense and Sensibility

Contents

Preface

In her 1981 mystery novel, *Death in a Tenured Position*, Amanda Cross constructs a scene in which the fictitious first woman professor of English at Harvard University is interviewed by a woman reporter from the student newspaper. The reporter articulates women students' need for women teachers: "Professor Mandelbaum, it matters a lot to us serious women students to have a new role model like you. We study here, we pay the same as the men, we work as hard, we get better grades, but when we look up at the faculty, there are hardly any women." Professor Janet Mandelbaum, however, needs to believe that her Harvard appointment has come *only* because she is an outstanding expert on seventeenth-century literature. The reporter recalls being rebuffed with the statement that she and other women students "could go to women's colleges if that was what we wanted." Professor Mandelbaum, for her part, "never wanted to hear the phrase 'role model' again."

As most admirers of the pseudonymous Amanda Cross now know, *Death in a Tenured Position* was written by a woman professor of English at Columbia University, Carolyn Heilbrun, who reflects knowingly on the dilemmas facing many academic women. Terms like "role model," "affirmative action," and "token women" would, however, be unfamiliar to the pioneer women profiled in *Lone Voyagers*. The concepts are products of modern consciousness and of recent programs to open opportunities to underrepresented groups. Yet, in 1910 an alumna of the University of Wisconsin, Helen Olin, understood what "role model" implies, without needing the term. She wrote:

> The men who are trying to manage the large coeducational institutions are in danger of becoming warped in judgment and crippled in execution, from being deprived of advice and direction which is sympathetic with the best interests of fully one-half their students. The women among the students lose the stimulus of association with the ideal toward which they are striving. The student men, especially those among them who think that they can be well taught only by men, have not the advantage of the proper perspective in intellectual life.[2]

There were also early efforts to intervene in the academic marketplace, to pressure institutions to employ more women faculty and treat them more equitably. The campaigns of the American Association of Collegiate Alumnae and the National Association of Deans of Women are examples. The idea of tokenism was also present among the academic officials who stated to the investigative committee on women of the American Association of University Professors in the 1920s that it might be necessary or important to have one woman on the faculty, but that one was sufficient.

The portraits of the seven women featured in this volume, all "lone voyagers," present a means of understanding the significance of the women who have taught in coeducational universities in the United States and Canada. They were a vanguard, trying to erase prevailing beliefs that women faculty indeed might never "belong" in institutions so long the exclusive preserve of male professors teaching male students. The women who followed these pioneers have faced many of the same besetting problems, experiencing similar feelings of grudging acceptance, buoyed by occasional male allies and by their students. The Introduction places these seven academic women in a broad framework, analyzing the lines of continuity and change in the situations of women faculty from 1870, when Maria Sanford was hired by Swarthmore College as a professor of history, to 1937, when Theresa McMahon retired from the University of Washington and Lucy Diggs Slowe's career at Howard University was cut short by her death. The biographies and documents that follow sensitively delineate each woman's individual character and situation. The Introduction, therefore, endeavors to present a context so that the reader may better recognize both the representativeness and the individuality of these lone voyagers. The book's aim is to recognize the rare distinction of these women's careers, however, more than to generalize.

While academic women have been ignored by most historians and biographers, the silence about early women in coeducational institutions is especially pronounced. They lacked the supportive colleagueship that might come with numbers—the "critical mass" of women teachers found in most women's colleges, for example. Most did not become the full professors and "academic power brokers" on their campuses, but survived as untenured assistant professors or "irregular" faculty. Moreover, most women faculty in the United States were confined to lower-status institutions: in normal schools and their successor institutions, the state teachers' colleges; junior and community colleges; public colleges and universities of lesser rank; and little-known church-sponsored colleges.

This anthology, then, reveals something of the institutions as well as the faculty usually omitted from historical surveys. Only Clelia Mosher (Stanford University) and Marion Talbot (University of Chicago) were located at universities that are invariably part of the recounted story of American higher education. The others taught at a public university for blacks (Howard University), at remote and provincial state universities (the Universities of Wyoming, Minnesota, and Washington), at an important Canadian institution (McGill University) unfamiliar even to specialists in the United States; or at a struggling Quaker college (Swarthmore). Our women are unusual in including one engineering graduate, two physicians, and an economist. But the far more common experience of women working in and around "women's fields" is also represented.

The authors of the biographical portraits of these seven academic women have selected documents that allow each woman to speak for herself—to reveal the range of her own scholarly and public interests, and the institutional challenges she confronted. In most cases aspects of the "woman question" bulked large in their thoughts and actions. A dedicated scientist, Clelia Mosher made gender questions a major theme in her research and teaching. Grace Hebard was a vocal suffragist, Maude Abbott a quiet one. Maria Sanford became one only after decades of struggle to assert herself. As deans of women as well as professors, Lucy Slowe and Marion Talbot struggled with institutional expectations that made women a sex apart. Maude Abbott left an autobiography that details the steps by which she acquired medical training and ultimately a position on the McGill medical faculty; if anything it understates the frustrations and lack of appreciation that she must have felt. In her old age and sightless, Theresa McMahon dictated fascinating recollections of experiences that led her from her days as a sixteen-year-old "subfreshman," through graduate study in the slums of Chicago, to a career of teaching labor economics, her appointment delayed by her sex and political liberalism. Despite the regional diversity they would have brought to this collection, it was the absence of personal writings that has excluded important early women professors in southern co-educational universities from this anthology. For example, neither Jo-belle Holcombe of the University of Arkansas nor Sarah Isom of the University of Mississippi left us her writings. Hence, a special effort was made in the Introduction to consider the situation of academic women in the South.

With the exception of Maria Sanford, the women featured in this collection were born in the second half of the nineteenth century—a time of potentially great opportunity for careers in college teaching, given the nearly ninefold multiplication of student enrollments that occurred in the United States between 1850 and 1900. Census data report an increase of professors from 943 to 7,272 during those fifty years, making college teaching one of the fastest growing professions. Faculty numbers at America's oldest college, Harvard, went from 23 to 545. As a private men's school, Harvard would not hire women teachers, as might a coeducational, public institution like the University of Michigan, whose faculty expanded from 11 to 210 in the same period; yet only five women were appointed to Michigan's regular faculty positions before 1900.[3] Certain less presitgious and smaller state universities, like South Dakota and Wyoming, offered women more opportunities. The Introduction provides an overview of the numbers and distribution of women in the professoriate.

The sources of assistance to women scholars and the sense of a sisterhood of professionalism are far better developed today than they were for the lone voyagers. The publication of this volume testifies to a widely shared determination to participate in the recovery from oblivion of women in the history of higher education. Our deep appreciation is extended to all who helped in this endeavor.

Notes

1. Amanda Cross, *Death in a Tenured Position* (New York: Ballantine Books, 1981), p. 103.

2. Helen, R. Olin, *The Women of a State University* (New York: G. P. Putnam's Sons, 1910), p. 297.

3. Alan Creutz, "Social Access to the Professoriate: The Pattern of Late Nineteenth Century America" (Unpublished paper, American Historical Association Annual Meeting, San Francisco, December 1978), pp. 1, 26, 29.

LONE VOYAGERS

Introduction

by Geraldine Jonçich Clifford

The current status of women's academic employment is fairly well known because of organized investigations of inequities in hiring, retention, and promotion and continuous monitoring by women's caucuses in institutions and scholarly organizations. The American Association of University Professors (AAUP), for example, now annually reports comparative rank and salary data for men and women. Its past performance was less helpful: After issuing a landmark report in the 1920s, its Committee W, on the Status of Women in College and University Faculties, went out of business for half a century.

Comparing the situations of academic women in different periods is also made difficult by changing definitions of what constitutes post-secondary education and by variations in how data were gathered by the United States Bureau of Education. Thus, it is unclear whether women's share of faculty positions actually declined during the 1930s, or whether women continued to be hired but in more tenuous positions.[1] Recalculations make it appear that women's share of positions reached and maintained its peak during the period from 1920 through 1946, when women held between 28 and 31 percent of faculty positions.[2]

Like the Civil War, World War I opened more employment to women in predominantly male fields; academic employment was no exception. A graduate of Newnham College, one of the two women's colleges of Cambridge University in England, recalled how depletion of the faculty in 1917 caused the head of the physiology department to

1

ask her to demonstrate laboratory techniques and to hire the first woman assistant.[3] Maude Abbott received a wartime offer that would have given her a regular faculty appointment. On the other hand, that same war aroused so much anti-German feeling in the United States that Theresa Schmid McMahon felt that she had to take a leave from the University of Washington to hide herself in research three thousand miles from her home. Nor did women always retain the positions opened to them by a temporary, wartime suspension of gender rules.

A persisting characteristic of women's academic employment has been the uneven distribution of women among different kinds of institutions. The women's colleges and other institutions that educated a preponderance of women, such as the public and private normal schools that trained teachers, employed most faculty women in this period. Lucille Pollard was able to identify so many academic women in the nineteenth century only because she generously included, as colleges, many southern institutions which, despite their names and charters, were female seminaries and finishing schools.

In the same vein, academic women were concentrated in fewer disciplines than were their male counterparts—although there was probably no field where no woman was present. The great majority of women faculty were found in the "service" professional schools, notably education, social welfare, librarianship, and nursing, and in departments of home economics, foreign languages, English, nutrition, health, and women's physical education.[4]

Feminism, Women's Culture, and Academe

The dissolution of organized feminism after female suffrage was achieved is often blamed for diminishing the passion for independence and career that motivated earlier women to demand higher education and fight for positions "outside of woman's sphere." A 1922 graduate of Newnham College remembered women students being "accepted, even if sometimes considered rather odd."

> But, whatever still remained to do to put the [women's] College . . . entirely in its proper place in the University, at our level as students the anti-feminism with which earlier generations had had to contend had disappeared completely. My contemporaries were for the most part hardly aware that it had ever existed. In my second year the principal speaker at our annual Commemoration Dinner . . . chose as her theme "The kingdom of heaven is to the violent and the violent take it by force," and round this

she wove a rousing, fighting speech of the kind which ten years earlier would have brought her audience shouting to their feet. We received it in silence, profoundly shocked. It seemed such dreadfully bad form.[5]

Rosalind Rosenberg suggests that in achieving a modicum of success in the "man's world" of the university, women graduate students and faculty cut themselves off from other women and their networks, without being able to establish new support systems. "Women academics came to identify more fully with their professional than with their sexual status," even though their professional associations continued to be male dominated and sexist.[6]

The battle was far from won. In *The Women of a State University,* published in 1910 to try to counter a movement to restrict women in American higher education, Helen Olin commented on prevailing attitudes about women's graduate education:

It would be recommended as generally useful in [teaching in] high schools, normal schools, and even women's colleges. It would be acceptable in infinitesimal quantities in higher coeducational institutions providing a woman would do a man's work for one half his salary, in a position giving no authority or influence in the control of the department.[7]

To the extent, then, that women students chose to study or teach in colleges instead of normal schools, and in coeducational instead of women's colleges, they were abandoning the very institutions that had the best records in employing academic women.

In one of the earliest surveys of women teaching in state colleges and universities, the author hypothesized why, in 1912, western institutions had more women than did eastern and southern schools: The thinly settled states were poor and it was cheaper to hire women.[8] As individual colleges and universities prospered, their willingness to hire women faculty often declined. When Swarthmore College was a new institution, and Maria Sanford taught there, nearly 40 percent of its faculty were women; by 1940 their percentage was halved.[9] A coeducational institution for black students, Fisk University, which opened in Nashville in 1866 offering secondary-level work, employed fourteen women (70 percent of the faculty) in 1890 and twelve women (20 percent) in 1961.[10]

More is known about faculty women in elite women's colleges because of these institutions' greater visibility in the nineteenth-century women's movement, their higher social status, and their clustering of women faculty into a relatively sizable group. The all-woman faculty at early Wellesley College has been studied and the nature of its collective culture analyzed, along with the factors propelling these women into college teaching.[11] A small number of biographies and autobiographies of academic women exist to be mined for information on factors like sponsorship and networking. For example, Lucy Salmon was hired at Vassar in 1887 on the recommendation of Dr. Eliza Mosher, who had known her as a student at the University of Michigan.[12] Alumnae of elite women's colleges were probably overrepresented in the American Association of Collegiate Alumnae (the precursor of the American Association of University Women). This organization was important in the network, bringing together, for example, Alice Freeman Palmer and Marion Talbot, both of whom joined the faculty of the University of Chicago when it opened in 1892.

Despite their lack of endowment to support research and graduate education, women's colleges exercised a disproportionate influence on the situations of academic women, especially in science. In 1921 they employed 40 percent of women scientists with academic appointments.[13] Like the men's colleges, the prominent women's colleges recruited among their graduates to fill faculty positions.[14] But the need was all the greater since women, especially in science and other "nonfeminine" fields, were greatly handicapped in getting employment in coeducational institutions and were almost never chosen by the men's colleges. So many women doctorates were unemployed or underemployed that even the deans of women in the well-known women's colleges held that degree, before it was commonplace among male faculty in American higher education.[15] Not surprisingly, therefore, it was only in the women's colleges that one could consistently expect to find women as presidents, academic deans, and registrars.[16]

Thus, the well-being of academic women in the nineteenth and twentieth centuries was closely tied to the fate of the women's colleges. The trend of student enrollments was, however, strongly toward coeducation. In 1870 fewer than half the female college students in the United States were in coeducational institutions; by 1890 it was 70 percent and still rising. Between 1872 and 1910, the number of women's colleges declined from 175 to 110.[17] Women's colleges, which comprised 20 percent of all institutions in 1890, were 8 percent by 1970.[18] Surviving women's colleges often responded to coeducation by bringing more men to the faculty and filling the important positions with males; women faculty began to cluster in the junior ranks. Agnes Scott College, the first college in Georgia to be accredited by the Southern Association of Colleges for Women illustrates this phenomenon. In

1895, women comprised 88 percent of the faculty; by the mid-1930s their proportion was 75 percent.[19]

While attending the University of Michigan in 1874, a future Vassar professor, Lucy Salmon, wrote an open letter to her pastor protesting his sermon on women's sphere; it was a statement on behalf of coeducation:

> If little children study together at their mother's knee, if the brother and sister go to the same school, at high school together, who shall draw the dividing line and say, that for these four years of college life they shall be separated? If a girl has no special capacity for music and the fine arts but desires to excel in study must she on account of her sex, fritter away her time on something for which she cares nothing while her brother with less capability enjoys the highest intellectual advantages?[20]

Whatever the respective merits of single-sex study as compared to coeducation, the fact was that the future of academic women would be increasingly determined by their ability to enter and advance in coeducational colleges and universities. Between 1870 and 1957, the percentage of all institutions that admitted both sexes rose from 29 to 74 percent, and such places enrolled over 90 percent of all college women.[21] Susan Carter calculates that the changing institutional mix within the college and university system—notably the demise of normal schools and most women's colleges—accounts for some two-thirds of the change between 1900 and 1940 in the proportion that women represented in the professoriate.[22]

There were two geographical holdouts to the coeducation movement in the United States. One was the Northeast, where a few institutions with strong connections to social and economic elites were able to persist and profit from excluding women students. The other was the South, where two principal factors explain the survival of many sex-segregated colleges and universities for whites. One was the hold of traditional ideals about genteel womanhood—ideals best nurtured in female seminaries, finishing schools, and women's colleges. Since these ideals were not extended to blacks, most black women who have gone on to secondary schooling have attended coeducational colleges. The second was the fact of the differential effects of the Civil War. It closed most southern institutions while in the North it merely depleted them of many of their male students, encouraging the institutions to accept women in order to survive. After the war it was impossible to dislodge female students and, finding that their presence did not damage the institutions but, in fact, gave them greater financial security, most other northern colleges adopted coeducation.[23] Consequently, except for Roman Catholic schools, very few new single-sex colleges were founded outside of the South.

Of institutions like Mary Baldwin Seminary in Virginia, and Lucy Cobb Institute and Agnes Scott College in Georgia, it was noted that many parents enrolled their daughters in the confidence that such schools "would instill in the girls the gracious values of the antebellum southern lady."[24] Gentility overwhelmed academic values. In 1913 the annual meeting of the Association of Colleges and Secondary Schools in the Southern States heard that the bachelor's degrees offered by thirty-eight southern women's colleges were approximately "equivalent to one year of college work," and the degrees of fifty-eight others did "not apparently represent any standard work at all."[25] Whether teaching in women's or coeducational schools, southern faculty women were held to codes of conduct fitting the "southern lady" image. [26] Not surprisingly southern institutions lagged behind in expecting women faculty to hold the Ph.D.[27] In private southern universities, women with doctorates barely outnumbered those with only a bachelor's degree.

Mathematician Dr. Jewell Hughes was an example of a southern woman academic who came to believe that scant opportunity existed in her homeland to gain appropriate recognition and salary. She evidently agreed with her friend Jobelle Holcombe, since 1901 a member of the University of Arkansas English department, that "if a woman has any ambition she can't stay here—unless she teaches home economics." President Futrall was on record as saying higher mathematics was a man's field and required a masculine approach. When Hughes and Holcombe were promoted to associate professorships in 1927, Holcombe thought "that was the end, for both of us."[28] Hughes left in 1930 for Hunter College in New York (then a women's college) where she headed the mathematics department. Holcombe was promoted to professor in 1941, the year before her retirement—repeating the experience of Maria Sanford and Clelia Mosher, among others.

Although the earliest state universities in the United States were founded in the South, their acceptance of women came late: In 1910 only five were coeducational. While the University of Mississippi led in the admission of women in 1882, and hired Sarah Isom as its first woman instructor in 1885, the University of North Carolina waited until 1927 to appoint a woman to the regular faculty: Sallie B. Marks, assistant professor of elementary education.[29] Of the eleven southern state universities from Kentucky to Texas in 1910, six had no women on the faculty—at a time when women comprised, nationally, about 10 percent of the faculties of state universities.[30] Gradually the regional average caught up with the national figure, however, and the prospects for southern academic women came to resemble those of faculty women generally.

How Academic Women Entered the Coeducational Institutions

In the later years of the nineteenth century the larger academic institutions in the United States were only beginning to take on some of the characteristics of bureaucracies. In today's more dominant bureaucratic framework, administrative staffs are increasingly drawn from outside the professoriate; nontraditional in attitude, they are more attentive to fiscal, legal, and public relations concerns. Such administrators are, in theory, more "neutral" than are professors about the threat that women faculty might pose to institutional "character" and ethos. The larger and more varied teaching loads that women carry and the greater likelihood of their employability as flexible part-time and irregular faculty, as well as the inconvenience that comes from government inquiries about affirmative action, together make professional administrators less inclined to keep the college or university an exclusive men's club. Such calculations have not generally animated the faculty, however, and male professors long dominated the processes whereby new members are sought out, nominated, and reviewed for hiring and promotion.

Academic employment operated in what is called an internal market: Faculty positions were held by current incumbents with openings reserved to persons with qualifications not widely found in the general labor pool, especially among women and many ethnic minorities. Unlike most internal markets, where selection criteria were quite explicit, the academic market operated with vague rules and unsystematic procedures that derive from custom and that stress "general competencies sought rather than specific behavior actually required for the job"; its "uncodified, unspecific and highly variable" standards for entry and promotion were most perilous to underrepresented groups.[31] The formal criteria of competence in teaching and research might qualify women; the informal criteria of "collegiality" and "fitting in" could exclude them. The nineteenth-century preference for faculty and college presidents who were Yale graduates, or who were sponsored by them, exemplifies a custom that effectively excluded women, since Yale College remained an all-male institution until 1969.

Such "old-boy networks" are believed by their members to protect institutions from taking overly large risks and making mistakes that will reflect badly on an institution's prestige or, where it has little prestige, cause embarrassment if a faculty member must be "let go."[32] Knowing someone in and having prior relations with a hiring department are major elements in the relatively closed system of faculty selection that characterized academe, especially in the more prestigious schools. In the words of the authors of a major study of faculty hiring and mobility, "Women tend to be discriminated against in the academic profession, not because they have low prestige but because they are outside the prestige system entirely and for this reason are of no use to a department in future recruitment."[33]

Institutions have long recruited faculty disproportionately from among their alumni, even with the rise of national labor markets and the existence of a small elite of important graduate schools to channel faculty mobility. Theresa McMahon gained from being an alumna of the University of Washington and being acquainted with the faculty. She lost out to a man, however, who was also known; only later were scruples about her sex and her suspect interest in labor issues overcome, and she was hired in 1911. Bacteriologist Mary E. Caldwell had both a Chicago doctorate and the advantage of being an alumna of the University of Arizona to ease her way at Tucson.[34] A researcher examining faculty conditions in four colleges—Bucknell, Franklin and Marshall, Princeton, and Swarthmore—between 1870 and 1915 concluded that "The emphasis upon institutional and religious affiliations rather than external standards of scholarship, reflected the expectation that faculty members would be subservient to the local and denominational authorities." Thus, President McCosh of Princeton encouraged talented undergraduates to pursue graduate studies in order to return as faculty, accommodating the preference for alumni to the new demands for specialization. A president of Bucknell University hired over 80 percent alumni, explaining that "the best men for us [are] our own men" since it took outsiders years to demonstrate the appropriate institutional loyalty.[35] Another study of the phenomenon of "ingroup membership" in academic hiring found that 43 percent of all outside faculty appointments at Indiana University from 1885 to 1937 were Indiana alumni, and one of five appointees had some kind of family connection with the university.[36]

Women were less numerous than men among the graduates of coeducational colleges and universities, and to some male professors, presidents, and trustees they seemed the ultimate outsiders. How, then, did women break into the faculties of U.S. coeducational institutions? In brief, many entered through the creation of a separate, gender-based labor market. In what follows we will see that *resistance* to academic women was weakest where positions could be justified as woman's work: restricted to dealing with women students and their "special problems," or in roles requiring women's "unique talents," or segregated in "female departments." Margaret Rossiter calls this the *territorial* form of academic sex segregation, as distinguished from the *hierarchical* kind where women are employed as subordinates to male scholars.[37]

Employment by Student Demography

In both public and private universities a direct relationship exists between the relative presence of women in the student body and the numbers and ranks of faculty women.[38] The Demia Butler Chair was established in 1869 as a memorial to the first woman graduate of Butler University in Kansas; by it, Ovid Butler intended also "to give emphatic recognition of the rights of woman to occupy any position for which she was qualified."[39] Historically the entry of appreciable numbers of women into coeducational institutions or into particular departments exerted pressure to engage one or more female faculty. Oberlin College pioneered in proposing in 1834 that young lady students needed to be supervised by a "judicious lady" who was also to be given a faculty appointment; for years the incumbent, the only woman on the faculty, implored the trustees to hire more women faculty, consistent with increases in female students.[40] In 1891 the Association for the Advancement of Women received a report on the discrepancy between women's presence as students and their near-total absence on U.S. faculties.[41] In 1892 its Association of Alumni petitioned the University of Illinois: "That in view of the fact of the large number of girls in attendance at the University each year, we recommend to the Trustees that a representative woman be made a member of the faculty." Katharine Merrill was subsequently hired as assistant professor of English literature.[42]

Fields like English, the modern foreign languages, history, and later the social sciences and psychology attracted numbers of women students—in part because these fields led directly to teaching positions in the fast-growing world of high schools. Male students, however, were by 1900 beginning to think of higher education as providing explicit training for business, engineering, and the male-dominated professions. As a result women became, by default, the majority of students in the humanities. Thus, women's appearance on the faculty in response to the presence of women students can be explained as the result of changes in student demography, or as employment by "gender example": women teaching women. The principle in academia resembled that which asserted that women patients had a right to women physicians—and which, between 1850 and 1890, helped open the then-weak medical profession to women.[43]

The United States Bureau of Education first requested information about the gender of faculty in men's and coeducational institutions in 1890, and in normal schools and teachers' colleges in 1900—accepting the premise that academic women were no longer found exclusively in women's colleges. The appearance of "one or two lady teachers to guide feminine activities" in the men's colleges that admitted women during and after the Civil War caused 1,083 women (or about 14 percent of college and university faculties) to be employed in 1890—compared to the 1,648 located in the women's colleges.[44] This widening of women's opportunities means that colleges might admit women as students long before they hired some as instructors. Bates College in Maine opened in 1863 as a coeducational school and employed its first faculty woman in 1901: Caroline Emily Libby, dean of women and professor of Romance languages.[45]

Some institutions tried to respond to the "special needs" of women students—or to some inner sense that the sex-role identity of women students must be reconfirmed—by enlisting the wives of male faculty and respectable townswomen in lieu of employing women faculty. Such a Woman's League operated at the University of Michigan from 1890 until 1896. An organization of faculty wives and faculty women, the Association of Ladies of the Faculty, long functioned at the University of Kansas as advisers and social mentors to women students.[46]

Since women's schools always employed women faculty, the merger of a men's with a women's college was another way for academic women to appear in coeducation. This happened when Evanston College for Ladies became part of Northwestern University in 1873. The college's president, Frances Willard—later to become famous as head of the multi-purpose feminist organization, the Women's Christian Temperance Union—became professor of aesthetics and dean of the Women's College, responsible for the morals, health, and manners of the women of Northwestern. A successor, Emily Huntington Miller, was assistant professor of English literature and principal of the Women's College.

As for the men's colleges, their position was clearly stated when the AAUP's Committee W, on the Status of Women in College and University Faculties, conducted surveys around 1920. Several responded that they did not employ academic women "as we are not coeducational."[47] Furthermore, the imposition of formal or disguised quotas for women students at coeducational institutions—such as happened at private Stanford and Cornell Universities and public Pennsylvania State University and the University of North Carolina—ensured that this demographic claim on behalf of employing academic women would be held in check.

Employment through Transfer—or "Promotion"

Published numbers of "faculty women" were not always reliable indicators of the opening of college teaching as a profession for women, especially before 1920. Substantial proportions of the first women employed by the women's colleges and coeducational institutions were a subfaculty of part-time teachers whose principal duties were disciplinary and social. They held titles like "matron," "lady principal," "preceptress," "women's medical examiner," and "dean of women"; the last-named position came to be nearly universally found in coeducational schools. Institutional concern with women students' housing or their health or social adjustment and the cheaper costs in employing women meant that supervisory positions were created that were reserved for women. Such women might, then, be granted faculty status as well. In some instances this meant no more than being listed under "faculty" in the college catalogue. In many cases, however, the result was an "academic hybrid of 'women's work' ": women faculty chosen for or partially assigned to nonclassroom duties directed at women students.[48] Marion Talbot was an example: Brought to Chicago in 1892 to be assistant dean of women and assistant professor of sanitary science, she was more visible as dean than in her professorial role. Such entry into the faculty can be understood as employment by transfer or promotion, in that a number of such women were eventually able to become full-time faculty if they chose. The careers of Dr. Clelia Mosher, Grace Hebard, and Maria Sanford illustrate variants of that process.

The dozens of women students at the University of California at Berkeley in the 1880s had become hundreds by 1891. That year a group of "co-eds" approached a woman physician practicing in Berkeley, asking that she give them the physical examination necessary to participate in the gymnastics that the men took for granted.[49] After two years of volunteered service, Dr. Mary Bennett Ritter was paid by the only woman member of the board of regents, Mrs. Phoebe Hearst, who next financed the building of a women's gymnasium. The position of woman medical examiner thus became established. Dr. Ritter became a faculty member because the students, by then 46 percent of the undergraduates, asked her, the only professional woman at the university, to offer lectures on personal hygiene and home sanitation. These quickly evolved into a course required for women students, until Dr. Ritter resigned her part-time post shortly after the turn of the century and left Berkeley with her faculty husband. This was "the wedge which opened the way for the grafting of several strong branches onto the old university tree," she recorded in her autobiography, along with the telling observation that

> I was considered a sort of pariah in the University. The innovation of an unwelcome course pushed into the fringe of the orthodox curriculum by scarcely acceptable women students, caused some resentment in the faculty when the work was considered worthy of any notice at all.[50]

After Ritter resigned no other woman was appointed to the faculty until 1904, when the second woman to receive a Berkeley Ph.D., Jessica Peixotto, was hired as a full-time lecturer in social economics. In 1905 she was joined by Lucy Sprague, who was promoted from reader in economics and English to instructor in English and assistant adviser to students on becoming Berkeley's first dean of women. In 1918 Peixotto was the first woman promoted to full professor rank at the University of California.[51]

A woman hired to direct women's use of a college gymnasium or to take charge of physical training was often one of the earliest of faculty women; she would be asked to instruct in physical culture, hygiene, or physiology as well as to administer the gymnastics program or coach women's team sports. In 1885, in response to a petition from "lady students" for "an amount of gymnastic training that will be an equivalent for the military drill that is provided for gentlemen," the Regents of the University of Nebraska paid Minnie Cochran for instruction in calisthenics. A male instructor in physical training for women was hired in 1891, but when the course was made compulsory in 1892, the university decided to find a woman instructor to give examinations and to lecture in physiology and hygiene. Women students hired as gymnasium assistants were often the source of future faculty, as in the case of Anne Barr, who became Nebraska's director of women's physical education in 1895.[52] The University of Kansas had such a woman instructor by 1894. The completion of a women's gymnasium at the University of Michigan in 1896 provoked the hiring of Dr. Eliza M. Mosher; brought in to direct the physical education work for women and be their medical examiner, she was given the titles of professor of hygiene and dean of women.

In like manner, librarians were sometimes given part-time faculty titles. Rosamund Parma (J.D., 1919) was law librarian and secretary of the School of Jurisprudence at the University of California at Berkeley when, in 1922, she was also made lecturer in legal bibliography.[53] But the emergence of the post of dean of women had the most consistent effect in bringing more women into the professional community at co-educational colleges and universities, and in allowing most of them eventually to hold faculty as well as administrative status. In 1874 President Gregory recommended to the trustees of the Illinois Industrial University (later the University of Illinois) that a preceptress to the female students would be doubly useful if she could "open and direct the studies in the School of Domestic Economy"; both the position and a new curriculum were thus established.[54] When Cornell changed the post of lady principal of Sage College (the women's dormitory) to that of warden in 1896, the incumbent became a member of the faculty. This development has been called "the first recognition at Cornell University of women's right to teach, as well as learn."[55]

Writing on behalf of the American Association of Collegiate Alumnae's accreditation committee in 1913, the University of Chicago's dean of women, Marion Talbot, recommended that coeducational colleges give the dean of women both regular faculty rank above that of instructor and the opportunity to teach.[56] A 1911 study of fifty-five institutions found forty-four having deans of women; most of the positions were established in the previous decade and already gave their incumbents at least nominal faculty status. A more comprehensive survey, published in 1928, found a dean of women present in 93 percent of the institutions enrolling women. Three-quarters of the deans had faculty appointments, and 71 percent actually taught.[57] It was probably the case, however, that most male administrators, like President Wheeler of the University of California at Berkeley, considered a dean's teaching position much the less important part of her duties, the professorship being only a strategy to recruit or retain an able administrator.[58]

When President Finney of Oberlin College responded to an inquiry from the University of Michigan in 1858 about handling coeducation, he specified that "You will need a wise and pious matron with such lady assistants as to keep up sufficient supervision."[59] Such pioneers in the education of women were animated by the need to protect women's reputations in an arena where they were not welcomed. In the words of the principal of Newnham College, Cambridge, there was so much suspicion of women students in Britain that "if any inconvenience followed from their being there, or if any individual among them deviated in the slightest degree from the ordinary standards of society, it would be considered as a complete justification of this attitude."[60] While much antisocial or unconventional behavior was tolerated among British and American male students, the "co-eds" were subjected to intense scrutiny and quick condemnation. The entrapment of the deanships of women in a discriminatory social system was more than some incumbents could tolerate. Psychologist Margaret Washburn found her work as warden of Sage College at Cornell "highly uncongenial" and was grateful when the University of Cincinnati and then Vassar College offered her professorships.[61]

The position of dean of women permitted women to move more readily than otherwise possible from one to another institution or from the faculty into the administration. Violet Jayne, whose graduate studies included work at the University of Zürich, moved from heading departments of English in normal schools to become dean of women and professor of English at the University of Illinois in 1897.[62] Margaret Washburn taught at Wells College before going to Cornell in 1900 where she doubled her salary. Elizabeth Powell Bond was an instructor in physical education at Vassar, among other posts, before becoming matron of Swarthmore College in 1886 where she did no teaching but was a social and moral guide, attending to "the needs of [women's] spiritual natures." Her successor, however, was previously dean of women at the University of Colorado and, by moving to Swarthmore, gained an opportunity to "increase [students'] mental equipment" by adding an appointment as instructor in Greek.[63]

It was inevitable that college officials would consider their own faculty women when developing deanships. Boston University added the title of adviser of women to Agnes Scott Black's professorship of elocution in 1915. When Luella Carson became the University of Oregon's first dean of women in 1899, she assumed this role in addition to her work as professor of rhetoric and English literature. Conversely, while contemplating the disestablishment of the office of dean of women in 1904, the University of Illinois divided its duties among the twenty-six faculty women. From the women who headed the Library School, School of Household Science, and Physical Education for Women, an executive committee was created that placed all women faculty on committees to oversee the clerical work of the Woman's Department and the intellectual, social, and rooming house lives of the women students. Yielding to the petition of the women faculty that another arrangement be made, the trustees eventually restored the position of dean of women but made it subordinate to that of dean of men.[64]

The growth of the deanship of women undoubtedly benefitted many women students, as did the appearance of women physicians. But the small numbers of women employed in any coeducational institution and the ambiguity and fluidity of their positions profoundly disappointed an observer like Helen Olin. Writing of the University of Wisconsin between 1863 and 1910, she complained that

> no woman of distinction has ever been called there. Only two full professorships have ever been given to women; one for domestic science, and one which was for six years incidental and subordinate to the administration of the dormitory for women students. One associate professorship existed for three years which was incidental and subordinate to the administrative work of the office of dean of women. At present neither of these administrative positions is accompanied by any instructional work.[65]

Later surveys, such as those published by Jane Jones and Lulu Holmes about deans of women in coeducational colleges and universities in the United States, bore out Olin's earlier complaint.

Although the deanship grew in the years between the two world wars, there were two developments that lessened its potential for the academic employment of women in many institutions. First, the position was increasingly professionalized as "student personnel work," with its own training and organizations.[66] Second, a number of institutions abolished the post by reorganizing services under a dean of students, who was usually a man.[67] At the University of Chicago in 1925 the dean of women was replaced by a Woman's University Council, made up of all women deans, representatives of women's athletic, residential, and social activities, a group of senior faculty women, and others appointed by the university; the council was succeeded by a dean of students in 1931.[68]

Employment by Institutional Division and Segregation

An alternative door opened to women faculty when a college or university created a program, department, or professional school in which the majority of students would be female. The formation of a "normal" or pedagogy course to train teachers was an early example. Later, departments of domestic science (home economics), social work, librarianship, and public health and nursing were occasions for adding women to the faculty. Exercise or sports activities were required of women students, some of whom might also wish to become physical education teachers in schools; women faculty were also hired to teach "physical culture" to all women students, especially in an era when there was much question about whether advanced education injured women's health and reproductive physiology.

Since it represented a process of growth in opportunity by addition and partition, rather than by opening fully to women faculty all of the arts and sciences, or those professional courses in which male students predominated, this approach to the hiring of academic women can be considered employment by institutional division and segregation. Entry to the academic profession through the principle of segregation has been a story of successes and failures. Although far more likely to be hired, given tenure, and promoted—and to have sympathetic colleagues—academic women in the "women's fields" also experienced the lesser pay, prestige, and power that their departments suffered on many campuses.[69]

A forerunner to the relative concentration of academic women in a separate academic unit was the "Female College" or "Ladies' Course" of such earlier coeducational institutions as Oberlin, Grinnell, Iowa State College, and the University of Wisconsin. These were intended to reproduce in coeducational colleges the more academic elements of the female seminary's curriculum, while restricting women's entry into the institution as a whole and limiting their opportunity to sit and recite with male students. Maude Abbott entered McGill University as a student in 1885, admitted into the Donalda Department for Women. These structural reminders of women's inferior status were disappearing by the 1880s. They were readily replaced, however, by a degree of segregation of the sexes based on the self-selection by women and men students within the liberal arts curriculum, and by the appearance of new, sex-segregated curricula designed to reflect women's and men's different social and employment opportunities. In 1900, of the 61,000 women studying in coeducational institutions in the United States, 43,000 were in teacher training and 2,000 in home economics courses; in either case, most of their cohort were women.[70] For their part, men were similarly concentrated in the colleges of agriculture, commerce, and engineering, in the physical science departments, and in what were considered the "harder" social sciences of economics and political science.

Unbalanced sex ratios prompted Mabel Newcomer to ask, "If the balance of men and women on a woman's college faculty is educationally sound might not men's colleges and the coeducational institutions find it equally sound?"[71] Although male professors were numerous in many "women's departments" of coeducational schools, the reverse was not the case. In fact, the addition of "men's fields" to the curriculum ordinarily had the effect of restricting the proportional growth of women students and women faculty. An astute economics professor at the University of Chicago assured his colleagues in 1902 that declining proportions of male students would be reversed "as soon as proper support and endowments are given to the work which offers training for careers in engineering, railways, banking, trade and industry, law, medicine, etc."[72] In the process women faculty also became less "justified."

Institutions with disproportionately large enrollments in women's fields had more faculty women. Conversely, campuses with their strength in male fields had scarcely any women faculty; the technical colleges and some of the land-grant universities illustrate this latter. Thus, Berkeley, with 40 percent of its entire regular faculty in agriculture, forestry, and engineering, in 1921 offered academic women few positions.[73] Additionally, a department might train a great many women graduate students, but not employ them on the faculty nor urge their hiring by other institutions. Botany at the University of Chicago was one of many examples.

Home Economics Probably no field exceeded home economics in its opportunities for women to become members of the faculty and build careers, especially women scientists. Public colleges were the most accommodating to this new specialization. The land-grant universities created whole departments of home economics, hiring women to staff them. Iowa State College offered "Domestic Economy" in the Ladies Course in 1871. The State Agricultural College of Kansas quickly followed with its several courses in household management, child rearing, and home nursing; with the emphasis on home economics the two women of the original faculty—an assistant in the precollegiate program and a teacher of instrumental music—were joined by other women.[74] Private Cornell University, being New York State's land-grant institution, added a department of home economics. An economist, Sarah Gibson Blanding, moved from dean of women and associate professor of political science at the University of Kentucky (1928) to dean of home economics at Cornell University (1941), to president of Vassar College (1946).[75]

Many private coeducational schools thought to cater to their women students by offering occasional courses in child development, consumer economics, and marriage and the family—in departments of psychology, economics, and sociology, taught by women if they were present on the faculty. Thus, Stanford University had Mary Roberts Smith offer a course on the family in 1894; although having previous experience as a high school teacher and instructor in history and economics at Wellesley, it was as the wife of an engineering professor, however, that Roberts received her initial faculty appointment at Stanford, where she taught for ten years.[76] The University of Chicago went the farthest. It launched a Department of Household Administration in 1904, relocating Marion Talbot's courses there from their original home in the Department of Sociology. Sophonisba Breckinridge, with a law degree and a doctorate in political science, was added to the faculty of the new department. However, Talbot concluded that the university was "either too handicapped financially or too fearful of increasing the proportion of women students to take any steps toward the enlargement or strengthening of the Department."[77]

One of the more blatant testimonials to the formal disregard that male faculties had for women scholars comes from Cornell. In response to the trustees' proposal "to appoint women to seats in the special faculties," the majority resolved in 1911 that "the University Faculty, while not favoring in general the appointment of women to professorships, interposes no objection to their appointment in the department of Home Economics."[78] Nonetheless, the first two women named to professorships were advised not to attend faculty meetings until the opposition had died down.[79]

While the initial complement of academic women at the University of Chicago was spread across several disciplines, the few subsequent appointments and promotions were disproportionately in "feminine fields." In 1924, when 147 men held full professorships, the 3 Chicago women full professors reported their grievances to the trustees. These included the fact that academic women had only a slight role in "providing and imparting opportunities for education to persons of both sexes on equal terms."[80] From 1892 to 1920, no woman progressed through the ranks to full professor in the social sciences at the University of Chicago; all its women professors attained that rank at another institution before being employed or had been promoted in women's departments like home economics and social work.[81]

While not as extreme everywhere, this general tendency in coeducational higher education persisted. A 1920 survey of academic women in 176 institutions found that home economics teachers numbered 53 of their 190 women full professors; the largest single group of women at all the other ranks was also made up of home economics faculty.[82] Given their concentration—as faculty and as full professors—in just a few fields, women were rarely department chairs or deans of professional schools except in those fields.[83]

Teacher Education   Over the past century and more, teaching became "appropriate" work for women: "It was genteel, paid reasonably well, and required little special skill or equipment."[84] As schooling grew in the United States, so did the opportunities for women to gain economic and psychic independence as teachers and, often, to move into other employment or into public affairs. Women teachers often used their savings to finance further education for themselves.[85] By experience and preparation they were especially fitting themselves to teach other teachers, as faculty women in normal schools, state teachers' colleges, and the proliferating colleges and universities that established departments for the education of teachers after 1900.

In college catalogues that listed teachers of both sexes, it was common in the early years to label male college faculty as professors and female faculty as preceptresses. Probably the first woman to hold the title of professor was Rebecca Pennell, a member of the faculty of Antioch College when it opened in 1853. An early graduate of a Massachusetts normal school, a successful public school teacher and normal school instructor, Pennell's presence testified to the gradual movement of normal (teacher) training into coeducational colleges and universities in the second half of the nineteenth century. It was, in fact, through the limited admission of women students into such normal courses or into summer sessions for teachers that many institutions became fully coeducational.[86]

The normal department was opposed by many faculties precisely because it brought females—students and professors—into the university. Still, many men were themselves averse to teaching pedagogy, with its low-status connections with the mass education of children and its predominance of women students who were expected to teach only provisionally—i.e., provided they remained unmarried. Women students could not be comfortably regarded as apprentice professionals as were male students in the proliferating commerce and engineering departments. This aversion forced colleges to hire women faculty to teach the prospective teachers whose enrollment was politically necessary in public institutions and whose tuition increasingly sustained many private colleges. Marion Talbot noted that the organization of the School of Education in 1901 "brought a considerable addition of women to the teaching staff" of the University of Chicago; this happened through the incorporation of the Cook County Normal School into the university.[87] As the women retired, however, their positions were closed or filled by men.[88]

Over half the faculties of the nineteenth and twentieth-century normal schools were women. Hence, the demise of these institutions or their conversion into state colleges—like the closing of many women's colleges—was a significant factor in the several declines in women's share of all faculty positions during the twentieth century. Also, in the

coeducational universities, women faculty in education had fewer opportunities to advance than in home economics, probably because their
student bodies were not so disproportionately female. In the AAUP
study, among full professors in education, there were 9 women and
190 men; among instructors, however, there were 38 men and 43
women.[89] Women had such an unexpectedly low rank among education faculty that a 1924 study of women's status on university faculties
in *academic* departments decided to question education department
chairs also in order "to get at the workings of the masculine mind of
those occupying our chairs of education."[90]

Such men had an explanation, however: They blamed other women.
When Marie Belle McCabe wrote to the head of the University of Chicago's Department of Education in 1936 about her wish to earn a Ph.D.
and embark on an academic career, Charles Judd replied that "It is one
of the characteristics of your sex that they do not like to be taught by
women. This is perhaps deplorable but is a fact and the result is that
universities and colleges take men even if they are comparatively inferior in quality as distinguished from women."[91]

Employment by Connection

In some instances, probably fewer than by using the routes described
above, women were able to exploit family and institutional connections
to gain a faculty place. The daughter of a prominent local citizen or
institutional patron, the wife of a well-placed member of the faculty, or
someone otherwise socially well sponsored might find herself employed to teach. This was more likely the case for faculty of either sex
in the provincial and newly established schools where access to an ex-
tralocal faculty market was weakly developed and the sense of propri-
etorship—"this is *our* school"—was strong. Holder of a Ph.D. and an
active researcher, June Downey, who chaired the psychology department at the University of Wyoming from 1911 to 1931, was also the
daughter of a founder and longtime president of the regents of the
university.[92]

Male relatives could be moved to exert pressure on behalf of their
daughters, sisters, or nieces, given the low rates of marriage among the
educated upper-middle class women coming to maturity in the late
nineteenth century, especially in the Atlantic coast states where there
were severe imbalances of marriageable-age men and women. Mary Livermore traveled around the United States in the 1870s lecturing on the
need to give "superfluous women" an opportunity to lead useful lives.
One woman wrote to her former classmate, Lucy Salmon: "How the

audience cheered when Mrs. Livermore referred to [Vassar College as-tronomer] Maria Mitchell as one of the superfluous women."[93]

Rebecca Pennell was aided by the fact that her uncle, Horace Mann, was president of infant Antioch College; knowing her qualifications, he did not hesitate to employ her. The University of Minnesota was a small and provincial place when Ada Comstock was appointed an assistant in Maria Sanford's Department of Rhetoric and Oratory in 1900. A student at Minnesota and Moorhead Normal School, Comstock had degrees from Smith College and Columbia University; but the connection to her fa-ther—a successful lawyer, a regent of the university, and a state legis-lator—meant that her abilities and qualifications got a fair (and favorable) hearing. Exploiting this opportunity, Comstock went on to become dean of women and professor of rhetoric, dean of Smith College, and president of Radcliffe College.[94] Academically well qualified for the fac-ulty of any college, her family's role in founding Bryn Mawr College was important in M. Carey Thomas becoming first its dean and then its president.[95]

Dr. Thomas Dudley Isom was one of the founders of Oxford, Mis-sissippi where the University of Mississippi was opened in 1848. In 1884 the trustees authorized the employment of "a suitable man, spe-cially fitted for that duty, to teach Elocution." In 1885 the board's sec-retary wrote to the president of Columbia University, enquiring whether "mere sex [is] a disqualification in a woman for appointment to a po-sition as a teacher in a male educational institution." F. A. P. Barnard replied:

> There are subjects for which women seem to possess a peculiar aptitude in teaching, and one of them certainly is elocution. . . . If the appointment of a female teacher in the University of Mississippi would be likely to create an excitement, even though on the part of a minority, prejudicial to the internal order of the institution, or to its outward prosperity, it would be better to delay any such action until this adverse feeling should be corrected or should, as it ultimately must, die out of itself.[96]

Oxford was evidently not opposed to Sarah McGehee Isom, Dr. Tom's thirty-one-year-old daughter and a professionally trained orator. She became the first woman member of the faculty, teaching from 1885 to her death in 1905. It was said of Miss Isom that, had her social class position not prevented, she would surely have used her talents on the stage. As it was, she was a pioneer among academic women in the South, not able, however, to break the male monopoly on the profes-

sorial titles; she remained instructor in elocution during her entire career at "Ole Miss."

Several presidents of the University of California in its less bureaucratic years showed little hesitancy in employing faculty on the basis
of personal and family connections. With few formal qualifications for
the position, Lucy Sprague was made Berkeley's first dean of women
because President Benjamin Ide Wheeler knew her surrogate family,
George Herbert Palmer and Alice Freeman Palmer, formerly president
of Wellesley College. The fact that Lucy Sprague's brother-in-law,
Adolph Miller, was chairman of the department of economics undoubtedly helped. President William Wallace Campbell met Jacqueline De La
Harpe when she was in Berkeley in 1926, visiting family that included
her brother, the university's astronomer. Quickly hired, she was to remain as professor of French for thirty-four years.[97]

The women highlighted above combined family connections with
the more universal criteria of relevant training and experience. Compared to their male counterparts, however, their advantages were fewer.
Outside of the personal network linking the women's colleges, no "old-
girls' club" existed to ease their way, as countless academic men were
assisted by their own well-established networks which, perforce, excluded women. Moreover, the families of ambitious, career-minded
women were predictably more likely to be ambivalent in pushing
daughters forward, unlike the situations that men experienced when
competing for faculty or administrative positions. Nonetheless, by the
late nineteenth century there was no shortage of women with the objective qualifications required for academic employment. All they
needed was a chance.

The Qualifications of Women for the Faculty

The equitable employment and advancement of academic women were
hindered by the conventional wisdom that conceives women to be
forced by biology and culture to pursue their careers less single-
mindedly than are men. On the average, women are led "to settle for
much less career preparation than men," writes Juanita Kreps.[98] Yet,
when their career preparation was equal or superior, women still faced
attitudes that diminished its value. When President M. Carey Thomas
of Bryn Mawr College required that all of her faculty have the Ph.D.
degree, a standard hardly contemplated for males at the turn of this
century, President Charles W. Eliot of Harvard belittled the effort:
"There is an intuitive something in ladies of birth and position which

enables them to do without college training, and makes (on the whole) better professors for women college students than if they had themselves been to college."[99] Le Clerc Phillips went further, in 1926, to demean women who pursued advanced education and academic careers. He wrote that "taken as a whole, they are distinctly lacking in physical attractiveness, charm of manner, and social agreeableness." He advised schools that employ women to take, "as a sort of counterbalance a thoroughgoing woman of the world who has been successful in love and whose triumphs constitute a refutation of the . . . frigid-reserve theory of training" presumably espoused by academic women.[100]

A strong cultural preference existed among men, and some women, that women students and faculty remain a breed apart, exemplifications only of "womanly women." Nonetheless, the movement to professionalize college studies and their teachers resulted in a pool of women with the formal qualifications to enter any faculty on equal terms with men. This removed one of the two major reasons not to hire academic women.[101] The other barrier, male antipathy, proved harder to root out.

Educational Qualifications

The earliest women faculty in women's colleges were themselves graduates of female seminaries or normal schools. Marianne Parker Dascomb, for example, graduated from Ipswich Female Seminary in 1833 and taught at Oberlin from 1834 to 1870; neither Carla Wenckenbach nor Mary Alice Willcox of the early Wellesley faculty advanced beyond normal schools.[102] By the end of the nineteenth century, however, women graduates of colleges and universities possessed qualifications equivalent to male academics. Coeducational universities were preparing future faculty women. The seven women on the initial faculty roster of the University of Chicago included graduates of the University of Michigan and Boston University.

Women's opportunity for graduate study grew with the success of Helen Magill as the first woman to receive a Ph.D. degree from an American university, in 1877, and the availability of women with European doctorates, such as M. Carey Thomas. By 1900 half of the graduate students at the University of Chicago were women.[103] If quality of graduate preparation is measured by the status of the institution from which one's degree comes, white women were receiving their degrees from as prestigious schools as did white men. A study of the years 1920 to 1959 found that the top-ranked universities granted 54.8 percent of the Ph.D.s awarded to men and 56.6 percent of those awarded to women.[104]

Largely excluded from white institutions, however, higher proportions of black academics and professionals were graduates of those black schools that retained the paternalistic traditions that did not promote the "initiative, independence and self-direction while in college" that Lucy Diggs Slowe thought necessary to the emancipation of the Negro woman.[105]

The one factor that did not favor women of either race was women's persistent concentrations in specializations different from men's. Around 1910 women also had to weather assorted threats to the gains made. To placate male sensibilities, coeducational colleges considered segregating their women students for instruction; medical schools and hospital internships set rigid female quotas; and patterns took hold that limited women's access to graduate fellowships. Helen Olin urged that faculties in public institutions be warned that "the personal opinion of no man may gainsay what the people have declared to be woman's 'equal eligibility' to these privileges."[106]

Women doctorates bravely faced other difficulties. With the passing of the earliest generations of college-educated women, their successors increasingly tried to combine a career with marriage. Too many found this impossible and abandoned their careers. In a large study of women who earned doctorates up to 1924, this group was most likely to advise other women not to take the Ph.D. And married or not, many women commented on the discrimination they faced in competing with men for positions.[107]

Doctoral degrees were increasingly mandated of both men and women in order to gain or retain faculty positions, especially in universities and fields outside the performing arts. Women doctorates were hired in all types of institutions, except the all-male colleges and technical schools, in numbers that helped to compensate for the loss of positions caused by the closing of normal schools and women's colleges. Their entry into the faculties of land-grant universities, most notably in home economics and such teaching-related fields as the humanities, meant that women became better represented on the faculties of elite schools. However, the historic discrepancy between women's educational credentials and their appointment and promotion rates at top-ranked institutions was first evidenced in this period.[108]

Teaching Experience

By experience, as well as by formal study, women fitted themselves for university positions. By the 1880s, their widespread presence as teachers in female seminaries, coeducational high schools, and normal schools lessened objections to them as college teachers.[109] Of the forty-nine women who served on the Wellesley faculty to 1920 about whom information is had, one quarter had taught in secondary schools. As women increasingly went to college to prepare to teach, their numbers alone created pressures to employ some faculty women. Since women graduates of the most prestigious women's colleges and coeducational schools entered teaching in large numbers, this also meant that teaching was affecting a segment of the social class structure that was especially ready and able to consider the career of college teaching. In England, which had a more limited and aristocratic system of higher education than the United States, the careers of university-educated women also showed teaching predominant. Among Newnham College, Cambridge graduates between 1871 and 1893, 53 percent became teachers; similar figures were reported from Somerville College, Oxford University's women's college.[110]

Most of the early deans of women had been teachers. Lily E. Kollack, who went from Vassar to the University of Illinois in 1907, had taught chemistry for eight years in a Louisville, Kentucky high school after taking a Ph.D. at the University of Pennsylvania.[111] Lucy Diggs Slowe left the principalship of a Washington, D.C. junior high school for the deanship of women and a faculty position at Howard University in 1922. Lucy Salmon preceded her graduate studies and eventual professorship at Vassar with teaching and principal duties in schools in McGregor, Iowa and Terre Haute, Indiana; her experiences were common to early academic women, as Maria Sanford's career also demonstrates. In the years following the Civil War, southern women began to enter the teaching profession to staff the new systems of public schools; by the 1880s they were 60 percent of all teachers.[112] This reduced the need of the South's more advanced institutions to hire northern women or to rely primarily on social qualifications in forming their faculties.

Superior Intellect and Motivation

By the late nineteenth century the professionalization of academe was well under way and the majority of new faculty were careerists.[113] The new emphasis upon formal qualifications was to the benefit of reformist women who were arguing that the ascribed characteristic of gender was irrelevant in this and other traditionally male professions. The women pioneers had, however, to be more than equal.

"If a woman has the presumption to teach philosophy, she has to be as good as a man," scolded Mrs. McIntosh, wife of a biology professor and partner in her husband's research. "She ought to be better."[114]

This character in a 1929 novel, set in a disguised version of the University of Minnesota, reflected real states of mind. Internalizing society's double standard, many academic women in science concluded they had to be exceptionably able. Margaret Rossiter calls this the "Madame Curie strategy": performing at superior levels in order to acquire what the ordinary academic man confidently expected. Among our "lone voyagers," Maude Abbott's career exemplified this phenomenon. In response to the inquiries about women on the faculty made by the AAUP's Committee W in 1920, the dean of an eastern university answered, "When we discover a woman who can handle some subject in our course of study better than a man could handle it, we shall not hesitate to urge the appointment."[115]

The academic honors and prizes won by [early women students] testify to *their* ability and drive. For a woman to try to breach the all-male faculties called for superior motivation, above-average evidence of talent and training, and extraordinary persistence. The women in this collection clearly demonstrated those qualities. While faculty women undoubtedly varied among themselves on many dimensions, it seems safe to assert that they varied less than did their male colleagues in that they were conspicuously absent from the lower end of the continuum of ability.

In 1910 Helen Olin inveighed against "the cultivation of the petty spirit of superiority that is in reality the last refuge of an inferior nature" and that persisted in higher education.[116] A few years later Le Clerc Phillips candidly discussed the reason for "the average man's dislike of the unusually intelligent and exceptionally well-educated women" who know more than does the average man:

> The old cry of the men, "Why don't you go home and mind the baby?" is heard no more; it is long since out-of-date; but there still lingers on a smoldering resentment, breaking every now and then into roars of disapproval, against those women, who, seeking and finding absolute independence in a career, are able to flout with impunity the authority of men. That is what economic independence has done for women, and there is little doubt that men have not been much pleased by it. . . . A man has to have a great deal of "luminosity" of his own before he is able to recognize any existing in women.[117]

The Status of Faculty Women
in Coeducational Institutions

Having made their ways onto faculties, despite their own socialization and that of the other sex, how did early academic women fare in their often hard-won positions? Again, fiction gives us insights. The opening scene in Wanda Neff's autobiographical novel, *Lone Voyagers,* takes place in the Women's Building of the University of Minnesota, during a lecture by a distinguished visiting German physicist. The seating of the audience follows the institution's prestige system: the front chairs filled with professors of philosophy, physics, mathematics, astronomy, and German; "behind them were the lower orders of academic arch-angels, other scientists, and beyond a lesser hierarchy, young men in history, in literature, and even in the classics. . . . Mixed with these lesser ones was a sprinkling of women teaching in the University."

More than fifty years later, zoologist Mariette Nowak ends her study of female anatomy, *Eve's Rib,* on a different note: "In the long run, on an evolutionary scale, the female has a proud and inspiring heritage. It's fine to be female in the natural world."[118] Academe, however, is not the natural but a social world—and one in which many women found it was *not* fine to be female.

The Responses of Faculty Males

Stanford's first president, David Starr Jordan, is often celebrated in the annals of women's education for his support of university women. Stanford opened as a coeducational institution in 1892 and Jordan wrote on behalf of coeducation. There was a cluster of women on Stanford's faculty. Yet, in Jordan's autobiography, one finds almost no mention of these women; and the faculty is referred to, repeatedly and proudly as "the Stanford Men." Jordan probably revealed his deepest feelings about women's place when he wrote, "Even less possible is it to do justice to individual faculty women whose faithful devotion has been so important a factor in their husband's success."[119] Were faculty wives the *real* "faculty women" in Jordan's ideal university?

Margaret Rossiter has demonstrated in her history of women scientists in the United States before 1940 that, both as graduate students and as faculty, women did have their supporters among the male professoriate; there were those who, despite prevailing opinion, lacked sex prejudice and championed the cause of individual women. But the common opinion of department heads in U.S. coeducational institutions in the 1920s was that male academics were not averse, in theory,

to the employment of women—in departments other than their own
and at the lower ranks.[120]

One explanation offered was that men "do not want education to
be regarded as an effeminate job"—fearing that college teaching might
become "feminized," as was elementary and secondary school teaching.[121] Another concern was that "sex solidarity" would be destroyed
by women's presence. As one man put it, "I think it is psychologically
impossible for men entirely to ignore in their dealings with women the
fact that they are dealing with persons that are not men, persons who
must be treated in a different way.[122] These explanations mask the influence that prestige plays in the workings of the academic system.
While dean of academic affairs at Brown University, Jacqueline Mattfeld
wrote of the pervasiveness in higher education of "the popular view
that the academic excellence and prestige of an institution are directly
proportional to the number of men in it and to the prevalence of their
values, interests, and concerns in all areas of its endeavors."[123]

The Fact of Marginality

As institutions in the academic hierarchy, the women's colleges have
always been marginal. But their faculties' sense of discrimination and
social isolation is reportedly less acute than that of women on coeducational campuses—where women are fewer in number, scattered, and
where their colleagues may consider their scholarly work, if it is at all
marked by gender, as being on the "fringes" rather than the "frontiers"
of knowledge.[124]

In her 1915 doctoral dissertation, Jessie Taft wrote that "women
who attempt to conform to both male and female worlds, as many are
compelled to do, find themselves face to face with conflicts so serious
and apparently unreconcilable that satisfactory adjustment is often quite
impossible on the part of the individual woman."[125] Through their advanced education and occupational choice, many of the academic
women mentioned in this volume had left one social group without
being able to gain acceptance in another. They put themselves on the
margins of both groups, full members of neither.[126] This clearly was true
of Clelia Mosher, Maude Abbott, Lucy Diggs Slowe, and Maria Sanford—
although not of Grace Hebard; perhaps early Wyoming's down-to-earth
ways helped. Many other faculty women were isolated. Consider the
small but symbolic matter of where women might eat. At "Chippewa
University" it was a reserved corner of the undergraduate women's
dining room.[127] On many campuses, denied the privileges of membership in "*The* Faculty Club," academic women sometimes joined with

librarians, administrative assistants, faculty wives, and women graduate students to form a women's faculty club. At Berkeley the existence of this separate organization confirmed an effective isolation, so strong that the earliest faculty women felt unable to attend faculty meetings lest their appearance strengthen prejudices against them and women students.[128]

Faculty women were, paradoxically, both invisible and extravisible.[129] Manifestations of invisibility included lack of support and recognition—through salaries, promotions, publication offers, holding association offices, offers of outside consulting, the quality of interaction with colleagues, university-conferred honors, and being taken seriously in general.[130] Extravisibility included the constant pressure of being in situations where one is the exception, where, like Maude Abbott, one is on trial as the representative of all other women who would aspire to academic labor. Ida Hyde's 1901 diary reports her sense of betrayal and vulnerability while head of the physiology department of the University of Kansas. Her feelings, while understandable in any conscientious person, may have been especially poignant given the extraordinary efforts required of the pioneer academic woman:

> I feel that my heart would break—to think that after I labored like a slave, to do my best, and be just and upright towards the institution and the students, that now they should go before the Faculty and rebel because I did not let them pass, those that failed . . . I have lost all hope and courage.[131]

The claim that women did not fit academic institutions took several forms. It was charged that they looked at things oddly, not playing the game quite as men did. "Latterly, they have combined and more or less to support each other," a department chairman complained in 1924; "instead of becoming an integral part of the university, they show a tendency to become a foreign, irritating body within the university."[132] But another male thought them excessively timid: They are imposed upon, he wrote, "because women as a class will not fight back quite as much as men."[133]

Nor were women immune to defensiveness and self-scorn, internalizing the doubts that society expressed. One compensating strategy was for women to act and "think as much like men" as possible, making the professional role prepotent. Maria Sanford's refusal to act "the lady" and her habit of wearing a plain black dress, a virtual uniform, seem to fit this response. On the other hand, the women featured in this volume do not fit Rossiter's description of academic women scientists, as having "developed a defensive attitude bordering on martyrdom," to be bitter, anxious, despondent.[134]

The Image of Deviance and Eccentricity

Only one of the women featured in this anthology, Theresa McMahon, ever married. She did so early in life, and remained childless. A study of women who earned the Ph.D. from 1877 to 1924 reported that one-fourth were married; another survey found 72 wives among 687 eminent women scientists.[135] Of the 77 black academic women employed in 1940, 57 were single.[136] Although the rates of marriage among academic women rose over what they were in the last quarter of the nineteenth century, they remained very low compared to male academics and to women in general.[137] This supports the image of their exceptionality, their deviation from cultural definitions of a healthy adulthood. Career women, like single men, do not conform to conventional expectations. They "will appear, however mildly, as deviant to the majority of their colleagues who are married males."[138]

Negative images of the single woman run through the popular culture. Single women are almost never portrayed in novels as eminent, successful, admired, highly trained, or even happy.[139] Compared to faculty wives, birds of "tropical plumage," academic women were sparrows with their businesslike clothes and shiny noses.[140] The unwillingness of Maria Sanford and Maude Abbott to give thought to their dress helped confirm their later reputations as eccentrics. During the 1930s, when intense pressure was applied to remove married women from the work force, especially from the better-paid and responsible positions, a counterattack reasserted the deviance of the single woman. Dean Virginia Gildersleeve of Barnard College protested both "the tendency of today to regard celibate teachers as 'frustrated' " as well as the "cruel and unwholesome discrimination against unmarried women."[141]

Lucy Sprague found that some of the older Berkeley men thought faculty women were unwomanly "freaks."[142] Their critics accordingly feared that unmarried women teachers were a bad influence on college women. There is some evidence, however, that their single status itself increasingly limited their influence as role models. Professor Carrie Harper of Mount Holyoke College wrote in 1913 that "the woman who teaches will always, I sometimes fear, seem to her pupils unsuccessful" for not being married. Of undergraduates, she wrote, "I sometimes think that at present they are honestly afraid to study hard lest by some accident they come to be what they think we are—poor underpaid women, who work hard and lead meagre, grey lives."[143] Although it ceased to be expected that single women faculty would live in student dormitories and "preside over table," attitudes about unmarried women were, if anything, hardening. As college-going became a common experience and as college-educated women began to marry at the same rates as the general female population, the dedicated unmarried female teacher was ever more likely to strike her students as a relic from another era.

It was expected that a woman who married would naturally give up her position. Although it was usual for married, college-educated black women to continue to work, the trustees of Howard University accepted, in 1913, President Boyd's proposal "that any female teacher who thereafter married while teaching at the University would be considered as having resigned her position."[144] Concessions were, however, sometimes won because of the value of the women themselves. Mossie May Waddington, Ph.D., author of a study of the development of British philosophy, was head of the Women's Union and teacher of English at the University of Toronto's coeducational University College in 1923 when she informed the College Council that she was to be married to Professor W. A. Kirkwood. The search for her replacement as head of the Women's Union was unsuccessful and she was asked if she would stay on in a position that she upgraded to dean of women. Despite having two children she was later made principal of St. Hilda's, the women's college of the university. In "Women's Right to Work" (1937) she argued for women's right to work even when men were unemployed: "Woman like man, has powers and gifts which must be used, if rust or bitterness is not to destroy both power and happiness."[145]

Overcoming Discrimination

During the lives of these seven "lone voyagers," higher education was a growth industry, drawing many men into the faculty ranks and making some places for women. As we have seen, however, academic women in coeducational schools experienced occupational stratification based on gender. As a group they were unable to achieve parity of position in rank, salary, tenure, status, or power. It is not surprising, therefore, that a survey of magazine articles on women's images in education concludes that the complaints remained the same from 1900 to 1977: "The only change is one of tone in the 1970s when legal recourse is advocated to eliminate some job discrimination."[146]

A degree of optimism existed around 1920, due in part to wider employment of academic women as a result of World War I. The numbers of employed academic women went from 6,397 in 1916 to 10,445 in 1922.[147] Both Harvard and Yale had hired their first women faculty members. In 1919, at the age of fifty, Alice Hamilton was appointed assistant professor of industrial medicine (the field she founded) at the Harvard University Medical School—with the understanding, however, that she not march in the commencement procession nor appear at the faculty club so critics might continue to believe that hers was only a research appointment. She retired, unpromoted, sixteen years later.[148] Yale University, which became a major site of doctoral study for women, appointed a woman in 1921 to the Department of Education. The danger that this department might, as it had elsewhere, become a conduit of women into the faculty was unrealized, however: Bessie Lee Gambrill was the only full-time faculty woman in the thirty-four-year existence of that department.[149]

A closer look reveals retrogression as well as advance. At the 1922 meeting of the National Association of Deans of Women, Nebraska's Louise Pound reported widespread feelings that their dismal prospects could not encourage women to pursue graduate work, and that positions they once held were "being quietly taken from the women in this generation."[150] At her own institution, according to the well-publicized report of an alumnae group, the number of women declined and their share of faculty positions dropped from 23 percent in 1915 to 16 percent in 1920.[151] At Chicago—the institution once described as the one place where women students and teachers were "so thoroughly on an equality with men"—women dropped from 8 percent of the faculty when Marion Talbot was hired, to 2 percent in 1970 when there were 11 women full professors (compared to 464 male full professors), 6 of them in social work.[152] Although faculty women's status on state university campuses increased slightly from 1920 to 1940, the rise failed to keep pace with that of the total faculty in many places, including the public universities of Rhode Island, Connecticut, Pennsylvania, Arkansas, Texas, Iowa, Illinois, Wyoming, and Nevada.[153]

In the 1930s a new tenure policy was instituted that might dismiss those judged ineligible for permanent positions after a maximum of seven years of service. The principle of "up-or-out" was justified as a means of ending the long-term exploitation of low-paid and junior faculty. It also promised to motivate and reward scholarly promise and productivity in the spirit of the research university. Accepted by the American Association of University Professors in 1941, it was widely adopted, although the vast majority of U.S. colleges and universities were not research institutions and a majority of their faculty lacked doctoral degrees. Women faculty were disproportionately located at the bottom of the faculty ranks and in irregular positions off the tenure-track. They suffered from a policy that was also motivated by the wish to make positions available, in a tight academic job market, to sponsored younger applicants, most of whom were male.

Wage Inequity   Maria Sanford and Maude Abbott repeatedly protested their poor pay. In 1913 a committee chaired by Marion Talbot recommended to the Association of Collegiate Alumnae that institutions on its list of accredited schools meet several tests, including that "women of the faculty shall receive approximately the same salaries as men of the same rank."[154] Institutional resistance to salary equity was strong, however, for pragmatic reasons as well as the sheer prejudice that women should not be men's equals. Poorly endowed colleges, unwilling to raise tuition charges to necessary levels, could use their ill-paid faculty to subsidize the real costs of education. Public institutions could operate more cheaply, reducing taxpayer resistance. These were common practices in over-built American higher education before the advent of women faculty, but women's employment enabled schools to recruit some men who could only be gotten if adequately compensated. Public and private black colleges, especially, lacked adequate financing. Hence, black women college teachers were even more exploited than were white women.[155]

Women's salaries were sometimes increased where they or the state demanded it. When the trustees of one private institution voted, around 1920, a maximum salary of $1,800 for women and $3,000 for men of the same rank, the action was rescinded when the women learned of it and planned to file a protest.[156] An individual's progress might also be more equitable in those departments where women were more numerous and well promoted. Clelia Mosher and Maude Abbott would surely have been promoted more rapidly had they been school of nursing faculty. But the general absence of women from the higher ranks also prevented them from gaining important campus positions on faculty committees and in the administration, where they might counter gender discrimination generally.

Antinepotism Rules   The reforms of the Progressive era of the earlier twentieth century included attempts to remove unethical patronage practices from public employment, and to substitute merit as the sole criterion for appointment. The private sector accepted a similar principle as part of the movement to use expertise and professional credentials in its personnel policies. Although family, social, and political connections continued to operate, they were more covert and regulations were adopted to limit or channel their effects. These included the

acceptance of formal or informal rules about hiring relatives: the antinepotism principle. Since the 1920s many colleges and universities
apparently used these, on an ad hoc basis, to limit the academic
employment of wives of the male faculty. They were most commonly
applied in public and prestigious institutions.[157]

Although husbands and sons could have been the victims, it was
usually married women who were prevented from being hired in or
were fired from faculty positions. Theresa McMahon battled relentlessly
against these practices at the University of Washington, where her husband was also a faculty member. Moreover, since the rules did not
prevent women from being hired as part-time teachers, researchers, or
administrative staff, institutions could gain the services of qualified
women at low cost and without making permanent commitments to
them.

The frustration of many women is captured in the experience of
Marguerite Hall Albjerg.[158] An honors graduate of Franklin College in
1917, a teacher in high schools in Indiana and Kansas, she entered the
premier department of history at the University of Wisconsin in 1922,
earning a master of arts and Ph.D.; with a four-year average of A + , she
was the first woman to hold the university's President Adams Fellowship. For two years she headed the History Department at Alabama State
College for Women, resigning in 1927 to marry Victor L. Albjerg whom
she had met in graduate school. From then until 1951 she taught (in
that revealing term she used) *intermittently* in the History and Government Department of Purdue University, where her husband had a faculty appointment. Despite the publication of four books and more than
thirty articles on history and education, Purdue's antinepotism policy
restricted her to the margins of the institution. Her only child, Patricia
Albjerg Graham, remembers how elated her mother always was when
a chance to teach was offered; she would hire a housekeeper and rejoice in doing what she was most fitted to do. The office of dean of
women later gave her further surcease from domesticity with the position of counselor. Although she was the daughter of a professor of
Greek at Franklin College and sister of a president of the University of
Oregon, Marguerite Albjerg was denied the opportunity to exploit her
background, training, and intelligence. In that regard she was typical of
uncounted women on the periphery of academic life. As admirable and
gratifying as academic life may be, the American university is not
an island of rational androgyny. It was, and remains, a mirror, not faithful to be sure, of a society so molded by sexism as to confound easy
analysis.

Conclusion

Feminist historians are discovering a wealth of women to inspire the women of today and tomorrow. Angie Debo exemplifies another woman of superior education, experience, motivation, and achievement who was unable to find her academic niche. Growing up in frontier Oklahoma, Debo taught school before entering the University at Norman, taught again to finance graduate study at the University of Chicago where she compiled a brilliant record, and was encouraged to become a scholar. Between her master's and doctoral studies she sought a college teaching job; of the thirty institutions that contacted Chicago's history department for nominations of its graduates, she reported in an interview years later, "twenty-nine of them said they wouldn't take a woman under any circumstances. One of them said they preferred a man."[159] Her refuge became tiny West Texas State Teachers College where she taught for ten years while earning a Ph.D. from the University of Oklahoma. Her pioneering dissertation on the ethnohistory of the Choctaws was published in 1934 to scholarly acclaim. Already at work on another of her nine books, she never gained an academic position, her path apparently blocked only by her sex. She spent the last eight years of her career before retiring, in 1955, as curator of maps in the library of Oklahoma A & M University.

The past speaks to the present in many ways. There is little doubt that the experiences of relative isolation or outright alienation are shared across generations of academic women, and that inner-directedness alone sustained many. Feelings of ambivalence, intense need to prove oneself, and betrayal redound in the writings of the early women as they echo among their present-day counterparts. It must, however, have taken more courage and willing acceptance of their deviance for these early women to enroll, persevere, and triumph in the academic life than for the women who followed. By them the path was broken and smoothed. Mildred Dresselhaus of the electrical engineering faculty of the Massachusetts Institute of Technology was motivated by a woman teacher of freshman physics at Hunter College and aided by the women faculty of the University of Chicago: "Women students had gone through the mill before me, and had been successful," she wrote. This was for her sufficient encouragement despite the lack of sympathy of her thesis advisor, who "was totally unsympathetic to career women."[160]

Not surprisingly, many women faculty and their students accepted key elements in the prevailing sex typing. Given the socialization to which they were subjected, it was the rare woman who could ignore *all* that she had been taught about women's destiny and innate character. Even a perceived "radical" like Theresa McMahon, a fearless activist on women's labor issues, declined to find financial support for women graduate students because their plans to marry did not, unlike male students, signify career commitments. In this same vein, when Luch Stebbins sent out questionnaires to departments after becoming Berkeley's dean of women in 1912, she ignored such fields as law because of the length of graduate study required. Writing in 1915 about the failure of many women to enter the new fields of study in higher education, Emilie McVea, dean of women and assistant professor of English at the University of Cincinnati, concluded that these fields had "little intrinsic appeal to women and . . . were highly specialized, and women do not generally take kindly to specialization." She spoke favorably instead about "a school of charities and philanthropy"—i.e., social work—and about women using their current interests in government and study of political science to fit themselves for "higher secretarial positions to governors and state officials."[161]

In their own era, the ideas these women espoused were progressive, but not radical. They allowed women to advance primarily through extending "women's sphere" rather than by challenging the status quo. Progress was not always evident. The proportion of women specializing in science has actually declined during this century. And, while many women early in the century took degrees in and taught mathematics, especially in the high schools, the later twentieth century "discovered" that girls and women have "math anxiety."

Women were 20 percent of the Berkeley mathematics department faculty in 1928 (three of fifteen) and none of eighty-one in 1968. "Women scholars are not taken seriously and cannot look forward to a normal professional career," two sociologists wrote during the peak years of academic hiring in the United States after World War II. "This bias is part of the much larger pattern which determines the utilization of women in our economy. It is not peculiar to the academic world, but it does blight the prospects of female scholars."[162] Like the earliest women students and faculty, primarily concerned with breaking into male education, their successors must still battle for access. But the present generation demands even more. It has been readied by feminist theory and scholarship to question the "competitive, egotistical, and entrepreneurial culture" of higher education itself.[163] The experiences of these women should fuel that challenge.

The women featured in this volume were alike confident of their intellectual and professional abilities, however much they might suffer—like the rest of humankind—doubts about their personal acceptance by others, especially those with more power. They were intrepid lone voyagers. Highly visible and remembered as unique and demanding of respect, these early academic pioneers were taken seriously by their students. Some were role models. Some were also leaders of new scholarly and educational efforts. Students and colleagues, male and female, sometimes recognized and acknowledged their effects, assisting the historian in assessing the personal influence and impact of women on higher education. "I just love you so much it hurts," one student wrote to Grace Hebard.

To continue the task of historical recovery requires many more biographies of individual women and collective studies of academic women in varying kinds of institutions and different eras. Lucille Pollard's survey, Patricia Palmieri's portrait of the women of the Wellesley College faculty, and Margaret Rossiter's study of U.S. women scientists have shown the way. The authors and compilers of this anthology hope their example will also stimulate further scholarship, and inform women and men of the contributions that both sexes have made to the history of American higher education—and of the talent and energy that are squandered when gender is put ahead of humanity.

Notes

1. Lois Scharf, *To Work and to Wed: Female Employment, Feminism, and the Great Depression* (Westport, Conn.: Greenwood Press, 1980), p. 92.

2. Susan B. Carter, "Academic Women Revisited: An Empirical study of Changing Patterns of Women's Employment as College and University Faculty, 1890–1963," *Journal of Social History* 14, no. 4 (Summer 1981): 675–99; Lucille A. Pollard, *Women on College and University Faculties: A Historical Survey and a Study of Their Present Academic Status* (New York: Arno Press, 1977), p. 190. After 1945 their percentages began to decline, the principal factor being a flood of men coming into colleges that swamped women as both students and teachers. Although there were more women faculty in 1962 (94,003) than ever before, women as a percent of all academics reached their lowest point in over seventy years: 21.97 percent. In Canada women's share of university teaching went from 11.4 percent in 1960 to 13.9 percent in 1974. Janet Scarfe and Edward Sheffield, "Notes on the Canadian Professoriate," in *Comparative Perspectives on the Academic Profession,* ed. Philip G. Altbach (New York: Praeger, 1977), p. 93.

3. Ann Phillips, ed., *A Newnham Anthology* (Cambridge, England: Cambridge University Press, 1979), p. 80.

4. In a survey of eighty-one institutions of all kinds, including women's colleges, in the eastern and southern United States, Pollard found the largest

proportion of academic women (12.5 percent of the total) were teaching in English departments. In the fields in which women are more numerous, they are also better rewarded.

5. A. Phillips, *Newnham Anthology,* pp. 157–58.

6. Rosalind Rosenberg, *Beyond Separate Spheres: Intellectual Roots of Modern Feminism* (New Haven: Yale University Press, 1982), p. 244.

7. Helen R. Olin, *The Women of a State University* (New York: G. P. Putnam's Sons, 1910), pp. 292–93.

8. C. H. Handschin, "The Percentage of Women Teachers in State Colleges and Universities," *Science,* 12 January 1912, p. 57.

9. Pollard, *Women on College and University Faculties*, p. 158.

10. Ibid., p. 159.

11. Patricia Ann Palmieri, "In Adamless Eden: A Social Portrait of the Academic Community at Wellesley College, 1857–1920" (Ed.D. diss., Harvard University, 1981).

12. Louise Fargo Brown, *Apostle of Democracy: The Life of Lucy Maynard Salmon* (New York: Harper & Brothers, 1943), p. 104.

13. Margaret Rossiter, *Women Scientists in America: Struggles and Strategies to 1940* (Baltimore: Johns Hopkins University Press, 1982), pp. 172, 174.

14. Luella Cole Pressy, "The Women Whose Names Appear in 'American Men of Science' for 1927," *School and Society,* 19 January 1929, p. 100.

15. Jane Louise Jones, *A Personnel Study of Women Deans in Colleges and Universities,* Teachers College, Columbia University Contributions to Education no. 326 (New York, 1928), p. 19.

16. In 1952, for example, 53 percent of such positions in women's colleges were filled by women. In Pollard, *Women on College and University Faculties*, p. 43.

17. Mabel Newcomer, *A Century of Higher Education for Women* (New York: Harper & Brothers, 1959), pp. 48, 88; Pollard, *Women on College and University Faculties*, pp. 178–79.

18. By 1960 the elite women's colleges, which had educated 30 percent of college women in 1880, enrolled only 3 percent in 1960. Newcomer, *A Century of Higher Education,* pp. 48, 88.

19. Male-female parity was reached by the 1970s. Amy Friedlander and Ayse Ilgaz-Carden, "Creeping Forward at a Snail's Pace: College as Instrument of Change in the Status of Women" (Unpublished paper, Agnes Scott College, 1982), pp. 12–14.

20. Brown, *Apostle of Democracy,* p. 59.

21. Newcomer, *A Century of Higher Education,* pp. 37, 48.

22. Carter, "Academic Women," p. 681.

23. Geraldine Jonçich Clifford, " 'Shaking Dangerous Questions from the Crease': Gender and American Higher Education," *Feminist Issues* 3, no. 2 (Fall 1983): 31–32.

24. Friedlander and Ilgaz-Carden, "Creeping Forward," p. 5.

25. C. Vann Woodward, *Origins of the New South, 1877–1913* (Baton Rouge: Louisiana State University Press, 1951), p. 439.

26. A recent anthology about academic women in the South is revealing, titled *Stepping off the Pedestal: Academic Women on the Move,* ed. Patricia A. Stringer and Irene Thompson (New York: Modern Language Association of America, 1982).

27. Among the academic women in a sample of eighty-one institutions in 1963, one-third of those in northeastern schools and 21 percent of southern-employed women possessed a doctorate; the comparable regional figures for male faculty were 57.6 percent and 56.6 percent. Pollard, *Women on College and University Faculties,* p. 284.

28. Robert A. Leflar, *The First 100 Years: Centennial History of the University of Arkansas* (Fayetteville: University of Arkansas Foundation/Bobbs-Merrill, 1972), p. 154.

29. Pollard, *Women on College and University Faculties,* p. 174.

30. Ibid., pp. 169–71.

31. William H. Exum, "Academia as an Internal Labor Market: Implications for Women and Minority Faculty" (Unpublished paper, American Educational Research Association Annual Meeting, New Orleans, April 1984), pp. 5, 6.

32. Ibid., p. 11.

33. Theodore Caplow and Reece J. McGee, *The Academic Marketplace* (New York: Science Editions, 1961), p. 111.

34. Rossiter, *Women Scientists,* pp. 187–88.

35. W. Bruce Leslie, "Between Piety and Expertise: Professionalization of College Faculty in the 'Age of the University,' " *Pennsylvania History* 46, no. 3 (July 1979): 252, 256.

36. A. B. Hollingshead, "Ingroup Membership and Academic Selection," *American Sociological Review* 3, no. 6 (December 1938): 826–33.

37. Rossiter, *Women Scientists,* pp. 51, 63.

38. Margaret Gordon and Clark Kerr, "University Behavior and Policies: Where are the Women and Why?," in *The Higher Education of Women: Essays in Honor of Rosemary Park,* ed. Helen S. Astin and Werner Z. Hirsch (New York: Praeger, 1978), p. 120.

39. Pollard, *Women on College and University Faculties,* p. 132.

40. Lulu Holmes, *A History of the Position of Dean of Women in a Selected Group of Co-Educational Colleges and Universities in the United States,* Teachers College, Columbia University Contributions to Education, no. 767 (New York, 1939), pp. 110, 115.

41. Rossiter, *Women Scientists,* p. 64.

42. Mary Louise Filbey, "The Early History of the Deans of Women, University of Illinois, 1897–1923" (Unpublished paper, University of Illinois, 1969), p. 6.

43. Joan Jacobs Brumberg and Nancy Tomes, "Women in the Professions: A Research Agenda for American Historians," *Reviews in American History* 10, no. 2 (June 1982): 285.

44. Pollard, *Women on College and University Faculties,* p. 189.

45. Ibid., pp. 144–45.

46. Holmes, *History of Dean of Women,* pp. 11, 12. Unless otherwise credited, further references to deans of women are from Holmes.

47. A. Caswell Ellis, "Preliminary Report of Committee W, on Status of Women in College and University Faculties," *Bulletin of American Association of University Professors* 7, no. 62 (October 1921): 22. As men's colleges were opened to coeducation in the 1960s and 70s, the earlier-seen principle worked as well. Thus, when Yale first admitted women as undergraduates in 1969, there were 20 women in a faculty of 675; by 1981 there were 123 women and 645 men on the faculty. Similar changes occurred at Colgate, Trinity College, Princeton, and Dartmouth.

48. Rossiter, *Women Scientists,* p. 71.

49. Mary Bennett Ritter, *More Than Gold in California, 1849–1933* (Berkeley: Professional Press, 1933), pp. 201–4.

50. Ibid., p. 206.

51. Jessica Blanche Peixotto Collected Papers, Bancroft Library, University of California, Berkeley; Lucy Sprague Mitchell, *My Two Lives: The Story of Wesley Clair Mitchell and Myself* (New York: Simon & Schuster, 1953), p. 192; Holmes, *History of Dean of Women,* p. 39.

52. Phyllis Kay Wilke, "Physical Education for Women at Nebraska University, 1879–1923, *"Nebraska History* 55 (Summer 1975): 193–219.

53. Sandra P. Epstein, "Women and Legal Education: The Case of Boalt Hall," *Pacific Historian* 28, no. 3 (Fall 1984): 18.

54. Filbey, "Early History of Dean of Women," pp. 4–5.

55. Holmes, *History of Dean of Women,* p. 38.

56. Ibid., pp. 25–26.

57. Deans of women's most common rank was professor, although only a minority of those in coeducational schools had doctoral degrees and it was already difficult for any person lacking a doctorate, especially a woman, otherwise to gain a professorship. Jane Louise Jones, *A Personnel Study of Women Deans in Colleges and Universities,* Teachers College, Columbia University Contributions to Education, no. 326 (New York, 1928), pp. 12, 23–24.

58. Holmes, *History of Dean of Women,* p. 13.

59. Ibid., p. 7.

60. Blanche Athena Clough, *A Memoir of Anne Jemima Clough* (London: Edward Arnold, 1897), p. 195.

61. Rossiter, *Women Scientists,* p. 71; Margaret Floy Washburn, "Autobiography," in *A History of Psychology in Autobiography,* vol. 3, ed. Carl Murchison (New York: Russell & Russell, 1961).

62. Filbey, "Early History of Deans of Women," p. 11.

63. Holmes, *History of Dean of Women,* pp. 31–34.

64. Filbey, "Early History of Deans of Women," pp. 41–44.

65. Olin, *Women of a State University,* p. 295.

66. Sarah M. Sturtevant, Ruth Strang, and Margaret McKim, *Trends in Student Personnel Work* (New York: Teachers College, 1940).

67. National Center for Education Statistics, *Digest of Education Statistics, 1981* (Washington, D.C.: United States Department of Education, 1981), p. 109.

68. Holmes, *History of Dean of Women,* pp. 89–90.

69. In the present period, it has been found that where women graduate students are numerous they are more likely to think themselves taken seriously and perceived by faculty as dedicated students than is true in fields that are male-dominated or have a masculine imagery. Saul D. Feldman, *Escape from the Doll's House: Women in Graduate and Professional Education* (New York: McGraw-Hill, 1974), pp. 70–71.

70. Newcomer, *A Century of Higher Education,* p. 91.

71. Ibid., p. 255.

72. Quoted in Rosenberg, *Beyond Separate Spheres,* pp. 48–49.

73. By 1930 the figure of total faculty in the male fields had dropped to 30 percent, giving prospective academic women a somewhat greater opportunity for employment. Gordon and Kerr, "University Behavior and Policies," p. 118.

74. Newcomer, *A Century of Higher Education,* p. 90; Pollard, *Women on College and University Faculties,* p. 135.

75. Obituary, *Oakland Tribune,* 4 March 1985.

76. Newcomer, *A Century of Higher Education,* p. 99. There is correspondence concerning Albert Smith and Mary Roberts Smith in the Stanford Archives. This fascinating woman, who had a second academic career at Mills College following a mental breakdown, service as a social worker in San Francisco, and remarriage to a novelist, richly deserves a biography.

77. Marion Talbot, *More Than Lore: Reminiscences* (Chicago: University of Chicago Press, 1936), p. 153.

78. In Ellis, "Preliminary Report of Committee W," p. 25.

79. Charlotte Conable, *Women at Cornell: The Myth of Equal Education* (Ithaca, N.Y.: Cornell University Press, 1977), p. 127. The first woman full professor in Cornell's College of Arts and Sciences did not appear until 1960 although the majority of Cornell's women students had always enrolled therein. Rossiter, *Women Scientists,* p. 65.

80. Talbot, *More Than Lore,* pp. 136–39.

81. Jo Freeman, "Women on the Social Science Faculties Since 1892, University of Chicago," in *Discrimination against Women,* ed. Edith Green et al., Hearings before the Special Subcommittee on Education of the Committee on Education and Labor, House of Representatives, 91st Cong., 2d sess., on Section 805 of HR 16098 (Washington, D.C.: United States Government Printing Office, 1970), pp. 273–85.

82. Ellis, "Preliminary Report of Committee W," p. 23.

83. In her 1963 study of southern and eastern institutions, Pollard found that women chaired departments in 11 percent of the cases; eliminating the fields of women's physical education, nursing, and home economics reduced

their chairs to 6 percent; had women's colleges been excluded the figures would have been still lower. Pollard, *Women on College and University Faculties,* pp. 265–67. One of the very few women presidents of colleges other than secular and Catholic women's colleges was Kate Galt Zaneis who headed Southeastern State College in Oklahoma from 1935 to 1937. Cited in Melvena K. Thurman, ed., *Women in Oklahoma: A Century of Change* (Oklahoma City: Oklahoma Historical Society, 1982), p. 157.

84. Nancy Hoffman, *"Women's True Profession": Voices from the History of Teaching* (Old Westbury, N.Y.: Feminist Press, 1981), p. xvii.

85. Clifford, "Teaching as a Seedbed of Feminism," (Unpublished paper, Fifth Berkshire Conference on Women's History, Vassar College, June 1981).

86. Clifford, " 'Shaking Dangerous Questions,' " pp. 24–27.

87. Talbot, *More Than Lore,* p. 133.

88. Woodie T. White, "The Decline of the Classroom and the Chicago Study of Education, 1909–1929," *American Journal of Education* 90, no. 2 (February 1982): 167.

89. Ellis, "Preliminary Report of Committee W," p. 23.

90. Ella Lonn, "Academic Status of Women on University Faculties," *Journal of American Association of University Women* 17, no. 1 (January–March 1924): 6.

91. White, "Decline of the Classroom," pp. 166–67.

92. Rossiter, *Women Scientists,* p. 187.

93. Brown, *Apostle of Democracy,* p. 72.

94. Barbara Miller Solomon, "Ada Louise Comstock," in *Notable American Women: The Modern Period,* ed. Barbara Sicherman and Carol Hurd Green (Cambridge: Harvard University Press, 1980), pp. 157–58.

95. Martha Carey Thomas, *The Making of a Feminist: Early Journals and Letters of M. Carey Thomas,* ed. Marjorie Housepian Dobkin (Kent, Ohio: Kent State University Press, 1979).

96. Courtesy of Joanne V. Hawkes, Director, Sarah Isom Center for Women's Studies, University of Mississippi. President Barnard had been chancellor of the University of Mississippi.

97. Mitchell, *My Two Lives.* A brief biographical sketch of Jacqueline De La Harpe is published in University of California, *In Memoriam, 1985* (Berkeley: Academic Senate, 1985), pp. 104–6.

98. Juanita M. Kreps, "The Woman Professional in Higher Education," in *Women in Higher Education,* ed. W. Todd Furniss and Patricia A. Graham (Washington, D.C.: American Council on Education, 1974), p. 81.

99. For M. Carey Thomas's rejoinder, see her *Education of Women* (Albany, N.Y.: J. B. Lyon Co., 1900), p. 26.

100. Le Clerc Phillips, "The Problem of the Educated Woman," *Harpers* 154 (December 1926): 58, 59.

101. Thomas Woody, *A History of Women's Education in the United States,* vol. 1 (New York: Science Press, 1929), p. 324.

102. Pollard, *Women on College and University Faculties,* pp. 104, 109; Palmieri, "In Adamless Eden," pp. 295, 304.

103. Rosenberg, "The Academic Prism: The New View of American Women," in *Women of America: A History,* ed. Carol Ruth Berkin and Mary Beth Norton (Boston: Houghton Mifflin, 1979), p. 337. The proportions of women among new doctorates peaked in the late 1920s.

104. In Carter, "Academic Women," p. 685.

105. Robert C. Johnson, "Affirmative Action and the Academic Profession," *Annals of the American Academy of Political and Social Science* 448 (March 1980): 114; Lucy Diggs Slowe quoted in Marion Vera Cuthbert, *Education and Marginality: A Study of the Negro Woman College Graduate* (New York: American Book—Stratford Press, 1942), p. 114.

106. Olin, *Women of a State University,* p. 292.

107. Emilie J. Hutchinson, *Women and the Ph.D.* Institute of Women's Professional Relations Bulletin, No. 2 (Greensboro: North Carolina College for Women, 1930), p. 22. Attrition rates remained greater for women: in 1965 they earned 52 percent of high school diplomas, 41 percent of college degrees, 32 percent of master's degrees, and 11 percent of doctorates. Oliver Fulton, "Rewards and Fairness: Academic Women in the United States," in *Teachers and Students: Aspects of American Higher Education,* ed. Martin Trow (New York: McGraw-Hill, 1975), p. 201.

108. Bonnie Cook Freeman, "Faculty Women in the American University: Up the Down Staircase," *Higher Education* 6, no. 2 (May 1977): 176–77.

109. Pollard, *Women on College and University Faculties,* p. 273.

110. Alice M. Gordon, "The After-Careers of University-Educated Women," *The Nineteenth Century* 37 (June 1895): 955–60.

111. Filbey, "Early History of Deans of Women," p. 56.

112. Amory Dwight Mayo, in *Southern Women in the Recent Educational Movement in the South,* ed. Dan T. Carter and Amy Friedlander (Baton Rouge: Louisiana State University Press, 1978), p. 168.

113. Alan Creutz, "Social Access to the Professoriate: The Pattern of Late Nineteenth Century America" (Unpublished paper, American Historical Association Annual Meeting, San Francisco, December 1978), p. 9.

114. Wanda Neff, *Lone Voyagers* (Boston: Houghton Mifflin, 1929), p. 3.

115. Ellis, "Preliminary Report of Committee W," p. 22. Such expectations in the sexist institutions of American higher education persist according to interviews with women presently in doctoral studies. As one put it, "I had to write better papers than the men. I have to have better documentation. I was called upon daily." In the same study another said, "In seminar, women had to be impeccable. Everyone else could be mediocre, but women had to be impeccable." Katherine Jensen, "Women's Work and Academic Culture: Adaptations and Confrontations," *Higher Education* 11, no. 1 (January 1982): 72, 79.

116. Olin, *Women of a State University,* pp. 297–98.

117. L. Phillips, "Problem of the Educated Woman," pp. 59–60, 62, 63.

118. Mariette Nowak, *Eve's Rib* (New York: St. Martin's Press, 1980), p. 246.

119. David Starr Jordan, *The Days of a Man: Being Memories of a Naturalist, Teacher and Minor Prophet of Democracy, Vol. I: 1851–1899* (Yonkers, N.Y.: World Book Co., 1922), p. 441. More positively, see Jordan's, "The Higher Education of Women," *Popular Science Monthly* 62 (December 1902): 97–107.

120. Lonn, "Academic Status," p. 7.

121. Clifford, "Shaking Dangerous Questions," pp. 48–54.

122. Lonn, "Academic Status," p. 7.

123. Jacquelyn A. Mattfeld, "Many Are Called, but Few Are Chosen," in Furniss and Graham, *Women in Higher Education*, p. 124. If their numbers are thought appreciable, women's presence subtracts prestige from the organizations in which they work—provided they are there as peers of men; their employment as clerical staff, waitresses in the faculty club, and as research assistants is accepted as helpful to men in doing *their* work. Adrienne Rich, "Toward a Woman Centered University," in *Women and the Power to Change*, ed. Florence Howe (New York: McGraw-Hill, 1975), pp. 26–27.

124. Newcomer, *A Century of Higher Education*, p. 164; Rossiter, *Women Scientists*, p. 206; Jensen, "Women's Work," p. 80.

125. Jesse Taft, *The Woman Movement from the Point of View of Social Consciousness* (Menasha, Wis.: Collegiate Press, 1915), p. 4.

126. Everett V. Stonequist, *The Marginal Man* (New York: Charles Scribner's Sons, 1937); Rosenberg, *Beyond Separate Spheres*, pp. xxi–xxii.

127. Neff, *Lone Voyagers*, p. 4.

128. Lynn D. Gordon, "Coeducation on Two Campuses: Berkeley and Chicago, 1890–1912," in *Women's Being, Women's Place: Female Identity and Vocation in American History*, ed. Mary Kelley (Boston: G. K. Hall, 1979), p. 178.

129. Sandra Acker, "Women, The Other Academics," *Women's Studies International Forum* 6, no. 2 (1983): 194.

130. In 1985 an astute alumna wrote to UCLA that "the *de facto* exclusion of women from the Faculty Research Lectures stinks." Only one woman, Lily Bess Campbell, in 1935, had ever been selected for this annually conferred honor that began in 1925. The selection committee is comprised of former lecturers. Sara Meric, "Lectures Blasted," *UCLA Monthly* 15, no. 5 (May–June 1985): 2.

131. Entry for 28 January 1901, Ida Hyde Papers, American Association of University Women Archives, Schlesinger Library, Radcliffe College.

132. Lonn, "Academic Status," p. 8.

133. In Ellis, "Preliminary Report of Committee W," p. 27.

134. Rossiter, *Women Scientists*, p. 164.

135. Hutchinson, p. 21; Pressy, "Women in 'American Men of Science,'" p. 100.

136. Cuthbert, *Education and Marginality*, p. 141.

137. Marital status continues to distinguish female and male faculty. Helen Astin, *The Woman Doctorate in America: Origins, Career, and Family* (New York: Russell Sage Foundation, 1969), pp. 26–32; Freeman, "Women on the

Social Science Faculties," pp. 171–75; Fulton, "Rewards and Fairness," pp. 204–7.

138. Fulton, "Rewards and Fairness," p. 233.

139. Rosemary Yost Deegan, *The Stereotypes of the Single Woman in American Novels* (New York: Octagon Books, 1967), pp. 123, 132.

140. Neff, *Lone Voyagers,* p. 11.

141. In Scharf, *To Work and to Wed,* p. 83.

142. Mitchell, *My Two Lives,* p. 193.

143. Carrie A. Harper, "A Feminine Professorial Viewpoint," *Educational Review* 46 (June 1913): pp. 48, 51.

144. Cuthbert, *Education and Marginality,* p. 36; Rayford Logan, *Howard University: The First Hundred Years, 1867–1967* (New York: New York University Press, 1969), p. 170.

145. Mossie May Kirkwood, *For College Women . . . and Men* (Toronto: University of Toronto, 1938), p. 67.

146. Linda L. Mather, "The Education of Women: Images from Popular Magazines" (Ph.D. diss., University of Pennsylvania, 1977), p. 250.

147. Pollard, *Women on College and University Faculties,* p. 182.

148. Barbara Sicherman, *Alice Hamilton: A Life in Letters* (Cambridge: Harvard University Press, 1984), p. 5.

149. Ellis, "Preliminary Report of Committee W," p. 21; John Brubacher et al. *The Department of Education at Yale University, 1891–1958* (New Haven, Conn.: n.p., 1960).

150. Louise Pound, "Graduate Work for Women," *School and Society,* 27 May 1922, p. 573.

151. Rossiter, *Women Scientists,* pp. 162–63.

152. Helen Reed, quoted in Mather, "Education of Women," p. 91; L. Gordon, "Coeducation," p. 188. See, also, Patricia A. Graham, "Women in Academe," *Science* 169 (September 1970): 1284–91.

153. Pollard, *Women on College and University Faculties,* pp. 170–71.

154. In Holmes, *History of Dean of Women,* pp. 25–26.

155. Cuthbert, *Education and Marginality,* p. 41.

156. Ellis, "Preliminary Report of Committee W," p. 27.

157. Heather Sigworth, "Issues in Nepotism Rules," in Furniss and Graham, *Women in Higher Education,* pp. 117–18.

158. Papers relating to Marguerite Hall Albjerg are courtesy of her daughter, Patricia Albjerg Graham, Harvard University (and herself the first woman appointed to the deanship of a professional school in Harvard's history). Also, Helen B. Schleman (former dean of women, Indiana University) to Geraldine J. Clifford, 1 November 1984.

159. Glenna C. Matthews and Gloria Valencia-Weber, "Against Great Odds: The Life of Angie Debo," *Organization of American Historians' Newsletter* 13, no. 2 (May 1985): 8–11.

160. Mildred S. Dresselhaus, "Electrical Engineer," in *Women and Success,* ed. Ruth B. Kundsin (New York: William Morrow, 1974), pp. 39–40.

161. Emilie W. McVea, "The Effect of Recent Educational Developments upon the Higher Education of Women," *Education* 36, no. 1 (September 1915): 13, 18–19.

162. Caplow and McGee, *Academic Marketplace,* p. 226.

163. Pamela Roby, "Women and American Higher Education," *Annals of the American Academy of Political and Social Science* 404 (November 1972): 118.

MARIA LOUISE SANFORD

"Best Loved" . . . *and Besieged*

MARIA LOUISE SANFORD
1836–1920

by Geraldine Jonçich Clifford

In July of 1880, William W. Folwell, president of the University of Minnesota, wrote to his wife from Baltimore. Midway in a faculty recruiting effort he was discouraged, despite the many applications seen and candidates interviewed. "It was a colossal blunder to make all these vacancies at once," he conceded. "I don't expect to find a man for Ag. & I fear we may not get 'prima facie' men for any place."[1] The recruiting circular listed six principal positions: mental and moral philosophy, mechanical engineering and physics, mathematics and astronomy, French language and literature, chemistry, and theory and practice of agriculture. The committee also mentioned a lecturer in the theory and practice of teaching and an instructor in vocal music, and proposed "to employ an assistant to the Professor of English, who shall be an elocutionist, and shall conduct the rhetorical exercises of the lower classes and the rehearsals of the upper classes, and teach Rhetoric and English if necessary."[2] This plethora of positions was caused not by a sudden prospering of the university but by dissatisfactions within the board of regents that led to forced resignations, and precipitated a rift in the faculty and circulation of a handbill attacking Governor Pillsbury, the most powerful regent.[3] Additionally, the professor of English was seriously ill and requested an assistant, and the Minneapolis resident who had been giving free instruction in elocution was unable to continue.[4]

The recruiting effort concentrated in the northeastern states; the majority of the trustees and early faculty of the university were Yankees.[5] The final statement of the recruiting circular reaffirmed that the university was willing to consider a woman. It had two women, an assistant in German and the preceptress and instructor in English, Mrs. Smith, who was among those leaving. It was also "preferred to put the department of French in charge of a competent lady, who shall at the same time discharge such of the duties of a preceptress as the circumstances allow." On July 9 Folwell wrote to an applicant, Maria L. Sanford: "We have a number of vacancies not arranged for, but I fear none that would suit your tastes . . . You will see that it is for the French Dept. that we are seeking a woman."[6] After interviewing her in Chautauqua, however, Folwell recommended hiring Sanford, a Yankee and professor of history at Swarthmore College from 1870 to 1879, as assistant professor of English, to teach rhetoric and elocution at $1,200 per year. The regents confirmed the committee's recommendation and Maria Sanford arrived in Minneapolis on September 22, 1880 to begin a tenure on the faculty that lasted until her retirement in 1909.

Undoubtedly Sanford's experience and reputation as a public lecturer, beginning with the large regional meetings of teachers called "institutes," helped convince the committee to upgrade the vacancy in elocution. But the efforts of Swarthmore's president, Edward H. Magill, on her behalf were also important.[7] During several years previous, Magill had recommended Sanford to such university presidents as Angell of Michigan and White of Cornell.[8] In later years Folwell boasted that the one service to the university

> for which I will claim to deserve the congratulations and the gratitude of all concerned . . . is the discovery of Professor Maria L. Sanford at Chautauqua, N.Y. one fine summer morning in 1880. An hours conversation, on the bench, shaded by a tree, satisfied me that we need look no further for the woman to be added to our faculty.[9]

This woman came to be called the "best known and best loved woman in Minnesota." Her statue was one of the two representing Minnesota in Statuary Hall in the nation's Capitol. Her name was given to a Minneapolis public school, a dormitory at the University of Minnesota, an academic building at Central Connecticut College in New Britain (the successor institution to the normal school from which she had graduated in 1855), to scholarships for senior college women, and was included in a window in a black church in the South. Carleton College awarded her an honorary doctorate. Such recognition was reached, however, only after a prolonged and lonely ordeal, and was accompanied by many doubters—for Maria Sanford was not universally esteemed. When she struggled for the Minnesota position, she was unemployed, in debt, and in love with a married man.[10] She knew of the opinion that women like herself far exceeded the bounds of appropriate feminine behavior. Writing on her behalf a friend noted, "There are as yet so few women who have achieved a right to ask for a professorship in a college, that it would seem as if there might be a chance for the few."[11] There was a chance, albeit a slight one.

The struggles between President Folwell and the regents' "Bourbon" faction, that sent so many faculty coming and going in 1880, reflected the unsettled conditions that afflicted many institutions in their early histories. Poor management of the university's funds, the small population of the state, the closure of the institution during the Civil War, and the more persisting lack of secondary schools able to prepare students for college work threatened the university's existence. The state's agricultural interests squared off against the "exponents of dead languages"; it was even proposed to separate the Agricultural College and its properties from the rest of the tiny university.[12] Of his board of regents, President Folwell wrote in 1869 that "They are good men, but do not yet know what a University is."[13] In turn, a majority of the regents eventually let Folwell know that "it might be advantageous to the University to call to its head some one else—some one, if possible, of established reputation in connection with the famous eastern Universities—some one with the prestige of a well known name."[14] His leadership questioned, Folwell resigned in March 1883 and was given the professorship of political economy. His successor, Yale professor Cyrus Northrop, took up the office in 1884. While her career had prospered under Folwell's presidency and they remained warm friends, Maria Sanford knew Northrop, welcomed his selection, and had no apparent reason to feel insecure at the change.

In fact the prospects of the faculty were always tenuous. Those, like Sanford, who survived a decade, had good statistical chances of a long career at Minnesota.[15] But they had little assurance of this in advance. Although the regents ceased, in 1882, the anxiety-provoking practice of requiring annual reappointments, and redefined employment as "terminable at the pleasure of the Board of Regents," resignations might be requested or salaries cut suddenly and without recourse.[16] Minnesota's situation was disparaged by Harvard's president, Charles W. Eliot. Enclosing the names of some candidates for the 1880 search, he advised Folwell that

> You expect to take rather young men, I suppose. The tenure is so insecure that you can hardly expect to get any others. I feel like expressing

my commiseration for you who are trying to build a university under such conditions. Bricks without straw are relatively easy to make.[17]

Some prospective faculty refused to consider such unfavorable terms. Frank Clarke was unwilling to leave his position in Cincinnati, even to be interviewed. The implication of annual elections, he thought,

> would deter many desirable men from becoming candidates. Above all things, stability in his position is important to a scientific man. If he is all the time to be worried about reelections, he cannot do his best work. In most colleges appointments are for life or during good behavior; and such institutions are all the time drawing away the best men from those schools which follow the other policy. I do not see how a strong, harmonious efficient Faculty can be kept together where annual elections are the rule.[18]

Refused his "prayer" to the regents to have his salary increased, the professor in charge of the Department of Agriculture left the University of Minnesota. Of the Minnesota regents he wrote Folwell, "I believe that they have yet to learn the greater importance of a first class, trusted, unfettered and unterrified teaching force."[19] The faculty became a mix of "locals"—loyal Minnesota alumni, devoted teachers, would-be scholars without the requisite credentials or standing to be sought by more desirable places, and "cosmopolitans," men like Alexander Osmund, hired at the same time as Sanford, but soon called away to Princeton, or philosopher John Dewey, who taught at Minnesota briefly, on the way to Michigan, Chicago, and Columbia.[20] Despite her growing reputation as a university extension lecturer and public speaker, Maria Sanford was forced by age, lack of academic degrees, and gender to cast her lot with Minnesota. She wrote to Folwell in 1883, "I see Professors of Modern Languages & of English & Eng. Literature come and go but I think my own thoughts and ask no questions."[21]

At that point her own future looked bright. Among those hired in 1880, she was paid as much as some men who had completed graduate programs, including a professor of chemistry with a Ph.D. degree.[22] After only one year Sanford was promoted to professor of elocution and rhetoric and her annual salary raised to $1,600; the next year there was a raise to $1,700 with an additional $200 "for her services as Matron of the Institution"—presumably recognizing the fact that she housed a number of students in her residence.[23] After Professor Marston's death in 1883, she was put in charge of the English department until his replacement was hired, and a further increase, to $1,900, came in 1885. The economic depression of the nineties slowed her progress, but the regents voted in September 1895 "that the salary of Prof. M. L. Sanford be made $2,250 for the present year and $2,400 thereafter."[24] Her lecturing around Minnesota, where she addressed farmers' wives, civic groups, and schoolchildren, was credited with playing a major role in establishing public confidence in the state university.

There was an additional sprinkling of women colleagues on the faculty. Mrs. M. J. Wilkins was made assistant professor of German and English in 1890, and new fields were broached at the end of the century with Josephine Tilden's appointment in botany, Elizabeth Beach's in history, Louise Kiehl's in physical culture, and Virginia Meredith's promotion to professor of home economics in the School of Agriculture. Sanford particularly admired Kiehl's successor, Anne Butner, for her "seeking to make others happy."[25] Ada Comstock taught in the rhetoric department from 1900 to 1912, also serving as the first dean of women from 1907, before leaving for Smith College and the presidency of Radcliffe College. Despite these achievements, Dr. H. Edith Robertson of the Department of Pathology did not exaggerate when she wrote to Professor Emeritus Maria Sanford in 1913, offering her membership in the Faculty Women's Club: "Our honorary members are so few and so loved by all that we beg of you to meet with us whenever you can."[26] Not numerous either were the club's active women faculty.

In Sanford's final year of teaching, Minnesota enrolled 4,800 students—a far cry from the 1880 institution of under 300 students and 18 faculty. At her first commencement, Sanford saw only 28 graduates, 8 of them women and 4 of these taking the bachelor of literature, rather than the more traditional bachelor of arts degree. As late as 1895, the College of Science, Literature, and the Arts awarded only 94 bachelor's degrees—a number some 50 percent smaller than the combined degrees awarded by the increasingly popular Colleges of Engineering and Law (the largest), and the Department of Medicine.[27] Into the twentieth century most women graduates continued to choose the bachelor of literature and newer bachelor of philosophy degrees.

At his inauguration in 1869, President Folwell proclaimed of the university that "it knows not male nor female, 'Barbarian, Scythian, bond, nor free.' The doors of its auditoria, its laboratories, its library, stand open to all worthy comers."[28] After Professor Ormund left for all-male Princeton University, he wrote to Folwell that it was a hopeless task at Princeton "to enlist the interest of every man in the class." In contrast to Minnesota students, "The proportion of dead beats is larger here than in the University and the teacher's work is consequently harder and more unsatisfactory."[29] Compared to Princetonians, Minnesota students were indeed unsophisticated. The lack of secondary schools had required the university, like many nineteenth-century colleges, to open with a pre-freshman program. In 1904 the regents authorized an examination in reading, writing, spelling, and English composition and established remedial courses. Sanford tried to enlist high school principals in the formation of a composition league; she would send out theme topics, receive from each school the better essays, judge them, and print the best in local newspapers. "It will not only open to the students a wide and healthful competition, but it will be a help to me in my department to know before they come to the University, the students who are ambitious in this line."[30]

While the university offered a free education that attracted students from beyond the state, the majority were residents of rural Minnesota— provincial and inexperienced for the most part. Not atypical was the former student who recalled the help Sanford gave her in registration: "I was a little sixteen year old country girl and that kindness meant much as did the five years which I spent in your classes."[31] Peter Fitzgerald contends that the midwestern land-grant universities, including Minnesota, were not democratic institutions since the students "came substantially from the mercantile and professional classes," and predominantly from native Scots-Anglo rather than immigrant families.[32] The regents, however, perceived financial need among the students and their parents. In 1882 they discussed a proposal to shorten the university year "so as to permit young men to return to the farm and young women to the country schools at the opening of Spring."[33] Thus, Minnesota officials were responding as had those at many older American colleges, including the now-elite schools of the northeast, when many of their students needed farm and teaching wages.

In Sanford's time most Minnesota undergraduates came from homes that contrasted markedly with the cosmopolitan character of the curriculum in literature and art history that she offered in her courses. Shakespeare, Kipling, and Browning were her heroes, and the pictures of works of art that she purchased and used in illustrated lectures were revelations. Students appreciated that she enlarged their horizons and promoted their ambitions to see more, do more, and translate their educational opportunities into "good works" when they returned home.[34] Those affected long remembered their days in her classrooms. Many years later, a former student wrote Sanford: "You did for me more than you can realize; since you don't know how hemmed in and brought to a stop my life seemed at the time when I first met you."[35] A teacher at the Boston Latin School wrote of his days at Swarthmore: "It is more than thirty years since I sat at Miss Sanford's feet and listened to her inspiring instruction; but no memory of my early schooldays abides so vividly still in my mind as that of this alert, vigorous, and stimulating teacher."[36] "She did more to create in me the love of knowledge than any teacher that I had the pleasure to go to," a physician remembered forty-two years after she taught him in the Parkersville, Pennsylvania common school.[37] Another rhapsodized: "To have been a pupil of such a teacher is a blessing rarely bestowed!"[38]

It was said of Maria Sanford that "in her time probably no member of the University faculty came in contact with more students."[39] Rhetoric was required of all freshmen. And, until the regents acceded to student petitions to end the practice when graduating classes got too large, each male senior gave an oration and each female senior read an essay—these at the compulsory chapel exercises or at commencement.[40] Because Sanford trained the students for these ordeals, she had prolonged contact with the graduating classes. To maintain an interest in oratory, Sanford built up the university's debating program, soliciting prize money from Minnesota alumni.[41] The regents' standard for classroom work of professors in charge of departments was fifteen hours per week. Sanford calculated that she spent an average of fourteen hours per day, five days a week, in teaching classes, training debaters, correcting papers, and supervising the work of the junior faculty in the rhetoric department.

The students called her "Maria"—pronounced in the New England way: Ma/rī/ya. Unprepared students learned that they could capitalize on her passion for her subject and get her to recite one of her favorite poems until the dismissal bell rang.[42] Not systematic as a thinker or teacher, Sanford rather was inspired and unsparing of herself. Allen Asher remembered the Shakespeare course he took in freshman year and the sophomore debate course the next. And, "I can never forget the interest you took in us boys."[43] Although her papers are filled with grateful letters from male former students, she had a particular meaning for Minnesota women. For her seventieth birthday celebration, one of these wrote to her, wondering if "you realize the love and esteem that the 'older girls' bear to you."[44] She received confidences that a male professor would not have heard, such as advice about how to handle "insults" from male faculty members. When she went to give the commencement address at the Hawley, Minnesota high school in 1919, a decade after her retirement, her 5:30 A.M. train was met by "all the girls of the graduating class, several teachers and townspeople including two or three who had been in her classes at the U."[45] Countless women's clubs, like the Married Woman's Tuesday Club of Amery, Wisconsin, thirsted for the Shakespeare readings and lectures on public issues that she was always ready to give.[46] In the words of a later woman member of the English department faculty, Maria Sanford became something of a "cult figure" to generations of women who thought her somehow representative of them. "Zealous and passionate, Maria was unique, however."[47]

In 1906 a "Woman's Building"—Alice Shevlin Hall—was opened on the campus. The occasion must have been a bittersweet one for Sanford, for it stood on the site of "Old Main." Consumed by fire in 1904, the building's loss had also taken Sanford's books and pictures, including those she purchased in Europe on a trip in 1899, financed by a local newspaper's "favorite teacher" contest and the additional contributions of her students. The loss, however, symbolizes a series of defeats in her relationship with the university. Student criticisms of Sanford began to surface in the late 1880s. Gathering because of her more frequent absences from the university for public lectures, although she never missed her classes, the student body was also expressing some of that passion for athletics and fraternity life and repudiation of paternalism that was sweeping American higher education. In 1888, a student sent Regent Pillsbury a ranking of the faculty by graduating seniors: "The best informed consider it just, fair and truthful—and . . . *thoroughly unbiased.*"[48] Of twenty-six faculty, Sanford was ranked sixteenth in "Ability" and twentieth in "Relative amount of work done." Students and colleagues complained to President Northrop that she assigned more work than the catalogue specified.[49] Her practice of purchasing books and then renting them to students for one dollar per term, even after the book was paid for, raised charges of profiteering. It was heard that private tutoring from Miss Sanford, for $25 per term, was required to pass Freshman Rhetoric. She was reported to have given grades to some students before their assignments were completed. The board of regents issued a regulation that no member of the faculty could tutor students for pay. A friend said of Sanford:

> In a passionate love for noble things, in her exalted aspiration for high achievement she was saintly and prophetic; in her daily relation with certain people, in her utter disregard for all that was *comme-il-faut* and conventional, she lent herself to disrespectful judgment. . . . She was so honest that she sometimes came near to dishonesty in small matters.[50]

What Geraldine Schofield calls "sex antagonism" may have played some part in student sentiment against her. Sanford was a friend of Susan B. Anthony but most male students boycotted Anthony's appearance at the university. Asked about this discourtesy, one responded, "We despise all she stands for."[51] Sanford's plain black dresses, which became a sort of uniform, made no concessions to fashion and flattered no man that she sought his admiration. She was emerging, in fact, as an eccentric: a woman who did the most menial house and yard work for a large number of boarders and lodgers, who reportedly swept out grain cars and collected scraps from boarding houses to feed her chickens, who walked everywhere to save carfare, who sat up all night in coach class when traveling to give lectures.

When he reiterated a series of student complaints, the president's tone was sharp:

> Now when you were struggling and pleading for a full salary, $2400, you said if you got it you would be the happiest woman in Minnesota. You did get it. All the time that you give to students belongs to the University. It is paid for by a full salary. The charging here and there five dollars or one dollars is wholly wrong and ought not to be done in any case. There is a good deal of excitement over it in certain quarters, as the fact has been brought out in one of the Faculties.[52]

On April 10, 1900 Northrop notified Sanford of a resolution introduced at the regents' meeting to terminate her employment, in 1901, along with that of a rhetoric department colleague and two other long-term professors. "I have been to see you several times to notify you of this fact but have failed to find you," he wrote. "I deeply regret the situation."[53] Instead the regents lowered the salaries of these and three other individuals. Sanford's was the severest cut; of the four professors earning $2,400, Sanford was reduced by $600, the three men by $400 apiece. Financial stringency was not the principal issue—since increases given in the College of Science, Literature, and the Arts almost offset the savings; there were also numerous increases to faculty in the professional colleges of mines, engineering, medicine, and pharmacy.[54]

Although Sanford made an attempt to secure the presidency of the University of Idaho, the struggles of the ensuing years were to prevent her dismissal or the closing of her department, and to restore her salary. The actions of well-placed friends helped to save her job.[55] Early efforts to raise her salary were not auspicious. In another effort to cut expenses, the regents reduced Sanford's salary further in 1903 (to $1,500), along with two others; the amount saved was one-third the amount spent in faculty raises. "It is awfully tough on those cut down," Northrop explained to his daughter. "But the Regents put in on the ground that the old people must be sort of pensioned [off] and the young people encouraged."[56]

Criticisms about her absences from campus and the regents' actions

of cutting her salary were bitter reminders of what had earlier happened
to Sanford at Swarthmore. She had begun lecturing to supplement her
salary. As she explained to a woman to whom she owed money, "You
will remember that I have had much to keep me back, and a woman's
salary is not very large at best."[57] President Magill recalled "the opposition thou had to meet from one [a woman member of the faculty]
who had better not now be named, and also from some members of
the Board, because thou would travel about and give lectures, (really
the best thing possible for the College at that time)."[58] In apparent response her salary was cut from $2,000 to $1,500 in 1878, precipitating
her departure the following year.[59] Such trustee action was common
given the "well-established tradition of balancing the budget at the faculty's expense and expecting them to accept financial adversity as part
of their duty."[60] Although a young college, Swarthmore was of the "old
time college" type. Its professors were dominated by the administration
and by trustees who preferred to use denominational loyalty and disciplinary success as criteria for hiring. Having no hand in selecting their
colleagues, with heavy teaching loads in addition to overseeing student
activities outside of the classroom, some might have felt justified in
resenting Sanford's absences—and her independence.

Sanford did not fight the Minnesota regents unaided. As she had
done in countering the effort to dismiss her, Sanford enlisted the help
of devoted former students, some of them prominent men. Judge S. D.
Catherwood made inquiries trying to prevent some members of the
board of regents from being reappointed.[61] Sanford wrote to Governor
Van Sant, expressing appreciation for an appointment to the Prison Association and what it symbolized:

> But what is most precious to me in this appointment is that it implies
> . . . that you do not sympathize with those who would belittle my power
> and worth. This, I assure you, is most gratifying. I believe I shall be able to
> prove that those who had confidence in me were right. I shall try to bear
> my present humiliation with dignity, and by my faithfulness and devotion
> to duty to convince all who are willing to be fair-minded, how grave an
> injustice has been done to me.[62]

The Woman's Council of Minneapolis wrote letters on her behalf.[63]
In 1904 the president of the Minnesota Federation of Women's Clubs
wrote to Sanford proposing a campaign to counter a reported scheme
"under way which is working against you."[64] By 1907, perhaps in an-
ticipation of her retirement, the regents' Salary Committee accepted the

recommendation of Dean Downey that "her salary be liberally increased." He explained that

> Miss Sanford is doing vigorous and valuable work, more concentrated and systematic than formerly. Last semester there were 962 students in the department, 217 of whom were in her own classes. She is much liked by her students, and she is widely known and highly esteemed throughout the state.[65]

By increasing her salary to $3,000, Sanford was made eligible for a Carnegie Foundation annual pension of $1,500. Spearheaded by women's organizations, a gigantic seventieth birthday celebration was held in December 1906, and the senior class in her final year of teaching chose her for its commencement speaker. Vindicated and triumphant, having outlasted her opponents, Maria Sanford entered a busy retirement.

Maria was an eccentric, not alone because of her behavior. She was certain to be watched—and satirized, if possible—because she was a woman, doing something hardly any woman did: teach in a university and travel about, speaking on issues on which women were supposed to be ignorant and silent. She was a "driven" personality, forced by an ingrained sense of duty to act in ways governed by conscience and not by social conventions; her Puritan heritage was stronger than Puritanism's restrictions on women. At her graduation oration at the New Britain Normal School, Sanford characteristically threw out the challenge: "Fear not! faint not! fail not!"[66] Lamenting the weak character of a great-nephew, she attributed it to his lacking a high purpose in life and the sense of obligation to God and humanity.[67] She tried to instill similar purposefulness in her students, telling them that she considered her duties to extend beyond rhetoric and composition, to form their characters, to help them "become better men and women."[68] Pride in self, ambition, and purpose were the desiderata of manly character—and no less required in woman's.

That her brother, Rufus, and some of her sisters' children disappointed her in meeting their responsibilities did not lessen her own Puritan sense of obligation. Rather she took upon herself the payment of their debts, and the support and education of their children. Her intense need to help others led her, imprudently, to advise friends in Pennsylvania to invest in a land speculation in Minneapolis in the 1880s. When the boom collapsed, she was some $30,000 in debt. Rather than declare bankruptcy she determined to repay everyone; the project took the rest of her life. She wrote a note to herself in 1916 rejoicing that, by dint of extreme frugality, with her pension and lecturing income, she was very nearly free of debt:

> This seems my day of emancipation. The beginning of life—the life I have always longed to live . . . while I still owe about $4000, it is all except my note to Mrs. Walker secured. So I need not worry about getting work, but I can work for others. . . . There is much to be done. *Improve every moment.*[69]

That she, who witnessed her father's long-endured indebtedness, was not cautious in money matters was an irony of her life. But, then, had the Puritan tradition persisted of naming children for their parents' expectations of them, Maria Sanford's cognomen would not have been "Prudence" or "Silence," but "Do Good" or "Resolute." Ina Firkins, one of the few persons in whom Sanford confided her inner feelings, said of her, "my Miss Sanford was a baffling combination of virtues and defects—I cannot use the word 'weakness' in regard to her because even in her mistakes she was strong."[70]

In present-day feminist thought her ambition is a virtue. In Sanford's own time, however, many thought the pursuit of opportunity wrong in a woman: moving from school to school for higher wages; allowing her supporters to put her forward for election as county superintendent of schools, a position thought reserved for men; contemplating the study of medicine; permitting her troubles at the university to become public knowledge in order to preserve her professorship. Sanford was proud. She relished the public recognition she received. When Folwell wrote of her achievements for a public ceremony, she thanked him: "It is a delight to have it said by one like you, and to believe that in my life work I have not, in the estimation of those who can calmly judge, utterly failed."[71]

Her pride prevented Sanford from having many confidants. Late in life she confessed her loneliness to Firkins. One of the few who knew her innermost thoughts was Edward Magill, president of Swarthmore College. At some point their friendship had become a love affair. Because he was married and their scruples prevented an illicit affair, Sanford eventually chose to leave Swarthmore, pledging at the same time to dedicate herself to her profession.[72] They remained friends. He occasionally visited Minneapolis and once hoped to see one of his daughters teach there, "that she might be near thee, and aided by thy wise counsels and directions."[73]

In her social views Maria Sanford was a representative figure of the Progressive movement. Her own works of social service—to preserve

Minnesota's forests, improve the health of Montana's Indians, raise funds for Negro churches and schools in the South, beautify Minneapolis, nominate the best candidates for public office—typify the social consciousness of the liberal reformer of her time. She believed in the good will and capacity of the "better classes" of people to lead the work of social and environmental regeneration. Her senior class in Literary Criticism was assigned speeches on the social problems of work and poverty, and issues like labor organization; all her students were encouraged to use their educations for the public good.[74] The first woman invited to address the Grand Army of the Republic, she proposed to the 1910 convention that northern veterans join with southerners to work for world peace.[75] Despite labor's views that colleges were dominated by antiunion professors, she received thanks from Terence Powderly, leader of the militant Knights of Labor, for "your letter came as a golden ray of sunshine to help and assist me."[76]

In responding to news of a seventieth birthday celebration for Maria Sanford, a North Dakota businessman wrote, "I am truly glad to see the rights of women thus well recognized in our State University and I shall certainly rejoice to see the day when women may enjoy all the rights and privileges that men as citizens of our commonwealth enjoy."[77] It was on this "woman question" that Sanford's own actions and opinions were the most consistently radical. Mary Clark Sanford had taught her daughter about the contributions of pioneering women like Mary Lyon; she learned early that women were clearly among those "best people" who must promote social betterment. Sanford's understanding and admiration of Susan B. Anthony must have been strengthened by the experience that these two outstanding teachers shared, subject as they were to the prevailing discrimination that gave women half or less of a man's salary. The Sanfords were also longtime supporters of temperance and Maria Sanford came to appreciate the woman suffrage movement through the Women's Christian Temperance Union, an omnibus reform organization led by another long-time teacher, Frances Willard. She earned the thanks of the director of women's physical education at Minnesota when she rebutted published criticisms of girls' athletic contests as unladylike and improper. "I saw nothing of which to disapprove in the tournament," she asserted. "It reminded me of what I have read of the Athenian games, where the girls were fitted for the duties of life by similar vigorous and strenuous contests in the arena." She wrote to Miss Butner, "For the basket-ball, I was only too glad to say what I did. I was highly pleased with the work the girls did and with their whole appearance."[78]

Sanford was a director of Northwestern Hospital, which treated only women and children, and all of whose physicians and administrators were women.[79] A founder of the Woman's Improvement League of Minneapolis, increasingly active in addressing other women's organizations, she was recognized as a leading exponent of women's rights before she came into the suffrage fold. In 1907 the Secretary of the Liberal Union of Minnesota Women sent its appreciation of her work "for all the women of the state for whose benefit your voice and pen have been so generously given."[80] That voice was magnificent— compelling and unforgettable, by all accounts; from 1912 she turned it, also, to the cause of woman suffrage.

Not previously outspoken on the question, Sanford was quoted in a 1909 newspaper story as thinking woman suffrage unnecessary.[81] But she was also becoming sure that it would come. After a trip through the Northeast she received a letter from a student at the normal school she had once attended: "Suffrage is uppermost in our minds now and I regretted after you left that I did not ask you if you wanted suffrage. We are so enthusiastic that we are planning to go to New York May 4 to join the parade."[82] Sanford's best answer to the query was the much-talked-of speech she gave to the General Federation of Women's Clubs convention in San Francisco—leading the woman principal of a St. Paul school to call her "the greatest inspiration of all the women of the country."[83] Sanford lived long enough to speak at a rally on the steps of the state capitol, celebrating congressional passage of the suffrage bill.

Yet, in the traditions of a lifetime, Sanford did not view woman suffrage in terms of equality of rights or privileges. The franchise represented another opportunity to be of better service in the cause of social reform—voting on those issues of child welfare, vice, and industrial oppression that most affect women.[84] She was herself tempered for such service "in the school of adversity," developing therein what she called the highest power in humankind: "I think it is power to *stand alone,* power to seek the best things."[85]

Notes

    1. William Watts Folwell to Sadie (Mrs. Folwell), 21 July 1880, William Watts Folwell and Family Papers, Minnesota Historical Society, St. Paul (hereafter MHS). By permission.

    2. University of Minnesota Circular, 5 May 1880, Folwell Papers, MHS.

    3. Elmer E. Adams, *Recollections of Early University Days* [Extracted from

the *Minnesota Alumni Weekly,* 5 May 1934 to 5 January 1935] (Minneapolis: Alumni Association of the University of Minnesota, 1935), p. 505.

4. University of Minnesota, *Board of Regents' Minutes,* vol. I, especially pages 178 and 184, University of Minnesota Archives (hereafter UMA). By permission.

5. Available data indicate that twenty-five of the seventy-four faculty appointed from 1868 to 1890 and thirty-eight of the fifty-four regents serving between 1851 and 1890 were born in the northeastern United States. In Peter Fitzgerald, "Democracy, Utility, and Two Land-Grant Colleges in the Nineteenth Century: The Rhetoric and the Reality of Reform" (Ph.D. diss., Stanford University, 1972), pp. 156, 169.

6. Folwell to Sanford, 9 July 1880, William Watts Folwell Papers, UMA. By permission.

7. Folwell to Magill, 31 July 1880, Maria L. Sanford Papers, MHS. By permission.

8. Magill to James B. Angell, 16 August 1877; Magill to Andrew D. White, 14 April 1879, Sanford Papers, MHS.

9. Folwell to Mr. Johnson, 13 December 1911, Sanford Papers, MHS.

10. Geraldine Schofield, "Four Minnesota Women: Lecture No. 2, Maria Louise Sanford," audio tape, 21 February 1978, Audio-Visual Library, MHS; Geraldine B. Schofield and Susan M. Smith, "Maria Louise Sanford: Minnesota's Heroine," in *Women of Minnesota: Selected Biographical Essays,* ed. Barbara Stuhler and Gretchen Kreuter (St. Paul: Minnesota Historical Society Press, 1977), pp. 77–93; Helen Whitney, *Maria Sanford* (Minneapolis: University of Minnesota Press, 1922).

11. Eliza S. Turner to Miss Eastman, 28 April 1879, Sanford Papers, MHS.

12. Fitzgerald, "Democracy, Utility, and Land-Grant Colleges," p. 86.

13. Folwell to A. D. White, 30 August 1869, copy in Folwell Papers, UMA. See also Folwell to C. Hewitt, 29 March 1872, Folwell Papers, UMA.

14. W. R. Marshall to Folwell, 6 April 1883, Folwell Papers, MHS.

15. Fitzgerald, "Democracy, Utility, and Land-Grant Colleges," p. 154.

16. University of Minnesota, *Regents' Minutes,* vol. I, p. 231, UMA.

17. C. W. Eliot to Folwell, 18 May 1880, Folwell Papers, MHS.

18. F. W. Clarke to Folwell, 15 July 1880, Folwell Papers, MHS.

19. C. Y. Lacy to Folwell, 5 March 1881, Folwell Papers, MHS.

20. University of Minnesota, *Regents' Minutes,* vol. I, pp. 182, 259; vol. II, pp. 304, 348, UMA. The analysis of professorial "types" is from Alvin W. Gouldner, "Cosmopolitans and Locals: Toward an Analysis of Latent Social Roles," *Administrative Science Quarterly* 2 (1957–58): 281–305, 444–80.

21. Sanford to Folwell, 26 July 1883, Folwell Papers, MHS.

22. Of the seventy-four members of the Minnesota faculty hired from 1869 to 1890, Sanford was the only member with a normal school diploma. Four others lacked college degrees and there were twenty-seven whose training is not known. In Fitzgerald, "Democracy, Utility, and Land-Grant Colleges," p. 157.

23. University of Minnesota, *Regents' Minutes,* vol. I, pp. 218, 231, UMA.

24. Ibid., vol. II, p. 462.

25. Sanford to A. Butner, 2 January 1910, Anne Maud Butner Papers, UMA. By permission. Butner was director of physical culture from 1900 to 1912, when she resigned, disappointed by her persisting struggles with the regents and administration. She remained in Minneapolis to become a successful businesswoman.

26. H. E. Robertson to Sanford, 6 December 1913, Sanford Papers, MHS.

27. University of Minnesota, *Regents' Minutes,* vol. I, p. 215; vol. II, p. 458, UMA.

28. Reprinted in Fitzgerald, "Democracy, Utility, and Land-Grant Colleges," p. 139.

29. A. T. Ormund to Folwell, 18 March 1883, Folwell Papers, MHS.

30. Sanford circular letter, n.d., Sanford Papers, UMA. By permission.

31. Gertrude G. Meier to Sanford, 18 December 1906, Sanford Papers, MHS.

32. Fitzgerald, "Democracy, Utility, and Land-Grant Colleges," p. 189.

33. University of Minnesota, *Regents' Minutes,* vol. I, p. 231, UMA.

34. Schofield, "Four Minnesota Women," MHS.

35. Helen A. Wilder to Sanford, 16 December 1906, Sanford Papers, MHS.

36. Henry Pennypacker to W. W. Woodruff, 26 February 1910, Sanford Papers, MHS.

37. T. E. Parker to W. W. Woodruff, 26 February 1910, Sanford Papers, MHS.

38. Louisa Hughes Cox to W. W. Woodruff, 24 February 1910, Sanford Papers, MHS.

39. Ina Firkins, "Maria Sanford" (typescript address to Daughters of the American Revolution, Mankato, Minnesota, 1 April 1922), p. 2, Sanford Papers, UMA.

40. Adams, *Recollections,* p. 506

41. Max West to Sanford, 9 November 1899, Sanford Papers, UMA.

42. Adams, *Recollections,* p. 521.

43. Allen P. Asher to Sanford, 15 March 1903, Sanford Papers, MHS.

44. Gertrude G. Meier to Sanford, 18 December 1906, Sanford Papers, MHS.

45. Florence P. White to Librarian of University Archives, 2 July 1963, Sanford Papers, UMA.

46. Mrs. John Howe to Sanford, 4 April 1900, Sanford Papers, MHS.

47. Schofield, "Four Minnesota Women," MHS.

48. "Student" to Gov. Pillsbury, 27 August 1888, Cyrus Northrop Family Papers, UMA. By permission.

49. Northrop to Sanford, 17 November 1890, Sanford Papers, MHS.

50. Firkins, "Maria Sanford," pp. 3–4, Sanford Papers, UMA.

51. Whitney, *Maria Sanford,* p. 146.

52. Northrop to Sanford, 31 March 1900, Sanford Papers, MHS.

53. Northrop to Sanford, 10 April 1900, Sanford Papers, MHS.

54. University of Minnesota, *Regents' Minutes,* vol. II, pp. 535–36, UMA.

55. David P. Jones to Sanford, 2 May 1900, Sanford Papers, MHS.

56. Northrop to Elizabeth Northrop, 23 April 1903, Northrop Family Papers, UMA.

57. Sanford to Hannah C. Partridge, 30 June 1874, Sanford Papers, MHS.

58. Magill to Sanford, 27 September 1904, Sanford Papers, MHS.

59. Whitney, *Maria Sanford,* p. 98.

60. W. Bruce Leslie, "Between Piety and Expertise: Professionalization of College Faculty in the 'Age of the University,' " *Pennsylvania History* 46 (July 1979): 245–65.

61. S. D. Catherwood to Sanford, 28 January 1903. The basis of Catherwood's regard for Sanford is indicated in his letter to her of 12 January 1906, both in Sanford Papers, MHS.

62. Sanford to Gov. Van Sant, 10 July 1903, Sanford Papers, MHS.

63. Women's Council Resolution, 28 May 1900, Sanford Papers, MHS.

64. Genevieve Ives Allen to Sanford, 25 April and 16 May 1904, Sanford Papers, MHS.

65. Downey to Sanford, 7 May 1907, Sanford Papers, MHS.

66. Whitney, *Maria Sanford,* p. 51.

67. Sanford to Elizabeth Murray, 12 August 1915. See also Sanford to Richard Murray, 24 February 1915, both in Sanford Papers, MHS.

68. Otto K. Folin to Sanford, 22 May 1893, Sanford Papers, MHS.

69. Sanford memo, 8 June 1916, Sanford Papers, MHS.

70. Firkins, "Maria Sanford," p. 3, Sanford Papers, UMA.

71. Sanford to Folwell, 30 December 1911, Folwell Papers, UMA.

72. After Magill's wife died, Sanford refused his offer of marriage out of pride; her debts were too large to have another person assume them. In Whitney, *Maria Sanford,* pp. 108–9.

73. Magill to Sanford, 24 June 1881, Sanford Papers, MHS.

74. Schofield, "Four Minnesota Women," MHS.

75. Whitney, *Maria Sanford,* p. 222.

76. T. V. Powderly to Sanford, 17 November 1890, Sanford Papers, MHS. On professors and the labor movement, see Fitzgerald, "Democracy, Utility, and Land-Grant Colleges," p. 158.

77. E. A. Curie to Linda Maley, 20 November 1906, Sanford Papers, MHS.

78. Clipping, n.d., in scrapbook of newspaper clippings; Sanford to Butner, 10 January 1907, both in Butner Papers, UMA.

79. Schofield, "Four Minnesota Women," MHS.

80. Elisabeth S. Way to Sanford, 30 March 1907, Sanford Papers, MHS.

81. Duluth, Minnesota newspaper clipping, 5 December 1909, Sanford Papers, MHS.

82. May E. Goodrich to Sanford, 29 April 1912, Sanford Papers, MHS.

83. Margaret Lennon to Sanford, 24 July 1912, Sanford Papers, MHS.

84. "Why a Suffragist?" *Alexandria (Minn.) Post News,* 19 December 1912, Sanford Papers, MHS.

85. Sanford memo, [1880s], Sanford Papers, MHS.

1. EXCERPTS FROM AN UNFINISHED AUTOBIOGRAPHY

Sometime before her death on April 20, 1920, Maria Sanford had begun writing a short autobiography, probably at the request of the Minneapolis Journal. *Apparently never finished, it was serialized in that newspaper shortly after her death. The portions reproduced here deal with her family and childhood.*

I come of good, strong New England stock. My ancestors were among the first settlers of the town where I was born, Saybrook, Connecticut, called later, since the town was divided, Old Saybrook.

My father's mother was Elizabeth Chapman. Her great grandfather, George Chapman, erected, about 1650, the first frame house in Saybrook. This structure, about twenty feet square, was so well built that it formed still the summer kitchen of the house in which I lived from my sixth to my eleventh year. I was told, as a child, that my ancestors in two lands, the Chapmans on my father's side and the Clarks on my mother's for three generations went up to the general court (legislature) together when the people sent their best men.

My uncle, William Clark, was a school teacher, and I used to tell my little companions with pride that I had an uncle who had taught school forty years. I little thought that I myself should teach fifty-four years. In those early days teachers had to be severe to be successful, and my uncle was a very successful teacher. My mother went to school to him, and he was so much afraid of being considered partial to her that he was so strict (nobody could be severe with her), that she called him "Mr. Clark" at home.

My father, Henry E. Sanford, was like the Chapmans, tall and straight, six feet in his stockings. His characteristics were strength, courage, energy, and skill, and a good cheer which no misfortune could crush. He learned the shoemaker's trade and worked at it, giving his wages to his father, as was customary, until he was twenty-one. Then he worked for himself, and by the time he was twenty-five he had laid up enough to warrant his marrying. And he won a prize. The marriage was an ideal one. My mother and father were so proud of each other, so ambitious, and looked to the future with such confidence and hope! I love to imagine those early prosperous years, when my father bought and paid for the comfort of a little house, which my mother's neatness and good taste, and their mutual affection, made a beautiful home.

But their love was not dependent on good fortune. In the darker years that followed, when loss and hardship came, there was never a flaw in their trust and devotion. Some time in the first seven years of his married life, my father went to Georgia and set up a shoe store, and he was successful. But the years 1836 and 1837 were not only years of financial panic, but also of anti-slavery agitation and of great prejudice in the South against Northern people. Somebody sent my father anti-slavery newspapers. He never saw them. They were taken out of his office and distributed among his customers. All at once his business fell flat. He could sell nothing, he could collect nothing, for even in the best days Southerners, at that time, paid their bills only once a year. He came home to do the best he could by his business creditors. He sold the place he and my mother loved so well, moved his family into part of his father's house, and when he had thus raised all that he could, there still remained a debt of a thousand dollars, for which he gave his note; and of which, I rejoice to say, he paid every cent. He might have taken advantage of the bankrupt law, but he said proudly: "No man shall ever look me in the face and say I wronged him out of a penny." It was just three months before my birth that, when the last things were placed on the load, my mother bade farewell to the home of much happiness and with her two little girls walked up to my grandfather's house.

In my young womanhood I was subject to deep depression, and my mother said to me: "It is no wonder to me, when I recall how I suffered in the months before you were born." Fortunately for me my father's spirit triumphed in me. I outlived the days of darkness and have been able, until bowed by the weight of years, like my father to square my shoulders to heavy burdens, and not only stand erect but keep a cheerful spirit.

My home was about three miles from the church, and in those days everybody except very little children went to church. My father hired a sitting for my mother in a neighbor's wagon; but of my earliest recollection, when I was about three years old I walked with my father. My mother was too scrupulous about infringing upon other's rights, when one sitting was hired, to have taken her little girl upon her lap. And so I walked; and when I was tired my father took me in his arms. I count this experience one of the valuable ones of my life: the close association of my father and the early formed habit of enjoying a long walk.

I was four years old when I began to go to school. There was a low bench around the stove for the little children and a high bench behind it for the older ones. There was no singing in the school. There was no mental arithmetic, no literature, and no history. And if we chanced to draw a picture on our slates we were severely reproved. We read round in turn from the New Testament; and the few fanatics who now advocate the reading of the Bible in school would be cured of the notion if they could but hear one day's blunders as I remember them.

I have two vivid recollections of this school term when I was four years old. One is that the teacher, anxious to make us acquainted with useful facts, crowded into our heads long lists of names of the Indian tribes of the United States, which I can reel off today, mispronunciation and all, just as I learned them. Useless lumber to give a child to keep in the brain for fourscore years!

The other vivid recollection of my first term at school was a thunderstorm. It was at the end of two weeks of August rain; and on that particular morning there came a crashing bolt, and the whole schoolhouse seemed to go up in flame. The lightning had really struck a haycock about ten feet from the schoolhouse. Why it didn't strike the building I have never known. There was more than one child who insisted the next morning: "The schoolhouse has burned down. I saw it afire." We rushed out, teacher and all. The street was flooded with water. We took refuge in the house of the nearest neighbor. It was almost noon; and father came in soon to his dinner and went up at once to see what had become of his little girls. I think he was very much relieved to find us safe in the house of the neighbor, for I remember that his right arm pressed me close to his breast as he carried me home. My next sister was holding his left hand, and the oldest clinging to his coat on the right. To me one of the most beautiful sights is a father caring tenderly for his little daughters; I think perhaps because the scene is tangled up in my mind with such precious memories.

Going back to the schools of my childhood. In summer we had women teachers and in winter men, because it was thought that women couldn't control the big boys; and in the brutal system of school government then prevailing, physical strength was an important matter. There were often twelve or fifteen boys of man's stature; and in some schools it was a favorite amusement to turn out the teacher.

The prejudice that believed women could not control older boys has passed away; but we still retain the prejudice that a man teacher is necessary for the dignity of a school. I admit that the influence of both men and women is desirable in the formation of the character of the young. But when people put inexperienced, callow youths in positions of importance in schools or colleges simply because they are "lords of creation," and pay them twice as much as is given to the really valuable women whose power alone keeps the man in his place and the school running, then there is a call for reform. The thing we need to guard against is that we do not in these days let the really priceless women who are in the profession leave it for want of proper pay.

By far the most valuable educational influence of my childhood came from my mother. I remember when I was not yet four years old following her about in her work, begging her to tell me more about the war. Her uncle had been a colonel in the Revolutionary War. Long before I was ten years of age I had in mind a gallery of worthies, embracing not only our Revolutionary heroes and men like Hamilton and Marshall and Henry Clay, but old world worthies: Oliver Cromwell, John Hampden, Alfred the Great, Gustavus Adolphus, and Charlemagne. I knew and delighted in the character and deeds of these men. My mother realized the value of the word "service" in its modern application; and she sought to inspire us to worthy lives by keeping before us the achievements of such women as Hannah More, Elizabeth Fry and Mary Somerville, and in this country of Mary Lyon, and later of Susan B. Anthony and Abby Foster and Lucretia Mott.

My mother took for her motto in the training of her children the saying of some distinguished man: "Fill up the measure with wheat and there will be no room for the chaff." I have often in later years recommended to mothers that they follow her example in teaching their children, instead of senseless jingles, noble poems which will be priceless seed grain in the mind of the child, bearing rich harvest in later years.

In the fall before I was six years of age my father moved his family back to Saybrook; and for four years he took charge of the farm of his uncle, George Chapman. My sister and I used to help on the farm. We dropped corn and potatoes in the spring, and picked up potatoes in the fall, and husked corn; and by this means earned a little money to buy our clothes. It was helpful and not hard work. It was while we were here on the farm that my father finished paying off the debt he had carried, and easier times dawned for us.

Maria Sanford's Unfinished Autobiography was serialized in the *Minneapolis Journal* on Sundays, from May 2, 1920 through June 2, 1920. It was reproduced in Helen Whitney, *Maria Sanford* (Minneapolis: University of Minnesota Press, 1922). These excerpts are reprinted by permission of the *Minneapolis Star and Tribune*.

2. MARIA L. SANFORD TO WATSON REEDER

Maria Sanford carried over into her college teaching the concern for her students' intellectual and personal development that she showed as a country schoolteacher—as this letter to Watson Reeder, a former Swarthmore College student, illustrates.

SWARTHMORE COLLEGE
Swarthmore, Del. Co., Pa.
2 Mo. 28 1875

Watson Reeder
New Hope
Bucks Co., Pa.

My dear friend

I was very glad to get your letter, and indeed answering it sooner but you know how full the days are here, and for two or three weeks past I have been unusually busy.

I feel sorry we cannot have you here anymore, and I miss you very much, but still I do think you are wise in your conclusion. It would be almost impossible for *you* to come back and "take it easy," you would I know work harder than you ought and so get sick again. But as your schooldays are done I know you will not feel that your education is complete, but will strive to widen your range of thought and increase your stores of knowledge.

May I give you a little advice? There are some things that you are deficient in which will be hard to gain at your age but which your earnestness and perseverance can accomplish: I did not feel like speaking of these things when you were here and had so much to do, but now you have time.

First make it a matter of duty not to try to do too much, take some leisure every day; there is education in leisure as well as in work and I know it would have been of great advantage to me if I at your age had learned how to be sometimes a[t] leisure. Now very likely you do not understand me. I know I should not once have comprehended such advice, or felt its value. You have something to do all the time and just as soon as one duty is done you take up some other, it may be of a different kind but still work, something that you feel you ought to do. Now I have learned that leisure like sleep makes work more valuable, it gives a person ease, the man (or woman) who never sits down in his home without book or work is awkward and ill at ease when visitors compell him to be idle. Learn to entertain yourself occasionally with games or conversation with the family—the children—to stroll about and think and observe and be at ease. I know that if I had told you to read all Cicero's works, or to perfect yourself in the history of France from the earliest time it would have been a far easier task than this but not to *you* half as useful; and if to that you would have cheerfully given time and effort, do the same for this. Now don't overdo the matter and make the effort painful [;] it is a few minutes now and then when you can drum on the piano or romp with Mattie or talk with your Mother or pick up stones just to see how far you can throw them—the idea is, breathing *space,* when you can do anything or nothing.

Speaking of stones, have you any taste for mineralogy? This is pleasant employment of idleness strolling about to find specimens and the arranging of a cabinet would be useful to you in another way; it would teach you to observe and compare and to write.

This *writing* was what I meant to speak of when I began but the other matter crept in accidentally. Now you need to take time to learn to write [;] it can be done at your age and has been under greater disadvantages than you have to overcome. You don't need copy books but practice. You would have given your $150. and five month's time here willingly had you been well, but for the accomplishment of writing easily and readily, and spelling correctly you need not give so much, and it will be as valuable to you as the other.

I would get some book like the Domestic Life of Tho's Jefferson, and a quarter ream of commercial note paper (good quality, you can't learn to write on inferior paper) and copy carefully those letters. Write an hour or two every day until going over common words the spelling and use of capitals become second nature, and by writing much with care you will acquire that ease of hand which marks a gentleman and scholar. You need not be a handsome writer, but you want to learn to write off hand a letter that will bear testimony anywhere that you and a pen are old friends. Do not always copy but try sometimes to put the ideas of the author into your own words.

If I have written too familiarly, pointed out too freely your shortcomings, I know you will pardon me and understand that it is because of my affection for you and my deep interest in your welfare.

Don't either be afraid to write to me and think I shall criticize; this is no new thought with me, only when you were so busy here you had no time for these things and it was useless to speak of what now you may profit by.

I have written a very long letter and if another time I should now write or write a very short one you must not think I have lost my interest in you but only that I have so much to do that many things have to be neglected.

Love to all.

Truly thy friend
Maria L. Sanford

3. MARIA SANFORD'S PLEDGE TO HERSELF

The probable occasion for this intensely personal note to herself was Sanford's realization of the depths of the mutual regard that she and Edward Magill, president of Swarthmore College, had for one another, and the hopelessness of their situation.

I thank thee oh my God for light.

"Till death us part," it shall be time. I can work for him, seek his happiness, live for him; and receive no sign.

Shall I not then be his good angel. That will not be coldness but the fullness of unselfish love.

Oh God help me!

My heart shall not grow cold for I will keep it warm with sympathy and love for others. I will throw my whole soul into my profession. Oh it is hard, but it is the rugged path that leads us upward always.

1st mo 22.'76

Reproduced from the Maria L. Sanford Papers, Minnesota Historical Society. By permission.

4. MARIA L. SANFORD TO WILLIAM WATTS FOLWELL

Having ended her association with Swarthmore, Sanford inquired of several universities about a position, including the University of Minnesota. William Watts Folwell was its president from 1869 to 1883.

Topeka, Kansas.7.1.'80

Pres[iden]t Folwell

Dear Sir,

Though you will probably remember meeting me at Swarthmore you will know something of what my work must have been to hold for nine and a half years a department in that college; and the enclosed letter will tell my reasons for leaving.

I knew I had reached all I could hope for there and I was willing to risk a year or two to obtain a position where after proving myself worthy I could obtain what I think is just compensation. I have looked to your institution for more than two years, and have been several times on the point of writing to you, but I hoped the way would open for me to go to Minnesota, and I know a personal interview is so much more satisfactory in such matters than correspondence.

I should hope to have ultimately a department, either History [or] Didactics; but I would take for a year any work that I could do, teaching Reading[,] Composition (I had the Senior and junior classes in Rhet[oric] & Comp[osition] for many years at Swarthmore), Eng[lish] Grammar, Arithmetic[,] Geography or History—anything in the College or Preparatory School that is in my line just to get a foothold and show you what work I can do.

I have been engaged in Institute work for the last year and if you wish to establish a Normal Department I can give you very strong recommendations from the highest educational authorities in Penn-[sylvani]a and some other states showing my success in training teachers.

If you have work for me and wish to see me before trusting to an engagement I will gladly come to Min[nesota] but I did not feel like taking the expense in uncertainties.

Please address   Maria L. Sanford
                                                                           Topeka
                                                                           Kansas

Will you please return to me this letter of Pres[ident] Magill's.

Reproduced from the William Watts Folwell and Family Papers, Minnesota Historical Society. By permission.

5. MARIA L. SANFORD TO CYRUS NORTHROP

Maria Sanford was acquainted with the Northrop family, prominent in Connecticut affairs. In 1884 she wrote to Cyrus Northrop urging him to accept the offer of the presidency of the University of Minnesota and revealing some of her impressions of the university. Note her misspelling of Northrop's name in the salutation.

                                                                           Univ.of Minn.3.17.'84
Prof. Cyrus Northrup,

My dear f[rien]d
    Your card just rec[eive]d gives me the privilege that I had wished to take, but feared to seem presuming.

I have conceived too high a regard for you to be willing, for your sake, to urge a course you might regret; and really it must be a mutual good or no good. I hope you will come, for I believe you will succeed. There are difficulties of course, if there were not there would be no credit in success; but if I am any judge of character the difficulties are not such as you should shrink from and the requirements of the place are those which you possess.

I know that standing before a great task all our knowledge and all our strength[,] compared with what we would be[,] seem weakness & ignorance, but we are not for this reason incompetent.

It was the word you dropped to me at Gov[ernor] P[illsbury]'s that made me want to write you. I have not spoken of it & shall not, but it struck me as possibly more than a mere casual remark. I am sure you need not hesitate on this ground. The Col[lege] cur[riculum] of our day is too wide for one man to grasp, and people are learning that mere book-knowledge does not constitute scholarship, and much more *ability*. We ask that our Pres[ident] should know something not that he should know everything—but we do ask that his knowledge shall have been moved into power. That he have ideas and dare to express them, that he take hold of his work with the vigor of manhood, believing in himself and in us.

I know it is hard to fill a place where great expectations have preceded us, but is it not good for us to be put upon our mettle, to feel obliged to stand for our topmost inch[?]

Our people are discerning but not disposed to criticize or carp, and I assure you you have made a most favorable impression. The students looked at you and said "he'll do," and I have not heard one dissenting voice anywhere. I think you will find this a most delightful place to work. Our Regents are liberal in thought and act, and if they are a little slow they have the good of the Univ. at heart. As a faculty we are united and cordial and we will give you our hearty support. Pres. Folwell, to whom of course the change will be somewhat embarrassing, is a Christian gentleman and will throw no obstacles in your way. We are not accustomed to much supervision but we understand that "new masters make new laws." Our students are remarkably obedient and law-abiding; and I can think of no reason which should deter you from coming *to rule over* us.

But indeed we do need you, and if you do not come the disappointment will be very great, and it cannot but have a bad effect upon the Univ. creating an unfavorable impression as to its character.

This is it seems to me an opportunity such as does not come often to any of us—to do a good work for which we are especially fitted & it is a work which any man ambitious to serve well his time might rejoice to accept. Therefore I do hope and trust that you will come.

I have written with the freedom of an old friend, and you may count on me for such frankness whenever I can aid you.

Yours with sincere regard.

M. L. Sanford

Reproduced from the Maria L. Sanford Papers, Minnesota Historical Society. By permission.

6. MARIA L. SANFORD TO CYRUS NORTHROP

In several of her letters, Sanford expressed her cognizance of the unusual situation she held as a professor and a woman. This letter to President Northrop is one example, and it also gives early insight into what was to be their steadily worsening professional relationship.

Univ[ersity] of Minn[esota] 1.24.'85
Pres[iden]t Northrup,

My dear f[rien]d

I wanted to bid you goodbye, but when I went to speak to Prof[essor] Folwell I saw you were ready to go, and occupied; and I had not quite courage.

I must thank you for the change this week has wrought. Your frankness has given me confidence, and your thoughtful kindness and encouragement have brought me back hope and faith.

You may perhaps feel that it is not much, and I can well understand that your generous nature could do no otherwise, but the kindness is none the less singular because it is natural; and to me who received it it is like life from the dead. Do not think that I speak too strongly, you cannot know the crushing weight that was upon me. The alternative which had stared at me for weeks was harder to look upon than my open grave, for death takes care of itself, or rather God takes care of us; you will say, so he does in life too, but it is not so easy to trust him.

I knew by what effort I had gained my present position, how few such places are open to women, and how absolutely ill success would close every door; but I could not and would not be "a cucumber of the ground." Then too my professional pride is the one selfish passion of my life. All that other women give to dress and establishment, wealth and social position, everything but my duty to God and my fellow men is absorbed in my love for and pride in my work.

I realize that there is much to do, that I must, as you said, "by a desperate struggle win back inch by inch what I have lost"; but I have confidence to try it now. My work, everything seems so changed. I no longer shrink from meeting the pupils and the professors, and most of all from meeting you.

May God bless you and grant that to many souls in need you may bring the light and strength you have brought to me.

You will not I hope fail to tell me with utmost plainness what you see amiss. I can bear anything. I shall rejoice in everything, however severe, that can help me in my task.

There is one little matter of business I wanted to speak to you of though perhaps it is entirely unnecessary. Mr. Rankin of Owatonna is warmly attached to the university, and he has influence. If he could be interested in the matter I think he might do much toward securing for our next commencement a rousing meeting of the Alumni.

This letter does not trouble you for a reply. I have written because I could not help it.

With sincere respect & gratitude

Maria L. Sanford

Reproduced from the Cyrus Northrop Family Papers, University of Minnesota Archives. By permission.

7. MARIA L. SANFORD TO CYRUS NORTHROP

During his presidency of the University of Minnesota, from 1884 to 1911, Cyrus Northrop had various occasions to rebuke and disappoint Sanford, and to receive her appeals. We should assume that she indeed sent him a version of the letter draft reproduced here.

[1901-Draft]

Pres[ident] Northrup,

I want to ask you earnestly to reconsider this matter concerning the work in my department. It is of vital moment to me. I have given time

without stint and money that I could not spare to build up debate in
the university. Success has not yet come, it necessarily comes slowly,
but it is coming. Now I cannot bear to have my efforts thwarted by this
adverse decision.

I am sure if you could see the work as it really is you would not
decide against me. I don't know why it is but I always feel when anyone
attacks my work that I have first to convince you that it is valuable. If
you knew the truth you would need no argument, and I could bring
overwhelming proof from the best of our students that my work is
good, equal to the best done in the u[niversity.]

[I] suppose I do not work in exactly the way Prof[essor] West does.
I can do as good and lasting work as he can. I had won wide reputation
by my success as a teacher before he was out of the grammar school,
and it is as much impertinence of him to interfere with my department
as with that of Dr. Burks or Prof[essor] Moore. I protest against it and
I ask you in kindness and in justice to take my part.

I enclose a letter which came to me in answer to the request for
help, and I know there are many more who would echo the same sentiment could they be heard from.

Very truly yours
M. L. S.

Reproduced from the Maria L. Sanford Papers, Minnesota Historical Society. By permission.

8. MARIA L. SANFORD TO THE BOARD OF
REGENTS, UNIVERSITY OF MINNESOTA

*Oppressed by her debts and aware that she had numerous influential
friends in the state, Sanford never ceased trying to reverse the actions
taken by the Regents of the University of Minnesota to reduce her salary and cause her to leave.*

Oct.1,'03 [draft]
Board of Regents, Univ[ersity] of Minn[esota]

Dear Sirs:
I have asked the privilege of making this communication that I may
make protest against the reductions which have been made in my sal-

ary, as an injustice which this Board would never have allowed if they had known the facts in the case.

I do not ask at this time any change in my salary. I appreciate the difficulties of the present situation and I am willing to wait for better times; but I do earnestly request you, as men who want to do what is just and right to inform yourselves as to the condition of my department and if you find as I believe you will find, that while it is one of the largest and most difficult departments in the university, it is in as satisfactory a condition as any other department; that the work is thorough, the students interested, the methods up to date and the teachers zealous and harmonious, and that all feel the hand of the head of the department directing and stimulating their work. I believe you will also find that parents and friends of the students look upon this department as one eminently helpful in building up character and implanting worthy aims. If these things are true, and I believe every one who knows the facts will testify that they are, I ask, why should my salary be reduced.

It is not the reduction of this year against which I protest, but all reductions from the rank I held.

I think I may modestly say that I am highly esteemed in the community; I am widely known in at least five different states and what happens to me for good or ill is heralded. My pride in my professional reputation is very great, and the degradation which I have suffered has been far harder to bear than the privation which the change has brought, though the latter would be considered very severe by anyone who knew its extent.

My age has been mentioned as the reason for this reduction, but where can you find a woman of thirty five or forty, or a man of that age, who has more vigor and endurance, and where a professor who puts in more hours of effective work? I am carrying now eighteen hours of recitation per week besides managing my department and giving to the supervision and preparation of public debates and oratorical contests a large amount of time.

[Is it] right that a person doing this work, and doing it well, should be hampered and crippled by a salary which compels her to do menial work to pay for a bare living? Under the circumstances in which I am placed, and which when all told would hardly be considered discreditable to me, I cannot live without such labor. Years ago I made pledges of monthly payments which I must keep, and I have with my present salary just *$13.* left each month to meet all my own expenses.

Trusting to your honor and sense of justice I shall go on working

hard and meeting privation cheerfully, believing the time will come
when I shall have the great delight of full vindication in the complete
restoration of my salary.

> Very respectfully yours,
> Maria L. Sanford

Reproduced from the Maria L. Sanford Papers, Minnesota Historical Society. By permission.

9. MARIA L. SANFORD TO THOMAS WILSON

*Unsuccessful in her earlier attempts to get her salary restored, Sanford
wrote to Regent Thomas Wilson, using comparative work loads and
statistics on student enrollment to make her case for fairness and justice.*

> The University of Minnesota
> Minneapolis

> April 24.'05

Hon[orable] Thomas Wilson,

Dear Sir:

President Northrop has advised me to send to you the enclosed
sheets.

I enclose to you as chairman of the Salary Com[mittee] the two accompanying sheets.

Sheet No. 1 is to show the justice of the request which I presented
to the Board of Regents in September 1903, for the restoration of my
old salary of $2400. when the appropriation should make such action
possible. It is a comparison of my work to that of five other heads of
departments closely associated with me. The figures were furnished by
the Registrar from the reports of last semester's work.

The upper line gives the whole number of students in each of the
departments. Then comes the individual work of each professor: his
classes, the number of students in each, and the number of hours per
week given to each class.

It will be seen that some classes recite once a week, some twice,
and most of them three times. In order to make a fair comparison, I

have multiplied the number of hours given to each class and added the products, so that the lower line of figures shows the whole number of student-hours of instruction given by each professor.

It will be seen that not only is my department the largest, but that I teach the largest number of classes, and by far the largest number of students. If the comparison were made for the present semester all my classes would number more, in the largest I have 155 students where last semester I have but 79.

I ask if it is not clear that the Regents are wronging these students by putting over them an incompetent teacher, or that they are wronging me by withholding from me the salary which my work should command. The students in my classes are eager and earnest, and I have found difficulty in driving them out, when since the burning of the Main Building I have, in some cases, to use a room too small to hold all who came.

I have worked and waited patiently believing that the Regents would do me justice when it was possible for them to do so.

The second sheet shows what I ask for my department. I have, where ever I could wisely do so, made changes that reduce the expense. In the place of Mr. Chase I can get a young man for $250. but I have not yet decided which of two men to recommend.

More earnestly than I ask for justice to myself I ask that I may have for my department the salaries which will retain efficient instructors, and encourage those who are doing good work for small pay.

Reproduced from the Maria L. Sanford Papers, Minnesota Historical Society. By permission.

10. STATE'S "GRAND OLD WOMAN" TELLS WHY SHE WANTS VOTE

In 1916, as the woman suffrage campaign was intensifying, the Women's Journal and Suffrage News *wrote a story about Maria Sanford's position on this issue. It quoted her extensively, and that part is reproduced here.*

The Bible says, "Thou shalt not muzzle the ox that treadeth out the corn." This may be interpreted, "Thou shalt not hinder and cripple those who are doing effective and valuable work." Women are doing effective and valuable work, not only in the home, but outside of it, for their city, State and nation. The men who are working side by side with women in these lines would feel themselves crippled and hampered without a vote. There are few women who have had experience in public work who do not feel the same way. We have, then, not only the Mosaic law, but logic and common sense on the side of woman suffrage.

But are there not some evil results to be feared—evil results to the women themselves? This fear kept me out of the suffrage movement for years. I am jealous for our womanhood. I would sacrifice no jot of its modesty or refinement. But I have lately had a chance to know and to work with women in California, Idaho, Utah, Illinois and other suffrage States—in States where women have had the ballot for a short time, and States where they had it for a long time—and I have nowhere found any justification for such fears. These women are not inclined to take up the tricks of scaly politicians. They are not eager for notoriety or for office. When responsibility comes to them, they take it with modesty and dignity, as our own women do. The feminine cranks who are caricatured in the comic papers do not even remotely represent the women of the suffrage States. They are workers for temperance, for justice to all, for chastity, for everything that makes for better homes and better children, just as our women are, but with this difference— they are working effectively and directly, while we are crippled and hampered because politicians think that women do not count. To all those who have the vision of a better republic, of better conditions in the way of temperance, of moral reform, of justice for high and low, of children safeguarded, my advice today is, join the suffrage movement, for votes for women will help every one of these good causes.

Reprinted from the *Woman's Journal and Suffrage News,* 20 May 1916. A copy of the article is in the Maria L. Sanford Papers, Minnesota Historical Society.

11. RESPONSE BY MARIA SANFORD AT THE UNIVERSITY OF MINNESOTA CONVOCATION CELEBRATING HER EIGHTIETH BIRTHDAY

The University of Minnesota hosted a grand birthday party and convocation for Maria Sanford on December 19, 1916. Her response to this tribute was printed in the university's alumni bulletin.

Mr. President, old colleagues, old students and friends, I thank you all today. Your gracious words, these flowers, the messages that have come from distant friends, your presence here and the multitude of written messages of love—these all are very grateful to the heart of one who bears the weight of eighty years. But I cannot flatter myself that I deserve these honors. I have sometimes thought that I could do good work, but in the perspective of years it diminishes and the things that I did not do loom up and overshadow it as the distant mountain does the foothills. But there is one thing of which the years have not robbed me—the love of my old students. It comes, it meets me wherever I go. It comes to me not only in ceremonial garb on state occasions, but in everyday dress, with warm handclasps, loving words, deeds of kindly service, perhaps from one whose name I have forgotten. It comes from strong men and women who are bearing life's burdens and it comes from young people, the sons and daughters of those who sat in my classroom—boys and girls who have never known me except through their parents' love, and I tell you friends it is a priceless treasure and it doesn't diminish as the years pass. It stays by and I have faith that it will endure until the end.

Perhaps I should stop here, but there is something more I want to say.

Because I have been so long strong and vigorous, I hoped I had ten years more to work as hard as I had always worked, and I wanted to give those years to our city and our state, doing some things that needed to be done. Understand me, I had no brilliant vision of great success but hoped to be able to lend a hand in a modest way. Others had been able to give money—I thought I might give intelligent service. But in the last few weeks, in spite of all the things that have been said for me, I have had to admit that I am old. Ill health has made me feel that I must take care of myself. I want to ask you, my old students and friends, to do with your youth and vigor and power, hundreds of things more than I ever dreamed of. I want you to do for our city and our state, the best that can be done. Minneapolis, Minnesota, ought to stand foremost in social progress. Splendid work is being done here by our intelligent business men. It is inspiring to follow such leaders, but they need a solid phalanx behind them—men and women who will do as they are doing, study social laws and conditions as they really are and then, with courage and wisdom apply to social betterment practical business sense. This is the call to you. It is this that I ask you today to take up. If you have wealth or social position or education or business ability, all these are doubled in their value to you if you use them for the common good. Use them not for yourself alone, but to stay the sources of ignorance and degradation and misery, to open the opportunity for all, even the humblest, for health and vigor, for ambition and success. If you will do this you may be able to close the gap between class and class—to make the poor man who is working in overalls, the mother with her little flock, the young boy or girl who is working in store, or factory, or mill, make them all feel that they belong with you because their interests, their pride and opportunity and highest welfare are so carefully conserved, and so secure. This is not an Utopian dream, it is the goal toward which our Civic and Commerce association is wisely leading us; it is Minneapolis when we all do our duty.

Will you not help?

Reprinted from the University of Minnesota *Alumni Weekly*, 25 December 1916, pp. 9–10.

MARION TALBOT

The University of Chicago Archives

For the *"Women of the University"*

MARION TALBOT
1858–1948

by Ellen Fitzpatrick

From the earliest years of her life, Marion Talbot found herself drawn into the changing world of nineteenth-century women's education. Over the course of her career, Talbot would prove to be a central figure in bringing women's education into the twentieth century. But her conception of female intellectual life, her approach to academic institutions, and her unswerving commitment to young women scholars were deeply rooted in her experience of late-nineteenth century America.

Talbot was more fortunate than many women of her generation. Born in 1858 to an upper-class New England family, she enjoyed the devoted attention of her gifted parents and she benefitted from their lively circle of friends, a group that included such luminaries as Julia Ward Howe and Louisa May Alcott. Her father, Israel Tisdale Talbot, was an admired practitioner of homeopathy, a sect of medicine that rejected the use of heroic measures in the treatment of illness and instead relied on infinitesimal doses of medicine to cure disease. His progressive interest in medical education led to Talbot's appointment as the first dean of Boston University's School of Medicine in 1873.[1]

Marion Talbot's mother, Emily Talbot, was something of a renegade, as well. She shared her husband's enthusiasm for reform, particularly as it related to the sphere of education. A few years of public school teaching, undertaken before her marriage, exposed Mrs. Talbot to the chaotic conditions that pervaded many nineteenth-century schoolhouses. And she vowed from then on to devote her energies to improving the character and extending the province of American education.[2]

Of utmost concern to Emily Talbot was the instruction of her own daughters, Marion and Edith. As the older of the two children, Marion served as a test case for her mother's ambitions. Discouraged by the poor opportunities for female education in public and private Boston schools, Mrs. Talbot arranged for Marion to be tutored in Latin at home at the age of ten, introduced to Greek three years later, and taught with future Harvard students at the predominantly male Chauncy Hall School. A fifteen-month family tour of Europe assisted Marion and her sister in acquiring foreign language skills.[3]

Nonetheless, it took her mother's best efforts to gain Marion's early admission to coeducational Boston University in 1876, mostly because all of Marion's schooling still left her less adequately prepared for college than the young men who had studied at Boston or Roxbury Latin. As a result of Marion's difficult experiences, and anticipating that similar obstacles would fall in her daughter Edith's path, Mrs. Talbot organized a campaign to open Boston Latin to female students. Although her crusade met with much opposition, Mrs. Talbot was able to savor a partial victory. A "Latin School for Girls" opened in 1877 for the purpose of offering young women a college preparatory course equal to that available to young men; Edith Talbot graduated in the new school's first class.[4]

In choosing to pursue a higher education, Marion Talbot set out on a path that ultimately brought her to an academic career. Once again, her mother's timely intervention helped Talbot to find her way. Like many of the country's first women graduates, Marion fell victim to a kind of aimlessness and uncertainty upon earning her bachelor of arts degree in 1880. Her college experience heightened Talbot's wish for an active life and an exciting career that would make use of her newly acquired knowledge. Yet little in the society at large or in her own circle of friends supported such an aim.[5]

If anything, her education widened the distance between Talbot, her surroundings, and her girlhood friends. The young women she knew best were either absorbed in the activities of the "sewing circle" and the Junior League or awash in excitement over impending debuts. Troubled musing apparently led Talbot to realize that "the satisfactions obtained in the pursuit of truth make other searches seem trivial in comparison, and the use of one's mind becomes not only fascinating, but a compelling task." She intended to continue her education, eventually choosing to study the new field of "sanitary science" with Ellen Richards at the Massachusetts Institute of Technology.[6]

Marion's mother sympathized with her daughter's social dilemma and her professional aspirations as she too pondered the discouraging prospects new female college graduates seemed destined to face. She wisely recognized that her daughter's predicament would be shared by ever increasing numbers as educational opportunities for women continued to expand. When a Vassar graduate sought her out for advice on finding a suitable career, Mrs. Talbot suddenly had a "vision" of college women from all over the country joining together to advance their own and other noble causes. She passed her thoughts on to Marion who quickly enlisted Ellen Richards's assistance in organizing a meeting of recent female college graduates at MIT in the fall of 1881. Out of this initial gathering came the Association of Collegiate Alumnae.[7]

The ACA provided Marion with the new company of like-minded friends and an organizational base for her growing interest in the issue of women's education. The association dedicated itself to refuting arguments that discouraged women from collegiate study, and worked to discover ways of assisting those already pursuing a higher education. In effect, the group operated as a lobby for women graduates from approved colleges although the association itself described its mission as "practical educational work." Talbot served first as a loyal secretary to the ACA and then as its president; she remained an active participant in the organization and never relinquished her membership in the group that it spawned, the American Association of University Women.[8]

While her work with the ACA filled an important void in Marion's postgraduate years, she never abandoned her quest for further academic skills. Her choice of sanitary science as a subject worthy of advanced study reflected an attempt to elevate the domestic interests widely accepted as woman's "proper" domain to a respectable position as a professional, scientific field. No one influenced Talbot's views in this more profoundly than Ellen Richards. A chemist by training and home economist partly by default, Richards pioneered in creating a new discipline that combined elements of chemistry, nutrition, public health, and domestic science.[9]

Sanitary science met compelling social needs and the purpose of enterprising women scholars such as Ellen Richards. Public health claimed an obvious hold on the attention of officials concerned about the proliferation of disease in the emerging urban, industrial society of late-nineteenth century America. Richards shrewdly made a virtue of what was clearly the professional handicap of her sex by arguing that women had a vital role to play in forging a science of sanitation. As homemakers they defined conditions in an important human environment, and thus were well placed to apply principles of sanitation once those principles had been tested in laboratories. At MIT, Richards taught her students (including Talbot) to test water for contamination, study the composition of foods, and construct model diets for the poor. Much of this work was carried out in a special "Woman's Laboratory" at MIT.[10]

Sanitary or domestic science, as it was increasingly called, ideally suited Marion Talbot's desire to find meaningful work that was socially useful, intellectually challenging, and available to her sex. She shared the romance of the post-Darwin generation with science, and the definition of sanitary study as scientific inquiry at once lent credibility to the discipline and made professionals out of its practitioners. Because Richards had deftly created a rationale for training women in an emerging field, an important entree into academic life appeared, assuming colleges and universities could be persuaded of the discipline's intellectual and practical worth.[11]

Not surprisingly, a new women's college, Wellesley, proved to be especially receptive to domestic science. The discipline fulfilled the institution's aim of educating young women well while reminding them of their proper sphere. In 1890 Marion Talbot joined the faculty at Wellesley as an instructor of domestic science. A female mentor once again played an important part in advancing Marion's career: She owed her position to Wellesley's president, Alice Freeman Palmer, who recognized the striking ability of the young woman who displayed such leadership in the ACA, an organization Palmer held in high esteem.[12]

Talbot's close association with Palmer soon took her from the quiet, refined college on Lake Waban to the parvenu, moneyed university rising up near Lake Michigan. The University of Chicago's first president, William Rainey Harper, was no enthusiast of coeducation, but he was saddled with a charter that mandated the equal instruction of women and men. Propriety required that the care of young women be placed in female hands, and Harper wanted Alice Freeman Palmer to assume that duty when the university opened in 1892. The largess of John D. Rockefeller fitted Harper with an important tool in winning illustrious academics away from their secure positions in the East. He needed all the help he could get. As Marion Talbot recalled, many considered Chicago "a very wild and woolly place."[13]

Alice Freeman Palmer accepted Harper's offer of a position as professor of history and dean of women with conditions that ensured Marion Talbot an appointment at the university as well. Palmer agreed to go West provided that Talbot be made her assistant. Since Mrs. Palmer negotiated an arrangement for herself requiring that she be in residence only three months of the year, it was certain that numerous responsibilities would be delegated to the assistant dean of women. With some misgivings about leaving home, Talbot agreed to join the University of Chicago and accepted an appointment as assistant to Palmer and assistant professor of sanitary science, as well.[14]

Her dual role as administrator and teacher comprised the essential core of Talbot's experience at the University of Chicago. Within just a few short years, Mrs. Palmer relinquished her ties with the school and Marion was given in title the duties she had been assuming in fact. By 1899 Talbot found all the women in the university—graduates and undergraduates alike—counted among her charges. Her position as dean of women made her a highly visible figure within the university community and brought to her a kind of recognition that her work as a professor never quite afforded. From her arrival in 1892 to her retirement in 1925, Talbot distinguished herself as a courageous advocate for University of Chicago women and a formidable opponent to anyone who chose to stand in their way.[15]

Several factors created a rather unique environment for women at Chicago, and Marion Talbot benefitted from some important institutional supports, not the least of which was the presence of a significant number of women on the campus grounds. Although women accounted for only a quarter of the undergraduates when the university opened in 1892, the composition of the student body changed swiftly and the enrollments of women advanced rapidly in Chicago's early years. Less than two hundred women attended in 1893; by 1897 their number swelled to over one thousand. In the academic year 1901–1902, women comprised 52 percent of Chicago's undergraduate classes.[16]

Female students assumed a central place in the graduate school from the very start. Indeed, the single largest collection of graduate students entering from one institution in 1892 (fourteen) came from Wellesley College. Women students never approached majority status in the graduate school, but the university quickly became one of the nation's leading institutions in awarding the Ph.D. degree to females. The university's performance as an *employer* of academic women was not as impressive. Still, Talbot was far from alone in her seat on Chicago's faculty; eleven women held faculty appointments by 1897.[17]

Although she looked primarily after female students, Marion Talbot appeared to consider all of Chicago's women as her constituency. In her annual reports to the president, she surveyed the "women of the university" as seen from her vantage point as dean of women. Talbot's summaries always emphasized the many achievements of female undergraduates, professors, and graduate students, partly as a demonstration that "the presence of women did not mean the lowering of any standards." Yet she scarcely missed an opportunity to remind the president of the necessity of additional institutional support. She pointedly observed, for example, in her 1905–1906 report that "the work in Physical Culture continues to gain in effectiveness in spite of the fact that the increase in the number of students is not accompanied by a corresponding increase in instructional force or equipment."[18]

At times she let her elaborate graphs, charts, and statistics documenting the status of Chicago's women speak for themselves. "The officers of instruction and administration of academic rank in all Departments of the University included fifty-two women in 1902–03, and forty-five in 1903–04," she wrote on one occasion. "Of these, sixteen in 1902–03 and seventeen in 1903–04 were members of the Faculties of Arts, Literature, and Science. Three in each year held a rank above that of Instructor." Whatever her technique, Talbot's insistent refrain ensured that nothing would silence the voice of what William Rainey Harper called "the woman side of the university."[19]

The sense of community Harper detected among University of Chicago women evolved in part from Marion Talbot's deliberate aims. Although she adamantly opposed sororities and secret clubs, she helped establish a "Women's Union" at the university in 1901 which was open to all Chicago affiliates who would pay their dues. The union proposed to "unite the women of the university for the promotion of their common interests." Talbot also took an active interest in the Club of Women Fellows, an organization that brought together graduate women holding university fellowships. At monthly meetings, club members updated the progress of their research and shared opinions on professional issues that troubled them. These formal and informal gatherings gave cohesion to the female community at Chicago thereby ensuring a highly visible presence for women students and scholars at the university.[20]

But if Talbot's savvy approach to the education of women seemed thoroughly modern, her social sensibilities appear to have been at least partially rooted in the traditions of the nineteenth century. She herself noted,

> At the time the University was organized, women were just beginning to feel the shackles loosen which had been fettering them. . . . The situation was confusing. No formulation of the principles which should guide the new freedom had been worked out to take the place of the old restrictions and taboos.

Marion Talbot's actions as dean of women mixed freedom and restraint in her care of Chicago students.[21]

As she assisted young women in their development, Talbot searched for a middle ground that would graft the behavior that characterized the "best of society" onto a setting that diverged rather radically from dominant social trends. Toward this end, Talbot advocated organizing the women's residence halls on a "house plan." Some aspects of the residence system gave evidence of a liberal attitude toward the inhabitants. The houses were largely self-governing, although each dorm had at its head a woman who held an academic post at the university. Graduate and undergraduate women boarded in the same halls; varying interests and age groups provided a lively mix of styles.[22]

But decorum was maintained in accordance with social values that Talbot considered fundamental. The drinking of wine and attendance at off-campus parties fell victim to Marion's proper rule at an early date. She defended her restrictions by pointing out that skeptics observed in her presence that the University of Chicago could not "be the dignified body of scholars you intend it to be if women are to be included." To prove otherwise, Talbot believed impeccable "social standards" would have to be maintained. Marion didn't hesitate to upbraid those who tested the limits of respectability even when the transgressor was the offspring of the university's president. Espying from her office one day the daughter of William Rainey Harper bedecked in a bizarre outfit and headed for a club initiation, Talbot halted her and lectured about the importance of proper public appearance. The young woman answered back that she had seen men do the same thing and wasn't it true "that women had the same rights as men in the university?" In her reply, the sagacious Dean drew an important distinction for the young woman. "Women had the same rights as men to do anything creditable," she explained, "but no right at all to do anything discreditable, even if the majority of the men set the example."[23]

Among the hardest lessons Talbot learned at the University of Chicago was the awful persistence of discrimination even among the enlightened administrators whom she freely called her friends. Her affection for Harper, for example, coexisted with a frustrating recognition that the Chicago president sometimes stood in the path of women's progress. Marion must have suspected as much when she requested an appointment as an associate professor upon joining the faculty and was given the rank of assistant instead. Encouraged by what seemed to be the limitless possibilities of the university, she came to Chicago with the dream of establishing her own department of sanitary science.

Harper adamantly rejected her plan as an unthinkable expenditure of university funds during the institution's early years.[24]

Yet, enough flexibility existed at the University of Chicago to permit Marion Talbot periodic victories. For example, in 1904 her persistence, and the growing acceptance and even enthusiasm for the "women's field" of home economics, led Chicago to finally establish a Department of Household Administration. Now promoted to full professor, Marion took her place as head of her long-dreamed-of department. From this position she secured faculty appointments in household administration for her gifted protégées, Sophonisba Breckinridge and Alice Peloubet Norton, and a few fellowships for a new generation of graduate women. In so doing, Talbot furthered a trend that saw women moving away from advanced study of traditional and predominantly male social sciences toward training in more "feminine" fields. Their marginal status may have been easier for women scholars to bear, however, ensconced in a department that provided some hegemony within the university.[25] The fledgling department offered such courses as House Sanitation; Administration of the House; Food and Dietetics; The State in Relation to the Household; The Legal and Economic Position of Women (with a description sounding very much like a contemporary women's studies course); as well as interdepartmental offerings in chemistry, zoology, physiology, pathology and bacteriology, education, and textiles and design.

The appointment of Breckinridge must have been especially gratifying to Talbot because she had tried for years to find her dear friend "Nisba" a secure place in the university. Breckinridge earned a Ph.D. from Chicago in political science in 1901 and then became the first woman to receive a J.D. degree from the university's new School of Law. But her continued presence at the university was not a sine qua non in Harper's view, as it was in Talbot's. Her personal interest in the young Kentuckian prompted a valiant campaign to convince Harper that the young woman should be kept on. Her success in this entitled Talbot to take more than a little credit for Breckinridge's subsequent distinguished service to the university as cofounder of the esteemed School of Social Service Administration in 1920.[26]

The battle over Breckinridge reveals a good deal about Marion Talbot's tenacious style. After succeeding in providing Sophonisba with a position as her assistant dean, she worked on Harper to increase Breckinridge's salary. In December of 1900, she stated to the university president her "hope that in making out the budget for another year, you will find it practicable to make Miss Breckinridge's salary more nearly commensurate with the value of her services than it is at present." Two months later Harper replied, "I wish I could have secured a larger appropriation for Miss Breckinridge for the coming year. I made the effort but failed. . . . Nothing is being done for next year that is not absolutely necessary. Perhaps I ought to have said so." Talbot's response typified her direct and forceful posture in dealing with Chicago's president. "I think that if you are willing to quote me you *can* say that this is absolutely necessary," she wrote.[27]

For Marion Talbot, the University of Chicago represented a microcosm in which the larger problems besetting academic women might be observed and removed. In a plea to President Harper urging a salary increase for Katherine Bates, Talbot stressed, "she is so valuable a woman in many respects, outside of her department, that I wish we might keep her. . . . It may be well for us to train men to go elsewhere, but I think we ought to keep the pick of our women, especially when we have so few of the intellectual and social equipment and experience which Miss Bates has."

The attitude of the popular press toward women frequently made Talbot bristle. And she rarely hesitated to confront the issue in a setting in which she felt empowered to do so. She complained to Harper in 1902 about the university's student newspaper. "The Weekly has been fairly truthful, if not always well-bred, in its attitude toward the women of the University," she wrote.

> I hope that some action has been taken to show the management that the administrative officers of the University will have little toleration of slurs and innuendoes concerning the character of the women and none at all of lies. We have a right to expect decent treatment from our own press at least.[28]

Toward the end of her life Marion Talbot looked back on her career at Chicago and reflected that "for thirty-three years I gave all I had to the university, and reaped a rich harvest of happiness and content." The testimonials that poured in from former students when she retired surely enriched her sense of accomplishment. One student evoked perfectly the early days in women's education when she recalled how much Talbot's "faith in women" had meant to her. "I had heard many stories of so-called 'college life' before I entered the University, and I wondered how I would feel when I went," she explained.

> I had to do serious work, I cared little for social life, and had no funds for such. It was a great comfort to find that the students at Chicago had come to work and to develop their talents. I had always been classed as

"peculiar" and it was good to know there were others who also lived seriously. My present work brings me with such companions always now, but earlier I had only one, and so the University meant more to me than, maybe, to some others.[29]

Marion Talbot died in 1948 at age ninety after twenty-three years in retirement from the university.

The official university paid Marion Talbot what was, perhaps, the institution's highest compliment at an early point in her career. In 1902 a decennial publication compared her to Chicago's legendary football coach, Amos Alonzo Stagg. "As Mr. Stagg is 'first in the hearts of Chicago men' " it boasted, "so she might well be proclaimed first in the affection of the gentler sex."[30] That an academic institution could celebrate the talents of a woman who made a career of critiquing the university's treatment of her sex is perhaps Marion Talbot's most impressive, and telling, legacy.

Notes

1. Richard J. Storr, "Marion Talbot," in *Notable American Women, 1607–1950: A Biographical Dictionary* (Cambridge: Harvard University Press, 1971), pp. 423–24; "Israel Tisdale Talbot," *Dictionary of American Biography,* vols. 17–18 (New York: Charles Scribner's Sons, 1946), p. 278; Rosalind Rosenberg, *Beyond Separate Spheres: Intellectual Roots of Modern Feminism* (New Haven: Yale University Press, 1982), pp. 2–4.

2. "Emily Talbot," *Dictionary of American Biography,* vols. 17–18, p. 276.

3. Marion Talbot and Lois Rosenberry, *The History of the American Association of University Women,* (Boston: Houghton Mifflin, 1931), pp. 3–4.

4. "Emily Talbot," *Dictionary of American Biography;* Storr, "Marion Talbot"; Talbot and Rosenberry, *History of the AAUW.*

5. Talbot and Rosenberry, *History of the AAUW,* chap. 1; see also Rosenberg, *Beyond Separate Spheres,* chap. 1, and Joyce Antler, "The Educated Woman and Professionalization" (Ph.D. diss., State University of New York at Stony Brook, 1977).

6. Talbot and Rosenberry, *History of the AAUW,* p. 6; Storr, "Marion Talbot."

7. Talbot and Rosenberry, *History of the AAUW,* p. 9.

8. Ibid., p. 12; Rosenberg, *Beyond Separate Spheres,* pp. 18–27; Storr, "Marion Talbot."

9. Margaret Rossiter, *Women Scientists in America: Struggles and Strategies to 1940* (Baltimore: Johns Hopkins University Press, 1982), pp. 68–69.

10. Ibid,; see also Dolores Hayden, *The Grand Domestic Revolution* (Cambridge: MIT Press, 1981).

11. Rossiter, *Women Scientists,* pp. 68–69.

12. Storr, "Marion Talbot."

13. Marion Talbot, *More Than Lore: Reminiscences of Marion Talbot, Dean of Women, The University of Chicago, 1892–1925* (Chicago: University of Chicago Press, 1936), chap. 1; Thomas Goodspeed, *A History of the University of Chicago* (Chicago: University of Chicago Press, 1916), p. 138; Talbot, *More Than Lore,* p. 5.

14. Talbot, *More Than Lore,* chap. 1.

15. Ibid., p. 158.

16. Thomas W. Goodspeed, *The Story of the University of Chicago* (Chicago: University of Chicago Press, 1925), pp. 137–38; Talbot, *More Than Lore,* p. 175.

17. Storr, *Harper's University* (Chicago: University of Chicago Press, 1966), p. 109; Rossiter, *Women Scientists,* pp. 35–37; Ellen Fitzpatrick, "Academics and Activists: Women Social Scientists and the Impulse for Reform" (Ph.D. diss., Brandeis University, 1981), p. 76; Talbot, *More Than Lore,* p. 131.

18. Talbot, "The Women of the University" in *The President's Report,* various years in the 1890s, regularly until 1925 (Chicago: University of Chicago Press); Talbot, *More Than Lore,* p. 64; Talbot, "Women of the University," 1905–1906, p. 30.

19. Talbot, "Women of the University," 1902–1904, p. 105; William Rainey Harper to Talbot, 24 October 1904, Marion Talbot Papers, University of Chicago Library.

20. Talbot, *More Than Lore,* pp. 75, 85–86.

21. Ibid., p. 101; Storr, "Marion Talbot."

22. Talbot, *More Than Lore,* pp. 62–64; Storr, "Marion Talbot"; Talbot, *More Than Lore,* chap. 6.

23. Talbot, *More Than Lore,* pp. 64, 161–62.

24. Talbot to Harper, 13 August 189–, Talbot Papers.

25. Fitzpatrick, "Academics and Activists, pp. 111–17; Talbot, *More Than Lore,* p. 150.

26. Christopher Lasch, "Sophonisba Breckinridge," in *Notable American Women;* Harper to Talbot, 28 March 1904, Talbot Papers.

27. Talbot to Harper, 1 December 1900; Harper to Talbot, 16 February 1901, President's Papers 1889–1925, University of Chicago Library.

28. Talbot to Harper, 16 December 1896; Talbot to Harper, 21 August 1902, President's Papers.

29. Talbot, *More Than Lore,* p. 217; Olga [?] to Talbot, 13 April 1925, Talbot Papers.

30. Robert L. Henry, Jr. and Charles W. Collins, *A Decennial Souvenir of the University of Chicago Weekly,* 1892–1902 (n.p., n.d.), p. 43.

1. "THE TREK" FROM *MORE THAN LORE*

Her decision to join the new University of Chicago and her early ex-
periences during the institution's opening days are recounted in Mar-
ion Talbot's autobiography, More Than Lore.

Life will always be full of adventures as long as human perspectives
change with age and values vary with experience. It was certainly very
exciting to have Santa Claus write me a real letter and tell me that he
was sending me a new doll and that I must be more careful and not
smash its china head, as I did my dear old dolly's head. Another great
adventure into a rich field was the Christmas gift of a set of the Rollo
books, twelve in number, bound in green and gold and packed in a
box, the most sumptuous Christmas gift I ever had, not excelled even
by the Davenport desk which was my birthday present when I was ten
years old. And life went on, and year after year brought thrilling experiences. One might perhaps become blasé, as it is said the present
generation early becomes. But no lapse of years or train of interesting
happenings in travel, education, or social life could deaden the sense
of adventure when the call came to help organize the new University
of Chicago. Stories of the new educational venture in the West had
reached Boston. Its novel features—such, for example, as unprecedent-
edly large salaries, continuous instruction throughout the year, the organization of Extension Work, a Press, University Affiliations, Junior
and Senior Colleges, and many others—gave rise to ridicule and sar-
castic comment; but underneath, the educational world felt very real
interest in the venture.

The gifted young president, William Rainey Harper, scoured the academic world for great scholars who would dare exchange comfortable
and safe positions for the hazards and excitements of a new undertaking. Among those whom he most strongly urged were George Herbert
Palmer, of Harvard University, to be head of the new Department of
Philosophy, and his wife, Alice Freeman Palmer, formerly president of
Wellesley College and at the time in the forefront of the chief educational movements in Massachusetts, to be professor of history and dean
(of women) in the Graduate School and College. For a long time Professor and Mrs. Palmer were unable to reach a decision, swayed, as they
were, on the one side by the many opportunities and inducements offered, and, on the other, by the strength of long-established ties and
enterprises already undertaken. Mrs. Palmer and I had worked in close
and intimate accord in the Association of Collegiate Alumnae, which
had been founded ten years previously and in which she maintained

an active part to the end of her life. This experience began the year after I received my Bachelor's degree from Boston University. As secretary for a long period, I had an unusual opportunity to study collegiate and university conditions in the United States. This experience was supplemented with study which led to the master's degree at Boston University and a more specialized degree in science at the Massachusetts Institute of Technology, with the secretaryship and later the presidency of the Massachusetts Society for the University Education of Women, with membership on the Board of Visitors of Wellesley College and later an instructorship at the same college, and with a term of service as alumni trustee of Boston University.

In April, 1892, Professor and Mrs. Palmer visited Chicago and met with much encouragement from influential men and women. Still in doubt, Mrs. Palmer wrote me, "Remember, if I come West you must come too—I mean it, my dear friend." Later on, in July, when the arrangement was made by which Mrs. Palmer would take an active share in the administration and be in residence at the University during twelve weeks of each year, she wrote me again, "I made my going conditioned on yours. Dr. Harper says that he distinctly wants you and will try to get you to Chicago for the start." When finally, in the late summer of 1892, the appointment came to be assistant professor of sanitary science and dean (of women) in the University Colleges, I had mingled feelings of interest and hesitation. The work at Wellesley in domestic science which I had started was full of promise. The secretaryship of the Association of Collegiate Alumnae brought important duties. My home ties were becoming increasingly close, and my circle of friends was large. My mother, however, had taken joy in training her children for service according to their several gifts. Moreover, she had been in Chicago—a rather unusual experience in those days for a Bostonian— and had been greatly impressed with its spirit. She was convinced that I should cast in my lot with the new University and the growing city. So, though it cost her many a heart pang, she encouraged me to accept. My father also, to whom I was giving clerical assistance in his medical and philanthropic work, set aside his wish to keep me near him and set his mind on the opportunities the future would bring to me. Chicago seemed a very wild and woolly place to my friends, and they were almost horrified at the idea of my leaving Boston, even though some of them had a glimmer of an idea of the honor and responsibility involved. Many of them expressed the hope that I would soon return, and some were quite certain that I would get enough of the West pretty soon. But preparations went on for my departure. There were clothes to be bought, suitable for many kinds of occasions and enough to last several months, and even seasons, for there would be no time or strength for shopping or dressmakers. The outfit seemed almost like a modest trousseau. To add to the impression that I was about to change my state, not only Massachusetts for Illinois, but spinsterhood for matrimony, kind and thoughtful friends provided me with silverware, attractive dishes and bric-a-brac, and even linen.

At last came the time for departure. Mrs. Palmer and Mr. William Gardner Hale were to be my traveling companions, and quite a crowd of friends assembled at the station in Boston to see us off on September 19, 1892. Florence M. Cushing, an honored graduate of Vassar College with whom I had done educational work for several years, pressed into my hand a small carved box. In gentle and rather solemn tones she said, "It contains a piece of Plymouth Rock." I felt the gift was rather symbolical of the attitude of Boston educators to the new undertaking. Those were shifting and perilous sands out there on the edge of the prairie, as it seemed to the dwellers on Beacon Hill. I must be reminded that the United States, at least my part of it, was founded on a rock; I might forget that four of my ancestors landed from the little ship "Mayflower," and be tempted to follow strange gods unless I had some forceful, though symbolical, reminder close at hand.

We carried our friends' good wishes for us in our undertaking, even though some of them quietly intimated that the pioneer conditions of life and education in the Middle West, for such they were supposed to be at that time, would not hold us long from the well-tried and highly approved mores of the Athens of America. But we were confident and light hearted. Even Mr. Hale's remark as we sped through the Berkshire forests, "Goodbye, Trees," failed to give us concern.

When we reached Hyde Park station the following afternoon, we were met by J. Laurence Laughlin, our old friend and associate. He waved a magazine in the air as he approached us on the platform, and said, "We have a real University; here is the student paper!" Ten days before the University opened!

We drove to the Hotel Monroe on Monroe, later Kenwood, Avenue, just north of Fifty-fifth Street, where we found a few of our new associates had already arrived: and soon we were all settled at dinner, one of the most extraordinary combinations of food I ever saw. We had barely finished when President Harper arrived and I met him for the first time, for he had appointed me on Mrs. Palmer's advice. There was, of course, no opportunity for intimate talk. One reason was that he had brought with him a student who had just appeared at his house, Elizabeth Messick. She had arrived that afternoon at the Union Station from Memphis, Tennessee. As was the custom, not only in Memphis, but in

Podunk and Boston, she took a "hack," had her trunk strapped on behind, and told the driver to take her to the Hotel Beatrice at the University of Chicago. Then the journey began. They drove and they drove. Night began to fall. City sights gradually disappeared and were replaced by bits of open country. Fully aware of the perils lying in wait for a young girl in the wicked city of Chicago, she made eager inquiries of the driver as to how much farther they had to go; but his assurances that they would soon arrive, even though frequently repeated, did not deter her from making ready to leap from the vehicle, speed across the prairie, and disappear in the dusk. In about an hour, the driver thought they were somewhere near the University, but he had to make inquiries, as he had never been there. It was, in fact, several years before the University actually got on the local map—years before it was on the academic map. Having located the University, consisting then of four unfinished buildings—Cobb Hall and three men's residence halls, or "dormitories" as they were called—the next problem was to find the Hotel Beatrice, the only clue being that it was on Fifty-seventh Street. The first attempt proved, on inquiry, to be the Hyde Park High School, which later gave way to a series of other schools, public and parochial. Of course, the schoolhouse was closed and dark. Finally, the Hotel Beatrice was located; but it, too, was closed and dark and not even completely finished. What could be done? The young southerner, with a wit which justified her attempting to enrol as a student in a great University, said, "Let us find out where the President lives—it must be near here." A drug store was found at the corner of Fifty-seventh Street near the railroad, and it was learned that the President lived just around the corner on Washington, later Blackstone, Avenue. Soon the journey was over. The President was somewhat disconcerted to discover that an actual student, an attractive young woman at that, had deposited herself on his front doorstep. Even if never again, he took great satisfaction on that occasion in the fact that he had two women deans at hand to help him out of his difficulty. And so he came to call on his new Faculty, not alone, but with a tall, slender young girl, clad in a circular cape and small cap with a patent-leather visor, her cheeks glowing with excitement and her large dark eyes nearly popping out of her head. There was no room in the little hotel for her, but she had to be housed, so the landlord said he would put a cot for her in the alcove in my room. This suited her so well that, taking advantage of the intimacy thus started, she hardly let me out of her sight for days except when I was at a Faculty or Council meeting or peremptorily engaged in some University duty where she would have been distinctly *de trop*.

It was not long before we moved into our new quarters, the Hotel

Beatrice on Fifty-seventh Street. Our experiences there make a tale in themselves and a unique feature in the establishment of a University. While Mrs. Palmer and I were trying to get some order out of the domestic chaos in which we found ourselves, the little group of students busied themselves by day, and even by night, getting ready for their entrance examinations, just as students were accustomed to do in the old-time colleges of the East. These examinations were an innovation in the Middle West, but it did not take much time or effort for the students to create the conventional atmosphere of dread and excitement or to adopt very foolish and wasteful ways of preparing themselves to meet the tests. The examinations were taken; and after a due period of suspense, word came that all of our group at the Beatrice were admitted to the University.

Marion Talbot, *More Than Lore: Reminiscences of Marion Talbot, Dean of Women, the University of Chicago, 1892–1925* (Chicago: University of Chicago Press, 1936), pp. 1–11. © 1936 The University of Chicago. All rights reserved.

2. MARION TALBOT TO WILLIAM RAINEY HARPER, AUGUST 13, 189–

When William Rainey Harper, Chicago's first president, invited Marion Talbot to join the university in 1892, she responded to his offer by outlining her vision of the role she might play in the new academic venture.

In reply to your question as to what I would be willing to undertake in the form of lectures, I would suggest the establishment of a "department of public health." I am encouraged to do this by Prof. Palmer's assurance that the Univ. of C. is to do pioneer and unique work along advanced lines in addition to its other functions. Such a department has recently been organized in some of the foreign universities but there is yet in this country no large opportunity for work in this field altho' to my personal knowledge there is a demand for it. Moreover such a department would be in close harmony with the broad sociological and economical work which you have planned as a special feature of the University. I realize that only the beginnings of such a department could be made at present but it seems to me imperative that its cornerstone should be laid at once. Altho the general plan has been in my mind for some years I have had but little time to consider its development with reference to the Univ. I can therefore present for your consideration only a brief outline.

Department of Pub[lic] Health

1. House Sanitation, including situation, surroundings, ventilation, heating, drainage, plumbing, lighting, furnishing.

2. Sanitary Aspects of Water, Food and Clothing including food analysis, food adulterations and dietaries.

3. Domestic Economy (taken in the sense in which Xenophon makes Socrates use it, i.e. the order and administration of the household) with a discussion of the scientific principles of the application of heat to food materials [and] the chemistry of cleaning & service.

4. Municipal, state, and national sanitation.

5. Vital Statistics.

6. Sanitary Jurisprudence.

Courses 4, 5, & 6 with similar courses might be given eventually by members of the faculty; at present special lecturers could be obtained. Courses 1, 2, & 3 I would give this year as minor courses to students in the Univ. College and Grad[uate] Depart[ment] who have had preliminary courses in physics and chemistry. Later it would be desirable to have additional prerequisites in physiology, pol[itical] econ[omy], Fr[ench] & German.

In addition to these courses I would offer this year a Seminar in san[itary] sci[ence] with special investigations in household and sanitary problems.

You must infer that I should feel much hampered if my work as a teacher were to be limited to "lecturing." Any success I have had as an instructor has depended on the use of other methods in addition, i.e. library, laboratory, written recitations, special investigations, theses. Books essential from the start should be ready in the library when work begins. It would be necessary to equip this year a small working laboratory whose outfit would not involve at present a large outlay of money.

Your second question is what responsibility I would be willing to take in the care of the young women. I have discussed this with Mrs. Palmer and while it is impossible to determine details until later we agreed that I should be in residence and for this year at least take the duties of Resident Dean of the Women in the Grad[uate] Depart[ment] & Univ[ersity] College.

In regard to your specific offer of position, may I suggest that the proposed work as a member of the faculty and as an adviser is a very responsible and difficult one and it could be carried on with more ease as well as dignity in the grade of associate rather than assistant professor.

Am I right in assuming that in living with the students I should have in addition to my salary (which I understand covers a term of 36 weeks) living expenses suited to the position.

There is one other point. My first question to Prof. Palmer was whether I should be in an atmosphere of intellectual integrity and co-operation. He assured me that I would, but an endorsement of this opinion would give me satisfaction. Prof. Palmer tells me that the Univ[ersity] is to begin by going to work without formal opening exercises. I have not heard anything that will do more to silence some of the doubts and ignorant criticisms that have been expressed.

I trust I have written in such a way that you can take formal and immediate action. My decision will affect a large number of interests and obligations and I do not wish to announce it until I have heard again from you and know officially the action of your Board.

I regret that my letter must be so long. I shall only say in addition that if I join in your great work it will command my entire loyalty and active service.

Marion Talbot Papers, University of Chicago Library, Department of Special Collections, Chicago, Illinois. By permission of the University of Chicago Archives. This letter was almost certainly written in 1892, although the year does not appear on the document.

3. EXCEPT FROM "PRESENT-DAY PROBLEMS IN THE EDUCATION OF WOMEN"

Her administrative status as dean of women and her keen interest in the development of women's education earned Talbot a reputation as a champion of her sex. She stoked the fires of women's rights with essays on the problems faced by women students.

The problems which face all who are interested in the education of women were never more serious, never more perplexing, never more worthy of careful study and incessant effort than they are to-day. The first of these problems which demands attention is the proper correlation of the physical powers with the mental. We are still seriously handicapped by the notion, which prevailed widely not more than a generation ago, that physical vigor is incompatible with mental strength or intellectual achievement. The scholar was supposed to be characterized inevitably by drooping shoulders, pale countenance, and all the marks of physical deterioration. Fortunately we are outgrowing that conception. A good many people are now convinced that "a sound mind in a sound body" is not a mere oratorical phrase generally impossible of realization in actual life, and they are being greatly helped in demonstrating their belief by the increasing favor shown to physical vigor independent of mental activity. It is now no longer the fashion, as it once was, for a girl, any more than a boy, to be feeble physically. The popular sports which have taken such a hold on the American people of late years are playing a great part in giving us, as a nation, the strength which we need in coping with our duties and responsibilities. This favorable attitude of the public mind will do much to lessen the difficulty by solving this special problem. The investigation of the condition of physical education among girls in colleges and universities, made by the Association of Collegiate Alumnæ thirteen years ago, showed how nearly hopeless was the state of affairs. Much of the strength of the Association was straightway put into efforts to promote an interest in physical education among girls and women, and the outcome is most encouraging. There is reason to be glad that so much has been done; yet how much remains to be done! Well-appointed gymnasiums and expert teachers in physical culture are not enough, though their value cannot be overestimated. We need more definite instruction in the laws of health, we need more attention to the quality of food supplied to students and to the sanitary condition of their homes; we need a better understanding of the physical disaster which follows a wanton misuse of the hours of sleep or of social diversion, and we need most of all a still stronger conscience in our college communities, whose voice shall be raised in constant condemnation of the student who violates the welfare of her physical nature.

Certainly of no less importance is the problem of the correlation of the moral and spiritual natures with the intellectual. This is a burning question, and one which needs courage as well as wisdom. It would seem as if there never could have been a time when the demand was greater than it is now for the true interpretation of the principles of right and honor. The nation should be able to look confidently to its educated youth as leaders in this time of need; yet they fail all too frequently. It is true that they know the principles; but they lack the courage to voice them. Every college student knows in her own college experience how hard it is to stand for the right, when popular sentiment among her associates is tending the other way. Is it not possible to contrive a course for the development of a moral backbone which shall be worthy of the brain power it has to carry? Should not there be more open recognition of the truth all feel that the ethical nature of youth deserves and demands training?

Almost the same thing is to be said of the spiritual nature. It is claimed now and again that colleges are hotbeds of atheism. The accusation is false. The condition which is thus characterized is the same spirit of unrest and of dissatisfaction with old forms which prevails in society at large. Underneath it is a deep yearning for an expression of all that man holds most sacred. There are many signs that this is true. The eagerness with which people are reading books which deal with the vital truths of the higher life, or are listening to great preachers of God's word, shows this. Far from being the enemies of spiritual uplifting, student bodies in reality are quick to respond to real leadership in the higher life. How this immense power for good can be best developed is the problem.

Experience and investigation have demonstrated very clearly another problem in college training for women. Over and over again the four years of college work have utterly failed in effective results because of the lack of an adequate basis of early training. Any consideration, therefore, of the college movement must take into account the home and school training of childhood. The two periods are closely dependent—they are, in fact, one and the same, and any attempt to dissociate them is doomed to failure. The modern movements in primary and secondary education are destined to bear fruit, and their ultimate value will depend largely on the readiness of university educators to profit by them. On the other hand, the spirit of the university must be felt through all the lower grades of schools. What serves one serves the other, and constant watchfulness and power of adaptation is necessary for both. The study of the development of little children by trained observers will do much toward unifying the whole system of education. There is certainly abundant opportunity for non-professional, as well as professional, educators to devise ways and means of securing for the years of childhood the conditions on which progress in later years will depend. A study of the principles involved and the methods to be chosen has been well begun, but a much wider interest in the problem is greatly needed.

A problem which comes more strictly within the narrower limits of our theme is the choice of subjects which properly belong to the collegiate years. Everybody knows how great a field for controversy this presents. There are a few general points which should be considered. In the first place, our heritage of university courses has come from the Church. The subject-matter of the university curriculum has been largely determined by the needs of the priesthood. The present generation has seen an immense revolution whose results are full of promise, but whose tendencies also present points of danger. The radical revolt of modern times against mediæval scholasticism has done a noble work, but there is a possibility that in our enthusiastic devotion to the results of modern research and scholarship we may hold in too light esteem the treasures of ancient thought and experience.

In the second place, education is not merely intellectual training, though that may perhaps be its first function. It should also seek to widen the range of knowledge. As Professor Earl Barnes nobly says: "The curriculum of any grade of school to-day aims to bring before the student through types an epitome of all that man has thought and felt, and a vision of all that God has built into his infinite universe." But here too lurks a danger. The spirit of our age and land is such that the utilitarian aspect of education has an immense hold on popular opinion, and there is a constant effort to place acquisition before training. Superficial knowledge which can immediately be made use of in bread-winning is too generally prized. Moreover there is the demand for specialization, and it is made to begin more and more early. The truth is overlooked that the specialist needs a broad, general education of the higher sort; otherwise he will fail in much of his power as a specialist through his inability to relate his own piece of work to the rest of the universe, even if he is able to grasp it in more than a limited and sectional way. On all sides we feel the pressure of an age of haste, an age of utilitarianism. The problem of the college is to maintain through the repose of true scholarship the ideals of genuine learning. The importance of uniting training and acquisition is sometimes overlooked by educators whose range of vision is limited. Impressed by the practical value of certain subjects, they fail to see that no scientific method of presenting them has yet been fully evolved, and that thereby they are not fully entitled to a place in an educational scheme. It is true, however, that some of these subjects—e. g., modern languages and English literature—are making rapid strides forward, and within a very short time have gained greatly in educational value as subject-matter for instruction. But there is yet much to be done before all the subjects which are urged as worthy a place in a college curriculum can be thus fully recognized by true educators.

Closely allied with this theme of the curriculum in general is the question of choice of subjects by women for their best development as women. It is not as easy to lay down the law for all on this point as some would assert. Any attempt to do this rests on the assumption, in the first place, that emphasis must be given to acquisition rather than to training; and, in the second place, that all women have need of the same kind of information. In reply it must be said that the work which women are now more and more called on to do in the world demands, first of all, the best intellectual discipline. For instance, there are few forms of activity among men which require more carefully trained powers than housekeeping,—an occupation which is supposed to be women's peculiar sphere. Soundness of judgment, keenness of perception, quickness of decision, promptness of execution, all the higher powers are needed at their best to meet the manifold responsibilities and emergencies which arise. Failure to recognize this fact and the assumption that housekeeping comes by nature to women undoubtedly lie at the root of the disasters which are but too common in household administration, and which would be still more frequent were it not for the quick wit and ready adaptability which generally characterize women. It is manifestly true that in general, when men undertake such cares, they meet with a larger measure of success than women do. The administration of household affairs on a large scale, as in clubs, hotels, or public institutions, is almost entirely carried on in this country by men. The explanation undoubtedly is that the ordinary training and experience of the boy are much more likely to fit him to estimate properly the relation of one fact to another. Girls are not usually brought in such contact with the affairs of the world as to learn how to see things in their right proportions, and consequently, unless they are given special training, are harassed and discouraged by non-essentials.

Again, if it is granted that union of training and of acquisition is practicable, the fact must be acknowledged that the kind of acquisition to be chosen is a matter for the individual rather than for the sex. This is recognized in the case of men. The facts studied by a lawyer are totally different from those studied by a physician. The difference between lawyer and physician is far greater than that between physician and housekeeper. The woman in charge of a family would have more need of the kind of information a physician uses than a lawyer would have. It is evident that there are many phases of this problem, that it should be soberly and wisely studied, and that women—and educated women—should be most competent to study it.

Another problem which faces the advocates of collegiate education for women is how best to bring the college training in touch with the world and its work. The old idea has not yet been given up that the life of a scholar is something apart from the common interests of mankind. The charge is made that the college woman often considers that her special training sets her quite apart from the rest of the world. If this is true, as may be the case sometimes, the result is farcical, for the one conception that a woman should certainly gain from collegiate study is that these few years of effort can after all merely open her mental vision to the vast stores which are yet beyond her reach, and train her to use them as time and opportunity come hand in hand. Her friends and acquaintances may sometimes be to blame. It frequently happens that a girl feels herself placed in an entirely false position by the adulation of her immediate circle of friends. She longs to be taken simply, as her brother is, and freed from the artificial expectations which surround her. Moreover, she feels more helpless as to her real place and value in the world than she would if the college had done its whole duty. Here again there are on the one hand tradition and conventionality, on the other the newly awakened soul ready and eager for its task; the question is how the chasm shall be bridged.

Finally, the best results cannot be obtained from collegiate training until an atmosphere of greater freedom prevails. Lucy Larcom once said that genuine liberty was essential for a poet. Women can never be great lyric singers as long as they have any sense of oppression or restraint. This is true also of the best intellectual expression, and is undoubtedly the reason why so little creative work of a high order has been done by women. Fortunately many of the conventional aspects of the woman's college are disappearing, and greater freedom in social life is everywhere accorded to women. How to maintain the restraint essential to a period of development and at the same time the spirit of independence, sincerity, and frankness,—in other words, the sacredness of individuality,—is the problem.

It may be claimed that the questions suggested are not peculiar to the education of women. Many of them belong as well to the education of men. This must be true in so far as the individual is regarded as a human being rather than as a member of one sex or the other. It must be granted that the collegiate education of women is now an integral part of the whole system of education. The young of the race are all to be trained as citizens whose ideals of honor, of right, of justice, of truth, shall be the same whether they are men or women. Certain fundamental principles which are common to both sexes must be established. Moreover, whatever a woman's specific work in life is to be, she should be given in the college the scientific training on which she can build her professional learning. This foundation is the same whether she is to be a physician, housewife, philanthropist, or mother.

True progress in education can be made only by constant study and vigilant effort. Every thoughtful and interested student should be ready to contribute from experience and investigation to the solution of the problems which to-day confront the education of women and which to-morrow will give place to others. Every college woman especially has a great responsibility, as well as opportunity, in standing as the sympathetic critic and loyal supporter of the men and institutions whose efforts in behalf of women are one of the wonders in a century of wonders.

Marion Talbot, "Present Day Problems in the Education of Women," *Educational Review* 14 (October 1897): 248-58.

4. EXCERPTS FROM "THE WOMEN OF THE UNIVERSITY"

As dean of women, Marion Talbot was responsible for preparing a summary each year of the activities of "the women of the university" for The President's Report. *She used the occasion to celebrate student and faculty accomplishments, and to highlight matters that concerned Chicago's academic women.*

The Women of the University

To the President of the University:

Sir: As Dean of Women I submit the following report for the year 1908-9.

The Faculties of the Schools and Colleges of Arts, Literature, and Science included 14 women, distributed according to rank as follows: Professor, 1; Associate Professor, 1; Assistant Professors, 2; Instructors, 5; Associate, 1; Assistants, 4. There were 21 women among the officers of instruction of the College of Education.

Women Fellows, 1908-9

Name	College	State	Department
Grace Abbott	University of Chicago	Illinois	Pol. Science
Minna Caroline Denton	University of Chicago	Illinois	Household Ad.
Sister Helen Angela Dorety	Convent of St. Elizabeth	New Jersey	Botany
Frances Fenton	Vassar College	New York	Sociology
Mabel Ruth Fernald	Mt. Holyoke College	Washington, D. C.	Psychology
Dora Johnson	Vanderbilt University	Tennessee	Latin

Jeannette Brown Obenchain	University of Chicago	Florida	Anthropology
Macy D. Rodman	University of Chicago	Wisconsin	English
Clara Gertrude Seymour	University of Chicago	Massachu- setts	English
Anna Louise Strong	Oberlin College	Illinois	Philosophy
Dagney Gunhilde Sunne	University of Minnesota	Minnesota	Philosophy
Edith Minot Twiss	Ohio State University	Ohio	Botany
Mary Sophia Young	Wellesley College	Nebraska	Botany

ATTENDANCE OF WOMEN STUDENTS

Graduate Schools	508
Senior Colleges	366
Junior Colleges	493
Unclassified students	447
University College	358
Divinity School	25
Courses in Medicine	32
Law School	4
College of Education	837
Grand total	3,070
Duplicates	260
Net Total	2,810

This is a gain of 624, or more than 28 per cent, over the preceding year. The chief gains were in the Graduate Schools, University College, and the College of Education.

The Woman's Union

The Woman's Union exists for the purpose of making more attractive, interesting, and profitable the life of women students in the University. Its activities fall into four classes:

1. The provision of material contributions to the physical comfort of the students, such as the accommodation of an attractive lunch room, where luncheon is served daily at a low price, and the reception room, which is always at the service of members of the Union for rest, social

enjoyment, or as a reading room, where the daily papers and the current magazines may be found.

2. Opportunities for social enjoyment, such as formal receptions to distinguished guests, social teas, and frequent entertainments of an amusing or instructive character. Special guests of the University, the University Preacher, and other persons of note from the city and elsewhere are entertained from time to time.

3. The service of attention and help to all women students needing sympathy or assistance, such as may be accepted by one student to another or by the Union as a body to any woman student in sickness or need of any sort. Every member of the Union is urged to report any such cases to the chairman of the special committee or to the president of the Union.

4. In addition to the activities named above, the Woman's Union is the connecting link between the students of the University and organizations for social and civic improvement in the city of Chicago.

Although it is the wish of the Union to extend its privileges and hospitality so far as possible to every woman student in the University, it is most anxious to count a large body of active workers who are ready to join in the activities described, receiving therefrom the inspiration to be found in working with others and in common effort in the interest of the entire body of women students. The fee for active membership is one dollar a year or fifty cents a Quarter.

The following record shows in outline the scope of the Union's activities during the year:

Addresses by Mrs. Ella Flagg Young, "The Education of Women in Europe;" Mrs. Lenora A. Hamlin, "The Municipal Museum;" Mrs. Harriet M. Van Der Vaart, "The Consumers' League;" Miss Frances A. Kellor, "The Opportunities for Women in Civic Life;" Mrs. Ellen M. Henrotin, "Women as Investors;" Miss Hester D. Jenkins, "The American College for Girls in Constantinople;" Mrs. Zella Allen Dixson, "The Book Plates of Women;" Associate Professor Myra Reynolds, "The Learned Lady as a Comic Type in Eighteenth Century Literature;" Miss Ellen Gates Starr, "Artistic Bookbinding;" Mrs. Charles R. Henderson, "Some European Institutions and Customs;" Mrs. Paul O. Kern, "Music in the Home."

Excerpted from "The Women of the University," in *The President's Report*, 1908–1909, 1902–1904, and 1905–1906 (Chicago: University of Chicago Press), 1910, 1905, and 1907.

5. MARION TALBOT TO MISS CLOUGH, DECEMBER 18, 1919

*In 1919 an Englishwoman asked Marion Talbot to describe her view
of separate instruction for men and women at the University of Chicago. Few events troubled Talbot more than the coeducation controversy that had rocked the university in 1902. She responded as follows:*

I wonder if the statement which I enclose explains in any way my
delay in responding to your request. I have had to make quite a little
search among our archives in order to secure the material, and the pressure of work day by day has made it difficult for me to prepare the
statement. I have tried to present the facts in an entirely objective
way, although the memory of the struggle, a bitter, heated and prolonged one, is still very vivid. There are a few impressions which may
interest you.

The men of the University have for the most part been trained in
schools where many teachers are women and a large proportion of the
students are girls, and it seems to them entirely natural to have the same
conditions in the University. I have noticed that when the different
deans, men and women, are engaged in registering students, the men
students go quite simply and naturally to the women deans if they wish
information or help. Testimony comes in continually, and from many
sources, that far from lowering the standard of scholarship, the influence of women students has been such as to raise it. This is shown
more directly from two angles. The proportion of women students reported for unsatisfactory work is distinctly lower than that of men, and
at the other end, the proportion of women winning honors is higher. I
may add that this is perhaps a source of embarrassment to some of the
men who emphasize sex lines. . . . May I add that I hope to see the day
when the riches of Oxford & Cam[bridge] will be offered to the women
of Eng[land]. The delay in giving this reception to them is difficult in
these days to understand.

Statement Concerning the Subject of Providing Separate Instruction for the Sexes in the Junior College Subjects of the University of Chicago.

When the University of Chicago was opened in October, 1892, the
proportion of women students to men students was rather small. Various causes led to a rapid increase in the number of women students.
The University offered exceptionally fine opportunities to women,

whereas the facilities and attractions for men were not, during the early years of the University, distinctly superior to those offered by several other institutions. The number of women students gradually approximated the number of men undergraduates.

In July, 1900, the University Congregation discussed the question: "Resolved, that better educational results would be secured in the University by teaching the sexes in separate classes." This recommendation was later modified to read as follows: "Resolved, that better educational results would be secured in the Junior Colleges by teaching persons of the two sexes in separate classes." In February, 1902, the Senate was asked to vote on the question as to whether the members would advise the Trustees to accept a large gift of money for the erection of buildings, including recitation halls and laboratories, to be used exclusively for women. It was not appreciated at first that an important educational question could not be discussed wisely in connection with the acceptance of a gift. During a long series of meetings of faculties, Senate, Congregation and Trustees, the question was seriously and actively debated. On October 22, 1902, the Trustees voted (ayes 13, nays 3, absent and not voting, 5) that in the development of Junior College instruction provision be made, as far as possible, for separate sections for men and women. It will be noted that this form is somewhat modified from the original proposition.

The new method was immediately put into effect. The matter has never been brought before the faculty for further discussion but there seems to be a tacit agreement that any possible advantages inherent in the system are more than offset by its disadvantages, and as the system was not compulsory it has gradually disappeared. During the present quarter, of the 62 Junior College courses offered, not one is entirely segregated, and only two are partially segregated. One course in English has 10 mixed sections, 9 men's sections, and 7 women's sections. Another course in English has 5 mixed sections, 4 men's sections and 3 women's sections. This is all that remains of segregation, except physical training and chapel exercises. In the latter case some division is necessary on account of the inadequacy of the space to accommodate all the students, and a division by sexes seems as rational as any.

It is interesting to note that the proportion of men has steadily increased. It would be absurd to attribute this to the gradual disappearance of segregation, just as in the opinion of some the decrease in proportion of men was never due, in any considerable measure, to coeducation. The University has gradually developed its resources in ways which seem to meet the needs of men more effectively. A distinct increase has taken place in such courses as lead to medicine, law and business of various types. A well appointed club house has been established and opportunities for physical exercise have been greatly enlarged. During the present quarter the registration of men students in the Junior College is 888, of women students, 608. Men thus constitute 60% of the total number of Junior College students. In the quadrangles as a whole there are 2696 men and 1712 women, the proportion of men being about 61%, and of women, 39%.

Marion Talbot Papers, University of Chicago Liberty, Department of Special Collections, Chicago, Illinois. Clough's first name is unknown, but she was probably Blanche Athena Clough, former head of Newnham College, Cambridge University. By permission of the University of Chicago Archives.

6. "THE WEAKER SEX" FROM *MORE THAN LORE*

As Marion Talbot later remembered her years at Chicago, the days were marked by many struggles, but the few victories sustained the academic women who were determined to press on.

During the decade preceding the opening of the University, a band of college women had been studying ways and means of giving to women freer entrance into the field of scholarship. The Association of Collegiate Alumnae, organized in January, 1882, and known after 1921 as the American Association of University Women, took as its first objective the improvement in the health of college women, since it was popularly believed that women were not physically able to bear the strain of a college education. This undertaking had been no more than started when, at its second meeting, the Association proceeded to investigate the subject of graduate study for women in spite of the view frequently held that women were not mentally equal even to college work.

Women had some grounds for confidence in their intellectual ability. Helen Magill (later Mrs. Andrew D. White) had taken the degree of Doctor of Philosophy at Boston University in 1877 and was the first woman in the United States to hold that degree. In 1884, Cornell University awarded a fellowship to a woman, Harriet E. Grotecloss, and gained distinction as the first institution in the United States to make such an award. These were, however, exceptional instances, whereas fellowships were readily available for young men whereby they might go to Germany or some other country for the advanced work in research which was not as yet generally attainable in the United States.

Assistance and encouragement were given to young men who might choose to be fitted to hold teaching positions in the colleges and universities throughout the land. But very few graduate courses of any kind were open to women, and no positions on college faculties outside of the women's colleges could be obtained by them. It was distinctly masculine procession that was advancing into the field of research and scholarship. There was plenty of work for the Association to do, and they set about it valiantly. They little dreamed that within two or three decades the Association would be holding endowments for more than ten fellowships and a little later would be well on the way toward securing a fund of one million dollars for the further endowment of national and international fellowships.

But for a long time the road was a hard and weary one to travel; and there was but slight hope that, even if women were well equipped in scholarship, places would be found for them among the groups of scholars in the universities. Every appointment, even to a laboratory assistantship, was a source of cheer and gave encouragement to the belief that such a footing would lead the way to higher positions. But in whatever direction one turned, the way seemed blocked. The world seemed to have forgotten that several centuries before women had held, with distinction, professorships in leading universities of the Old World.

Such was, in brief, the status of women scholars in academic life when the educational world was startled and the Association of Collegiate Alumnae greatly heartened by the announcement of the new University of Chicago that women were appointed on its faculty and as fellows. Three months before the University opened, the first number of the *Quarterly Calendar,* dated June, 1892, gave the names of the following women as members of the prospective staff: "Alice Freeman Palmer, Ph. D., Litt.D., Professor of History and Acting Dean [of women] in the Graduate School of the University Colleges; Julia E. Bulkley, Associate Professor of Pedagogy and Dean [of women] in the Academic Colleges; Zella Allen Dixson, Assistant Librarian; Luanna Robertson and Elizabeth C. Cooley, Academy Tutors; Alice Bertha Foster, M.D., Tutor in Physical Culture; S. Frances Pellett, A.M., University Extension Reader in Latin." There were also six women fellows announced: "Senior fellows: Mabel Banta and Myra Reynolds; Junior fellows: Elizabeth Wallace and Mary Frances Winston; Honorary fellows: Maud Wilkinson and Madeleine Wallin."

In the following September two new names appeared on the Faculty list, viz., Martha Foote Crowe, Ph.D., Assistant Professor of English Literature; and Marion Talbot, A.M., Assistant Professor of Sanitary Science

and Dean (of women) in the University Colleges. The distinction between senior and junior fellows disappeared in this same issue of the
Calendar, and the names of Julia B. Platt and E. Antoinette Ely were
added to the list of honorary fellows.

This was the situation when the University opened October 1, 1892.
No wonder the road ahead seemed clear. But the vision proved to be
somewhat of a mirage. No new appointments of women and no promotions were made for two years. In 1894 the wheels seemed to move,
for Elizabeth Wallace, who had been a docent for a year, was promoted
to a readership! In 1895 Myra Reynolds, who had held an assistantship
for one year, became an instructor, and I was advanced to an associate
professorship. There was, however, no woman even nominally a professor, for Mrs. Palmer, at the end of three years of advisory service,
retired from her connection with the University. In 1896 Kate Anderson, who had succeeded Alice B. Foster, was raised from a tutorship to
an instructorship. In 1897–98 there were eleven women of all grades
on the Faculty—a merely nominal increase in proportion to the enlarged number of men. The years that followed proved to be rather
dark ones for women, although no whispers were heard against their
efficiency and devotion. A few bright spots should be noted. I was
made a professor in 1904. Sophonisba P. Breckinridge, who was fellow
in political science from 1897–1901 was docent in the same department
from 1902 to 1904, and instructor and assistant professor in household
administration from 1904 to 1920, when her distinguished career in
social service administration began officially. Ella Flagg Young was an
outstanding member of the Faculty from 1899–1904. Gertrude Dudley's inestimable and memorable services began in 1898. Edith Foster,
who began as assistant in English on her graduation in 1897, reached,
as Mrs. Flint, a professorship in 1923 and occupied many positions of
trust and responsibility. Elizabeth Wallace's story was almost parallel,
and her influence and activity of great value. Edith Abbott, who had an
appointment in the University as fellow in 1903, came again to the
University in 1914 as lecturer in sociology and in 1920 was appointed
associate professor of social economy. Later, as Dean of the Graduate
School of Social Service Administration, she began the magnificent work
which has placed the School in the front ranks of social-welfare schools.
In 1901 the organization of the School of Education brought a considerable addition of women to the teaching staff, notably Zonia Baber
and Alice Peloubet Norton. When the medical work was developed,
several women appeared on the scene, but mostly as assistants.

The list of women who have contributed to the upbuilding of the

University must close here, although among those not named are some not less distinguished.

Meanwhile the professorial groups were increasing very rapidly in the number of men, several of those who had reached the highest professorial grade having received their baccalaureate degrees later than women, who were still held in the lower ranks. Had the women failed to make good; and, if so, were there not others who might replace them?

Some comments on the situation may have interest.

Among the twenty women who held fellowships in 1899 and the two following years are eight whose names appeared in *Who's Who in America* in 1935, besides three who were listed in *American Women,* the official women's *Who's Who*. Fifty-five per cent to achieve national recognition is a gratifying proportion.

Generalizations concerning women in the field of scholarship have offered frequent opportunity for investigation. One instance resulted from the statement of a University professor known to be sympathetic with the aims of young women scholars. He said, in a public address, that both the wish and the ability of young women to take a college course had been abundantly proved (and consequently the old charge of their unfitness had been disproved); but, he went on to say, except in rare instances they showed little inclination to pursue their studies in the Graduate School. What did a study of the recorded facts show as to the validity of personal impressions? By that time the University had conferred the Bachelor's degree on 700 men and 598 women. During the preceding year, July 1, 1902–July 1, 1903, 88 of these men and 85 of the women had enrolled as members of the Graduate Schools of Arts and Sciences, or 12.6 per cent of the men and 14.2 per cent of the women were pursuing their studies. It was significant that of the 88 men, 10 were holders of fellowships, while of 85 women only 3 had been granted this assistance in continuing their studies.

Another statement was made to the effect that, in general, women who pursue higher studies are not so persistent as men and their scholarship is not of so high a grade. The statistics of the University showed that the first point was true, but the difference was surprisingly small. Of the 377 men who had held fellowships, 153, or 41 per cent, had attained the degree of Doctor of Philosophy. Of the 76 women who had held fellowships, 27, or 36 per cent, had received the same degree. In view of the limited opportunities and few inducements open to women scholars, it was rather surprising that there was not a greater difference.

In regard to the scholarship of those who had received the doctorate as determined by the grade of the degree, the accompanying table, compiled at the same time (1903), proved interesting. It shows that, while a slightly larger percentage of women than men fall in the two lowest classes, the percentage of men in the very lowest class is much larger than that of women. The figures for the highest class are slightly in favor of the women. It must be remembered, however, that with so small a total number of women a difference of even one in either the highest or lowest class would make a very appreciable difference in the percentages of those classes. In spite of these, and other creditable records, little advance was made in giving recognition to women.

	Men		Women	
	Number	Percent	Number	Percent
Rite	58	22.4	5	10.4
Cum laude	91	35.1	24	50.0
Magna cum laude	94	36.3	16	33.3
Summa cum laude	16	6.2	3	6.3
Total	259		48	

In December, 1924, the latent discontent among the women came to a crisis, and the three women who held professorships out of a total of 150 decided that drastic action must be taken, and, after careful deliberation, addressed the following communication to the President of the University and the President of the Board of Trustees:

Gentlemen:

The undersigned women members of the University Senate beg leave to call certain matters to your attention and ask your consideration of them in connection with plans for the future development and administration of the University. Their deep interest in the University and their loyalty may be measured in part by the ninety-five years of their joint connection with it.

I. The articles of incorporation include among the objects for which the University exists, the following:

To provide, impart, and furnish opportunities for all departments of higher education to persons of both sexes on equal terms.

These objects seem to us to be not adequately fulfilled in the following respects:

a) There is no woman on the Board of Trustees.

b) The Faculties of Arts, Literature, and Science have on their teaching staff too small a proportion of women, not even furnishing a sufficient number to fill the positions of Deans and Heads of Houses.

c) Although women comprise over 40 per cent of the graduate students and show by the grades accompanying the doctorates they receive that they reach a very high plane of achievement, they receive only about 20 per cent of the fellowships, including special fellowships designated for women.

d) Of the University of Chicago Bachelors who received the Doctor's degree between 1919 and 1923, seventeen received appointments to the Faculty. Seven men received appointments of professorial rank and the two women in this group received instructorships.

e) Promotions and increase of salary are awarded to women more slowly than to men. There are three women Faculty members who received their Doctor's degree in 1907 or earlier and who are still only associate professors; whereas twenty-one men who received their Doctor's degrees in 1907 or later hold full professorships. No one of these men has received the honorary degree of Doctor of Laws, whereas two of the women have received it.

II. The slight rôle given to women in "providing and imparting opportunities for education to persons of both sexes on equal terms" is supplemented with slight recognition given to them in other academic relations, viz.:

1. There have been 134 convocations with but four women orators.

2. Only one honorary degree has been conferred upon a woman.

3. Only twice has any woman been asked to speak at homecoming or Trustees' dinners.

4. With very rare exceptions women are not invited to give University Public Lectures.

5. Women do not receive appointments on important Faculty committees.

6. Women are not always represented in social functions given in the name of the University.

7. Women of the Faculty are given no opportunity to enjoy or to offer hospitality except under strict limitations at the Quadrangle Club.

8. No opportunity has been given the Faculty women to aid in working out plans for the development of the University, especially as it concerns the women of the University.

III. In view of the preceding facts we would urge—

1. The appointment of a woman Trustee.

2. The appointment to the Faculties of several women of distinction and power in scholarship, teaching ability, or administrative skill.

3. The granting of greater encouragement to young women scholars of promise.

4. A larger recognition of women in semi-academic ways.

5. Better facilities for agreeable social life.

6. Further opportunity to make known the needs of women Faculty members and students which either exist today or will be felt in the near future.

We believe that the measures here proposed will work advantageously in raising the status of young women students in college activities and that they will tend to produce even more women graduates of distinction and a body of women whose influence on boys and men through the school and the home will bring to the enrichment of the University a stream of young and able youth.

Finally, the University of Chicago, if true to the ideals on which it was established, can make a great contribution through the encouragement it gives its women members, toward the development of those resources of the world which are in the keeping of women and which they are called upon more and more to contribute to the progress of civilization.

[*Signed by*] Edith Foster Flint
Marion Talbot
Elizabeth Wallace

We waited with some trepidation for the repercussions from this bolt. A formal acknowledgment came from President Burton, but no more definite response. A rumor reached us, however, that the communication was read to the whole Board of Trustees and its statements were challenged. One member claimed that if any of the alleged facts were untrue or were misrepresentations, all the signers should be at once dismissed. A special committee was appointed to learn whether the statements could be verified. Their report was that the statement was not only true in every respect but might have been made even stronger. The women were gratified when, on the next announcement of promotions, Miss Abbott, Miss Katherine Blunt, and Miss Breckinridge were named as professors. Some other results followed, such as the appointment of a woman as Convocation orator; but on the whole no great progress was made.

The need of more women skilled in administrative matters and interested in promoting this phase of the University's activities has not yet been met, greatly to the detriment, as many observers believe, of the women students. It may be added that a fairer recognition of scholarly women would not only have a good influence on the younger students—but would widen the competition, thus raise the marginal level, and even do the men scholars some good, though it is possible that neither men nor women would be conscious of any altruistic motive underlying such a policy.

This brief résumé of the participation of women in the work of the University gives little hint of the whole-hearted devotion they showed. With hardly an exception, they worked as a team for unholding and advancing the intellectual and social standards of the University. Their common goal had no trace of self-seeking. Their common objective was the constant subject of their discussions and conferences. According to the notion current in some quarters, it might be assumed that differences of opinion would lead to petty personal antagonisms, or even spite. Many occasions, however, occurred when visitors from other academic groups were impressed by the friendly atmosphere and the devotion to a common cause which gave creditable and rare distinction to the group.

This résumé of the history of women on the Faculty has its disheartening aspect and seems to confirm the widespread conviction that present-day conditions offer little opportunity for women to receive recognition for their intellectual and administrative gifts. Discouragement is quite general, but here and there the battle cry is heard. The women of today must not falter in claiming the right to use their powers, and they will find more to encourage than to dishearten if they scrutinize this sketch of what has happened at Chicago in less than forty years. At the beginning the outlook was black indeed. The difficulty, if not impossibility, of believing that there were to be women on the Faculty of the new University may be shown by a little incident. Shortly after the University opened, the ladies of a neighboring church invited the Faculty and their wives to a Turkey Dinner. The invitation addressed to Mr. and Mrs. Marion Talbot was delivered to me. Nobody disputed my right to the share of the dinner, which I enjoyed. A glance forward of only twelve years from that time shows a woman holding a seat in the highest educational body, the Senate, of an institution which had a right already to a place among the great universities of the world. God's mills do not always grind slow, and history may be a tonic when courage and hope waver.

Marion Talbot, *More Than Lore: Reminiscences of Marion Talbot, Dean of Women, the University of Chicago, 1892–1925* (Chicago: University of Chicago Press, 1936), pp. 127–43. © 1936 The University of Chicago. All rights reserved.

7. MARION TALBOT TO ROBERT HUTCHINS, JUNE 8, 1940

Marion Talbot responded to a tribute from Robert Hutchins, President of the University of Chicago, in June of 1940 with some reflections on the changing nature of collegiate life. She was eighty-two at the time.

I am especially pleased that you recognize the two major objectives I had in mind in organizing the life of the women students. It seemed to me at the outset fifty years ago that as the student body was made up of both men and women they should share equally the responsibility of caring for and administering their common activities. On the other hand the women should be solely responsible for such activities as they deemed advisable to maintain. Moreover as the University was planned to be "a community of scholars" I did all in my power to cultivate so high a standard of scholarship that the university should always benefit from the influence of women. Responsibility and intelligence were indeed the keynotes one struck in those pioneering days and [maintained for a number of years. Unfortunately the women have recently been "slipping" due in considerable measure to the pernicious influence of the Maroon* which has been clearly felt in many ways, in part also to their ageold subjection to] habit and social standards. An organ supposedly representing student interests which ranks as its best representative man the one who can grow the most hair on his face and the best woman she who wins in the competition to be called Queen of the University and supplements this with some conspicuous and ill bred act which attracts public attention has had a vicious influence and I do not wonder that well bred parents in our community as well as in others inquiring concerning the activities and interests which will be likely to attract the attention and ability of their children choose institutions where standards of taste and manners are likely to be higher. Mr. Noyes gave the building as a memorial to his wife in order that the University might offer its women students some of the advantages which mark the women's colleges of the East. The Maroon now calls it the Student Club House and it is certainly true that men use its privileges without having to meet the costs involved in the use of their own club house The Reynolds Club without reciprocal advantages. . . . At the risk of making this expression of appreciation a bad tempered screed I must add that I regret the steadily decreasing number of our women students (and men) whose ability is receiving recognition through fellowships, schol-

---

*The Maroon was the University of Chicago's student newspaper.

arships, and grants in aid from colleges, universities, and learned societies.

Marion Talbot Papers, University of Chicago Library, Department of Special Collections, Chicago, Illinois. This letter was a draft and the material in brackets was crossed out. By permission of the University of Chicago Archives.

GRACE RAYMOND HEBARD

American Heritage Center, University of Wyoming

The Independent and Feminine Life

GRACE RAYMOND HEBARD
1861–1936

by Virginia Scharff

On March 6, 1932, the Professors' Club of Laramie, Wyoming (an all-woman organization) held a seventieth birthday party for its founder, Dr. Grace Raymond Hebard, head of the Department of Political Economy at the University of Wyoming. In arranging for testimonial speeches, the planners sought out women who might address the many facets of Hebard's career. Upon her death four years later, Hebard would be eulogized as "engineer, administrator, librarian, historian, champion of womanhood, citizen, teacher, and friend of youth."[1]

Those who gathered at the birthday celebration were inclined to more personal tributes. A friend from suffragist days called Hebard "the wise virgin who has always kept her lamp filled with oil and burning." A former student extolled Hebard as "the embodiment of the teaching virtues, love, patience, and confidence." Hebard drew praise for her work in Western history, in studies of the Americanization of immigrants, and in organizing and promoting the library of the University of Wyoming. But one speaker summed up all the laudatory words. "To speak of Dr. Hebard's work for women," she said, "is to speak of her whole life."[2]

Grace Raymond Hebard used the university, her own historical research, and women's culture to achieve feminist goals. Her politics and personality seem to have been particularly fitted for professional work in a state like Wyoming and a town like Laramie. Born in the young town of Clinton, Iowa in 1861, Hebard was the creature of a West that had rubbed off the rawness of the frontier, but in which many social, educational, and institutional paths remained to be broken. In towns like Clinton and Laramie, a citizen might combine self-promotion with civic idealism, reform zeal with local boosterism. Hebard's West embraced the legal rights of women and the dying romance of Indian culture, but not the rights of most racial or ethnic minorities. Her Wyoming affirmed cowboy independence, but not sodbuster radicalism. Her Laramie liked to think of itself as a forward-looking center of learning, but it sometimes emulated other college towns further east in its snobbery and petty feuding. Grace Hebard was the feminist personification of the individualistic egalitarianism and adventuresome conservatism of the high, dry country.

Hebard arrived in Wyoming in 1882, bearing a newly minted bachelor of science degree from the University of Iowa. She had been the first woman at that university to major in engineering, and later recalled that:

> I met with many discouragements and many sneers, and much opposition to my enrolling in the scientific course, which was then entirely a man's college. . . . All kinds of discouraging predictions were made that I would fail, that it was impossible for a woman to do the kind of work I was undertaking.[3]

Such condescension probably fueled Hebard's determination to succeed. She was a die-hard suffragist from an early age, and would never be daunted by sexist estimates of women's capabilities. Upon graduation, she would have a chance to prove herself in a drafting job in the United States Surveyor General's office in Cheyenne, Wyoming Territory. While she polished her mapmaking skills and ascended through the ranks of the bureaucracy to become deputy state engineer, she also worked on a master's degree in English literature, by correspondence with Iowa, completing the degree in 1885. She continued active in the suffrage movement and spoke on behalf of woman suffrage before the Wyoming state constitutional convention in 1889.

Hebard moved to Laramie in 1891 to take a new job as secretary to and member of the board of trustees of the fledgling University of Wyoming. This unusual combination of positions probably represented a recognition of her ambition, her administrative skills, her family connections, and her sex. She handled the university's finances as well as all official correspondence, and admitted that "the trustees gave me a great deal of power, and I used it."[4] Combining power politics with manipulative tactics, Hebard used her dual appointment to influence events covertly where she could not control them directly. F. P. Graves, an early president of the University of Wyoming, recalled that, "She zealously guarded all knowledge of the weaknesses I had exhibited and credited me with many successful projects which she herself had originated."[5] Her detractors saw such secretarial self-effacement differently, one professor complaining that "her power is recognized not only by the University people, but by many townspeople, yet her clerical position enables her to throw responsibility for any policy upon the executives."[6]

When a university funds scandal forced the resignation of several trustees in 1907, Hebard was attacked not for any dishonest action, but for running the school. The *Laramie Daily Boomerang* put the matter bluntly:

> It is a standing remark in Laramie that no professor or employee of the institution can hold his job without being branded "ok" by Miss Secretary Hebard, and whenever she decrees it the president's head will fall in a basket. The scalps of Presidents . . . may hang for many a moon in the Secretary's office as a practical demonstration of what a woman can do.[7]

Perhaps tiring of a job that entailed much responsibility and little glory, Hebard had already launched her campaign to get into the classroom. Partly in order to gain increased contact with students, she took on the unpaid job of university librarian in 1894, a position she would hold until 1919.[8] In 1893 she had earned, by correspondence, a Ph.D. degree in political science from Illinois Wesleyan University.[9] She began her work as a college professor by substituting for the regular instructor of an economic class. By 1906, having demonstrated a flair for teaching, she secured a faculty appointment in the Department of Political Economy, becoming head of the department little more than a year later. Her disgruntled predecessor accused her of buying a phony doctorate from a "loose and disreputable" institution, but Hebard defended her credentials and insisted that she had taken the job because she wished to be of service to the university.[10]

Judging from the terms "loose and disreputable," the charge against her appears to have been aimed as much at Hebard's moral character as at her academic credentials. However odd a correspondence doctorate may appear to us now, academic structures, particularly in the West, were considerably less formal than they are today.[11] Hebard's dissertation, a study of immigration and Americanization, represented her most serious scholarly effort up to the time, and she would devote many articles and lectures to presenting the nativist side of the immigration question in later years.[12] Further, her unorthodox career path should be seen in the context of the small but growing University of Wyoming which, in 1904, had only 19 faculty members and 182 students. Here a nascent professional specialization often bowed before the claims of expediency.

Despite the national trend toward offering increased numbers of specialized courses,[13] the members of the tiny Wyoming faculty performed as generalists. Hebard offered courses in state and national civics, federal constitutional law, Wyoming law (having been herself admitted to the state bar in 1898, the first woman to be so recognized), international law, English constitutional law, sociology, money and banking, political parties, labor problems, railroad organization, children's literature and storytelling, and library science. She also taught night classes in Americanization and patriotism for immigrants. Among her surviving students, she is best remembered for her exciting rendering of Wyoming history.[14]

However unconventional her preparation for teaching, literally hundreds of notes from affectionate students testify to Hebard's skill, enthusiasm, and magnetism in the classroom. Hebard's devotion to teaching might be interpreted as acquiescence to a traditionally female vocation, except that she understood the crucial role of education in empowering women over the course of the nineteenth century. She ascribed women's improving status in America not only to political agitation, but to the influx of women into the teaching profession.[15] She also strove to be a friend to and role model for students. One student made her feelings plain in a letter to Hebard: "I just love you so much, it almost hurts."[16] Another former student declared that she had "heard many young women of Wyoming say they made it a point to attend the university just to be able to say they had studied under Dr. Hebard."

The university community regarded Hebard as an advocate for all students and a particularly adamant supporter of women students. She fought hard for professional treatment for herself and her female protégées, particularly where pay was at issue.[17] Hebard held that economic issues were, like legal discrimination, part of the broader problem of women's rights, and could not be addressed as separate, negotiable items in a political laundry list. She seized the opportunity afforded by a 1920 suffrage speech to attack economic discrimination against the women who had contributed to the recent war effort: "It was that woman, whether she be a scrubwoman or a professor, who gets the salary of a scrubwoman."[18]

The University of Wyoming barred faculty and staff from participating in partisan campaigns, but this political prohibition did not prevent her from speaking out on such issues as woman suffrage, child labor protection, immigration restriction, or prison labor reform. The eminently political Grace Hebard (protesting, withal, "I do not like to go into politics"[19]) agitated and organized around all these causes. She was particularly tireless in her suffrage work. Active on the national as well as local level, she counted Carrie Chapman Catt among her good friends, and corresponded with many women prominent in the movement. Virginia Roderick, editor of the *Woman Citizen,* the magazine of the National American Woman Suffrage Association, praised Hebard's regular contributions to the publication, writing Hebard, "You are—I say it without a qualm—our star contributing editor."[20] Hebard also wrote the Wyoming chapter for *The History of Woman Suffrage.*[21]

A conservative suffragist of the type personified by Carrie Catt, Hebard's views on race and class relations and immigration can best be described as reactionary, tinged with the Westerner's geographically reinforced provincialism. For Hebard, American society remained a meritocracy, flawed only in its shameful refusal to give women a fair chance at individual achievement. Wyoming, she insisted, presented the rest of the nation with a model. Marketing woman suffrage as the fruit of frontier individualism, she made a point of referring to the passage of the Nineteenth Amendment as "inevitable" and always reminded her audiences that Wyoming had led the way in enfranchising women.[22] Hebard's work in Wyoming brought her a national role in the 1920 ratification campaign, when she spoke at the Victory Day dinner in Chicago and served as a member of the "Suffrage Emergency Brigade," a group that went to Connecticut to try to persuade the governor of that state to call a special session of the state legislature so that Connecticut might become the crucial thirty-sixth state to approve the Nineteenth Amendment. Hebard professed incredulity that the East had so tenaciously resisted enfranchising women, telling a reporter from the *New York Tribune,* "I never before saw an anti-suffragist. You know, out in Wyoming we have had woman suffrage for fifty years, and there is no such thing as an anti-suffrage man in our state—much less a woman."[23]

Though she portrayed Wyoming as an undivided bastion of feminism, Hebard's own problematic relationship with Wyoming's Nellie Tayloe Ross, the nation's first woman governor, belied her claim. When Ross became governor upon the death of her husband in 1924, Hebard rejoiced that Wyoming should have scored another political first for women. Soon, however, disillusionment set in when Ross turned out to be more a party-line Democrat than an advocate for women or women's concerns. Wyoming feminists complained that Ross did not appoint enough women to public office, and that she paid little attention to reform measures they supported. Hebard, long a central figure among activist women in the state, had frequently presented her constituency's case to people in power in Wyoming, and Ross proved less responsive to Hebard's entreaties than had other Wyoming politicians.[24] Hebard put aside her lifelong Republicanism to support Ross's losing bid for reelection in 1926, but she seems to have done so with reluctance. She wrote Catt, upon Ross's defeat, suggesting that Ross's lack of support for feminist positions had contributed much to the Republican victory.[25]

It is not surprising that Hebard's dedication to women's rights would have affected the direction of her scholarship. She was a Westerner, an identification that prompted her to write several books, many articles, and endless speeches about the male side of the history of Wyoming and the West. Her best known and most controversial work, however, dealt with women's part in the Western adventure.[26] Frankly romantic, she idolized Washington Irving and sought to create female heroes in the Irving mold. She popularized the idea that woman suffrage had first been introduced into the Wyoming territorial legislature in 1869 because one Esther Morris, a suffragist from the gold mining settlement of South Pass City, had invited candidates standing for the district's legislative seat to a women's tea party before the election. According to Hebard, Morris convinced both candidates to agree to introduce a woman suffrage bill into the legislature if elected, since the candidates knew how much influence the South Pass prosuffrage wives had with their enfranchised husbands.[27]

In strong-minded, tea-pouring Esther Morris, Hebard created an historical figure in her own image. These two women did resemble one another in style (assertive), temperament (volatile), and political ideology (feminist). Yet Hebard probably distorted the facts in pleading her case for giving Morris credit for woman suffrage in Wyoming. If Esther Morris rather too closely resembled members of Hebard's own circle of feminist friends in Hebard's rendition of the historical data, the historian would succumb even more completely to present-mindedness in her biography of Sacajawea, the Shoshone woman who accompanied Lewis and Clark across the continent. Hebard spent thirty years in a passionate effort "to rescue Sacajawea . . . from semi-oblivion . . . [and] to right previous historical wrongs."[28] Her interpretation of what many historians refer to as "the Sacajawea problem" is undeniably long on romance and short on hard evidence, suffering from a sentimentalization of Indian culture as well as an almost unconscious impulse to Americanize the Shoshones.[29] Yet though historians ought to take a skeptical view of Hebard's data on Sacajawea, it is interesting to probe her motives in devoting much of her scholarly life to this project. Hebard portrayed Sacajawea as valiant guide to white men and respected wise woman to the Shoshone people. The biographer wanted her subject to stand for the nobility of the uncorrupted Indian character and the innate dignity and heroism of women. Like Esther Morris, this Sacajawea was, in Hebard's eyes, a Westerner pathbreaker who demonstrated that women's role in the frontier epic deserved more attention and respect. No one would deny that much of the history of the West has been written more in the spirit of forging a cultural identity than in the interest of meticulously reconstructing the past. Like many Western historians of her day, Hebard was a mythmaker, yet her sagas were intended to immortalize heroes who had been ignored. Hebard's protégée, Wyoming historian Agnes Wright Spring, would say that "Dr. Hebard's historical work . .,. [came] as the direct result of her interest in women."[30] Wyoming psychology professor June Etta Downey wrote, in the introduction to *Sacajawea,* that the book was a thirty-year "labor of love."

There is no doubt that Grace Hebard valued the companionship of women. Her closest, longest-lived relationships were with women. She maintained ties with the female community through political, civic, social, and cultural organizations. Especially active in the Daughters of the American Revolution, she sometimes used conservative women's groups to push for projects dear to her own heart. The DAR, for example, sponsored an Esther Morris monument in South Pass City. Hebard also joined a host of professional and collegial organizations for women, including the American Association of University Women, the National Business and Professional Women's Club, the Wyoming State Teachers' Association, the National Association of Women Lawyers, Pi Beta Phi, and the Wyoming Public Health Association.[31] In 1924 she founded the Professors' Club. According to Wyoming folklore, she gave the club that title, reasoning that if male faculty members wanted their own club, they could call it the Men Professors' Club.

Lillian Faderman has written that women professionals of Hebard's generation "viewed themselves as pioneers, and as such they assumed the right to create a whole new lifestyle."[32] A number of historians have pointed out the significance of intimate emotional relations between professional women in the United States of Hebard's day, a time when few people believed in the compatibility of marriage and careers for women.[33] Hebard and her friends, many of them women professors at Wyoming, reconciled intellectuality, ambition, and emotion by affirming intimacy between women.

Hebard successively lived with two women who served as heads of the Wyoming history department, Irene May Morse and Agnes Mathilde Wergeland. These relationships appear to have been happy and productive. Hebard and Morse lived together for several years, up to the time Morse went to Massachusetts to study medicine. Their lodgings were a popular gathering place for students and staff, and they commemorated their domestic life in a snapshot album titled "Old Maids' Paradise," featuring themselves, looking very young, as the "two old maids." Each photograph had a humorous, yet revealing caption, one such proclaiming, "They say they prefer to marital strife/Their own independent and feminine life:/Truthful old maids!"[34]

Hebard's relation with Wergeland, spanning twelve years and ending only with Wergeland's death in 1914, was clearly the deepest emotional attachment of her life. Wergeland had charted a distinguished academic course, leaving her native Norway to teach at Bryn Mawr, the University of Illinois, and the University of Chicago before settling in Wyoming. A musician and poet as well as historian, Wergeland shared Hebard's love of outdoor sports and mountain landscapes.[35] Their house, "The Doctors' Inn," was refuge and work space for both. Wergeland's death devastated Hebard, though she sought to extract some good from her loss. She endowed two scholarships in Wergeland's name, a practice she also employed in commemorating June Downey and her sister Alice Hebard, who had been a schoolteacher and principal in Cheyenne.

Interestingly, not even a shred of gossip has survived to indicate that anyone in Wyoming regarded Hebard and the women she lived and worked with as unnatural in their unconventional living arrangements or their rejection of marriage. Hebard lived until 1936, long after the sexologists had begun to condemn women's romantic friendships as examples of "inversion." Those who eulogized Hebard made special mention of her "fine loyalty to close personal friends." Perhaps Wyoming, deep in the West, was simply too isolated from cultural trends to trade a Victorian image of old maid schoolteachers for the sophisticated notion that women who lived and worked together were sexually suspect. Upon her death, U.S. Senator Robert Carey would simply say, "No woman in Wyoming was ever held in greater esteem."[36]

Rosalind Rosenberg has written that women's community within the academy represented a professional as well as emotional response to increasingly narrow specialization within the university.[37] At Wyoming, women had the chance to develop generalized knowledge and skills, to avoid being marginalized in "women's fields" such as home economics, at the same time enjoying the support of a community of female scholars. Both Morse and Wergeland had been generalists like Hebard. Though she did devote more and more time to specialized historical research, Hebard had become professionally obsolete by the time of her death in 1936.

Laura White, who succeeded Wergeland as history department head, represented a new, discipline-identified model of scholarship. She wrote to Hebard in 1935, asking for information about the early days of the university. Hebard replied testily:

> I stand ready to help in any way and I do not want to run in conflict with anyone who is a newcomer who might try to write history according to Hoyle, but history was not written in the early days of any institution or country in just that way. There were emergencies to be met and the efficiency of the frontiersman was measured by his abilities to meet irregularities in a judicious way.[38]

Yet Hebard was not simply a crotchety dying pioneer; she was still primarily an advocate for women. In Wyoming she had found a sustaining community and a wealth of opportunity. Cancer had almost claimed her when she wrote White to caution her against despair. "An elderly woman does not get discouraged," said Hebard. "It is the young woman who generally lets her talents rust through sheer modesty and lack of appreciation."[39] Her legacy lies in such encouraging words, in holding out the promise of the independent and feminine life.

Notes

I want to thank Karen Anderson, Katherine Jensen, Kate Swift, and Casey Miller for their help with this chapter, in its various forms.

1. *In Memoriam: Grace Raymond Hebard, 1861–1936* (Laramie, Wyo.: Faculty of the University of Wyoming, 1937), p. 2.

2. Professors' Club scrapbook, 6 March 1932, Grace Raymond Hebard Papers, American Heritage Center, Coe Library, University of Wyoming, Laramie.

3. Hebard to Aven Nelson, 11 February 1928, Hebard Papers.

4. Janelle M. Wenzel, "Dr. Grace Raymond Hebard as Western Historian" (M.A. thesis, university of Wyoming, 1960), p. 10. Wenzel's thesis is the most

thorough treatment of Hebard's historical research, and it offers useful information on her life.

5. *In Memoriam,* p. 24.

6. Wenzel, "Grace Raymond Hebard," p. 10.

7. Ibid., pp. 11–12.

8. Hebard, "Dedication of the New Library," speech transcript, Hebard Papers.

9. *In Memoriam,* p. 3.

10. Ibid.

11. See Patricia Albjerg Graham, "Expansion and Exclusion: A History of Women in American Higher Education," *SIGNS: Journal of Women in Culture and Society* (Fall 1978): 759–73.

12. See, for example, articles in the *Woman Citizen,* 18 January 1921, 2 September 1927; also *Illinois Wesleyan Magazine,* October 1896.

13. *Recent Social Trends in the United States: Report of the President's Research Committee on Social Trends* (New York: McGraw Hill, 1933), p. 338.

14. Hebard, "Report to the President, 1913," Hebard Papers. Also interview with Caroline Mortimer, Green River, Wyoming, 23 July 1984.

15. See excerpt of Hebard's speech transcript on women and education, Document 3 of this chapter.

16. *In Memoriam,* p. 32; student to Hebard, n.d., Hebard Papers. On the issue of women's role in the academy, see Katherine Jensen, "Women's Work and Academic Culture," *Higher Education* 11 (1982): 67–83.

17. Hebard to C. A. Duniway, 14 April 1917; also Hebard to Aven Nelson, 4 April 1918, Hebard Papers.

18. "Hebard Appeals for Suffrage Cause," *Wyoming State Tribune,* 11 May 1920, Hebard Papers.

19. "Advance Guard of Suffrage Emergency Corps Arrives," *New York Tribune,* 2 May 1920, Hebard Papers.

20. Virginia Roderick to Hebard, 3 June 1922, Hebard Papers.

21. See Woman Suffrage file, Hebard Papers, for early drafts of this chapter.

22. I am indebted to Melanie Gustafson for the idea that Hebard marketed suffrage as a Wyoming export.

23. "Advance Guard Arrives."

24. Hebard and Ross apparently differed on the issues of prison labor reform and the proposed child labor amendment to the U.S. Constitution. See Mrs. Walter McNabb Miller to Hebard, 27 August 1925; Hebard to Nellie Tayloe Ross, 8 December 1924. For more on Ross, see Barbara J. Aslakson, "Nellie Tayloe Ross, First Woman Governor" (M.A. thesis, University of Wyoming, 1960).

25. Woman Suffrage file, Hebard Papers; Hebard to Carrie Chapman Catt, 9 November 1926 (see Document 2 of this chapter).

26. T. A. Larson, *History of Wyoming* (Lincoln: University of Nebraska Press, 1979), pp. 522–23; also Larson, "Woman Suffrage in Wyoming," *Pacific Northwest Quarterly* 56 (1965): 57–66.

27. Hebard's version of the advent of woman suffrage has survived Larson's well-founded criticisms and continues to be disseminated in history textbooks. See for example Mary Beth Norton et al., *A People and a Nation: A History of the United States, Volume Two: Since 1865* (Boston: Houghton Mifflin, 1982), p. 550. Hebard, "How Woman Suffrage Came to Wyoming," 1920, Hebard Papers; Larson, *History of Wyoming,* pp. 78–94; Virginia Scharff, "The Case for Domestic Feminism: Woman Suffrage in Wyoming," *Annals of Wyoming* 56, no. 2 (Fall 1984): 29–37.

28. Hebard, *Sacajawea* (Glendale, Calif.: Arthur C. Clark Co., 1933), pp. 17–18; Hebard to June Etta Downey, 13 October 1930, Hebard Papers.

29. Hebard and Oregon historian Eva Emery Dye sought to establish the claim that Sacajawea did act as guide to Lewis and Clark. Hebard also tried to prove that Sacajawea lived on the Wind River Reservation in Wyoming until 1884. This claim seems shaky in light of stronger evidence indicating that Sacajawea died in 1812. See Donald Jackson, ed., *Letters of the Lewis and Clark Expedition, with Related Documents, 1783–1854* (Urbana: University of Illinois Press, 1962), pp. 638–39.

30. *In Memoriam,* p. 10.

31. Organizations list, Hebard Papers.

32. Lillian Faderman, *Surpassing the Love of Men: Romantic Friendships between Women from the Renaissance to the Present* (New York: William Morrow, 1981), p. 204. Faderman's comments on passion and physical contact, p. 19, are also pertinent of this discussion of Hebard's relations with women.

33. Blanche Wiesen Cook, "Female Support Networks and Political Activism: Lillian Wald, Crystal Eastman, and Emma Goldman," *Chrysalis,* no. 3 (1977): 43–61; Nancy Sahli, "Smashing: Women's Relationships before the Fall," *Chrysalis,* no. 8 (1979): 17–27; Nan Bauer Maglin, "Vida to Florence: 'Comrade and Companion,' " *Frontiers: A Journal of Women Studies* (Fall 1979), pp. 13–20. The most comprehensive treatment of friendships between academic women is in Rosalind Rosenberg, *Beyond Separate Spheres: Intellectual Roots of Modern Feminism* (New Haven: Yale University Press, 1982).

34. "Old Maids' Paradise," Hebard Papers.

35. Agnes Mathilde Wergeland file, Hebard Papers.

36. *In Memoriam,* pp. 24, 25, 29, 32.

37. Rosenberg, *Beyond Separate Spheres,* p. 204. Also see Graham, "Expansion and Exclusion."

38. Hebard to Laura White, 14 February 1935, Hebard Papers.

39. Hebard to Laura White, 4 December 1935, Hebard Papers.

1. EXCERPT FROM JOURNAL OF TRIP IN
WYOMING FOLLOWING AND MARKING TRAILS

In 1915, Hebard traveled across Wyoming, camping, making speeches, and marking historical trails. Her delight in the awesome landscape and the chance to enjoy "pioneering" was tempered by the recent loss of her dearest friend, history professor Agnes Mathilde Wergeland.

August 11.

In camp at 6:30 P.M. at "Reeds Hotel." Reeds Hotel is nothing but a one roomed, dilapidated log cabin too filthy to enter, but has upon its top the sign "Reed's Hotel" which we have since learned was taken from a hotel of that name in Jackson.

We certainly did have an electric storm in the mountains. Sharp lightning and rattling thunder, but no rain. We experienced no danger or "grief" as the driver says when the horses have to work hard. When an auto finds difficulty in climbing a hill, it is called trouble. Not very far from where the Hoback runs into the Snake is where we fished and where Mr. Q caught four good fish for our evening meal. I saw him fighting and pulling at a large fish which finally escaped. Mr. Q says this would have weighed three and a half pounds and that it jumped out of the water just as he was pulling it in almost to land. This is near the spot where the Horse Creek empties into the Snake River. The Snake River is narrow, about one hundred feet wide, dark green, and looks tricky. Q. says it has an undercurrent and "will swing a horse any-place." This was the river that fooled the huntsmen of the Astoria Expedition and forced them, after they had abandoned their horses and built their boats, which were easily upset, to go on foot. We arrived at camp in good condition and hobbled Dick and Buster. B. "peeled the spuds" while Q. cleaned the fish and J. slept in the wagon. After a while J. and I got the wood for the supper fire and things at this moment are looking pretty good on this Horse Creek which here empties into the Snake. There are many quaking aspens here, and along this day's journey we have seen many of these trees trimmed from the ground up to the height of seven feet, the elk having eaten the limbs in the winter as high as they could reach. Then many of the Aspens show the effect of the weight of three, four, five, six or seven feet of snow and they look like this [Hebard illustrates with a squiggly line drawing]. Such a struggle for life! A. M. W. would have been touched by it all, but would have enjoyed every mile of our over twenty-seven miles this day. She has been constantly in my mind all day as we have been running along in the midst of this grandeur and this struggle and success of nature that always filled her heart with admiration.

The sun has now gone down behind the mountains and the fire is burning low and the coals are now hot enough for the two Dutch Ovens,—one with fish and the other with potatoes—and also the coffee pot.

B. and I are to sleep in a Wickieup, sometimes called a Wickie and familiarly known as a tepe tent. This is a small round, peaked tent, the floor of which is of canvas and not detachable from the rest of the tent. This is to keep water out in case of a freshet, and also to prevent snakes and lizards from crawling into the bed. J. is to sleep in the wagon, and Q. most anywhere, I fancy, but he has decided to sleep under the wagon. We certainly have been unusually fortunate in obtaining him and we wish he were to take us to the Park and even to the eastern entrance. We are running on schedule time. Everything is very beautiful, comfortable, and so enjoyable. In fact, everything is so superlative that one runs out of words with which to describe it all. I walked a long way today, while Q. fished, taking long strides, not "choppy and nervous" ones as W. said I took. I walked and thought with those early Wyoming people had made possible this great Western country. [sic] We hate to leave the Hoback River because it is one of our great delights. The North Platte is a wide, dirty stream, the Sweetwater river narrow and crooked, the Hoback rapid, clear. At this time of the year the Snake has an ugly look and very high banks.

Thursday, August 12.

The sleep in the Wickieup was comfortable enough, but I only slept two hours. The country made me think too much of W. and I had a night of silent grief. We breakfasted at the campfire—trout, potatoes, and hot biscuits, each cooked in a separate camp kettle, and coffee. I took a few photographs after breakfast, but as the sun was hardly showing above the horizon we cannot hope for good results.

This was a beautiful morning ride up the mountain and once in a while we got a glimpse of the glorious Tetons. We passed today also many aspen groves nibbled and trimmed as far as the elk could reach, and twisted and knarled [sic] with many winters of snow.

Grace Raymond Hebard Papers, American Heritage Center, University of Wyoming, Laramie. Used by permission.

2. GRACE RAYMOND HEBARD TO CARRIE CHAPMAN CATT

In 1924, Wyoming's Nellie Tayloe Ross acceded to the governorship on the death of her husband, becoming the first woman state governor in American history. While Hebard and other Wyoming feminists expressed delight and high hopes for what Ross's administration might bring, they found her less sympathetic than they would have liked. When Ross was defeated in her 1926 bid to be elected in her own right, Hebard wrote to Carrie Chapman Catt to explain the complex relation between feminist politics and Wyoming's premier female politician.

November 9, 1926.

My dear Doctor Catt:

The election in Wyoming, so far as the Governor is concerned, did not terminate as a great host of people had anticipated. The concensus of opinion was that the state would go Republican as it has tremendously so,—the entire state being Republican and the majority of Republicans in the House and Senate, as well as county and city officers.

Governor Ross came nearer being re-elected than any other Democrat on the ticket. Her defeat was between twelve and thirteen hundred votes. She carried ten out of the twenty-three counties. If I were to be able to talk to you I could tell you perhaps things that would not be wise for me to write, inasmuch as we at the University must keep out of politics, but I feel perfectly safe in communicating to you what I am communicating.

I should say that the outstanding reason for the result of the election as it was, was due to the advisors that Governor Ross selected, all men. I do not mean because they were all men, but I just give you that data. Next, and some people think this is the outstanding reason, was that toward the last of the campaign, there was injected in campaign literature by the Democrats that if Mrs. Ross were not re-elected the cause of woman suffrage would be defeated, which, of course, is a fake. The Republicans, I think, rightly took the stand that woman suffrage was a question, so far as Wyoming is concerned, that was settled on the tenth of December, 1869; that the era of sentiment to elect Mrs. Ross due to the tragedy of her husband had passed; that she had recognition as no other woman in the United States had had, and that she had proved herself a success and all the credit that was coming to her as a widow of a former Governor had been given her.

The next, which is a part of the second, was due largely to Mrs.

Teresa Jenkins' article, which, by the way, is not accurate in regard to that woman who died, the statement that Mrs. Ross had never taken any part in winning suffrage nor had she identified herself in any way with people who had been instrumental in getting this suffrage. In talking with a woman last night, who lives in Cheyenne, this Mrs. A. told me twice, so I may make no error, that she had heard Mrs. Ross make the statement, before she was governor or had thought of being governor, in a group that was trying to do something for suffrage and women who did not have the opportunity to vote, that she was not in favor of the woman suffrage movement because she believed the home was the place for the mother. Now this saying was forgotten because women did have suffrage and the majority of the state was glad to see Mrs. Ross made Governor, but when it came for her second term, there was a woman who was not in favor of suffrage and never lifted her hand to bring about suffrage. Why should she be twice honored?

The fourth reason, which, of course, is intimately associated with the third reason, was that Mrs. Ross had splendid opportunities to appoint able women to positions of importance and trust, and she never made any appointment of women whatsoever except five, and I know that two of those five were filled by women before. One was that when a Republican woman's term expired as trustee of this University, and when the Republican woman in charge of the Children's Home was removed, Mrs. Ross appointed two women to fill those places. I should not wish to repeat, except to Miss Roderick or your intimate group, what I am saying.

I wrote to Mrs. Ross, as a Republican, making the statement that I was sure that the women of the State of Wyoming would feel very gratified if she would make an appointment of a woman for trustee of the University and in charge of the Home. She never answered the letter, but she did immediately make an appointment of two women for these places in a position where men had previously at sometime, if not directly previous, filled these positions.

You can see why it is not wise for that to be known because it would look as if I were trying to appoint trustees who were over me in office. I had no thought of that whatsoever. There were many fine positions which Mrs. Ross could have given to women who worked for her, not Republicans, but Democrats, whom she might have honored.

There are doubtless other reasons, and the reasons that I have given may not be universal, although in many parts of the state and the majority of the state, what I have stated is a fact. All interesting, is it not, my dear Mrs. Catt? I am more of a feminist, of course, but in all my talks for women to go into activities, political and otherwise, or to occupy positions of responsibility, we women should never back up a woman because she is a woman, but back up the woman if we can find one who is as good and efficient as a man, and in some cases, I have advocated that the women will do better than a man in certain special places.

I think you will be glad to know that the sun is shining in Wyoming and the winter birds are singing and things are going on as usual, except in the home of Mrs. Ross and a group of Democrats. I think I should have said that there were many prominent Democrats that did not endorse Mrs. Ross for the second term on account of her petticoat.

Lovingly,

Grace Raymond Hebard Papers, Woman Suffrage file, American Heritage Center, University of Wyoming, Laramie. Used by permission.

3. EXCERPT FROM SPEECH: "THE TRAINING FOR CITIZENSHIP"

In this transcript of a 1930 speech, Hebard argued that women's increased access to education constituted the foundation of female emancipation. Reminding her audience of university women of the long struggle that had enabled them to go to college, she urged them to take citizenship as a serious, even "sacred," obligation.

A By-Product of a College Education

In order that one might be adequately prepared for citizenship, she must first go through a process of education.

In presenting this subject at this time to a group of well trained and carefully educated young women, it has been thought that perhaps it would be of interest and help to bring to you a realization of the trials and difficulties through which the movement for the education of women has passed, and then after having obtained an educated position in one's life journey, how franchise or the ballot came to women in America, of the difficulties through which this movement for political freedom has had to be in order that you young women may be able to vote when you are twenty-one years of age. Then having obtained your position in the educational world and your standing in the political or franchise world where women are allowed to vote, may I then speak of the natural and logical obligations for these privileges which have come to us through centuries of conflict? I ask you, then, what are you going to do with these opportunities to which women were not born, but to which they have obtained admission? What are we going to do with the education and the franchise that has come to women through years and years of contest and strife by our fathers and mothers, grandfathers and grandmothers for centuries? What are we going to do with these privileges and how are we going to use them in order to give to posterity those rights and privileges that have been *given* to us?

Woman's divine function seems to have been, according to the consensus of opinion of men who made the laws governing the action of women, that she had really no intelligence and she had been generally accepted as inferior to these men and it was also decreed that she had no sphere in education. Even though a woman gave the ground on which the first school in Bay Colony, Massachusetts, was erected, her sex was excluded from the benefits of schooling and it was believed and decreed that girls being educated and going to school was inconsistent with the design of the Divine Power in making women.

In early days in Connecticut we find that girls were permitted to attend school, but to do this they must go early in the morning and arrive and receive their instructions before the boys came and then come back to the school after the boys had gone home in the evening.

Woman's preparation for her allotted sphere, the home, was attained through an apprenticeship to her mother in the home and it prohibited any attention being given to formal schooling, which led her away from the fireside of that home. In fact, in the best families in New England the education to women extended to nothing more than reading, writing, and arithmetic. Colleges of those days were given over to the training of ministers, and since women could not enter that profession there was not the slightest reason for women contemplating such a step as a college education. Even more serious than this was the idea which prevailed that an educated wife was an infringement upon the domain of man, and even so important a woman as the wife of Winthrop "lost her mind because she left her proper domestic duties and indulged herself in literary pursuits!" In other words, to seek culture equal to that of man was to transgress the law of God, who had given her the home and fixed her in it!

It was indecent for a woman to appear upon a business street without a male escort, or to go to a bank to cash a check without her "legal protector."

Beautiful Harriet Martineau once visited the public library and sat at a reading table—alone. The public verdict upon this outlandish action was that Harriet Martineau was not a fit person with whom to associate. . . .

Perhaps the first entrance of woman into man's domain of work to [*sic*] which she had been prohibited was most clearly attained as a result of the Civil War, when women were forced to take the industrial places of the men who had gone to war, very similar to what our women did during the recent World War. We find in print at that time the following jingle, "Just take your gun and go, for Ruth shall drive the oxen and John and I will wield the hoe."

According to Harriet Martineau, one hundred years ago, it was declared that there were only seven occupations open to women. They were teaching, needle work, keeping of boarders, labor in cotton mills, book binding, typesetting, and domestic service. At this time scant attention was given to women in regard to education. It is true that we gradually attained female seminaries, high schools, common schools, and normal schools, but beyond this no woman was to aspire.

Perhaps one of the steps where women first appeared in public was at the Quaker meetings, where any member of the religious gathering, should the spirit move them, might proclaim an inspiration that came to him or her.

As late as 1819, just over a hundred years ago, to about the middle of the nineteenth century, we were taught about separate "tasks assigned to women," "the maternal relation," "the sphere of female influence," "mothers' counsels, "mothers' care," "mothers' touch," emphasizing and laying stress upon the genus female rather than that of homo.

The evolution which took place, shifting the sphere of women from the fireside to the outside world was a slow process of long duration. Ultimately as the women were allowed to teach in schools, largely during the period of the Civil War, this teaching school from a platform made a somewhat easy step to be taken from the platform to the rostrum, to which elevation women readily and intelligently stepped.

Looking back over the past three hundred years, it is clear that political emancipation is a great symbol of woman's victory, but *intellectual* emancipation, because of its prior and fundamental character, is of more vast significance. Without freedom from the educational subjection, without the opening of even a few and at first very inferior institutions of higher learning, women would never have been able to conceive of their complete political emancipation. As citizens they would not have been able to profit by it because of their lack of understanding had emancipation first been given to women before education. . . . The progress in education demanded the elimination of the last barriers to their emancipation, guaranteed by an equal rights amendment to our Constitution, the nineteenth, in August of 1920.

Grace Raymond Hebard Papers, American Heritage Center, University of Wyoming, Laramie. Used by permission.

CLELIA DUEL MOSHER

Stanford University Archives

The Making of a "Misfit"

CLELIA DUEL MOSHER
1863–1940

By Elizabeth Griego

This splendid modern woman, approaching the old Greek ideal of phys-ical perfection, is the mother of finer sons and daughters, the promise of a stronger race. This same achievement is now possible to all women. In the municipal playgrounds, swimming pools, gymnasia, and girl scout activities, woman to-day has such an opportunity as was never before given. It rests alone with her, whether she rejects it, clinging to the old ideal of physical weakness and dependence, or with open mind takes the opportunity of tasting the richness of physical perfection and the fullness of life which comes in its train, making of herself a better citizen, a better wife, a better mother.[1]

These challenging words conclude Clelia Duel Mosher's popular book, *Woman's Physical Freedom,* which was published in six revised editions during her lifetime. Mosher had seized the opportunity pre-sented by her book to recapitulate the findings of her various studies in physiology and to emphasize the overriding implications she be-lieved they held for women: that women were as physically and intel-lectually capable as men of undertaking advanced study and any kind of employment. Women were hampered in realizing their potential only by self-imposed limitations that they were socialized to accept. As a physician, researcher, and professor at Stanford University at the turn of the century, Clelia Mosher saw her "great responsibility" in life as that of arousing her women contemporaries to reject the barriers to their full and equal participation in life. Through her teaching and research she endeavored, in her words,

> to lead women to ideas of health, to hold out to each one an attainable physical ideal, to teach the mechanism of our wonderful bodies so that she obeys the laws of her body, laws learned so perfectly that they are obeyed automatically.[2]

This recusant from false medical doctrine and popular opinion was born on December 16, 1863, in Albany, New York. She grew up as the favored daughter in a household that included her parents, paternal grandparents, an aunt who was a portrait painter, and an invalid younger sister who was to die when Mosher was twenty-two. Learning received special emphasis in her extended, emotionally close, upper-middle class family. With no son as heir apparent to family affairs and his medical practice, Clelia's physician father made Clelia, as the older daughter, the focus of his attention and encouragement. A favorite childhood pastime of Clelia's was accompanying her father in his carriage while he made his doctor's rounds. Along the way they would discuss the classics that Dr. Mosher had given her to read from his extensive private library, and he would teach her the elements of botany and horticulture, lifelong interests for them both. When she wrote her unfinished autobiography in 1931, Clelia gratefully acknowledged her father's intellectual patronage, dedicating her notes "to my father, who believed in women when most men classified them with children and imbeciles."[3]

Dr. Mosher seems to have been comparatively less culture-bound than other fathers of the period in that he also encouraged his daughter's independence and physical prowess, unusual attributes in the stereotypic ideas of Victorian femininity. When Clelia was eleven, her father enrolled her in the Albany Female Academy, the oldest women's preparatory school in New York State, where her course of study was fairly typical of the more rigorous of the female seminaries and coeducational high schools of the period. After graduating in 1881, Clelia had planned to go on to college but her father, concerned for her health, kept her at home. She was "too slender, too pale and her color was too high."[4]

The subject of women's health under the conditions of advanced education was a popular topic among the middle class; many fathers and mothers were gravely concerned about their daughters' physical well-being while higher education was yet on trial in the eyes of the world. Clelia's father was no doubt informed by the arguments of his medical colleagues who advanced the Spencerian ideas of the body as a closed energy system. They argued that the mental strain caused by higher learning would divert a crucial amount of the body's limited supply of energy to the brain from the uterus and other reproductive organs, possibly permanently impairing women's health and ability to reproduce.

Although Dr. Mosher seemingly rejected the anti-women's education arguments, his ambivalence about female independence was reflected in his actions toward Clelia. For the next seven years he was successful in keeping Clelia at home. He allowed her limited autonomy by helping her to establish, under his supervision, a flourishing little florist's business on the Mosher family property. The ambitious Clelia was steadfast in her wish to attend college, however, and by 1889, when she was twenty-five, she had saved two thousand dollars—enough for four years' tuition at Wellesley College, to which she had just been accepted.

Unfortunately, after she enrolled, her father's earlier fears for her health were confirmed. Mosher battled unspecified illness from the very beginning of her residency at Wellesley. She withdrew in November of her sophomore year with references from the college secretary that she was overworked, ill-prepared for her courses, and frequently sick. No doubt the unanticipated death of her beloved father two months earlier contributed to her problems.

By the fall of 1891, Clelia had recovered enough to announce her intention to embark upon a career in medicine like her father and two of his brothers. She enrolled in science courses at the University of Wisconsin at Madison. There the curricular emphasis was on the scientific method and the German seminar; investigation and reason were supposed to prevail over prejudice and intuition. Mosher excelled in her classes and thrived in the directed atmosphere of the research university. She was, however, to transfer one more time—drawn by the romantic story of the founding of Stanford University in Palo Alto, California, she joined her good friend and former Wellesley instructor, Mary Roberts Smith (later Coolidge), and several of her Wisconsin professors, and transferred to Stanford for her senior year, during the second year that students were admitted.

Mosher graduated with a degree in zoology in 1893 and went on to receive her master of arts in physiology in 1894, at the age of thirty. It was while she was serving as an assistant in the Stanford Department of Hygiene, from 1892–94, that she independently began the research that was to sustain her interest for the rest of her life. Mosher was concerned that nineteenth-century science invariably described the nature and capabilities of women as being biologically substandard to men.

The current beliefs about physiological differentiation held that women had smaller frames and less muscular strength than men and thus needed to be protected; their brains were smaller, thus they were less intelligent; they menstruated, and thus were physically incapacitated for a period of time each month. The Victorian construct of women's sphere, developed largely in response to this prevalent Darwinian notion of the weaker, less intelligent, more emotional sex, served ultimately to isolate women from full participation in society. At the same time, it contributed to the generalized belief that women were inferior to men. Hence was developed the almost universally accepted nineteenth-century belief that men's and women's social roles were rooted in biology, with women being limited by their innate capabilities and interests to the home and family while men were comparatively free to participate in public life.

Science had always been dominated by male theorists. Despite seeing so few women predecessors, Mosher's confidence in her own intellectual capabilities caused her to question such constructs—quietly at first, in her teaching career; vociferously, later, when her medical training provided her with a base of knowledge and an authoritative credential, the M.D. degree. Her lifelong insistence that the vast majority of observable sex differences could be traced to cultural conditioning rather than inherent capabilities was to violate the fundamental belief of Victorian science that biology predominated over culture.

Mosher began her quest to disprove the stereotypes about the physical and mental incapacities of women by examining the physiology of respiration. In 1892, she concluded from her series of measurements on Stanford students and on unmarried, pregnant girls from the Pacific Rescue Home that there was no physical reason for women to breathe differently than men. She found the reason many women breathed costally, from the chest, rather than in the more physiologically efficient diaphragmatic way, was that the corsets, waists, and other constricting underclothing then in vogue forced women to breathe in this unnatural way. Remarkably, she was the first researcher to measure respiration when her subjects were unclothed. But then, she was the first woman researcher of this subject. Reticent Victorian women reportedly were reluctant to undress in front of Mosher's counterparts, the male physicians, who were previously the only persons qualified and interested in conducting research in physiology.

In the fall of 1896, Mosher determined that "to do such work in Hygiene and practical physiology as I wished to do, a medical course in the best school in the country was necessary," and she enrolled in the fourth class of the newly opened Johns Hopkins Medical School.[5]

While there, she published her first article, "Normal Menstruation and Some of the Factors Modifying It," which served simultaneously to de-mythologize a second topic of women's physiology and to introduce the research for which she was to become best known. At Stanford, Mosher had gathered over 3,000 records that her students had kept of their menstrual periods and daily health. These records represented the first collection of written reports about menstruation made by normally healthy women over time. Most previous research consisted of single observations made by male physicians on the basis of caseloads in which pathological women patients predominated.

Backed by the evidence from her data, Mosher felt confident enough to refute publicly the prevailing belief that menstruation was an inca-pacitating disease that caused women to become chronic periodic in-valids, disqualified from regular work and advanced study. She argued not only that women could be active during their menstrual periods, but that they should be. She contended that dysmenorrhea should be treated not by bed rest but through regular exercise, proper diet, aban-doning the constricting underclothing that also forced unnatural respi-ration, and most importantly, through revising expectations about the deleterious physical effects of menstruation. Mosher wrote that men-struation was so thoroughly identified with incapacity that the woman "who is free from pain is almost apologetic and inclined to question if her sense of well-being . . . is not abnormal." Later, she developed a series of isometric and deep breathing exercises designed to shorten the length of her students' menstrual periods and to make them less painful; these became widely known as "moshers" after their inventor.

Following her graduation from medical school in 1900, Mosher was selected to serve as an externe in the Johns Hopkins Hospital Dispen-sary and also as gynecological assistant in Dr. Howard Kelly's private sanatorium in Baltimore. After she was refused the opportunity to train to become a gynecological surgeon because, as Dr. Kelley confirmed, "no man would be willing to work as a surgical assistant under a woman," she returned to California and began a decade of private gen-eral medical practice in the university town of Palo Alto. Life was not easy; her practice in the sparsely settled countryside grew slowly and she suffered real financial constraints. Mary Roberts Coolidge described her practice this way: "A few established (male) physicians turned over to her their deadheads and neurasthenic women." During this time, she embarked on a long round of unsuccessful applications to obtain fund-ing for her studies of menstruation. Then in 1910, when she was forty-six, she received an offer to return to Stanford as Assistant Professor of Personal Hygiene, Medical Advisor for Women, and Director of the

Roble Gymnasium. She accepted these positions, seeing this as the opportunity to resume the research activities she had neglected in the
previous decade for want of time and funds.

Founded with the personal fortune of railroad magnate and former
governor of California Leland Stanford, Stanford University from the
outset had been among the best endowed and most physically beautiful
universities in the country. It combined a reputation for academic excellence with the Western pioneering spirit in an environment that attracted first-rate scholars who were innovative and often willing to
depart from the thinking and educational practices established in the
East. Women students had been purposely encouraged at Stanford—
over one-third of the students had been women at its opening in 1891.
From the beginning they distributed themselves across the curriculum,
except in the professional fields of engineering, mining, and pre-law,
and the graduate schools of law and medicine. The proportion of
women students rose steadily until it reached 44 percent in 1900, when
a fearful Jane Stanford imposed her notorious limit of five hundred
women in the student body. When Mosher returned to Stanford in 1910,
the number of women students was still limited to five hundred, representing a shrinking third of the student body, but still a proportion
higher than found in most other universities. The relative freedom of
choice in studies, the proportionally large numbers of women students,
and the unconventional academic climate at Stanford represented an
attractive environment for women students.

The Academic Council of more than one hundred faculty included
several women. Among the better known in Stanford's first twenty years
were Mary Sheldon Barnes, historian of the Pacific slope; Anna Botsford
Comstock, ecologist; Mary Roberts Coolidge, sociologist; Irene Hardy,
poet; Lillien Jane Martin, psychologist; Margaret Schallenberger, educator; Clara Stoltenberg, physiologist; Margaret Wickham, professor of
German; and Jessica Vance, educator. Despite their evident representation at Stanford, and notwithstanding the tolerance accorded women
students, women faculty were nonetheless subject to discriminatory
employment practices that reflected the treatment women received in
education nationwide. They were largely clustered at the ranks of instructor and graduate assistant with little hope of promotion. Retention
of women faculty was dismal. At an increasing rate, those who left
Stanford were replaced by men. Lillien Martin, Clara Stoltenberg, and
Mosher were the only women to attain the rank of professor during
Stanford's first four decades; Stoltenberg and Mosher both filled the
rank for one year only, the year before their retirement. Mosher was
able to advance because she was one of the few women with the proper

credentials to teach physical hygiene. There was little competition from men in this discipline taught for women largely by women.[6]

Physical hygiene was offered in virtually every college or university that enrolled women. The interest in physical training in America had begun during the coeducational public school movement in the mid-nineteenth century, when the relative merits of military drill versus Swedish gymnastics for the health of male students were debated fiercely. Gymnastics for female students was subsequently introduced as an outcome of the debate and interest in physical education for males. The female seminary educators encouraged calisthenics as a stimulus to mental alertness. The women's colleges, and later the coeducational universities, required physical training for women as an aid to good health and as a preventive against the physical drain supposedly imposed by study. Usually taught by a physician, instruction in physical hygiene generally included initial and periodic physical examinations and measurements; instruction in exercise, athletics, and the rudiments of physiology and anatomy; and, when taught by a woman, courses included what was often the first information on sexuality to which Victorian women were exposed.

Within her first year at Stanford, Mosher published an update of her menstrual studies that confirmed her earlier findings. She was soon at work on another research interest: female posture. She was convinced that bad posture contributed to dysmenorrhea and internal problems. Mosher collaborated with Stanford engineering professor E.P. Lesley in the invention of a "schematograph," an apparatus with a light bulb that worked by reflecting a silhouette onto graph paper. The outline could then be traced to illustrate variations in posture. Mosher and Lesley patented their schematograph and sold it to physical training departments all over the country.

Mosher was a devoted, if somewhat dictatorial, teacher. She saw her students as "under her care" and considered it her duty to use her contact with them to expound her theories on good citizenship, honesty in all situations, sensibility in dress and lifestyle, unselfishness, and the need for regular exercise. She declared that "good results" followed from her patient supervision and consultation with individual students. She tried to demonstrate to each student "the relation between what she has been doing or failing to do" and the resulting symptoms in the student's health.[7]

She directed the students in her class in active physical training and athletics. If a woman was menstruating, she was required to don her gymnasium suit like her classmates and then report to Dr. Mosher in the mat room. Here she was to fill out her menstrual record, complete the "moshers" series, and then the remainder of the hour she was to listen to Dr. Mosher lecture on "some hygenic subject, eugenics, vocational opportunities, dress or kindred topics which have some vital interest and relation to the woman's every-day life." Students were encouraged to ask questions and suggest topics of the day. If Mosher was prevented by other duties from lecturing, her students were assigned reading and asked to repeat the exercises at the end of the hour.[8]

Mosher developed an extensive library of reading material for her students, including manuscripts, books, and articles on nutrition and other health concerns. She included articles by and about and pictures of such well-known feminists as Gertrude Stein, George Sand, Elizabeth Cady Stanton, Susan B. Anthony, Mary Wollstonecraft, George Eliot, Reverend Anna Shaw, Mary Astell, and her own cousin, an East coast physician with whom she maintained an active correspondence, Eliza Mosher. She stated that her reasons for collecting this information were "to call women's attention to the attainments of women and familiarize them with the work and names of women who have contributed to their present freedom" and to show her classes "the past conditions of women" and how the stereotypical viewpoints regarding women's abilities persisted in limiting women's capacities and interfering with "their health and ideal development."[9] As she grew more and more firmly to endorse feminist principles, Mosher resembled many other women professionals of her time for whom feminism provided the moral and psychological constructs that enabled them to understand better their place in a culture generally hostile to feminine achievement. The scrapbooks in the Mosher papers provide evidence that not only did Mosher increasingly turn to feminism to support her ideas, she also wished, even instructed, her students to do likewise.

Mosher should be viewed as being in the vanguard of the movement that encouraged women toward greater activity and development of their physical capacities. She urged her students to take up additional sports to the ones, like croquet and golf, that were heretofore considered appropriately ladylike. She advocated tennis, swimming, hiking, bicycling, horseback riding, basketball, and later, volleyball and softball for women. During a time when men's intercollegiate athletics, particularly football, were the focus of a great deal of attention, Mosher arranged the first intercollegiate games between the women students of Stanford and those of the University of California.

While physical educators by the turn of the century were in agreement that athletics were valuable for women because of their healthful and social benefits, they differed on many issues, especially whether it was fitting that women engage in strenuous sport with the opposite sex, whether women could maintain their modesty while participating, and whether women should engage in sport during their monthly periods. Thus, although the number of acceptable activities for women increased during this period, it was widely agreed, even among women educators, that women's participation had to be yet more limited than men's.

Mosher agreed that athletics should be taught separately to each sex, and that women should play under separate rules, with women coaches. She conceded that women probably should not compete while menstruating, but she was unusual even among her physical hygiene colleagues in urging women to exercise and remain active during this time. She was less interested in emphasizing the popular aesthetic, transcendent female image than in training women to form healthy life habits and sound personal philosophies. She believed that physical hygiene as a discipline should aim beyond the present-oriented goal of helping women become physically fit; instead, it should become part of the larger goal of lifelong personal development. She wrote:

> That a girl is an athlete while in college, that she senses the joy of clean vigor, and physical freedom is something, but this will not carry over past the barriers imposed by the complexities and increasing demands of modern life unless we have made so clear the relation of health to her great primal obligation that she longs with all her heart for the perfection of her womanhood, and to attain it will rigorously imposé on herself that training which we have only begun.[10]

She wrote and spoke extensively about the early socialization of each sex—socialization then being a concept not widely known by name, but understood in context especially by the female scientists and researchers. Mosher explained that inhibitions in adulthood were caused by early training; e.g., preparing a pink layette for the girl and blue for the boy; the early admonishments to girls to be ladylike and to play quietly with a doll; "and if her muscles demanded activity, her restless spirit to voice her feelings by shouting, if she ran and played ball with her brother, she was designated a 'Tom-boy,' " Mosher wrote. Instead of their recognizing the natural inclination of all children to want to be physical, Mosher argued, adults created a "habit of expectancy" by discouraging activity among girls while encouraging it among boys.[11]

As a child, Mosher herself had not fit the polarized Victorian feminine identity and conduct that she described so clearly. Now, as an adult, she wished to point out the restrictions that behaviors labeled as sex-appropriate imposed on females. She resented society's expectations that women should suppress their intellectuality and aspirations and found herself particularly suspicious of opinions expressed by men about the nature of women:

> Where the women problem is concerned, it is rare to find a man able to discuss any phase of it with coolness and on an impersonal basis. His knowledge of women is usually confined to a small group—wife, daughters, sisters; what they are, how they react to a given question, obscures the larger view,

she declared.[12]

In the spring of 1915, officers of the Young Women's Christian Association invited Mosher to address their national convention. Her speech was so well received that they helped her publish her remarks in *The Relation of Health to the Woman Movement,* published that year by the YWCA National Board. Mosher's years of teaching and research bolstered her conclusions: In the early twentieth century, economic conditions had lessened the demands on women in the home; the result of increases in leisure time combined with the diminishing number of children per family meant that numbers of women were seeking ways to occupy their time. World War I was serving the function of a proving ground for women's capabilities, both in the trenches and replacing men in industry.

Where was the proof that women who worked would be incapacitated by their monthly menstrual periods? Mosher reiterated the findings from her work on menstruation and advocated her exercises as the principal means of avoiding dysmenorrhea. She also lectured on menopause (caused by social changes, inactivity, and woman's predisposition to viewing menopause as a disease), constipation (caused by inactivity and poor diet), water (the need to drink eight to twelve glasses a day to avoid constipation and bladder irritation), bathing (the need for cleanliness, especially during menstruation), alcohol (to be avoided), feet (damaged by the dictates of fashion), fatigue (cured by proper diet and regular habits and rest periods), fashion (scorned as the province of the "unthinking" woman), and exercise (to be performed daily).

During World War I Mosher served with the Red Cross in France as Assistant Medical Advisor for the Children's Bureau and later, as Medical Director of the Bureau of Refugees and Relief. These administrative positions were typical of those held by American women physicians during the war. Women were not permitted to receive army commissions—a fact that gave Mosher cause to chafe at the inequality afforded American women, especially when compared with their British sisters, who

did receive service commissions, and French women, who capably replaced men in the shops, fields, and factories. Devastated by the events
of the war, but happy to play a useful function assisting in French re-
location and reconstruction efforts, Mosher filled her journal of the
period with prose richly descriptive of French rehabilitants and war
events. Four of her short stories, collectively titled "As Seen by the
Doctor," were published in the *Women's Medical Journal* after her
return to California.

While she was still in France, Mosher published with Stanford physiologist Ernest Martin a monograph reporting their study on the relative
strength of women, finding—overconfidently—no physiological basis
for the differences in strength between men and women. They contended it was use, and not sex, that determined the strength of muscles.
Women had been supposed to be weaker than men only because their
constrictive clothing and social mores encouraged their more sedentary
lifestyle.

Mosher and Martin's conclusions seemed to have validity because
their research design accommodated for women's smaller size rather
than making direct comparison to men's strength. The methodology
they chose, however, unfortunately weighted the results in favor of
women. By summing various flexor muscle measurements and dividing
by body weight to determine a "total strength factor," the person with
the smaller body weight retained the larger dividend representing
greater strength. Because women, in general, are smaller than men, they
have a comparatively shorter range of motion to complete in flexing.
Mosher and Martin's flex tests thus gave women an artificial advantage
when compared with the longer range of motion required of men. To
compensate for this fact, most tests of innate strength at the present
time are conducted using explosive strength measures rather than flexor
strength measures. While it since has been conceded that men's greater
muscle mass and the contributing influence of the male hormone tes-
tosterone cause men, on the average, to be stronger than women, it is
nevertheless generally agreed that what Mosher called "the habit of
expectancy" contributes to the muscular development of both sexes by
working powerfully to encourage men and women toward different
levels and kinds of physical activity.

There is no evidence that Mosher and Martin's findings about the
greater strength of women were disproved in their lifetimes, but neither
was there a move to replicate their tests or to cite their work in scholarly publications. Perhaps this indicated a residual discomfort with the
findings, even though no one knew then how to measure innate strength
more accurately. The findings did receive a fair amount of media cov-

erage and generated an invitation in 1924, which she accepted, to address the International Conference of Women Physicians in London on the subject.

In 1928, at the age of sixty-five, Mosher was promoted to a full professorship at Stanford. Because she was beginning to feel the effects of recent illnesses and her advancing years, she resigned her post the next year, to live alone in the "dream house" of her own design on the Stanford campus and to devote herself to her Italian garden of rare plants and semitropical fruits. In 1934, she received an honorary doctorate from Mills College, a college for women across the bay. She died in 1940.

Mosher was probably best known in her lifetime for her studies on functional periodicity and the relative strength of women. The contribution for which she is best remembered, however, is a study that remained unpublished in her lifetime: the survey of women's sexual attitudes and practices that historian Carl Degler discovered among her papers and introduced in his 1974 article for the *American Historical Review.*

Beginning in 1892, when she was a junior at the University of Wisconsin and continuing throughout her years as a physician and teacher, Mosher administered a remarkably candid questionnaire that asked married women of her acquaintance questions of exceptional delicacy. In it she addressed directly the complex system of rules and norms that Victorian society had developed to regulate sex roles and the occurrence of sexual relations. The responses contradict the stereotypical beliefs that Victorian women lacked sexual feelings—for most of the educated wives Mosher studied viewed sexual relations as a natural part of healthy living. A few women felt that reproduction was the only acceptable reason for intercourse; the vast majority, however, reported that pleasure and furtherance of intimacy between husband and wife were the primary purposes. Almost all the women reported that they felt sexual desire independent of their husband. Almost all found sexual intercourse agreeable.

The answers given by the women Mosher surveyed provide evidence to counter other sexual myths of the nineteenth century: that female sexual desire occurred in relationship to the menses, with some physicians claiming desire occurred just before menstruation and others contradictorily claiming that it occurred immediately after (Mosher's respondents reported desire throughout their cycles); that men were possessed of greater sexual needs and desires (Mosher's women respondents often reported equal or greater need); that contraception

would lessen sexual satisfaction (not according to those Mosher surveyed—in fact, they often reported a heightening of satisfaction as the
fear of unwanted pregnancies abated); and that sex education would
lead to promiscuity (no evidence of such among Mosher's highly educated sample).

Carl Degler recognized the historic value of Mosher's survey: It is
the earliest known data on the sexual habits of American women that
we have, predating the Kinsey report by some forty years. The highly
modest women of the nineteenth century just did not write about information so intimate. Degler notes that even if we were able to find
references about sexuality among the private correspondence or personal diaries of nineteenth-century women, interpretations of such random comments would necessarily be highly subjective and difficult to
analyze in the aggregate. Not only did Mosher leave us information
about a little understood and fugitive subject, she provided it in a survey form in which the answers can be analyzed systematically.

Mosher had always been single-minded about her research. Beginning from her own egalitarian principles, she ferreted out the physiological roots supporting the beliefs in women's inferiority, and then
devised ways to conduct comparative measurements that would "sci-
entifically" prove that there was no significant difference between the
attributes of men and those of women. Sometimes her zealousness
caused her to be less critical of her measurements than she should have
been; this was true of her strength tests and of a study showing mirac-
ulous abatement in her students' menstrual periods after their daily
moshers practice. On the whole, however, her research was conducted
carefully and objectively, particularly when judged by the somewhat
lax standards of her day.

There was a sensitive, romantic side to Mosher's nature that she
largely kept concealed, presumably because it was too much in accord
with the emotional stereotypes of the feminine character that she
preached against to her students. On campus, she strove unreservedly
to model the ideal of the active, self-reliant, sensible, unsentimental,
productive, healthy, intellectual professional. In doing so, she made
self-conscious decisions about her personal life that both enhanced and
at times conflicted with the decisions she made about her professional
life. She traded traditional family life for the opportunity to pursue a
career. She remained self-centered and aloof from others, reserving the
most intimate and private of her thoughts not for friends, but for short,
unfinished autobiographical writings and disjointed prose that she kept
hidden among her private papers. Some of her writings contain sensual

descriptions of her garden and of nature; others, complaints about students or colleagues; still others reflect her longing for companionship and understanding.

During periods of her life she was pathetically lonely, yet it is apparent that she chose not to maintain intimate friendships. Sociologist Mary Roberts Coolidge was her friend of longest standing, but Coolidge was exceedingly busy and after she left Stanford in 1903, she traveled a great deal of the time. There is no evidence of real intimacy between the two in their correspondence; instead, they wrote about their professional work and shared information about the continuing public dialogue on the "woman question." Mosher maintained a similar relationship with her admired older cousin, Dr. Eliza Mosher. The voluminous correspondence between Palo Alto and New York City describes the busy activities of each. Though they visited each other several times, there is little evidence here, too, of emotional closeness.[13]

Mosher never had a known romantic involvement. Although she was on good terms with the Stanford male faculty members and even collaborated on her strength studies with Professor Ernest Martin, she did not count any of them as friends. Neither did she develop friendships with their wives or with the several accomplished women on the faculty. There is extensive correspondence between 1926 and 1929 with a young woman, possibly a former student, named Elena, and with a younger distant cousin named Phyllis Bartlett, but Mosher's interest in both was colored by the fact that she had asked each to work for her as her secretary. Neither did.[14] She was unusual among professional women of her time in eschewing professional and women's organizations, consistently declining invitations to membership on the grounds that she was too busy with her research.

It was apparently during the difficult decade 1901 to 1910, when she was in private practice and longing to return to her research, that Mosher began to alleviate her loneliness and to invent the personal support and understanding that she sought by writing letters to an imaginary friend. Her eccentricities prevented her from becoming a role model to her students, at least in her personal style. A student who later became a physician recalls her resolute daily march across the Stanford campus, dressed in her "mannish black suit" and prepared to preach up women's abilities in her physical hygiene classes. It is possible that Mosher, consciously or unconsciously, might have encouraged her status as an eccentric because she relished her privacy and preferred to be alone to concentrate on her research. This was one way of avoiding such responsibilities as mothering coeds and hosting ladies' teas—expectations for most women faculty of her time.

Clelia Mosher's private writings—her prose, diaries, and correspondence—together with the publications of her remarkable pioneering research, comprise a rare and extraordinarily rich record of the attitudes, values, and experiences of one highly educated, upper-middle class American academician at the turn of the century. Her intellect and ambition placed her in the challenging but unenviable position of contending with the distinctive mores and expectations of the contrasting worlds of academic professionalism and women's sphere of domesticity. Through her private writings Mosher was able to satisfy her personal needs in a manner that left her time to concentrate on her primary interest, the physiological research that enabled her to affirm women's capabilities and potential.

Notes

1. Clelia Duel Mosher, *Woman's Physical Freedom,* 3rd ed. (New York: The Woman's Press, 1923), p. 87. This book is the third revision of Mosher's *The Relation of Health to the Woman Movement* (New York: National Board YWCA, 1915).

2. Mosher, *Health and the Woman Movement,* 2d ed. (New York: National Board YWCA, 1916), pp. 44–45.

3. Mosher, "The Autobiography of a Happy Old Woman," 5 April 1931, Box 1, folder 10, Mosher Papers, SC11, Stanford University Archives.

4. Mosher, "Guilding the Lily," n.d., Box 1, folder 8, Mosher Papers.

5. Mosher to Frederick Burk, n.d., Box 2, folder 2, Mosher Papers.

6. Helen Sard Hughes's 1918 study for the Association of Collegiate Alumnae found that women nationally held only 3.5 percent of professorships at coeducational universities. Her findings were corroborated three years later in a major study conducted by the American Association of University Professors which found no women at all on the faculties of twenty-seven of the one hundred coeducational schools studied. Women employed at the remainder of the schools were clustered at the rank of instructor, holding only 4 percent of the full professorships (less than 3 percent if the highly feminized fields of home economics and physical hygiene were omitted). Helen Sard Hughes, "The Academic Chance," *Journal of the Association of Collegiate Alumnae* 12, no. 2 (January 1919): 79–82; A. Caswell Ellis, "Preliminary Report of Committee W, on Status of Women in College and University Faculties," *Bulletin of the American Association of University Professors* 7, no. 6 (October 1921): 21–32.

7. Mosher, "The Physical Training of Women in Relation to Functional Periodicity," *Woman's Medical Journal* 25, no. 4 (April 1915): 73.

8. Ibid., p. 74.

9. These articles are compiled and bound in five thick volumes entitled *Biography,* Box 4, Mosher Papers. The volumes are subtitled Vol. 1, *Women;*

Vol. 2, *The Woman Movement;* Vol. 3, *Mary Astell;* Vol. 4, *Paul Bert and His Family—His Friends;* Vol. 5, *Eliza M. Mosher, M.D., Pioneer Woman Physician.*

10. Mosher, typewritten essay, no title, n.d., Box 6, Mosher Papers, Archives of the Hoover Institution for the Study of War and Peace, Stanford University; Mosher to Lou Henry Hoover, telegram, January or February 1923, Box 2, Mosher Papers, Hoover Institution Archives.

11. Mosher, typewritten essay, no title, n.d., pp. 10–11, Box 6, Mosher Papers, Hoover Institution Archives.

12. Ibid.

13. Mary Roberts Coolidge's papers, including two letters from Mosher, are with those of her husband, Dane Coolidge, in the Bancroft Library, University of California, Berkeley. Letters from Coolidge to Mosher are in the Mosher Papers in the Stanford University Archives and the Hoover Institution Archives. Eliza Mosher merited a separate bound volume in Mosher's personal papers: Mosher, *Eliza. M. Mosher, M.D., Pioneer Woman Physician,* Biography, Vol. 5, Box 4, Mosher Papers.

14. Correspondence with Elena and with Phyllis Bartlett is in Mosher Papers, Hoover Institution Archives, especially Box 1. Elena's last name is unknown.

---

1. RESEARCH EXCERPTS

Clelia Mosher's first physiological research was conducted while she was a master's student in the Department of Physical Hygiene at Stanford University. She constructed elaborate measuring devices in the Stanford gymnasium in order to investigate her hypothesis that women breathed no differently than men, a speculation contrary to medical doctrine that she determined after observing her own breathing. The excerpts are reprinted by permission of the Stanford University Archives.

In 1892 every physiology still taught that women breathed costally, and men abdominally. The costal respiration of women was believed to be a provision against the time of gestation. In 1894 the writer [1] while at Stanford University, and Dr. Fitz [2] at Harvard, independently and almost simultaneously, demonstrated that there is no sexual difference in the type of respiration. My own experimental work in respiration has demonstrated that pregnancy interferes less with the respiration than has generally been believed. The respiratory movements in the different regions tend to become equalized, but the diaphragmatic respiration persists as late as the eighth and even the beginning of the ninth month of pregnancy. The movements of the diaphragm materially aid the expulsion of the bile from the common duct, as has been experimentally proved by Heidenhain and his pupils according to Naunyn. We may here have one of the factors in the production of gall stones which are of more frequent occurrence in woman than in man, another undesirable result of the unnecessary costal type of breathing. Moreover, strong abdominal muscles are essential to a good figure. They aid in the second stage of labor, are the chief support of the kidneys and abdominal organs, and, as we shall presently see, are very potent factors in preventing menstrual pain and excessive flow. Both the experiments of Dr. Fitz and my own clearly demonstrate that clothing is the most potent factor in the production of the costal type of respiration in many women.[3]

Woman's Physical Freedom, 3rd ed. (New York: The Woman's Press, 1923), pp. 18, 19.

Mosher's "Report of Progress," written in 1894 as she was conducting her respiration research, stated her conclusions specifically:

1. That clothing may interfere with the mechanisms of respiration, changing abdominal or other types to costal, making the mechanism work uneconomically and interfering with other organs and their functions.
2. That costal breathing is not a provision against the period of gestation, and finally, perhaps most important of all,
3. That women may breathe abdominally, costally, or at the ninth rib, or may have any modification of any one of these principal types. Pending further investigation this would lead to the conclusion that costal breathing is not a secondary sexual character but an individual variation.

"Respiration in Women: A Report of Progress in a Study of Respiration in the Roble Gymnasium, Leland Stanford University" (May 1894), *Hygiene and Physiology of Women, Vol. 1 Respiration,* Box 3, Mosher Papers, SC11, Stanford University Archives, pp. 2–10.

Mosher's original research on menstruation, or functional periodicity as it was then known, ultimately included serial records of 400 women

of her acquaintance, primarily students, these records collectively ex-
tending over more than 3,350 menstrual periods. A large number of
these records were supplemented by observations written monthly by
Mosher herself. They included preliminary statements; careful inter-
menstrual notes; data on the dates, duration, and amount of men-
strual flow; and subsequent letters. To this was added Mosher's
measurements of respiration rates, blood pressure, blood counts, he-
moglobin estimations, and other physiological data measurements. She
was to find that her conclusions refuted the popularly held views of
menstruation:

The argument on which this study is based may be briefly stated as
follows: Menstruation is apparently a more or less serious disability in
a large number of women. One writer has described it as "a constantly
recurring infirmity that occupies seven years out of thirty of a woman's
adult life." It can be of no advantage to the race to have one half of it
incapacitated one week out of four. Unquestionably, therefore, relief
from whatever incapacity may be associated with this physiological
function is important not only to woman as an individual, but to her as
the mother of the race.

The following questions therefore arise:

1. Does the above description represent the normal or even average
condition of women?

2. If not, what is normal menstruation?

3. What are the factors which modify normal menstruation?

4. What can be done to modify existing conditions?

The generally accepted view of menstruation is that it is a periodic
flow of blood from the genital tract of a woman, which is accompanied
by varying degrees of incapacity. This idea of disability and suffering
has been so thoroughly inculcated in women that one who is free from
pain is almost apologetic and inclined to question whether her sense of
well-being at this time is not abnormal. . . .

I should define normal menstruation as a periodic flow of blood
from the uterus of a woman, occurring at fairly definite intervals (reck-
oned from the first day of the onset of the flow to the first day of the
next onset) in the same individual, but the intervals varying in different
individuals, this function being unattended with pain or incapacity due
to it as such. If we can divorce our minds from all preconceived no-
tions in regard to this function, be they derived from individual experience, sex tradition or accepted teachings, and consider it as we do the
other periodic functions, this definition will not seem unreasonable. In
the first place, it must be admitted that there is no reason for treating

this function differently from the other periodic functions, such as sleep, digestion, defecation and urination, which likewise have their departures from the normal. We do not find these abnormal manifestations incorporated in the definitions of them. Take sleep, for instance: however common insomnia may be, we never consider it otherwise than a departure from the normal; indigestion is only the pathological expression of an abnormal condition of the digestive function; while constipation is quite as frequent as the so-called dysmenorrheas which are associated invariably with the definitions of menstruation.

In the second place, the observers of menstrual disturbances do not by any means agree as to the numbers affected or the degree of the infirmity. Moreover, the various bodies of statistics giving the percentage of women suffering at the menstrual period have all been based on single statements from women examined. . . .

1. Statistics based on single observations are necessarily inaccurate, for the following reasons:

a. The details of menstrual experience are quickly forgotten; probably more quickly by those who do not suffer than by those who do.

b. When asked what their usual condition is, many women reply by describing the most recent menstrual period, and forget the variations incident to previous periods.

c. It is more difficult to obtain records from well women than from those who suffer, because their condition, being normal, makes slight impression upon the mind; consequently the available data inevitably exaggerate the number of women who suffer.

d. Gynecological records are always available, and many of our statistical records are made up from the same sources. They certainly do not represent accurately the experience of average women, even when they are the patients' statements as to their condition before the illness which took them to the gynecologist. Not only is the present time of suffering bound to color their statements, but the importance of giving emphasis to every symptom they have ever had is unduly prominent in their minds. Under such circumstances, the occasional pain or discomfort becomes the habitual condition.

e. Increased discomfort may occur from cold and exposure in the winter season; therefore single observations made in inclement weather would increase unduly the proportion with painful menstruation.

f. The greater part of the observations on which the current view of menstruation is based were made by women, for the simple reason that women will speak more freely to one of their own sex than to a man, even though he is a physician.

2. Is all of the so-called dysmenorrhea true dysmenorrhea? Let us

clear up the subject by dividing all dysmenorrhea into two classes: (a) those cases due to organic trouble of the generative organ, which belong to the gynecologist, not to the physiologist; (b) cases of functional dysmenorrhea. The functional dysmenorrheas, must be again subdivided into (1) the true functional dysmenorrheas, and (2) coincident functional disturbances occurring in other organs at or near the menstrual period, but in no way due to the menstrual function as such. . . .

I am convinced that many of the so-called dysmenorrheas are not dysmenorrhea at all, but coincident functional disturbances in other organs.

"Functional Periodicity in Women and Some of the Modifying Factors," *California State Journal of Medicine,* January and February 1911, pp. 1, 2, 6.

In an update published three years after her first article on functional periodicity, Mosher recounted the factors that she was convinced led to dysmenorrhea in women:

(1) the upright position (Moscati), (2) alteration of the normal type of respiration by disuse of the diaphragm and of the abdominal muscles; (3) the lack of general muscular development; (4) inactivity during the menstrual period; (5) psychic influences. . . .

This periodic physiologic congestion of the uterus in woman, which occurs about the time of menstruation, [4] is frequently so excessive that it produces congestive dysmenorrhea. The upright position, lax abdominal muscles, costal instead of diaphragmatic breathing and constriction of the body by clothing which interferes with the use of the abdominal muscles and diaphragm—all combine to develop and promote this excessive pelvic congestion. As a result, there is pain at the menstrual period, prolonged hemorrhage and undue loss of blood. . . .

"A Physiologic Treatment of Congestive Dysmenorrhea and Kindred Disorders Associated with the Menstrual Function" (third note), *Journal of the American Medical Association,* 25 April 1914, pp. 1297, 1298.

After analyzing the causes of dysmenorrhea, Mosher set out to find ways to relieve menstrual pain for the women who experienced it. She developed a series of exercises for the students in her physical training classes that she believed would keep women healthy by both preventing

*and relieving dysmenorrhea. In the following description of her in-
struction, Dr. Mosher revealed the underlying assumptions that she
tried to get her students to understand and endorse:*

No woman is allowed to do this laboratory work (active work in
physical training or athletics) during the menstrual period. If she is able
to do her other university work, she is required to come to the gymnasium, get into her gymnasium suit, and report to the medical adviser
in the mat room.[5] Here she is required to enter on the following blank
her name and the date on which her menstrual period began.

As soon as this is done she takes her position on one of the mats
and does the following exercises:[6] Having taken the horizontal position
on her back, she flexes her knees and places her arms at her sides to
secure perfect relaxation. "One hand may rest on the abdominal wall
without exerting any pressure, to serve as an indicator of the amount
of movement. The woman is then directed to see how high she can
raise the hand by lifting the abdominal wall, then to see how far the
hand may be lowered by the voluntary contraction of the abdominal
muscles, the importance of this contraction being especially emphasized. She is cautioned to avoid jerky movements and to strive for a
smooth, rhythmical raising and lowering of the abdominal wall."[7] Before the exercise is begun the bladder should be emptied. The remainder of the hour is devoted to an informal talk on some hygienic subject,
eugenics, vocational opportunities, dress or kindred topics which have
some vital interest and relation to the woman's every-day life. If the
medical adviser is prevented by other duties from giving the talk, a well
developed library of current articles, books, magazines and manuscripts
on these subjects is available for reading. Suggestions for this reading
are found on the blackboards in the mat room, these suggestions being
frequently changed. At the end of the hour the exercises are repeated.

The reasons why we do the exercises in the mat room, why certain
exercises are given in the gymnasium and why other things are prohibited, are fully given. These talks are illustrated with charts, schematograms, [8] and demonstrations of the structure of the body by use of the
skeleton and manikin. These anatomic and physiologic reasons of such
prohibitions and requirements ensure an interest and an intelligent co-
operation on the part of the student which could not otherwise be
obtained. . . .

Good results follow from this patient working out with the individual woman, over and over again, the relation between what she has
been doing or failing to do and the unfavorable symptoms arising at
any menstrual period. At the same time the truth is constantly empha-

sized that no woman should be satisfied with anything less than perfect health and absolute freedom from any symptoms whatever during menstruation; that ideally a woman should feel just as well, just as efficient at her menstrual period as at any other; and that many women do so feel. A habit of mind is thus established in the woman which makes her relate any undesirable symptom to its cause. . . .

The women are also taught that, although to do the exercises twice during the required hour may relieve immediate symptoms, yet little permanent improvement can be expected unless they repeat the exercises at home in bed night and morning every day in the month. In fact, the one great reason for requiring these exercises in the mat room is to establish a habit of mind which will make the women associate the exercises with menstrual relief and so remember to do them whenever there is need. Since the chief cause of the undue congestion of the uterus is due to the insufficient use of the diaphragm and the weak abdominal muscles, the exercises must be continued over a considerable period of time to accomplish any marked results, long enough to develop these muscles and to establish their more or less constant use without conscious effort. . . .

Since physical development and perfect health are equally vital to every woman, whether as a preparation for motherhood or for economic independence, the fundamental idea in all the work is to make it of some practical value to the individual woman; to give her the work she is able to do and will enjoy most; to make it of interest enough to have her elect physical training and personal hygiene as one of her subjects; and by securing her co-operation to do away with questions of discipline, there being only such few rules and requirements as we mutually agree are fair and necessary.

"The Physical Training of Women in Relation to Functional Periodicity," *Woman's Medical Journal*, April 1915, pp. 3–5, 9, 11.

In 1912, two years after Mosher had returned to Stanford to head the physical hygiene department and become medical advisor to women, she made some cursory comments summarizing the questionnaires on women's sexual attitudes that she had administered over the preceding twenty years. These reflections are incomplete and disappointing in their brevity; they do, however, reveal some of Mosher's own thoughts on the subject as she began to compile her data. (If Mosher's comments were written in 1912 as noted, some of her questionnaires evidently have been lost to us as Mosher reports the total completed by 1912 as forty, over twice as many as remain in her papers today with either no date listed or a date recorded as 1912 or earlier. Additionally, her remarks written in 1912 could not have covered the seventeen to twenty-six questionnaires completed after 1912.)

Data Compiled about 1912

Marriage: 40 complete blanks
            Incomplete data 1 and 2
            Dyspareunia cases 3
            Second hand information 2

College women	30
Not stated	5
High Normal or Public School	9

Colleges:		
Penn. State	1
Cornell	6
Seminary	1
Pub. School	1
Ripon Col.	1
Smith Col.	1
Syracuse	1
Cambridge, Eng.	1
Canadian Weslyn	1
Oxford, Ohio	1
High School	2
Univ. Pac.	1
So. Bend Acad.	1
Radcliffe	1
Indiana Univ.	1
Normal Sch'l	2
Wellesley	1
Not Stated	3
Walker Col.	1
Vassar	2
Stanford	5

California	1
Iowa State Univ.	1

40

Effect of Menopause on Desire

a-Sex instinct still persists in women but is less insistent.
b-Absence of or increased frequency of absence of orgasm following
  menopause.
  No difference (no 45) no 43

The Fall Off of Birthrate Is Due

1-Voluntary restriction of birthrate by contraceptive methods for economic reasons
2-a) To increasing selfishness of (I) men:
  man wishes companionship of wife
    unhampered by children   3 cases
  (II) women:
  dangers of childbirth to women   1 case
  women who desire a life of ease
    and social freedom   1 case
3-Physical maladjustments due (to)
  a) lack of consideration of the woman by too frequent coitus de-
     stroys psychologic sex impulse
  b) lack of understanding of slower time reaction in women making
     marital relation for the woman without the normal physical re-
     sponse. This leaves organs of woman over congested.
4-Physical maladjustments
  A. Dyspareunia due to
     1) Physical terror though mutual consent   1 case
     2) Unusual angle of long axis of vagina causing
        undue suffering to woman   2 cases
     3) Physical disproportion.

Note: The maladjustments in marriage occasionally occur at the first
consummation of the marital relation. The woman comes to this new
experience of life often with no knowledge. The woman while she may
give mental consent often shrinks physically. Her slower time reaction
deprives her of all physical response, or (2) too often her training has

instilled the idea that any physical response is coarse, common and immodest which inhibits proper part in this relation.

6 June 1926, Box 1, folder 10, Mosher Papers, SC11, Stanford University Archives.

The national interest in anthropometry at the turn of the century promoted interest in annual height and weight measurements in both men's and women's departments of physical training in colleges and universities. Mosher found, for example, that the average height of Stanford coeds had increased 8/10 of an inch during the first three decades of Stanford's existence, from 63.2 inches in 1892 to 64 inches in 1920. She attributed her findings to two major factors:

(1) Increased Physical Activity of Women

It is a matter of common knowledge that the modern college girl is more physically active than the women of thirty years of age, but the Vassar studies make a real contribution to this subject. From 1896 to 1900, 26.5 per cent. of the entering students at Vassar College had engaged in no form of sport before coming to college; from 1916 to 1920, only 0.6 per cent. reported no sports before admission to the college. This almost universal physical activity during the preparatory years has been fostered, not only by the laws for compulsory physical training in the secondary schools, but also by the municipal play grounds and swimming pools. This eagerly to be desired, more fully developed woman will, therefore, be found in constantly increasing numbers among all classes of women, those who go to college and those who do not go, thus inspiring better wives and mothers, and consequently a better race.

(2) Influence of Fashion

The other factor is the influence of fashion. It has already been noted that, with increasing physical activity, a change to lighter and looser clothing was made and fashion was forced to adapt itself to the introduction of the bicycle and automobile.

"Some of the Causal Factors in the Increased Height of College Women" (third note), *Journal of the American Medical Association,* 18 August 1923, pp. 536, 537.

Continuing her diatribe against the dictates of fashion and women's habit of inactivity, Mosher wrote:

Constrictive dress and inactivity apparently interfere more with the abdominal muscles than with the diaphragm. The degree to which they induce menstrual pain may be suggested by a comparison of my observations made in 1893–96 with others made in 1910–14. In the earlier group a larger proportion of the women had pain and discomfort of severe type and of relatively long duration. In the later group the larger number of cases have no disability, and such pain as the remainder have is rarely severe and is of short duration. In 1893–96 the average width of skirts worn by 98 young women was 13.5 feet—the widest 15 and the narrowest 9 feet. The weight of the outside skirt alone was often nearly as much as the weight of the entire clothing worn by a modern girl. At that period, too, every woman must have a wasp-like waist while several under petticoats were also carried from the waist. It is certainly not difficult to understand why so many women had menstrual pain at that period.

In the year 1894 in the group of college women studied [9] there were 19 per cent. who were free from pain at their menstrual periods, while in 1915 and 1916 the number of women entering the university who were free from pain had risen to 68 per cent. . . . An extraordinarily close correlation was found between the fashion of dress and the menstrual disability of women. As the skirt grew shorter and narrower and the waist grew larger, the functional health of women improved. This narrowing and shortening, which are advantageous to the health of women, of course do not include such vagaries of fashion as the excessively narrow skirt, which hinders freedom in walking, or the extremely short skirt, which afforded insufficient protection against the cold; these would be almost as unhygienic as the skirt of the earlier period with its extreme width and great weight. We should rejoice in the freedom of the modern girl with her large normal waist.

Woman's Physical Freedom, 3rd ed. (New York: The Woman's Press, 1923), pp. 29–31.

The results of Mosher's investigations and measurements of women's strength served to confirm her belief that abilities differentially attributed to each sex were a result of social convention and upbringing more than they were inherent physical distinctions:

Forty-five average healthy college women, most of whom had always been physically active, although, in the majority of the instances, not specially athletic, were studied. . . .[10]

The following groups of muscles both on the right and the left side of each woman were tested: pectorals, latissimus dorsi, anterior and posterior deltoids, forearm extensors and flexors, wrist extensors, thumb adductors, and either wrist flexors or finger flexors. The wrist flexion test was found by some of the women to cause lameness. The finger flexion was substituted in the later testing. These muscle groups were tested with the subject standing. The following tests were made in the horizontal position: dorsal flexion, inversion and eversion of foot, adduction and abduction of thigh, hip extension and flexion, knee extension and flexion.

Thus a full test included observations of thirty-six groups of muscles. Each test was repeated two or three times, thus insuring as accurate observation as possible by securing the maximum cooperation of the woman on whom the tests were made. The highest record correctly made was used in each case.

These forty-five women were tested 120 times; there were ninety-five full tests and twenty-five partial tests. Every woman was tested from two to five times, and 3,576 muscle groups in the forty-five women were tested. Dr. Mosher made schematograms[11] of all the women studied.

A convenient method of classifying the persons studied is in terms of "the strength factor," which is simply the figure obtained by dividing the total strength, as determined by the tests, by the weight. . . .

A general comparison of the series of forty-five college women with the series of athletic college men by Dr. Martin and Mr. Rich, [12] yields some suggestive results. Let us consider briefly the strength of the different muscle groups.

The pectoral muscles are commonly relatively stronger in man than in woman, the average percentage of total strength being 2.35 in man, and 2.1 in woman. Twelve women have equaled or exceeded the average of the men. Case 35 from the second group, a married woman who has borne two children, has in her pectorals 2.52 per cent. of her total strength. This difference between men and women, which is apparently not one of sex, may be explained as due to the difference in use. Constant ball playing, punching and thrusting make up a very large part of the boy's exercise. His clothing does not limit the use of the pectoral muscles, as do a woman's waist, brassiere, etc. Moreover, although dress and convention have discouraged the use of the pectoral muscles in woman, their weakness is a distinct racial disadvantage. If the pectoral muscles were well developed in the woman, we should find fewer pendulous breasts in the young girl, as well as in the older woman.

The latissimus dorsi is better developed in woman than in man, contributing 1.65 per cent. of the total strength of woman and only 1.45 per cent. in man. The buttoning of women's waists and skirts in the back brings this group of muscles into constant use from childhood, while the boy's clothes are always more conveniently buttoned on the side or in front.

The anterior and posterior deltoids in woman create from 2.45 to 1.80 per cent. of her total strength, while in man they create only from 2.1 to 1.35 per cent. of his total strength. This difference again is readily explained as due to difference in use, that is, to woman's constant practice of putting up her hair. . . . There is no occasion for a habitual use of the deltoids among men, and, furthermore, their heavy coats tend to limit the freedom of action of the deltoids.

Forearm extensions and flexions are better developed in man than in woman. . . . Here again woman's close-fitting waists and sleeves and the conventional view of her physical delicacy, which would protect her from lifting all heavy weights, must at least partially explain this difference. . . .

There is no difference in the muscular strength of women and men which is due to sex as such. Such differences as are frequently found are due to differences in the use of the muscles, brought about by the conventional limitations of activity or by dress. Marked overweight or marked underweight tends to lower the strength factor, as does also lack of coordination, which is too frequently found in women and exaggerated by their scant physical activity in childhood. The effects of muscular training persist long after the particuar exercise has ceased. A high degree of muscular power in a woman in no way lessens her racial efficiency. Lack of muscular power, as in the pectoral muscles, may be a distinct racial disability.

It has been shown that periodic disability in a woman when no organic disease exists is readily eliminated.[13] We may therefore conclude that sex is not necessarily a disability, and that if some method be found of adjusting work to the individual strength under proper hygienic conditions, without reference to sex, there is no reason why the potential power of woman may not be used without danger of lessening her racial efficiency.

References and Works Cited by Mosher in the Original Documents

1. Clelia Duel Mosher, "Respiration in Women" (preliminary report as thesis for M.A. degree, Stanford University, May 1894. Also paper presented at California Science Association, January 3, 1896).

2. G. W. Fitz, "A Study of Types of Respiratory Movements" *Journal of Experimental Med.* 1, no 4 (1896).

3. Mosher, "The Frequency of Gallstones in the United States" (Paper read before the Johns Hopkins Hospital Medical Society, March 4, 1901), *Johns Hopkins Hospital Bulletin* 12 no. 125 (August 1901).

4. Mosher, "Normal Menstruation and Some of the Factors Modifying It" (preliminary note), *Johns Hopkins Hospital* Bulletin 12, no. 178 (1901).

5. Mosher, "Report of the Director of Roble Gymnasium to the President." *Ninth Annual Report of the President* (Leland Stanford Junior University Publications, Trustees' Series No. 21, 1912), p. 42.

6. Mosher, "Functional Periodicity in Women and Some of the Modifying Factors" (second note), *California State Jour. Med.*, January and February 1911; reprinted in *Woman's Medical Journal,* April 1911; *Sargent Normal School Association Proceedings* (1911), p. 14; *American Physical Education Review,* November 1911, p. 493; abstr. the *Jour. of A.M.A.,* 29 April 1911, p. 1295.

7. Mosher, "A Physiologic Treatment of Congestive Dysmenorrhea and Kindred Disorders Associated with the Menstrual Function" (third note), *Jour. of A.M.A.,* 25 April 1914, pp. 1297–1301; *Mind and Body,* December 1914.

8. Schematograms are graphic representations of posture and other conditions of the body made by the Mosher-Lesley Schematograph in use in Roble Gymnasium.

9. Mosher, "Normal Menstruation and Some of the Factors Modifying It" (preliminary note), *Johns Hopkins Hospital,* Bulletin 12, no. 178 (1901).

10. Miss Etta L. Paris and Miss Inzetta Holt of the Department of Physical Training for Women, Stanford University, have given invaluable assistance in making these tests.

11. Mosher, "The Schematogram," *School and Society* 1 (May 1915).

12. Rich, to be published.

13. Mosher, "A Physiologic Treatment"; *The Relation of Health to the Woman Movement,* (New York: National Board YWCA, 1915).

2. "THE SECOND GENERATION OR THE MAKING OF A MISFIT"

In this autobiographical sketch, Mosher traces her legacy as a "misfit" to her relationship with her father. The reference to having been named for her father is explained by the fact that "Clelia" was a derivative of the masculine "Cornelius," her father's first name. She refers to herself as the "second one" because her parents' first child died at birth.

The picture of a man, fine as a woman in all of his instincts, a physician who shrank from the sight of blood and whose sympathies were so tender, adored by his patients because of his capacity for deep sympathy and understanding of the woes and sufferings of others.

A man who had genius and yet by the circumstances of his life found no outlet. A lover of all that was beautiful but could not express in color as would an artist.

A lover of music and the drama with only the sympathetic understanding of the work of others and yet (illegible) with the instincts and emotions of the drama.

A student and scholar but with no power of self expression in words.

A man whose rich and varied nature found no expression of his own genius.

He marries as a young man a sweet gentle efficient practical wife who loves him devotedly a truly help meet in all practical relations of life but one who has not the faintest glimmerings of the real nature of this reserved man.

He idolizes his children and with the second one who is also a girl, names her for himself and devotes the unsatisfied side of his nature to giving her the interests and power which he lacks.

Realizing that the women of her generation not only miss all that is best and worthwhile in life. And with the knowledge he has of men and their frequent unfitness to make a woman really happy he bends every energy to keep this much loved child from the danger of love and marriage.

The beautiful companionship which exists between this father and daughter is a rare and precious thing.

The girl with her outlook on life, straight fearless, independent as a boy, with capacity for thinking her own thoughts, with tastes cultivated by the scholarly father. Surrounded by the best books, seeing all that is best in the drama, surrounded with the talk of writers, poets, artists, dramatists and actors. To build up her delicate body, encouraged to ride down hill with boys, play ball, run skate. A tom boy of her period. A grief to the mother with her boyish ways but a joy to the father who sees the possibility of the realization in this girl of some of the things he has missed.

She grows up boyish, independent, thinking she has to make good. Her masculine point of view and boyish ways in curious contrast to her very feminine embodiment.

"The Second Generation or the Making of a Misfit," n.d., Box 1, folder 8, Mosher Papers, SC11, Stanford University Archives. Reprinted by permission.

3. DIARY EXCERPTS

Sometime between 1901 and 1910, in an effort to alleviate her lone-liness, Mosher began to compose letters to an imaginary friend. The following letter was written in 1915, after she had been teaching at Stanford for five years. The excerpts are reprinted by permission of the Stanford University Archives.

As I ate my breakfast in my booklined study I looked past the half opened daffodil and the violets, past your empty chair, through the open door to the miracle of beauty and awakening life which we call spring. Truly my life is cast in pleasant places. The velvety green and white velvet of the quince, its dainty suggestion of purple in the un-opened blossoms, the very shape and color of the lemon bloom, the artichoke leaves, on to the feathery wisteria, the blue sky, the silence unbroken save for the notes of the birds, the distant larks bringing before my minds eye visions of lucious meadows with the tiny golden poppies, the great blue mountains—and my thoughts turned to you and our friendship—I realized suddenly why I have cared for you as no other friend—I saw you in the midst of the fairy like bloom of the miriad blossoms of that day we spent in Saratoga, I could see you with your hands full of the tiny golden poppies—or bending over the little pink roses you love so well dreaming and feeling their beauty as I do and as no other friend I have ever had has cared for them. You in your own beauty adding to my joy of form and color—I know that you will understand me when I say that the beauty of this perfect California spring almost hurts—the peace, the rest, the emotional satisfaction in all this beauty satisfies that side of my nature—and when I see and feel it all—I long for you to share the beauty of the spring with me so adding companionship and understanding—the doubled joy—it would be too perfect.

Diary, 20 March 1915, Box 1, folder 10, Mosher Papers, SC11, Stanford University Archives.

From all the evidence, Mosher had no intimate relationships or close friendships. This brief passage from her diary, written in 1919, suggests why she thought this so.

I am finding out gradually why I am so lonely. The only things I care about are things which use my brain. The women I meet are not much interested and I do not meet many men so there is an intellectual solitude which is like the solitude of the desert—dangerous to one's sanity.

Diary, 15 June 1919, Box 1, folder 10, Mosher Papers, SC11, Stanford University Archives.

After her mother died in 1920, Mosher probably felt the lack of daily companionship most keenly and turned increasingly to her imaginary friend. It was not until this time, after the war, that Mosher acknowledged in writing that her confidante was imagined and not real. In 1919 she began a letter, "To you my friend who does not exist." The following segment from her journal describes her imaginary friend and the purpose she served.

(You are) only a creation of my brain who never existed—and although you bear the beautiful embodiment of my dream—your behavior is that of the woman of the world—and not of my dream lady—and you are bored and amused at times. So I write my letters now to you, dear, only they are not sent. I get the sense of companionship and you are spared the boredom of reading them, and still I am content and still I am rich, with the joy of friendship which asks you nothing.

Diary, 30 January 1921, Box 1, folder 10, Mosher Papers, SC11, Stanford University Archives.

Mosher described her concept of the ideal friendship as one of mutual support and encouragement between two women. There is never a reference in her journal to her wishing for a friendship with a man. The following passage is one of the few that reveals that Mosher's need for a friend might have been served by a daughter.

There is a kind of friendship which may exist, between two women, where their individual interests are so merged, that each has for the other the same vital interest in the other's success as the mother has in her daughter's affairs, or father in his son's life. It has all the wonderful community interest one finds in ideal marriage and only differs in the absence of the physical relationship. It is emotionally satisfying. One seldom sees it. It is only possible to a very high type of woman, spiritually and intellectually.

It supplies to the working woman and compensates her for what she has missed in not marrying but cannot make up to her for her lost motherhood.

Diary, n.d., Box 1, folder 10, Mosher Papers, SC11, Stanford University Archives.

Writing in 1926, she seemed to resign herself to her solitude and her contrived means to achieve intimacy with her imaginary friend:

Dear "Friend who never was:"

I have given up ever finding you. I have tried out all my friends and they have not measured up to my dreams. They still are friends, and other friendships give joy and richness to my life but I cannot share my dreamland with them. I wander alone there and show the world my prose, my common sense. But I keep normal and wholesome by going ever alone in this land of dreams. It would not take long to be as drab as most of my contemporaries were it not for this land of my dreams.

Diary, 16 April 1926, Box 1, folder 10, Mosher Papers, SC11, Stanford University Archives.

It is evident from her diary that Mosher treasured most her solitude and thinking time, that she was perhaps happiest when alone in her study or her garden. At the age of sixty-three she wrote revealingly about her conflicting needs for solitude and friendship.

Friendship asks too much, takes too much of one's priceless leisure, interrupts one's time and lessens one's accomplishment. And yet, can one go on being a balanced, sane person, with only the casual companionship of one's acquaintance—or is a certain give and take of daily companionship necessary to keep one at one's best? Who knows?

Diary, 22 October 1926, Box 1, folder 10, Mosher Papers, SC11, Stanford University Archives.

MAUDE E. ABBOTT

Osler Library, McGill University

The Lonely Heart

MAUDE E. ABBOTT
1869–1940

by Margaret Gillett

The story of Dr. Maude Elizabeth Seymour Abbott is extraordinary, yet it contains many elements in common with those of the pioneering professional women of her day. Dr. Abbott was a distinguished medical researcher and teacher, a member of the Faculty of Medicine of McGill University, Montreal, who became world famous for her work on congenital heart disease and for her development of the medical museum as a medium of instruction. Her contributions to the writing of the history of medicine and to the professionalization of nursing education were also significant and widely acknowledged. During her career, she broke many barriers, scored many "firsts," won a number of awards ranging from gold medals to honorary degrees, participated prominently in international medical societies, had two scholarships and a lectureship founded in her name, was invited to the White House, was accorded honorary membership, *inter alia,* in the New York Academy of Medicine, and was greeted with affection by her colleagues and students. To record all this, a full-scale biography was published scarcely a year after her death. Such acclaim would seem to indicate unqualified recognition and success—and yet, and yet . . .

Like the lives of many professional women of her day and ours, Maude Abbott's career was haunted by a reservation. She was, after all, a woman. Though she was famous abroad, she was not given academic promotion at home; though she was gregarious and hospitable, she was ultimately lonely; though she escaped from the anonymity that was the

185

usual lot of her female contemporaries, she had to find refuge on the border of eccentricity.

The unusual nature of her story began in infancy. Maude was the daughter of Frances Elizabeth Seymour Abbott, whose husband, Jeremiah Babin, was a French-Canadian Protestant clergyman. The couple lived in the village of St. Andrews East, Quebec, about thirty miles from Montreal. In January 1867, Jeremiah Babin was accused of murdering his disabled sister, who, in true Victorian gothic fashion, had been kept in the attic of his home and whose body had mysteriously been found in a nearby river after the floods of the previous spring had abated. Though Reverend Babin was eventually acquitted, local feeling and circumstantial evidence were heavily against him. His wife, however, faithfully supported him throughout his long ordeal. Shortly before the trial she gave birth to a daughter, Alice, and two years later, to a second daughter, Maude. By then Frances Abbott Babin "had suffered all she could endure and a few months later she died of pulmonary tuberculosis."[1] Meanwhile, Jeremiah Babin had taken himself off to the United States and left his babies to be brought up by their widowed grandmother. She had their name legally changed to the maternal Abbott.

It is impossible to say how deep an effect this family tragedy had on Maude and Alice, but it must have left a residue of sorrow in its wake. However, it seems that the girls' childhood was essentially happy and their love for their grandmother very great. Alice proved to be musical; Maude was obviously intelligent but she was not certain of her talents or her virtues, suffering the awful personal doubts of the teenager. She wrote in her diary on April 1, 1884:

> I wonder what my life will be like and if I will have any opportunity to do something good or great with it. . . . How can anyone think anything nice about me? It must be that they don't know me well enough.[2]

Then again on June 25:

> When I come to turn myself over and pick myself to pieces, it is really awful how few lovable points I have in my character. I am half convinced I am clever . . . but my idea of cleverness is entirely different from what I am.

Both girls had their early education at home with a governess, not an unusual practice for children of their class at that time, yet Maude clearly wanted more. In 1884, at age fifteen, she wrote in her diary:

> One of my day-dreams which I feel to be selfish, is that of going to
> school. I know Alice would like it herself ever so much, but I do so *long*
> to go. . . . Oh, to think of studying with other girls! Think of learning Ger-
> man, Latin and other languages in general.

On another occasion she wrote, "I don't think it's the other girls' society I want, or anything of the sort, but the good education I would
love—how I long for one."

Later that year she resolved seriously:

> If it ever does come to pass and I get my wish, I will try to keep my
> resolutions (1) to study hard and conscientiously (2) not to get wild etc, as
> many girls do (3) not to care for competition but for the real study and the
> benefit I will derive from it (4) to remember that I go to school for educa-
> tion, not for fun.

This intense yearning for education was characteristic of many young
women of the era. (One, M. Carey Thomas, later to be president of
Bryn Mawr, recorded in her diary a burning desire almost identical to
Maude Abbott's.) This ambition was both a cause and effect of the expanding educational opportunities for women in the 1870s and 1880s.
In Montreal the available options were the Montreal High School for
Girls, which opened in 1875, or several private establishments for young
ladies. Maude Abbott's dream came true within the year, for she was
sent to a small school run by Miss Symmers and Miss Smith. She confided to her diary in December 1884: "I have gone to school, so now
I have a chance to keep those resolutions I made." But she added, "We
are never satisfied. My next wish is to go to college and now I am
wishing for that almost as ardently as I did last March for my present
good fortune."

Happily for her, college, too, was now a possibility. Montreal's
English-language institution of higher learning, McGill College, char-
tered in 1821, had opened its doors to women in October 1884. This
followed spirited efforts to gain entrance on the part of some girls from
Montreal High, their spectacular matriculation examination results, and
a sudden endowment for women's education by Donald A. Smith (later
Lord Strathcona.)[3] So in 1885, after winning a scholarship, Maude Abbott was admitted to the McGill Faculty of Arts or, more accurately, to
the Donalda Department for Women. As she records in her "Autobiographical Sketch," she attended for three weeks but, since there was a
serious outbreak of smallpox in Montreal that fall, she returned to the
safety of St. Andrews. The following year she reregistered at McGill and

became president of her class of nine women. At that time, women were instructed by the regular professors but were separated from male students in the arts course. They were permitted to attend coeducational classes for honors work in their senior year and welcomed in some informal campus activities. Maude participated fully in student affairs; she loved college life and, in fact, confessed in 1928, "I was literally in love with McGill, or so the girls said. I have never fallen out of love with her since"—though there were times when she well might have.

In 1890 she attained the then much-coveted B.A. degree, graduating as a gold medalist and also simultaneously acquiring, as an insurance policy, a teaching diploma from the McGill Normal School. As class valedictorian she made a speech that was the very model of sincere youthful exhortation, reminding the women students of their "duties and privileges," urging them to accept their individual responsibilities for the honor of the entire sex, begging them to "remember that at this early stage of women's education in Canada, you, as members of the advance-guard, are in your own persons to be pointed out as instances of its success or failure."[4]

If Maude Abbott appreciated being a student at patriarchal McGill and was grateful that women had been accepted in the Faculty of Arts, she was by no means content to leave it at that. She wanted admission to a field that continued to resist women's encroachment: medicine. This was a relatively unfamiliar professional area for women. The first M.D. degree to be earned by a woman was awarded to Elizabeth Blackwell at Geneva, New York in 1849; the first Canadian woman doctor, Emily Stowe, got her degree from New York Medical College for Women in 1867; Stowe's daughter, Augusta, was the first woman to take a medical degree in Canada and did so only in 1883. Medicine was commonly deemed inappropriate for nice young ladies and many medical schools forthrightly refused to accept them. McGill's Faculty of Medicine is the oldest unit of the university—it existed independently before McGill actually functioned, was "engrafted" onto the college, and for many years remained a law unto itself.[5] It did not welcome the idea of the female physician. In 1888, Grace Ritchie, the first woman valedictorian at McGill and close friend of Maude Abbott's, had courageously defied official censorship of her speech and called for the doors of the Faculty of Medicine to be opened. She was met with cries of "Shame!" and "Never!" and she was forced to take her medical training elsewhere. When Maude Abbott asked her grandmother, "May I be a doctor?" she might well have received a similar answer. But, according to Abbott's recollection in her "Autobiographical Sketch," that wonderfully supportive woman replied, "Dear child, you may be anything you like."

As the time approached for her to begin her medical studies, Maude also found encouragement from some of the upper-class women of Montreal—even from some of the men and from the newspapers[6]— when she was prominent in organizing an Association for the Professional Education of Women. Yet her high hopes were dashed. The Faculty of Medicine remained as Grace Ritchie had found it: impenetrable. Traditional arguments were advanced once more: The study of anatomy would produce hardening effects on the emotions; it would be impossible for any woman to pursue the long course in dissecting without losing her maidenly modesty and true womanliness which are her essential charms; women were unsuitable for public life, their nerves were weak, their powers of endurance limited, their health uncertain; they should not unsex themselves by leaving their own domestic sphere for that of men. One professor threatened to resign while another allowed that women "may be useful in some departments of medicine *but* in difficult work, in surgery, for instance, they would not have the nerve." "And," he added, "can you think of a patient in a critical case, waiting for half an hour while the medical lady fixes her bonnet or adjusts her bustle?"[7] Prejudice, sometimes camouflaged by "wit," carried the day and Maude Abbott was also forced to study elsewhere.

Though she was actually invited to enter the Medical Faculty of the University of Bishop's College, a rival medical school, she still had difficulty getting permission to "walk the wards" at the McGill-dominated teaching hospital, the Montreal General. She described in her autobiography how public pressure—a "newspaper storm" and threats to withhold all-important private financing—finally forced her entry. She also noted how embarrassed she was by the publicity and how lonely she was away from her women friends of McGill, isolated in an alien crowd of young men. Perhaps she was fortunate that her fellow students seem to have ignored her, for in other coeducational medical schools pioneering women were the constant butt of brutal "practical jokes," coarse language, and obscene graffiti. One woman pioneer wrote in her diary, "No one knows or can know what a furnace we are passing through these days at college. We suffer torment, we shrink inwardly, we are hurt cruelly."[8] Maude may have had a comparatively easy time of it. She did not complain of discrimination in grading or awards— indeed, she again graduated with two high prizes—but she was very conscious of the fact that she was treated differently from the rest. Either she was not asked to participate in class or she was given too much to do. She realized that she might have been "over-sensitive" but she found hurtful the apparently jocular remarks about "troublesome lady-students" by an apparently friendly professor. She was probably also aware of antipathy from a quarter from which she might have expected support.

The Lady Superintendent at the Montreal General, Nora Livingstone, did not welcome the idea of women medical students. She was categorically against coeducation, believing that "mixing of the sexes at lectures is bad and might give rise to complications, when the lady students get strong and brutal," and she rejoiced when the hospital decided to exclude them. When Maude was so grudgingly accepted, Livingstone wrote in a letter to her sister, "Miss Abbott is to be admitted here. There is no way out of it. I am sorry, for she is aggressive, but she being the only one, will mind her p's and q's."[9]

In the nineteenth century and even later it was not uncommon for North Americans to seek their graduate education and research training in Europe. Maude Abbott did so, spending almost three years abroad, studying with famous clinicians and bringing back knowledge, notes, and a collection of newfangled microscopic and lantern slides of medical specimens. She was accompanied on her trip by her sister Alice who, unfortunately, became very ill. The disease, so devastating for Alice, so heartbreaking for Maude, was manic depressive psychosis.[10] Though she survived for almost another forty years, Alice remained a chronic invalid. She was a dear but demanding responsibility that Maude alone had to bear. Their grandmother had died in 1890. Other members of the Abbott family included some distinguished personages such as cousin Sir John, who became prime minister of Canada, but Maude had to make her own way in the world. That meant supporting herself and Alice.

On her return to Montreal in 1897, she established herself in a private medical practice but was soon drawn back into the McGill orbit. She tells how Dr. Charles Martin of the McGill Faculty of Medicine, after a chance encounter, invited her to work part time at the Royal Victoria Hospital, another McGill-associated institution. The paper she produced from a statistical study on heart murmurs had to be read by a male doctor to the Medico-Chirurgical Society because women were excluded from membership, but it resulted in her being proposed and elected as the first woman member of that society and it started her off on her way to fame. Before many years had passed, Dr. Maude Abbott was considered a world authority on congenital heart disease. In 1905, Dr. William Osler (1849–1919), one of Canada's most distinguished physicians and medical educators who later became Regius Professor of

Medicine at Oxford, invited this young woman to write the chapter on congenital heart disease for the basic medical textbook he was preparing. This was a signal honor and Maude Abbott was worthy of Dr. Osler's trust. His pleasure in the paper she produced was only exceeded by her delight in his letter of praise for its "extraordinary merit," deeming it "far and away the very best thing ever written on the subject in English—possibly in any language." For years, Dr. Abbott carried that glowing tribute with her in her handbag."[11]

Osler also set her off in another important direction. He encouraged her to take serious interest in the McGill medical museum. Despite her initial misgivings, she put her prodigious talents and energies to work so that the course in pathology she developed using the museum became a voluntary,[12] then a not-to-be-missed, integral part of the McGill medical program. This was well before the era of TV and high-tech teaching aids, but Maude Abbott clearly understood how effective real objects and visual presentations could be in teaching. She also refined the system for classifying medical museum specimens and produced a monumental catalogue of the McGill holdings. Before long, she found herself organizing the International Association of Medical Museums, becoming its secretary and the editor of its journal. She held these positions for more than thirty years, breathing life into the organization, so that it was said that a meeting of the association without Dr. Abbott was like a performance of *Hamlet* without the Prince of Denmark.[13] She also created an award-winning international medical exhibition and wrote very successful histories of medicine in the Province of Quebec, and of the profession of nursing, and a life of Florence Nightingale. The writings on nursing grew into a course at the McGill Graduate School for Nurses, while the text and set of slides she prepared for her lectures were published and then adopted by many schools of nursing across North America. After the death of Sir William Osler in 1919, she undertook the editing of a massive collection of medical research studies and essays in his memory. When another gigantic undertaking, *The Atlas of Congenital Heart Disease,* was completed, the publisher inscribed the first copy to Dr. Maude Abbott, "The Madonna of the Heart."

By this time her fame was clearly established so that any Canadian medical person traveling abroad was likely to be met with, "Ah, then you must know Dr. Maude Abbott."[14] She was one of McGill's most renowned staff members, but what kind of a career had she had?

Dr. Maude E. Abbott, B.A. (McGill, 1890), C.M., M.D. (Bishop's, 1894), LRCR&S (Edinburgh, 1897), FRCP(C) (1931), FRSM (London, 1935), outlined her "progress" at McGill as follows:

I was appointed to the McGill staff in 1899, with the title Assistant Curator of the Medical Museum, and was promoted to the full Curatorship in 1901. This was a teaching appointment, so that my name appears in the Medical Calendar in the line of ascent of the Teaching Staff from the year in this capacity. In 1905 I was made also Research Fellow in Pathology, and in 1912 Lecturer in Pathology. . . . I retained my post as Lecturer in Pathology from 1912 until the year 1924, when I was promoted by the Governors of the University to the position of Assistant Professor of Medical Research. My appointment as Curator of the Medical Museum ran concurrently with the above posts . . . [15]

It is painfully obvious that this productive and well-respected scholar was advanced with spectacular slowness. The positions she was given were all peripheral until the lectureship in pathology, after thirteen years in the faculty. Even the assistant professorship, after another twelve years, was not in a regular department, but in a specially created area with no real future. Still, to show that it was not entirely unappreciative of her worth, McGill took the unusual step in 1910 of awarding her the degree of M.D., C.M. *honoris causa.* That is, it gave her the medical degree it would not let her earn, awarding it on the basis of her "distinguished career as an undergraduate at Bishop's College and for her high reputation as a writer on medical subjects, especially on the subject of Cardiac anomalies."[16]

Not surprisingly, other institutions sought Dr. Abbott out. During World War I she was offered an acting professorship at the University of Texas until the end of the fighting (when the men would be back) and an associate professorship thereafter. She did not accept that post but, after considerable persuasion, she spent two years (1923–25) as professor and chairman of pathology at the Women's Medical College of Pennsylvania. Then she returned voluntarily to McGill to her long-delayed assistant professorship. No man would have accepted this lowly status; no man would have been asked to. Why did she?

Her work, McGill, Montreal, and the care of Alice were obviously more important to Maude Abbott than her own career advancement. Yet she had considerable professional self-respect, once refusing a job at a Montreal hospital because she would have had to work under one of her former classmates and was afraid she would "get credit only when I asserted myself, which I find hard to do. I do not like the idea of doing higher work and being called only a second assistant, even for good pay."[17] Nor was she so much "in love with McGill" that she meekly accepted her lot. Over the years she wrote many times to the chairman of pathology or the dean of the faculty requesting promotion, more security, additional assistance, or salary increases, complaining that "I am at the breaking point financially and in other ways."[18] Minor adjustments were made from time to time, but real promotion was denied. Explanations for decisions were not always given—except that McGill was chronically short of money—and since, in those days, lecturers and assistant professors did not have seats on the faculty, she was unable to argue her case at any collegial forum. A lone woman, she remained an outsider.

The years went by and, as she approached sixty-five, she wrote to the principal of the university begging not to be subject to a new regulation requiring retirement at that age because:

> I am still in the vigorous exercise of all my faculties and am actively engaged at the present time in the consummation of researches and publications of recognized importance, the results of my years of experience, and which cannot from their nature be relegated to or adequately carried on by anyone but myself. Interruption of these by my retirement at the present juncture would appear to be little short of a calamity.[19]

Like other McGill professors (including some prominent people such as economist/humorist Stephen Leacock), she was bitterly disappointed when the appeal was denied and the regulation enforced. She asked "one final favour: namely that I be retired with the status of Professor of Medical Research."[20] Again the answer was "No" and the best the university could do was to grant her a three-month extension as assistant professor while attempting to soften the blow by awarding her a second honorary degree, the LL.D. (1936).

Since Dr. Abbott's work was of unquestioned merit, was it only because she was a woman that she was not promoted? Speculation about other reasons produces unconvincing results: (1) Objections to her family history? This is possible in a conservative milieu but farfetched here since no one at McGill seemed to know that her father was an accused murderer and it was not mentioned in any published biographical material until 1978. Furthermore, her maternal family, the Abbotts, were very highly respected; (2) Conspiracy? During Dr. Abbott's thirty-seven years at McGill, there were six deans of medicine and four principals of the university. It is very unlikely indeed that they would all have agreed to suppress a particular individual; (3) Personal dislike? Maude Abbott was generally on friendly terms with members of the faculty, as many letters, written tributes, and oral evidence indicate. A notable exception was Dr. Horst Oertel with whom she did not enjoy a happy working relationship and with whom she clashed over museum policy. He was her contemporary and a glance at his career pattern provides a considerable contrast to hers.

As anyone who has ever attempted peer assessment knows, simple comparisons can be dangerously misleading, yet the differences in these cases are astounding: Dr. Horst Oertel was born in Germany in 1873 (Dr. Abbott in 1869); he received his M.D. from Yale in 1894 (the same year she earned hers from Bishop's); he undertook graduate studies in Europe for four years (she for three); after working at the Russell Sage Institute of Pathology, New York, and Guys Hospital, London, he came to McGill in 1914 as an assistant professor (a rank she did not achieve for another decade); he was named full professor and chairman of pathology in 1919, and later to the prestigious Strathcona Professorship (distinctions never to be hers). World War I helped the advancement of his career (as it might have hers, had she been willing to leave McGill). Oertel was made acting chairman when the incumbent left for military service and was confirmed in this position after the war. He was apparently able to overcome prejudice against him because of his name and German origins better than she could compensate for her gender. One professor resigned over Oertel's original appointment on the grounds that he was "a member of the enemy race,"[21] but the faculty resisted that pressure more decisively than it overcame ingrained antipathy to women in medicine—promoting him, merely retaining her.[22]

Apart from Dr. Oertel and Dr. J. C. Meakins, chairman of the Department of Medicine, with whom she had a series of running battles concerning women's rights in the faculty, Maude Abbott's relationship with men was generally cordial. Like at least half the highly educated women of her generation, she never married but she was by no means a man-hater; on the contrary, she "keenly enjoyed male society," and appreciated the help received from "the generous-minded men on the Faculty of Medicine."[23] It was remarked that the vast majority of the pictures around her rooms were of men, mainly professors and personages in medicine from Canada and abroad.[24] Indeed, she was something of a hero worshipper. Preeminent among her heroes was Sir William Osler whom she (and others) called "the greatest clinical teacher of his time." His influence on her career has already been noted; his impact on her feelings can be seen in her "Autobiographical Sketch"—"I shall never forget him as I saw him walking down the old Museum with his great dark burning eyes fixed full upon me." It may not be stretching too far to place a Freudian interpretation on her account of her first meeting with Dr. Osler— "And so he quietly dropped the seed that dominated all my future work," and on the last words of her autobiography—"Sir William Osler, whose keen interest in my work and broad human sympathy pierced the veil of my youthful shyness with a personal stimulus that aroused my intellect to its most passionate endeavour." Her editorship of the Osler memorial material and the compilation of a complete Osler bibliography were clearly labors of love.

Maude Abbott had at least one other interesting relationship with a man and that was with her half-brother, the Reverend Harry M. Babin of Dixon, Illinois. He was a child of her errant father's second marriage and they came into contact around 1916 when she was in her late forties. A married man with a family, he visited St. Andrews where he was apparently not well received by the Abbotts. Maude, however, began a correspondence with him and parts of this remain, at least fifty-two of his letters to her between 1916 and 1920. In the beginning these communications were mundane affairs, but for about two years they became more frequent (arriving every few days) and more personal; then they lapsed again into formality. Both Maude and Harry seemed to have found a kindred spirit, someone in whom to confide and especially someone to whom they could speak of their father. He said, "I think it will give you greater peace to be reconciled to your father and to learn many of his good qualities."[25] She must have found expression for long-pent emotions.

Their letters had an intensely passionate quality, which probably would have surprised people who knew Dr. Abbott but which is clearly revealed in his words at the height of the exchange, words that must have responded to hers:

August 30, 1916

My dearest Maude

. . . That you should think of me so kindly and deeply moves all that is good in me to never disappoint but always strive to realize your good opinion and love. . . . Yet the better part in me responds gladly and strongly to your affection and goodwill and you mean very much to my happiness and peace. . . . I know that your sisterly love and interest act as a stimulating influence in my work even at this time and will continue to help elevate and beautify all life for me. It is such a precious thing in this world to find a disinterested love that I prize it above all things. . . .

Your loving brother
Harry[26]

There is no trace of this friendship in Maude Abbott's "Autobiographical Sketch." It was a very private and personal matter and, when the correspondence faltered, she must have felt a great sense of loss and renewed loneliness.

Despite the report that almost all the photographs in her rooms were of men of medicine, Dr. Abbott's relationship with women was also cordial. She kept in touch with a great network of female friends from McGill College days and was welcomed by women acquaintances wherever she traveled. She did not forget that women had supported her career—from her grandmother, to her teachers Miss Symmers and Miss Smith, to the rich matrons of Montreal who wanted to help her study medicine, to Grace Ritchie who had advised her how to get her ticket of admission to the hospital wards, to Dr. Helen MacMurchy (cofounder with Maude Abbott and National Corresponding Secretary of the Canadian Federation of Medical Women) who thought she ought to be a Fellow of the Royal Society of Canada.[27]

Though she worked for many years in an all-male environment, she did not—as others in her situation have sometimes tended to do—join the patriarchy and become condescending to members of her own sex. Among her closest friends were such avowed feminists as Dr. Grace Ritchie England and Professor Carrie Derick[28] who both worked for the female franchise, birth control, and social reform. Her own efforts at liberation were more specifically confined to matters of her own immediate concern; she had little time for more. An editorial in a Montreal newspaper at the time of her death declared that she was "never what is popularly known as a 'feminist.' And yet she did much to advance the emancipation of women from the shackles of all sorts of limitations and prohibitions from which they suffered."[29] It is clear where her sympathies lay from a note to her by a former chairman of pathology announcing his engagement, "Won't it delight you to think that I am allying myself with an advanced feminist."[30] And when she was elected as the first woman member of the Osler Society, the secretary said, "I thought that invitation would fetch you home and right glad am I that you have succeeded in smashing and crashing one of our last anti-feminist gates."[31]

Contributions to feminism may take many forms and very rarely do they have the violent aspects stereotypically ascribed to them. Dr. Abbott's feminist activities included energetic efforts on behalf of the Association for the Professional Education of Women in the late 1880s; helping to professionalize the curriculum of the Graduate School For Nurses, stimulating pride in that "female" profession and praising the heroism of Florence Nightingale; appointing a fine team of women when she had the opportunity at Philadelphia; and her own professional achievements. She also did what she could to help women students get into the McGill Faculty of Medicine—but since she had no voice in faculty affairs could not directly affect policy decisions. When women were finally admitted she was entirely supportive. One member of the first graduating class of 1922 remembered appreciatively how she hosted a celebration:

> Dr. Abbott was very proud that her beloved Alma Mater was at last bestowing the medical degree on five women undergraduates and I do not believe she ever exhibited one of her rare congenital cardiac specimens with more enthusiasm than she displayed over her human exhibit that day.[32]

Later, she organized the Women's Medical Society and helped in many practical ways to make it function. One of the first winners of the Maude Abbott Scholarship recalled that her acquaintance with Dr. Abbott began when she was asked to accompany Abbott to the society's annual banquet. She said:

> I dreaded the prospect wholeheartedly, as one would dread being the official entertainer of any public monument. To my surprise and pleasure, Dr. Abbott was not at all monumental; she was, indeed, a delightful companion who did not wait to be entertained but contributed generously to the enjoyment of us all.[33]

She and her peers recognized that Dr. Abbott was one of the pioneers who had made the younger scholars' path through medicine much less thorny than her own had been.

And, of course, the one person in her life to whom Maude Abbott was inextricably bound was her invalid sister Alice. Throughout her very busy career, despite serious financial problems, regardless of health difficulties of her own, she always managed to find some time to visit St. Andrews, to send gifts, and to reply to Alice's letters. These communications add to the massive amount of evidence from many sources that Maude Abbott was generous, affectionate, and kind, or, as one admirer put it, "a beneficent tornado" who was constantly on the move, helping, giving parties, writing letters. The flurry of keeping up with friends near and far, old and new, contributed to her busyness but did not entirely disguise the fact that she lived alone in Montreal nor that she seemed to have had no constant close companion and confidant ·with whom to share her troubles, frustrations, and triumphs.

Pioneering women professors in coeducational institutions, or any milieu where they first braved entry to a male domain, were by definition intruders, outsiders, not of the mainstream. Where they were few

in number, they were bound to miss out on personally and professionally enriching collegiality; they could not belong to the "old-boy network." Yet some were grateful, some proud, some humble, some felt
a sense of wonder, a feeling of disbelief that they had actually made it
into the university. They felt their difference even as they chose to
ignore it and concentrate on the task at hand. Their male colleagues felt
it, too, and quite frequently codified the gap with differential regulations of various kinds. Dr. Abbott's experience in being grudgingly employed by a university was not unique but rather reflected a willingness
of patriarchal institutions to accept females when there were exceptional circumstances. Limitations imposed on these exceptional women
no doubt reduced the precedent-setting effect they might otherwise
have had.[34] She was the victim of standard ploys of dominant males,
subjected to "teasing": tricks that belittle the victim, fail to take her
seriously, and are very difficult to counteract. A contemporary witness
attests that Maude Abbott did, indeed, encounter much of this kind of
thing:

> One of [Dr. Shepherd's] favourite jokes was to begin an argument on
> some technical point, and when he had her fully aroused, he would grad-
> ually back to the door, and standing at it would fire his final shot: "Woman!
> Ugh—simply undifferentiated Man!" And out he would go laughing, while
> Maude vainly strove to find a suitably crushing reply.[35]

It is highly unlikely that he treated his male junior colleagues in this
way.

Irrelevant distinctions based on gender are particularly difficult for
young women to manage; older women may suffer less. Aging can have
its compensations through a growth in self-confidence, a stronger sense
of identity, and perhaps a recognition that much of the academic poli-
ticking that goes on does not really matter—and also that it can ad-
versely affect men as well as women. As Maude Abbott grew older, she
acquired a degree of acceptance in the Faculty of Medicine, a special
niche; she developed into a personality and then became something of
a character. The adjectives used to describe her changed from "plucky,"
"brilliant," "aggressive," and "touchy" in youth to "gregarious," "in-
defatigable," "generous," "lovable," and "impossible" in later life. Over
the years, she became busier, more short-sighted, more financially
pressed, had more correspondence to keep up, had more difficulty dividing her time between Montreal and St. Andrews, had less time for
herself and less concern for her personal appearance—for whether there
were a stain on the front of her dress or if the hem of her skirt were

held by safety pins. The inevitable student-endowed sobriquet, "Maudie," she considered irksome and undignified at first, but came to accept as a sometime replacement for "Dr. Abbott"—though she still resented it when colleagues called her "Miss." Anecdotes were told about her—some of which she happily contributed. A limerick was spun:

> There was a young lady named Maude
> Who was a most terrible fraud.
> She never was able to eat at the table
> But out in the pantry—Oh Lord![36]

She became known as a terror for coopting students to run her errands or perform "small" tasks, so that they sometimes took to hiding in the bathroom when they saw her approaching.[37]

She also became more absent-minded and accident-prone. These accidents caused her physical pain and self-scrutiny reminiscent of her youthful, insecure self. Following a close call with a taxi, she wrote in her diary:

> I have stood in the valley of the shadow and [was] almost killed. What a strange, awe-inspiring thought. A little more speed of the taxi, a little variation in the angle at which it struck me and the world would have swung on without me. The bright, beautiful world so full of people I care for and who care for me. Was it a warning against carelessness? Oh, my dear, *what* do you believe?[38]

The strategies for survival are many. Becoming a character, embracing a mild form of eccentricity is one of them—especially when, from the beginning, one is deemed to be deviant or different and when the orthodox route to advancement is blocked. If Maude Abbott became slightly eccentric, it is no wonder. She worked in a very ambivalent professional world where she was greatly admired but still remained "other." She was both larger than life and lesser; world famous and a figure of fun. She had support from significant men in high places—especially Osler—but she did not have a mentor, a champion who fought all the way for her, pressing her case for promotion. She was given important but relatively small opportunities which she herself transformed into major accomplishments. Yet, in one of the host of affectionate and respectful tributes published after her death on September 2, 1940, Charles Martin, who had first brought her back into the McGill orbit to do research, wrote that she was "a scholar at McGill who, with but few exceptions, had greater international repute and contacts than anyone in the Canadian profession," that she was a person with "vivid personality, with engaging traits of character to give an example to future generations."[39] Ultimately, despite the ambivalence, there can be no serious doubt that Maude E. Abbott was genuinely different, special, an extraordinary woman who made a significant contribution to medicine and higher education.

Notes

1. Stanley B. Frost, "The Abbotts of McGill," *McGill Journal of Education* 13, no. 3 (Fall 1978): 264.
2. Maude Abbott, Diary, Osler History of Medicine Library Archives, accession #438/34.
3. See Margaret Gillett, *We Walked Very Warily: A History of Women at McGill* (Montreal: Eden Press, 1981), chap. 2.
4. McGill University Archives, Maude Abbott papers, MG1070, container 4.
5. It required a formal agreement between the faculty and the university in 1905 to bring Medicine fully into the administrative mainstream.
6. The Montreal *Gazette,* for example, reported on the movement for women's medical education sympathetically and on March 27, 1889 editorialized, "There are few to-day who question the wisdom of giving women the opportunity of studying medicine. . . . The outcome of the movement will be watched with interest and with many hopes for its success."
7. "Women and Medicine—A Meeting in the Interest of Their Medical Education," Montreal *Gazette,* 24 April 1889.
8. Elizabeth Shortt Smith, *Historical Sketch of Medical Education of Women, Kingston, Canada* (Ottawa: private printing, 1916), p.11.
9. Quoted by H. E. MacDermot in *Maude Abbott: A Memoir* (Toronto: Macmillan, 1940), p. 50.
10. Dr. Harold Segall, a renowned cardiac specialist and quondam student of Dr. Abbott, wrote in a private communication to the author dated 84.07.25, "When I met her in St. Andrews in 1936—and discussed the illness with Maudie—the diagnosis was manic depressive psychosis."
11. When the paper of Osler's letter threatened to wear out, Dr. Francis, curator of the Osler History of Medicine Library, had it bound for her on condition that she leave it to the library. It is accession #9545.
12. Members of three consecutive classes (1902–1904) expressed their appreciation by presenting her with gifts. While this gesture must be applauded, it should not obscure the fact that Dr. Abbott gave very demanding courses for no pay other than a small "purse" or book tokens.
13. As reported by MacDermott in *Maude Abbott.*
14. See Jessie Boyd Scriver, "Maude E. Abbott," in *The Clear Spirit: Twenty*

Canadian Women and Their Times, ed. Mary Quale Innis (Toronto: Canadian Federation of University Women/University of Toronto Press, 1967), p.142.

15. Maude Abbott to Dr. F. Owen Stredder, Bursar, McGill University, 20 December 1935, Osler Library Archives, #606.

16. "Honorary M.D.: Unusual Degree to be Conferred on Lady Doctor," Montreal *Witness,* 13 May 1910, McGill University Scrapbook #2, p. 325.

17. Abbott to Professor J. G. Adami (chairman of pathology), n.d., quoted by MacDermot, *Maude Abbott,* p.67.

18. Abbott to Colonel J. G. Adami, 3 August 1918, Osler Library Archives, #606.

19. Abbott to Principal A. E. Morgan, McGill University, 5 November 1935, Osler Library Archives, #606.

20. Abbott to Principal A. E. Morgan, November 1935, Osler Library Archives, #606.

21. Stanley B. Frost, McGill University: *For the Advancement of Learning, 1801-1895.* Vol. 1 (Montreal: McGill-Queen's Press, 1980), p.170.

22. In 1905, when McGill took over Bishop's Faculty of Medicine and Dentistry (the school from which Maude Abbott received her M.D.) there was an agreement that all Bishop's' graduates would automatically be accorded McGill degrees. *This was honored in the case of the men but not of the eligible women.* See Frost, *For the Advancement of Learning,* pp. 44–45 and n. 28, pp. 57–58.

23. Abbott, "Autobiographical Sketch," *McGill Medical Journal* 28, no. 3 (October 1959): 152.

24. H. E. MacDermot, "Dr. Maude Abbott," *McGill News* 22, no. 2 (Winter 1940): 21.

25. Harry M. Babin to Maude Abbott, 19 September 1916, Osler Library Archives #438/52.

26. Harry M. Babin to Maude Abbott, 30 August 1916, Osler Library Archives, #438/52.

27. Dr. Helen MacMurchy to Abbott, 17 January 1934, Osler Library Archives, #438/34.

28. Carrie Derick was also a McGill graduate of 1890, and somehow closer to the life of the university. Her career at McGill in the Faculty of Arts was more successful than Abbott's in Medicine. She advanced from demonstrator in botany, 1891, to lecturer in 1895, to assistant professor in 1904 and, in 1912, to professor. She was the first woman full professor in all Canada. There is no indication that Maude Abbott was envious of her old classmate's academic progress.

29. *Montreal Daily Star,* 3 September 1940.

30. Dr. George Adami, Vice-Chancellor, University of Liverpool, to Abbott, 14 February 1922, Osler Library Archives, #604.

31. Dr. William Francis to Abbott, 28 January 1973, McGill University Archives, #1058/86.

32. Scriver in *The McGill You Knew,* ed. Edgar Andrew Collard (Toronto: Longman, 1976), p.135.

33. Elizabeth MacKay, "Dr. Abbott and the Students," *McGill Medical Journal* 10 (1940): 48.

34. Women were excluded from the McGill Faculty Club until 1936. Maude Abbott was the first to break this barrier. A room was named in her honor in 1984.

35. MacDermot, *Maude Abbott*, pp. 80–81.

36. Courtesy of Dr. Edward Bensley, former Dean of Medicine, McGill University.

37. Ibid.

38. Abbott, diary entry, 7 November 1929, written in the Ross Pavilion, Royal Victoria Hospital, Montreal. McGill University Archives.

39. Dr. C. F. Martin, Emeritus Dean of Medicine, McGill University, "Maude Abbott—An Appreciation," *McGill Medical Journal* 10 (1940): 29, 32.

---

1. EXCERPTS FROM AN "AUTOBIOGRAPHICAL SKETCH"

Had it not been for an invitation to speak to the Women's Medical Society of McGill, Maude Abbott might never had gotten around to writing down recollections of her early life. We are fortunate that she prepared her "Autobiographical Sketch" for presentation to that group on March 31, 1928. History can be preserved by such apparently insignificant events.

Just the other day, in clearing out a certain cupboard, I came upon an old diary of my sister's into which she had thoughtfully pasted many years ago, some newspaper cuttings giving an account of an attempt which I made when in my third year in Arts at McGill, now nearly forty years ago, to obtain admission to the Faculty of Medicine as an undergraduate student. This old account has brought the facts before me so vividly that I thought it might be of interest to you to accompany me back in a bird's eye view across the past in a brief autobiographical retrospect.

Brought up in the country by my beloved grandmother, and educated with my only sister entirely at home except for one year in Montreal at Miss Symmers and Smith School, I was fortunate in that this school was for the first time sending up a class to McGill for the June Associate in Arts examination, as the matriculation was then called. I had been very unevenly prepared in the country, well up in French and history and literature, and yet knowing nothing whatever of Latin or algebra or geometry and very little of arithmetic; but I was consumed by a great thirst for the school work, and hurled myself into it with a tremendous zest, with a result that I was so fortunate as to win the Scholarship into McGill from that school. Had it not been for this happening, I should probably not be here today, for an Arts education for a girl was at that time considered a quite unnecessary luxury and it was exceedingly difficult for me to be spared a second year from home. But Miss Symmers wanted her first scholarship taken up for the honour of her school, so pressure was brought to bear at home, and I was permitted to come. Accordingly I came down (this was in the middle of September 1885), the plan being that I was to enter upon my first year in Arts and engage rooms for us all, where my grandmother and sister were to join me for the winter, in October. I had been just three weeks in Arts and all our winter's arrangements were made when I was obliged to give it up and return to St. Andrews. That was the time of the great smallpox epidemic in Montreal, and my dear grandmother was anxious and decided not to come, leaving me free to do as I thought best. It was a great struggle. I had just begun Greek, and the University life seemed to me to have opened the gates of Paradise, but by all the laws of fair play it was my "turn" to stay at home and let my sister come down when the epidemic had abated, and this was what did come to pass. That quiet winter at St. Andrews was not altogether fruitless however, for a kind old friend in the City sent me the modern Greek Textbooks and our own old Anglican clergyman coached me in this subject all winter long. Our lessons were mostly from the Greek Testament and interwoven with much sound doctrine. "ava, my dear", he would say, "means upward, $\tau\rho\epsilon\pi\omega$, I turn, $\omega\pi a$, my face, $av\theta\rho\omega\pi o\Sigma$, a man turns his face upward to God." "See that you do likewise." While for Latin I had the Presbyterian minister, also a very ancient man. "We will begin our lesson, my dear," he would say, "by kneeling together in prayer," and so we did.

This was the reason that although I matriculated in 1885, I did not actually embark on my Arts course until the session 1886–1887, and so graduated in 1890 with the third class of women in Arts from McGill. My three weeks in the first year in 1885 gave me at first a certain advantage over my fellow Freshmen who, consequently, elected me President, a post I retained until my final year. At that time we were called the Donalda Department of McGill after Sir Donald A. Smith, later Lord Strathcona, who had just given his first endowment for the higher education of women at McGill, and we were housed in that part of the Arts Building which [was] . . . called the East Wing, and we thought it a palace. Very enthusiastic we all were, but I think perhaps I, who was

country-bred, and had not had my fill of school or directed study before I entered Arts, felt our new advantage most acutely of us all. I was
literally in love with McGill, or so the girls said, and I have never really
fallen out of love with her since. I mention this because I think it best
explains all that happened since.

Being as we were the third class of women to graduate from McGill,
we helped to make our little page of history, for our nine members
raised the women students to twenty and that was a large enough number to organize from. During the four years I was in Arts, we helped
our seniors of class '88 to found the Delta Sigma Debating Society (in
1888) and in our last Session 1889–90, we ourselves founded a religious
society, which is now the College Y.W.C.A., but which we called our
Theo Dora or Gifts to God Society. A few weeks after our graduation
in June 1890, we got together and organized a Soup Kitchen on Jurors
Street for factory and working girls, which we and the accruing band
of Women Graduates maintained as such for a number of years, and
which finally became the University Settlement; and we banded ourselves at this time as the future McGill Alumnae Society.

As an undergraduate I was Editor for the Donaldas of the *McGill
Fortnightly,* then our only college publication, and a hectic time I had.
Arts, Science, and the Donalda Editors, the latter being I, united in a
vote of censure against the Editor-in-Chief, who was a graduate in Arts
but an undergraduate in Medicine, because he insisted in putting in over
the heads of the Editorial Board what we and our constituencies considered over-broad medical jokes. Many a time have I mounted the stair
in the East Wing to hear some such words as: "Father says he is not
going to let us have the *Fortnightly* in the house; there's another medical joke in it this morning." The men in Arts and Science also objected
to certain Editorials which appeared without having been submitted,
favouring the views of Medicine which were usually agog with those
of the other Faculties rather than Arts. Our Editor-in-Chief, however,
was impervious to our reprimands; he failed to resign and repeated the
offence, and we three resigned in a body, whereat he and his junior
medical editor triumphantly brought out the last number of the Session
alone. From this I learned a lesson I have never forgotten, which is that
to resign one's office is to abandon one's trust, and therefore any other
form of protest is to be preferred to withdrawal from office, if one
really cares for the work it represents.

I was Class Valedictorian too, a matter which was a more serious
undertaking then than now, for the men and women in Arts graduated
with Science . . . and we read our three valedictories (which had been
strictly censored the day before by the Principal Sir William Dawson

and all references not completely in accord with the then University policy, sternly deleted), in open Convocation. They were published in the May number of the *University Gazette* of that year and I would like to quote some paragraphs from my own if only to show how seriously we took ourselves, and how deeply we sensed our relationship to the School that had admitted us within her sacred precincts. It began,—

> As we stand together here on the vantage ground of our Graduation day looking backward over the past and forward over the future, the one supreme thought that comes to us out of the kaleidoscope of memory and hope is that of this mysterious *work*. To what it ultimately tends we know not, but we press forward in it to this the mark of our high calling. Work is fundamental to the onward march of science, it is at the bottom of every great and good action that was ever done, it underlies the foundation of all true character; and it is the sin of idleness that is to be counted as the deadliest, just because it chokes, with the stifling pressure of stagnation, every noble deed and eventually, every holy inspiration.

And it ended

> . . . It is with full hearts that we turn to repeat the word to our Alma Mater herself. But surely, there is no need (of vain repetitions here). The *"ego polliceor"* that we have just vowed is still vibrating on the air; and can we ever dream of ceasing to love and cherish and reverence, of ceasing to keep holy and undefiled the memory of that University that has made us her own children. Let us be still, and let our whole future life-work prove that from our hearts far more than from our lips, arises to our Alma Mater a wish that is a prayer "Farewell."

Owing to my domestic conditions, which were those of a very small family circle, it was impossible for me to remain away from home for two consecutive years. Accordingly, after my first year in Arts our little household moved into the city. Owing to illness at home I was obliged to drop my Classics honour course in my third year, but as I had had Greek throughout, I was able to qualify in the final year for the Lord Stanley gold medal, which I won. Of the five medals awarded that year, the nine girls in Arts '90 got three, and very proud of each other we were.

But what about medicine? The idea of studying it was not in the first place my own. My childhood "best friend," now Mrs. C. H. Eastlake, who is by the way one of our leading Canadian artists to-day, said to me during my second year in Arts, as we sat one day together in the fields at her home in Almonte. "What are you going to do when you leave College?" "I never thought about it," said I. "If I weren't an artist," said she, "I would be a doctor. It's a lovely life. So human and full of people." I came home and said to my grandmother, "May I be a doctor?" "Dear child," said she, "you may be anything you like." This was not a full decision, however, and I thought and spoke of the plan only in a desultory way, my great desire at that time being to remain on as a student at McGill. At the end of my second year, in May 1888, when the first class of women graduated, their valedictorian Octavia Ritchie, afterwards Dr. Grace Ritchie England, who was my very dear friend, made a stirring plea for the admission of women to medicine at McGill. The authorities were however strongly opposed to co-education and the matter rested there. Then, in my third year (1889), some kind ladies in the city, of rather advanced views, hearing that I wanted to study medicine, sent for me and offered to support any step I might take in the matter, and even undertook to go with me to call upon some of the leading doctors, to ascertain their views. The result was that I did send in, on February 12th, 1889, with the approval of some of the physicians who were more or less sympathetic or rather, not unfriendly, the following petition which I quote from the newspaper cutting above referred to.

"To the Dean and Faculty of Medicine of McGill University:

I, the undersigned, having decided upon adopting the medical profession, and being desirous of obtaining the necessary instruction in Montreal, do hereby petition the Dean and Faculty of Medicine that some provisions be made to this end. And I further most earnestly pray that the said provision be made for the approaching session of the college year, 1889–90.

I would solicit an early reply to this petition.

I am, yours respectfully,
Maude E. Abbott.

111 Union Avenue, Feb. 12th, 1889.

Shortly thereafter some of these lay friends, who were interested, formed themselves into a Society which they called the "Association for the Professional Education of Women" (A.P.E.W.), and they also petitioned the Faculty to consider my request favorably, to inform them what requirements financial and otherwise would be needed for our admission (for there were now two of us), and they pledged themselves to raise whatever funds were considered necessary to meet these, and to this end asked for a conference. The Faculty granted this, and a deputation from it met representatives of the A.P.E.W. and us two petitioners, but the Faculty finally ruled that it was impossible for them to consider the subject favorably at the present time. This was in the autumn of 1889.

Shortly after my graduation in Arts, in 1890, I had a message from the Medical Faculty of the University of Bishops College (a small school . . . which was more or less in rivalry with McGill, but whose students had their hospital work from the McGill Teaching Staff at the Montreal General Hospital), informing me that it contemplated opening its doors to women the following autumn and that three women had already enrolled themselves, and inviting me to do so. Dr. Ritchie (a graduate of the first class in Arts from McGill) then in her Third Year at Queens in Kingston was one of the three enrolled for her final year at Bishops, and September found me there a medical undergraduate in my first year. Those were dark days. No longer within the walls of my beloved McGill, among rough students, many of whom seemed to me to have lower standards than those among which we had worked together for the pure love of the working, and struggling, as only a first year student in medicine does struggle, with the bare bones of anatomy,—it was a dreary round. . . . Before the end of my first year, however, in the spring of 1891, I was warned by Miss Ritchie to apply at once for my student's perpetual ticket for the Montreal General Hospital, and *to pay the money down immediately,* and I accordingly did, that same day, pay in my $20.00 for a perpetual ticket, which was duly receipted; but my hospital ticket, which had to be issued later by the Committee of Management, did not come to me. Miss Ritchie (whose brother the late Dr. Arthur Ritchie was a fellow graduate of Dr. Osler's from McGill and a friend of the men in power), had already walked the wards throughout the session 1890–91, with success and popularity, but some of her old fellow-students at Queens had written in, asking for permission to attend the summer session, and the Committee of Management saw with alarm that they had taken a step that might open the flood gates for an ill-considered innovation, and they had accordingly actually ruled that no more tickets should be issued to women students, so that, in spite of the fact that my $20.00 had been paid in and acknowledged, the matter was still in abeyance and my ticket withheld. It was now July of 1891, and I was beginning to lay my plans to go to Philadelphia,* when the newspaper storm broke. It was the time for the payment of annual subscriptions to the Montreal General Hospital, and the situation had

*To attend the Women's Medical College, founded in 1849, the oldest medical institution for women in North America.

somehow got through to the consciousness of the Governors, and a number of these . . . quite spontaneously and entirely as a matter of fair play, took up the cudgels on my behalf, saying it was unfair to refuse a ticket for hospital attendance to me, an Arts graduate of McGill of good standing, when this privilege had just been accorded my fellow graduate Miss Ritchie and in no way abused by her; and they refused to pay in their subscriptions until a ticket had been issued also to me. The papers were again full of the pros and cons of the situation, of the "poor little men-students" who were about to be invaded and who needed protection from the "great big lady student," who was about to descend on them if allowed, but on the whole they were quite favourable to the cause of women in medicine. I felt the publicity of it, both then and earlier, greatly, and it made me very unhappy. I felt quite sure that none of importance in my world would ever want to speak to me again after all this newspaper exposure, and indeed I think many people did probably think of me askance and blame me as too young a woman to be flaunted in the papers so. In the middle of it all one day by mail at St. Andrews the ticket suddenly reached me. The battle had been suddenly won for me entirely in absentia, by men I had never known or seen. But a Resolution had been passed by the Committee of Management that no other tickets for hospital attendance were to be issued to women students.

During the next three sessions I was in full attendance at all the M.G.H. clinics that were open to McGill and Bishops students. I was the only woman, for Miss Ritchie had graduated, and a Miss Fyffe to whom a second ticket really was allowed through the influence of the late Dr. Kirkpatrick, did not attend the Third and Fourth Year clinics. I enjoyed the work greatly and on the whole I was very kindly treated, but I was more or less at a disadvantage, for I was rarely quizzed or called down on the floor, and there were painful moments in the operating room, when I had to decide for myself whether or not it was best to leave the room for certain operations not attended by the nurses, the thought of which still gives me a tingle of embarrassment. Of all the teachers, Dr. Shepherd was the kindest to me in a practical way, for he often let me assist in operations on my cases, or would reward what he regarded as a well worked-up case report by allotting me extra beds, taking them away for this purpose from "that fellow who is never here when he is wanted." I had as many as four beds at a time under him. On the other hand he took a delight in plaguing me by such announcements as "I have to let you out early today gentlemen to attend a meeting we're having to keep out those troublesome lady-students." The stamping and applause that greeted such a remark as this was the only unchivalrous act on the part of the men which I remember. A number of them had been my fellow graduates in Arts, and I used to look longingly across at them, but I was now in an alien school, and I think over-sensitive, and somehow, we did not grow intimate; and I was very lonely.

I graduated in Medicine in 1894, winning the Senior Anatomy Prize, and the Chancellor's Prize for the best examination in the final branches, and in July following, sailed with my sister for Europe, my dear grandmother then having died on December 12th, 1890. The Captain was an old family friend and we sat one on each side of him at the table, but they called us the Infants of the Ship, for we had never travelled before, and yet we were bound for Heidelberg, and after that, we knew not whither. But Vienna was at that time the Mecca of the Postgraduate, and our idea was first to learn German in a less expensive locality and then go there. We had a month first in London with old friends, and Professor Moyse, who had crossed with us, had given me a card of introduction to Sir Victor Horsley, then at University College and Queens Square Hospital. Between him and facilities provided by the London School of Medicine for Women, I had all the medical sight-seeing I could carry. Sir Victor was very good to us, had us at the house for lunch, got us tickets for admission to the House of Lords, and sent me notices for his daily private operations. On the morning of the day we left for the Continent, I attended one of these operations and after it went up to him to say goodbye. "Did you say you are going to Heidelberg?" he said; and when we arrived there, a week later, I found a letter from him addressed to me *Poste restante,* containing introductions from him, to Czerny the great surgeon, Erb the great neurologist, and Hoffmann the medico-legal expert. As I was at that time steering for gynaecology (or so I thought) and as this meant a knowledge of surgery, I decided to follow Czerny, and I went to his operations daily. The very evening of the first morning I spent in his operating room, all Heidelberg was astir with joy because he had just refused a call to Vienna to succeed the great Billroth. In his honour the students held a *Fackelzug,* or torchlight procession, marching before his house and cheering him sword in hand, after which they marched to the *Studentenplatz* which lay just under the walls of the beautiful castle, and danced their sword dance, striking their swords above their heads to the tune of the song they sung together . . . and ending by throwing their swords together in a heap in the middle of the *Platz.* This was a great sight that met our unaccustomed eyes in the streaming moonlight; for our kindly hostesses of the Pension Caemmerer steered us so that we saw it all.

Three weeks in Heidelberg and one in Bern (where I saw the great Kocher operate) and six in Interlaken, and then September 1894 saw us in Zurich, where I matriculated into the University (since this admitted women) for the winter session, while my sister settled down to music at the conservatorium. As is usual abroad we found old friends there and had a cosy apartment and a happy winter. I concentrated on pathology, for which purpose I got a place in Prof. Ribbert's laboratory, and struggled there alone and with very little personal supervision over my first microscopic sections, almost the only help he gave me being *"Zeichnen Sie, Fräulein,"* "draw, draw *everything* you see under your microscope"; but I followed his wonderful courses to the students on combined gross and microscopic pathology with great interest and profit; and I concentrated also on gynaecology . . . with Prof. Wyder, in which capacity my still insufficient grasp of the language brought me up against various difficulties, but he was extraordinarily kind throughout, and in the end opened the way to Vienna by introducing me to Wertheim there. I also followed Forel (Charcot's great co-worker in hypnotism) in his lectures on nervous and mental diseases, and had a neuropathology laboratory course with the distinguished von Monakow and I learnt to use the ophthalmoscope on rabbits' eyes, and had a special course in otolaryngology.

At last, in March 1895, we reached Vienna, and remained there or in the vicinity nearly two years. I began my medical work with the post-graduate courses in gynaecology and obstetrics, taking two in each subject to make up for my lack of student experience, at least in gynaecology. In the obstetrics courses, we followed the regular schedule then in vogue, which consisted in spending three days and nights on the Schanta *Gebärklinik* where we were accommodated with flea-infested beds, and were given a part in the many cases that came off, under the able, though it seemed to us cold-blooded tutelage of Dr. Wertheim, at that time a *Privat-Docent;* then came three days' intermission and then three days on duty again . . . [The best] of three sets of courses in internal medicine open to women were Dr. Ortner's, the other courses admitting men only, not because these teachers objected to taking women, but because the "Americans" who were responsible for filling the places in them had made this ruling. Each course was shared by six postgraduate students who paid 20 guldens apiece for 20 bedside quiz clinics given by the Docent, and his methods were of the best. All that could be got from the patient by inspection and palpation we had to glean before proceeding further, and often from the character of the pulse and other general features we had so narrowed the field by exclusion, that the diagnosis jumped out at one as soon as the main facts of the case were exposed. As soon as one internal medicine course ended, another by the same teacher began, and once one had secured a "place" one usually held it throughout one's stay in Vienna, either taking it along with other courses, or when one needed the time for other work, putting in a substitute who paid for it while he used it, and yielded it up again at request. This very convenient arrangement gave the advantage to those who had been longest in Vienna, or who had had friends there before their arrival, for the Docent cared not at all who was there so long as he was paid, and it was quite easy for old members to get control of other "places," and hand them to friends on their arrival. It is readily seen that such a system might undergo abuse, and I believe a time did arrive later when "Chicago" held one course and "Boston" another, and an outsider could not get in at all. But in my time it was merely a convenience, and at least in the Ortner courses everyone was friendly and obliging. When we arrived we found two old Montreal friends there, Dr. W. F. Hamilton and Dr. George Mathewson, who were nearing the end of a winter's stay, and Dr. Hamilton got me a "place" immediately in one of Ortner's courses, and explained the value of it to me, so that I owe it to him that I held it during the entire 22 months I was in Vienna, either filling it myself or by substitutes, who were always to be obtained. Thus it came about also that when in September 1896, four old fellow graduates of mine in Arts . . . arrived unexpectedly for three months work, I "owned" no less than four places in Ortner's courses that had been handed over to me by departing friends, and was therefore able to "place" all four men immediately, with a result that they gave me a grand Christmas dinner at the Riedhof with an invitation addressed to me as the "President of the Montreal Medico-Chirurgical Society of Vienna" (a pleasant harbinger as women had not yet been admitted to the Medical Society at home), at which there were presents for everyone and many promises of mutual good will and good fellowship were exchanged.

    In the same way, the gross pathology which was given once or twice weekly by Kolisko on all the accumulated material and was simply magnificent (no other word applies) was always attended by practically all the post-graduates throughout their stay in Vienna. We had splendid courses, too, from Albrecht in pathological histology which gave us a good outline and sent us home with a fine collection of slides. The two courses which I followed with him I had the pleasure of sharing with Dr. A. S. Warthin of Ann Arbor, and laid there the foundation of a friendship that has lasted since. I had many other courses, neurology . . . , neuro-pathology . . . , bacteriology . . . (and myself got diphtheria), blood diseases . . . , otolaryngology, ophthalmology and the rest . . . but it was the grounding I obtained into internal medicine and pathology from Ortner and Kolisko and Albrecht that determined my bent, and made possible my later work at McGill.

In the spring of 1897, en route at last for home, I passed the examination at Edinburgh for the Triple Qualification Licentiate . . . and I interned as locum tenens for a short time in a small Woman's Hospital at Glasgow, where the new Listerian methods of asepsis were followed in one surgical ward, while the old pre-Listerian practices of sluicing out the abdomen with tap water were practiced in the other (to my great consternation), and later during the summer I served as Clinical Assistant for three months in the great City Asylum at Birmingham. Returning to Montreal in September 1897, I set up my office and door plate at 156 Mansfield Street in the November following, next door but one to Dr. Shepherd, upon whom I left a card with some trepidation. A few weeks later I had occasion to call him in consultation on a case of stone in the kidney, and he operated on my patient, and has ever since been one of my best and kindest friends.

While in England I had joined the British Medical Association, and I had been in practice only a few weeks when I attended a meeting in Montreal at which Dr. James Stewart and Dr. Adami reported a case from the Royal Victoria Hospital of pigmentation cirrhosis in bronzed diabetes, the first in the English language, and the first in any literature in a woman. The tissue reaction is peculiar, in that the iron pigment reacts to ferrocyanide of potassium turning a bright Prussian blue (Perl's test). I had seen such a case in Albrecht's laboratory in Vienna and had the microscopic slides with me. I have them still. Next day, in walking through the college grounds I happened to meet Dr. Martin, who was Medical Superintendent of the Montreal General Hospital during the latter part of the time I was a student there. He stopped me with the question, "Are you practising here?" and when I said "Yes," he invited me to come up and work at the R.V.H.; whereupon I asked him if I might bring my slides of pigmentation cirrhosis and show them to Dr. Adami, and he made an appointment for me accordingly for the following day. When Dr. Adami saw my slides, he turned over the case of "Blue Mary," as it came to be called in the literature, to me to work up, while Dr. Martin set me to work from the clinical side on a statistical study on functional heart murmurs, based on the records in the Hospital since its opening some five years previously. I finished Dr. Martin's paper first, and he criticized it for me from Berlin, Germany, where he had gone for post-graduate work, and Dr. James Stewart read it for me (in Dr. Martin's absence in Germany, and as I could not present it myself not being a member), at the Medico-Chirurgical Society to which women had not yet been admitted. It was very well received and immediately after it had been read Dr. Adami proposed a resolution that women be admitted to membership in the Society, and nominated me for election to membership. This resolution, which had been proposed a year earlier on behalf of another medical woman and had then been turned down, was now carried practically unanimously, only one member voting against it. This happened on March 21st, 1898, and this article "On so-called Functional Heart-Murmurs" appeared in the *Montreal Medical Journal* for 1899, xxviii, 1 of that year.

The pigmentation-cirrhosis was a more extensive affair. As it was the first piece of pathological research I had ever done, Dr. Adami told me to work it over as completely as possible first, and after this was done, to make a survey of the literature. I accordingly wrote to Vienna for the full records of the case from which I had the slides, and they very kindly sent me material from two others with a paper by Kretz. . . . In the light of this article I proceeded to examine the livers from all the autopsies done at the R.V.H. since its origin five years before and to test those which showed pigment for haemosiderin, and incidentally I found it necessary to perfect the technique of Perl's test, which did not give a Prussian-blue reaction on formalin-preserved material unless the solutions were heated, and the hydrochloric acid used in excess of the ferrocyanide of potassium. In his work on haemosiderosis in copper poisoning Professor Mallory gives me credit for this point in its technique. It was nearly two years before this work, and my study of the literature, was finished, and meantime Dr. Opie of Baltimore brought out a study of a case that had occurred at Johns Hopkins. Fortunately, the fact that Drs. Stewart and Adami had made a brief report of our case at the Montreal meeting of the British Medical Association established its priority, but Opie's case has frequently been quoted by American writers (though never by English ones) as being the first in the English language. My article was ready for publication by December 1899, and it was presented for me by Sir Humphry Rolleston before the Pathological Society of London in January 1900, and published in its *Transactions,* and also in the *British Journal of Pathology and Bacteriology* in February 1900. I may add that it was the first communication ever made by a woman before that Society.

While this work was in progress, Dr. Adami set me to work also on a bacteriological problem, namely the possible transmutation in form of the colon bacillus under the action of certain serous effusions (ascitic fluid). Two papers were published by us on this work but no observation of any importance was made by me, partly I think because my own training in bacteriological technique was quite inadequate for any advanced problem of this kind. But I spent many harassing and hectic weeks trying to change a perfectly good colon bacillus with typical cultural features into a diplococcoid form by inoculating successive series of guinea-pigs and putting it through repeated changes of ascitic fluid media. This was the only really depressing bit of medical research I ever did.

In the summer of 1898 I had been appointed Assistant Curator of the McGill Medical Museum, and a year later to its Curatorship, Dr. Adami holding the title of Director as head of the Pathological Department. In January 1899 the Faculty sent me down to Washington and the other great centres in that vicinity to see museums, before embarking on my task of classifying and cataloguing the historical McGill collection and completing its teaching series. I went down with Dr. Wyatt Johnston's decimal classification in my hand (which I afterwards applied here) for discussion with other museum workers, and I carried a suggestion from him that I and the Curator of the Army Medical Museum at Washington should together try to organize a "Society of Curators" as none such existed. No action followed this suggestion at the time, but it led later to the development of the International Association of Medical Museums. On the way to Washington I stayed over at Baltimore and there for the first time I met Dr. Osler, and had the privilege of making rounds with him and a group of his students and physicians. Not only this, but he invited me to dinner at his house, and afterwards I was present at one of his famous student evenings, at which nine young men and two young women, his case-reporters at the Hospital, sat around the large dining-table, and I beside him at one end. After showing us all some rare first editions from early masters of medicine, and then discussing with them the problems and points of interest in their cases for the week, he turned suddenly upon me, as I sat there with my heart beating at the wonderful new world that had opened so unexpectedly before me, with the words: "I wonder, now, if you realize what a splendid opportunity you have in that McGill Museum. When you go home look up the article by Sir Jonathan Hutchinson on his "Clinical Museum," in the *British Medical Journal* for 1893. Pictures of life and death together,—wonderful, and then see what you can do." And so he quietly dropped the seed that dominated all my future work for very many years. . . .

Returning to Montreal from this rather strenuous and wholly stimulating trip, to the conflicting calls of a practice that had fallen somewhat into arrears through my absence, the multitudinous claims of a Museum collection that, in Dr. Ruttan's words at the time "needed a lover," and to personal problems of various kinds, I had a sort of nervous breakdown from worry and overtiredness, and was off work for some six months, and after that I gave myself up almost entirely to work in and upon the Museum collection, though for many years I still did some desultory practice, partly because I needed the money, and partly because of my desire to cling still to the clinical side which my time in Vienna had so endeared to me. This Museum work was very demanding and seemed at first a dreary and unpromising drudgery; but, as Dr. Osler had prophesied, it blossomed into wonderful things. Of these the most important as its immediate outcome were (1) the application of the Wyatt Johnston System of museum classification, (2) the museum teaching, and (3) the development of what I call the Osler catalogue. . . .

The museum teaching was a quite spontaneous development. As I came to know the specimens intimately, the students began dropping in and asking questions about them, and Dr. Adami, who as Professor of Pathology held the title also of Director of the Museum, put up a notice for the final year, stating that those students who wished to have the specimens demonstrated to them might arrange with me for this at hours mutually suitable. Very soon the entire final year had enrolled itself in groups which came weekly in rotation, so that I met every student once weekly in serial demonstrations which covered all the material that was worth studying by the end of the session. In 1902 I went again to Europe . . . and I took pathology courses with Vesterreich and others. I came home in August 1902 with fresh material for demonstrations and with the first edition of Kaufman's *Special Pathology,* which was exactly what we needed to answer the questions that arose in the course of the discussions from the informal nature of the "grind." Partly I think as a result of this, the demonstrations became in the next few years so popular that some of the best students would return every morning at 8 A.M. to go over again the same material. In 1902 and 1903 they had given me a purse in acknowledgment of the volunteer nature of these demonstrations, and in 1904 this was accompanied by a letter signed by the President and Secretary of the Class of warm appreciation which they said they felt it a duty to put on record before they graduated. This letter so impressed the Faculty that on account of this and other reasons they placed the museum demonstrations on the curriculum as a compulsory part of the course, and they remained so until 1922. . . .

In the year 1904 [Dr. Osler] came to the Museum for the first time in my Curatorship. I shall never forget him as I saw him walking down the old Museum towards me with his great dark burning eyes fixed full upon me. His delight that his own beloved specimens were being conserved and catalogued and their histories and references from the literature attached was very great and he insisted on being allowed to raise a sum for its publication. This the Faculty authorized him to do and he raised an amount sufficient to cover the estimated cost. . . . At this time too, he asked me to write up my museum teaching in an article which he sent for publication to the *Journal of the American Medical Association* where it appeared in 1905. In this year also the Faculty appointed me Governor's Fellow of Pathology, an appointment which I held for some five years.

Two other activities arose out of my work on the museum collection or rather upon one particular specimen in it. This was a remarkable cardiac anomaly, an adult heart with no ventricular septum, but a small supplementary cavity at its right upper angle, giving off the pulmonary artery. When I came across it in the year 1900, it was in a perfect state of preservation, but carried a label reading "Ulcerative Endocarditis." On the advice of Dr. Wyatt Johnston, I wrote Dr. Osler enquiring if he could inform me what it was. He replied that he had often demonstrated it to the students, that it was a special type of cor triloculare biatriatum, and that it had been reported by Dr. Andrew Holmes, first Dean of the Faculty, before the Edinburgh Medico-Chirurgical Society many years ago. After a little search I found the article in the *Transactions of the Edinburgh Medico-Chirurgical Society* for 1823, with a copper plate engraving of the heart. I republished this article with a description of the heart, and a little biographical sketch of Dr. Holmes in the *Montreal Medical Journal* for 1901. Next year the Faculty invited me to write up the New Medical Building of that year which was thrown open for the meeting of the Canadian Medical Association in 1902. I decided to embody this in an Historical Sketch of the Medical Faculty of McGill University and of its building and for this purpose spent some time in the Archives at Ottawa . . . , and I also had the benefit of the advice and assistance of the late Mr. William McLennan, Dr. Shepherd, and other authorities on the history of the School. The book was heavily illustrated too, at the request of the Faculty and the photographs taken for me by Notman at that time, of the founders of the School, from the oil painting in the old Faculty room, preserved them to posterity, for these original portraits were all burnt in the fire of 1907, and the ones now in the Assembly Hall were painted from my photographs. Moreover, . . . I published everything I had found in the Archives or elsewhere as an Appendix to the volume which was brought out as a special number of the *Montreal Medical Journal* for August 1902, and was distributed by the Faculty free to all the members of the Canadian Medical Association meeting. . . .

The other very important outcome of my early article on the Holmes heart was that in 1905 Dr. Osler invited me to write the section on Congenital Cardiac Disease in his new *System of Modern Medicine*. I asked him how to treat it, and he said, "Statistically." So I began on the *Transactions* of the Pathological Society of London and summarized all the cardiac anomalies there and from this passed to other articles until I had records of 412 cases with autopsies. I analyzed all the individual cases in large charts spaced for the special features and symptoms, which I had printed at the Gazette office, and finally I had a large mass of facts and figures from which to draw conclusions, with illustrations of many of the types of conditions drawn from our museum specimens. The work was not completed until December 1907, but that it was a great success is shown from the following beautiful letter which Sir William Osler wrote me when he had read the proof.

> Jan. 23rd, 1908.
> 13 Norham Gardens, Oxford.
>
> Dear Dr. Abbott:
>
> I knew you would write a good article but I did not expect one of such extraordinary merit. It is by far and away the very best thing ever written on the subject in English—possibly in any language. I cannot begin to tell you how much I appreciate the care and trouble you have taken, but I know you will find it to have been worth while. For years it will be the standard work on the subject, and it is articles of this sort—and there are not many of them—that *make* a system of medicine. Then too the credit which such a contribution brings to the school is very great. Many many thanks.
>
> Sincerely yours
> Wm. Osler.
>
> P.S. I have but one regret, that Rokitansky and Peacock are not alive to see it. Your tribute to R. is splendid. My feelings were the same when I read the monograph.

There was a new edition of the *System* in 1915, in which I raised the number of cases studied in my monograph to 631 and a third in 1927, in which my monograph was enlarged to twice its size in the first edition and the number of cases analyzed was raised by me to 850, with new chapters on many subjects and many new illustrations. The recognition which this work received has actually made me, in Dr. Osler's words, the first authority on this subject, at least on this continent.

In the spring of 1907 had come the great fires which burnt the "old Medical Building of McGill" (with its additions and alterations new in 1901), and a week later the Engineering Building. The flames gutted the central part of the Medical Building which enclosed our bone and obstetrical collections, but though they played havoc in the front part of the Museum where the clinical teaching series were, including practically the whole Osler collection and the wonderful Holmes heart, this was fortunately not burnt out for the fire was arrested here, and my catalogues were also saved with the help of an intrepid student. Nearly everything, however, was on the floor, in the midst of burst jars and ashes, and students and Museum Secretary and I worked for some 48 hours on end carrying them across from the floor, or basement where they had dropped through holes in the floor, on wire screens to a room behind the bursar's office, where we washed, identified and salvaged them. Dr. Martin was in Berlin and he got us some 200 picked specimens from Prof. Orth and from the London Museums to take the place of the loss we had sustained, and a few weeks later when I was in Washington, I put in an appeal and the Army Medical Museum gave us no less than 1,200 specimens to replace the splendid bone collection which had been entirely destroyed.

At this time too, . . . with the approval and support of Professor Adami and Sir William Osler, I organized the International Association of Medical Museums and brought out its first *Bulletin* which was published free by courtesy of the Surgeon-General of the United States Army, and contained an appeal for specimens to replace those destroyed by fire at McGill.

This Association is now a large and well organized International Society, the American and Canadian Section of which is ancillary to the American Association of Pathologists and meets yearly in conjunction with this and it publishes a substantial Bulletin bearing the title, "Journal of Technical Methods," which embodies its Proceedings.

In 1910 the Faculty was pleased to bestow upon me the McGill degree of M.D., C.M., *honoris causa,* at its convocation on June 9th, and my fellow graduates in Arts presented me with a silver tray in honour of the occasion. Also, my fellow townsmen in the little village of St. Andrews, Quebec, where my people have lived for three generations and which is still my home, led me on my arrival from the train one evening to the town hall where an assembled gathering presented me with an amethyst necklace and an illuminated address which expressed their affection and congratulation on the honour which the University had done me in the following touching and beautiful words:

We, the people of St. Andrews, who have long admired the unselfishness of your life among us, and many of whom have had personal experience of your kindness, wish to express to you the pride and joy felt at home in the honors that have come to you abroad.

From the successes won in your early girlhood to those recently conferred upon you by your Alma Mater, your attainments have been to your fellow-townsmen a source of increasing pleasure and satisfaction.

We rejoice that you have done for our own university a work that has made your name to be remembered in her annals, and that you have rendered to science a service which has already expended your usefulness beyond the bounds of your own country.

We beg that you will accept this small expression of our esteem, and to our hearty congratulations we would add the earnest wish that you may long continue to reap the reward of self-sacrifice in the success of your work and the love and appreciation of our fellow country-men.

June 9th, 1910

In March 1911 I went to Europe again, with the idea of organizing Local Sections of the Museums Association, and also hoping that I might see Dr. Osler. Owing to the unexpected development of a phlebitis following tonsillitis just after landing, I was laid up in London and he and Lady Osler took me with them to Oxford, where I spent three happy weeks with them reading delightful books fresh from the Oxford Press and seeing the surrounding country. . . . On my return to London [I] attended a meeting of British pathologists at the Royal College of Surgeons . . . at which a British Local Section of the International Association of Medical Museums was organized, and it was arranged that we should be invited to take charge of the section of Museum Technique of the International Congress of Medicine meeting in London in August 1913. . . .

In August 1913 I went across again, this time at the expense of the Faculty, in charge, as Secretary of the International Association of Medical Museums, of the Section of Museum Technique of the Congress. . . . We had circularized our international membership well, and exhibits were sent in from all over the continent, which made this one of the finest parts of the Congress Museum. A very favorable article appeared in the *Times* describing it, and I cut this out and sent it to Lord Strathcona who was living in London as Lord High Commissioner for Canada, and asked him if he would support this international un-

dertaking which had emanated from McGill, and largely from the efforts
of one of his own "Donalda" graduates, by donating a small sum which
would place the International Association of Medical Museums on a
securer basis and would act also as a nucleus for an Endowment Fund.
Dr. Shepherd, who was then Dean of the Faculty, supported this appeal
later by a personal visit, taking me with him, to Lord Strathcona, who
received us very graciously and enquired what amount of money was
needed, and when I suggested £1,000 he did not seem to think the
request unreasonable. This visit was followed by letters supporting it
from Sir Thomas Barlow and later from Sir William Osler, and shortly
thereafter Lord Strathcona sent me his personal cheque for $5,000.00
to be applied to the uses of the Association. . . . In this connection I
worked up a series of some 200 lantern slides illustrative of this subject
and later published these lectures with a descriptive list of the slides in
the *Canadian Nurse.* Since then these slides have been purchased from
us (William Muir and myself) by Teachers College, Columbia, and most
of the Training Schools in Canada and some in the U.S.A. In November
1927, the History of Nursing Society of Teachers College made me an
Honorary Member in acknowledgment of this contribution, and it led
also to my appointment in 1922 to the post of Lecturer on this subject
in the McGill School of Graduate Nurses. . . .

In 1918 I was given charge of the Canadian Medical Association Exhibit at Hamilton, Ont., at which the first exhibit of the Canadian Army
Medical Museum, prepared and mounted at McGill under my direction,
was shown. After the meeting, being in the vicinity of Ann Arbor, Mich.,
I went on there to be initiated into the Alpha Epsilon Iota fraternity of
medical women. . . . In the summer of this year, also, the University of
Texas offered me the appointment of Acting Professor of Pathology for
the duration of the war, with the permanent one of Associate Professor
of this subject after its cessation. I was however retained at McGill.

At this meeting of the Museums Association in London its Constitution was perfected from the international side, and I was made its permanent International Secretary. . . .

In August 1914 came the Great War, and the McGill Hospital drilled
in the corridors of the new Medical Building, and nearly everyone we
cared for went across. My part was of course to carry on at home, and
I was given the Acting Editorship of the *Canadian Medical Association
Journal* from 1914–18, and did my best to keep it from going under
during that troubled and short-handed time. In 1915 I did some work
in the anatomical department of the Harvard Medical School with Fred-
eric T. Lewis in anatomic reconstruction . . . and published an article
with him on the problem of transposition of the arterial trunks. . . . In

1915 also, . . . I delivered an illustrated lecture on Florence Nightingale before the Harvard Historical Club, which was afterwards published . . . in three successive numbers of the *Boston Medical and Surgical Journal,* under the title of "Florence Nightingale as Seen in her Portraits." One thousand copies of this article were reprinted in book form and sold by me by subscription for the benefit of the Canadian Red Cross Society. This led to my being invited by Miss Hersey to give the Valedictory Address to the Nurses graduating from the Royal Victoria Hospital Training School in May 1916. I ended this address with a plea for the introduction of the study of the History of Nursing in the curriculum of every Training School. As a result Miss Hersey invited me to give an introductory course of lectures on this subject at the R.V.H. Training School. . . .

On December 29th 1919, our loved teacher and friend Sir William Osler died at the age of 70 years, though still in his prime. The following April, 1920, at the Cornell meeting of the Museums Association it was resolved to bring out our next *Bulletin* as a memorial number, with myself as Managing Editor. This took six years to accomplish, the first Impression being issued in June 1926. . . .

In 1919 the Woman's Medical College of Pennsylvania offered me their Chair of Pathology, and, as I was not in a position to consider their offer at the time, they appointed an Acting Head of this Department. In July 1923 their Board of Corporators again approached me, informing me that their Faculty was undergoing reconstruction and offering me double the salary they had previously named, and the appointment of my own staff, if I would accept the Chair of Pathology and Bacteriology, either on a temporary or a permanent basis. I accepted this offer temporarily, on loan from McGill, for a period of one year, which was afterwards extended to two, from September 1923 to September 1925. I took with me to form the staff of my new Department Dr. Lola McLatchie (Toronto University) as Associate Professor of Bacteriology, Dr. Winnifred Blampin (McGill '22) as Teaching Fellow in Pathology, and Miss Iseult Finlay (Infants' Hospital, London), as Technician in Bacteriology and Pathology. With their assistance we successfully reorganized the Department (which was graded A by the State Board of Inspection), and when I returned to McGill at the end of the two years, my entire staff was retained, and Dr. Helen Ingleby, M.R.C.P. (University of London) was appointed on my recommendation to succeed me in the Chair of Pathology, and has carried on successfully up to this time. During my stay in Philadelphia, I was admitted by bedside examination to the Licentiate of the State of Pennsylvania, and elected to membership in the Philadelphia Medical Society, Philadelphia Physiological Society, Philadelphia Pathological Society and New England Heart Association, and to Fellowship in the American Association of Clinical Pathologists, and American Association for the Advancement of Science. . . .

I cannot close this little account of my academic activities to date without a word of tribute to those generous-minded men on the Faculty of Medicine who gave me so freely of opportunity and recognition during my early years, at a time when women were not yet admitted as undergraduate students to McGill (for this only happened in 1918, the first class graduating as all know, with high honors in 1922). Among these, I must mention especially Dr. Wyatt Johnston, perhaps the greatest genius McGill has ever numbered on its roll; Prof. J. G. Adami, . . . who was always to me a most generous and inspiring Chief; Dr. F. J. Shepherd, under whose Deanship in the years 1908–1914 my greatest advancement took place, and who was from my student days on, the kind and liberal supporter of what he saw to be honest work; and Dr. C. F. Martin, who has always been my best friend in the University. Nor may I omit from this list Dr. W. F. Hamilton, who first gave me a hand in Vienna; John McCrae, who revealed himself on more than one occasion my true friend; and last but not least, Sir William Osler, whose keen interest in my work and broad human sympathy pierced the veil of my youthful shyness with a personal stimulus that aroused my intellect to its most passionate endeavor.

McGill Medical Journal 28, no. 3 (October 1959): 127–52. Reprinted with permission of the Faculty of Medicine, McGill University. The original manuscript is now in the Osler Library.

THERESA McMAHON

Practical in Her Theories

THERESA McMAHON
1878–1961

by Florence Howe

On the campus of the University of Washington in Seattle today stands a dormitory named for Edward and Theresa McMahon, who were students together in the very last years of the last century, alumni for a decade, and then served the university as professors together for most of their adult lives. They were married in 1900, a year after her graduation and two years after his. He died in 1950, shortly before their fiftieth wedding anniversary on July 4. She lived until 1961, largely in nursing homes, increasingly blind and disabled by the debilitating arthritis she had suffered since middle age. During that last decade, in 1958, at the request of Henry Schmitz, president of the University of Washington, she wrote the unique document she called "My Story."[1]

Edward McMahon spent his life as a teacher, first in the public schools and then at the university. By all accounts, he was an especially fine public speaker and teacher. One of his university obituaries notes that he was "one of the few educators to attain the rank of full professor without holding a doctor's degree," and that he was "known to faculty and students as a teacher who presented his subject in the vernacular, disregarding unwarranted but popular conceptions of history." Although he did graduate work in history at the University of California and at the University of Wisconsin, where he earned an A.M. in 1907, he seems to have preferred teaching in Seattle's public schools to writing a dissertation. In 1908 he left his job as chair of the history department of "old Seattle High School" to join the university's history department.[2]

Theresa McMahon's life stands in contrast both to her husband's and to the lives of other women academics of her day. Unlike these professional women, she did not choose between work and marriage. She had them both, though she had no children. Unlike her husband, and like other "lone voyagers," she was a productive scholar and an off-campus activist, even as she was also a beloved teacher and counselor to students. Unlike other "lone voyagers," she had a lifelong partner who shared her philosophy and social ideals. Their half-century relationship, by her own account and the good-natured jesting of students' reports, would seem to have been companionate and supportive. Her exceptional achievements signify that she made the most of it.

Theresa McMahon was unique in her own time, and would probably be unique even in ours. She wrote a feminist doctoral dissertation in 1909. She divided her energies among her marriage, her teaching life, and her work on behalf of decent working conditions for working-class women. She was an economist in the early days of the profession, and, like Emily Greene Balch of Wellesley, she taught courses about women and work sixty years before the invention of women's studies in our time. Her activism outside academe made her a radical in the eyes of many on campus, though she eschewed the label. Finally, she left behind "My Story," dictated when she was nearly paralyzed and blind. In it, she recalls the lean line of her life, and dwells especially on the years of satisfying relationships with colleagues, including her husband, at the university. With the help of this document and other unpublished bits of typescript, the professional life may be glimpsed, and, perhaps as important, several hints about the historical development of women's place in academe may be assembled. Her life helps us to see more clearly the lives of "lone voyagers," surviving without female support networks.

Theresa McMahon's isolated childhood on what was then a remote island on Lake Washington helped to establish what she regarded as her principal character trait: courage, or what she rather diffidently calls in "My Story," "an absence of fear." She offers an unforgettable image out of that childhood: "I wasn't afraid to ride bareback through the woods on cowtrails."[3]

In 1894, the young Theresa Schmid, then sixteen, and having attended only an "ungraded" school on Mercer Island, was placed into the university's subfreshman class.[4] She entered the university with three "life-long friends" who themselves entered as freshmen, she tells us, one of whom was Edward McMahon, all of whom were five years older than she. They graduated in 1898; the precocious Theresa in 1899. She and Edward married in 1900. He was teaching in the public schools. She received an A.M. degree in English from the university in 1901. The same year, she and Edward left Seattle for California and a year of graduate study. They both returned to teaching jobs in Seattle the following year, and left again in 1906, this time for graduate study at the University of Wisconsin. Edward received an A.M. degree in history in 1907, and apparently returned to teach and chair the history department at Seattle's high school. Theresa received a Ph.D. in sociology in 1909 from the University of Wisconsin.

One can surmise that the couple were separated from 1907–1908, and that perhaps Theresa returned to Seattle with Edward, while she wrote her dissertation. In the middle of 1909, following her degree, she went to work in Chicago's Hull House, apparently leaving Edward at the University of Washington, where he had begun to teach in 1908. Theresa returned to Seattle in the fall of 1910, to accept an appointment as a graduate assistant in political science. In 1911, she was made instructor; in 1914, assistant professor; in 1926, following the publication of her only book, associate professor; in 1929, full professor. She retired in 1937.

In Theresa McMahon's "My Story," several factors emerge as essential to her development both as a strong student and as a teacher. First, there is her own young brand of courage. She describes an early experience in class at the University of Washington when a faculty member berated her for her ignorance, and afterwards, when she bearded him in his office and said, "I will not tolerate being humiliated." She was fueled not only by courage, but by her sense of justice, and she was fortunate in that the professor had a sense of humor as well as his own sense of justice. She apparently never forgot both how ignorant she felt as a student, and how significant to her was the encouragement from teachers who regarded her as a "good student." In her eighties, writing her memoir, she remembers how the simple "belief" of the professor "did wonders for me."

Of course she also had what she describes as "a philosophical mind. I could see things as other students couldn't see them, see them as a whole." And in the midst of a college career headed for English literature, she came under the influence of Professor J. Allen Smith, a man fueled by his own sense of justice. One can gain a sense of Smith from the titles of the courses central to the new Department of Political and Social Science, established in 1898, with Smith as its head and, for a year, its only faculty member. The university catalogue's description of the new department read: "The work in this department emphasizes the duties and responsibilities of citizenship. Its object is to inculcate worthy social ideals and lay the basis for sound independent thinking on political and economic questions." The courses included Elements of Political Economy, Economic Theory, Industrial Revolution, Political Institutions, and Elements of Sociology. Bolder, perhaps, were the courses titled Monopoly Problem, Socialism, Labor Question, Public Finance, and, simply, Money. A course called Industrial Problems offers the following description: "A study of the evils of unrestricted competition. An investigation of the meaning of 'survival of the fittest,' as applied to modern business."[5] Unlike modern catalogues, these titles and course descriptions define perspectives as well as subjects to be studied. They told students interested in social issues that these courses were prolabor.

In "My Story," Theresa McMahon notes Smith's influence on her: "I not only understood monopolies but I hated them. I hated the injustice that occurred in the industrial field." Surprisingly, however, and despite the fact that she doesn't mention women friends or the suffrage movement in "My Story," she wrote her doctoral dissertation on the history of injustices against working women. And as interesting, after receiving her Ph.D., she used it first at Hull House, both in activist projects and in research, again focused on women. As she tells us, Chicago and Hull House were her crucible. If she learned about injustice through books and Professor Smith's teaching, the palpable experience of the poverty, especially of women and their industrial exploitation, made a visceral difference to her work both as a teacher and an activist.

When she returned to the University of Washington as a faculty member in 1911, it was at the invitation of J. Allen Smith, and though at a level beneath her dignity as a Ph.D., she accepted the appointment as graduate assistant and began to teach Elements of Economics, the introductory course. By 1915, she was also teaching Labor Problems ("strikes, trade unions, employers' associations, arbitration, immigration, child labor"), Labor Legislation ("American and foreign. A study of wages, hours, accidents, industrial hygiene"), Standards of Living ("A study of the consumption of wealth with reference to the household and other economic units"), and Labor Movements in Europe.[6]

The catalogue of 1916 records the reorganization of the new Department of Economics and Commerce. For political and other reasons, some of which McMahon describes in "My Story," the political and social science department was split in 1916 into three parts. J. Allen Smith was sent off to head the new political science department, his and McMahon's friend Walter Beach to the new sociology department. And McMahon herself remained in economics as labor economist, within the newly organized College of Economics and Business Administration. The catalogue of that year and the next notes that the "reorganization has not been completed," and that "courses, therefore, are tentative." The most startling innovations are two: The introductory course has become Man and His Economic Life: "An analysis of man's original nature, a description of the evolution of his economic environment and a statement of his problems of adjustment in modern life." Theresa McMahon is not listed as teaching this introductory course, as she had taught others, but instead, she is teaching two new courses: Women in Business and Industry, and Vocational Opportunities for Women in the Pacific Northwest.[7] The following year the catalogue lists the introductory course as General Economics, with no description, and McMahon's course as Women in Industry.[8]

For all of the next decade, and most of the following one, Theresa McMahon taught twelve different courses, some every year, some in alternate years. They included Economics of Consumption, History of the American Labor Movement ("This course aims to show the relation between the development of the American labor movement and free lands, immigration, economic organization, prices and industrial crises"), Modern Labor Problems ("An analysis of the modern labor movement with special emphasis on craft unionism, industrialism, the cooperative movement, and profitsharing; the psychology of laborers as influenced by modern industrial tendencies"), Women in Industry ("A study of the evolution of women's work; the relative importance of women in industry; social reaction in labor legislation"). She also taught Immigration and Labor, European Labor Problems, Labor Legislation, American Labor Problems, Labor in Industry, and Seminar in Labor. One of her perennial courses, Social and Economic Standards of Living ("Their origins and development; class standards and their influence on industry. A comparative study of budgets"), led to the publication of her book on that subject in 1925. Typescripts in the archives and correspondence with former students suggest the makings of another book based on the course called Economics of Consumption ("Historical development of human wants in relation to the economic laws of consumption; influence on the production and distribution of wealth. Attempts to control consumption through private and governmental agencies").[9]

"My Story" allows us to glimpse the teacher in action, not usually in the classroom, but in the legislative hearing, at a committee meeting on behalf of labor, or as a journalist and "investigative reporter." Theresa McMahon also tells us that she made the connection, probably because of her Chicago experience, between immersion and learning, and hence, she encouraged her students to do what we would today call activist research. In a typescript not included in "My Story," McMahon describes how she made economics come alive to the students:

> For instance, in labor problems; I attended the Central Labor Council meeting every Wednesday. I sat there when a general strike was called, during the first world war. The workers in the ship building industry were apparently losing their strike and so one of their members harangued the council to call a general strike, tie up all the industries in Seattle, and labor will be able to dictate its own ways. The motion was made, seconded, and as I remember, carried unanimously. . . . The strike went off very quietly. I think it lasted only a few days and the men went back to work. Naturally, I kept my class informed. . . . Occasionally my students, when they had time, attended the Central Labor Council meetings. Frequently they had term papers to write on specific unions and specific movements. In other words, the subject was alive.[10]

Perhaps because she measured her classroom teaching style against her husband's renown as lecturer, Theresa McMahon judged her "greatest achievement" as a teacher neither in the classroom nor as activist, but rather as an advisor in one-on-one relationships with students. In another typescript she tells a series of anecdotes in which she teaches a failing student to take notes, for example, and advises a student "slow" at writing which courses required only the writing of term papers rather than examinations. In many instances she loaned or gave money to students. On other occasions, she describes her pleading before university committees for failing students she thought deserving of another chance; or her urging students to make their own vocational decisions, reminding them that, "if you do as your father wants you to do, and are unhappy all your life in your work activities, you have no one to blame but yourself." "I think a number of students thought I was a wonderful woman when I helped them out of predicaments," she says. "But I wasn't a wonderful woman. I simply was an understanding woman," and she reminds herself of the understanding she had needed and had received as a student.

Finally, in this much-scribbled-over typescript she recalls discussing with a retired colleague the limited value of academic publications, that scholarship produced by professors that sometimes disappears from view even in their own lifetimes, and she adds:

> I know my publications are never read any more. But my students who are grandfathers speak of erecting a monument to me when I am gone. I

told them that . . . the only monument either Edward McMahon or I wanted erected in our honor when gone was intellectual integrity. Pass it on to their children: that was the most valuable asset that we could give them.[11]

Until her death, Theresa McMahon corresponded with and received visits from former students. One letter from Ewan Clague, who in 1957 was Commissioner of Labor Statistics for the U.S. Department of Labor, fearlessly and heartwarmingly corrects his teacher's perceptions about her own influence on him:

> You are quite wrong about your own contribution to my career. It was you (and Ed [Edwin E. Witte, professor of economics] indirectly) who started me on the road I finally took. J. Allen Smith was a great thinker, a man of ideas, but he was not much force in the practical world. If I had remained under his tutelage, I would probably have gone out teaching civics in high school, and perhaps would never have gone on for an advanced degree.
>
> It was you who wrote back to John R. Commons at the University of Wisconsin and obtained the fellowship which made it possible for me to go there. It was you who advanced the money which I needed in order to get through that first year. And it was you who put me firmly over into the field of labor economics, which is where I really belonged. I have always considered that this was the real turning point in my career.
>
> . . . In one way Ed Witte was very much like you; he was practical in his theories.[12]

Ultimately, we must view Theresa McMahon's life and achievements within the frame of the period she lived through. As she describes it herself, it was "a muckraking period in American history, when the crusade was being carried on against the great financial interests who were the exploiters in American industrial history." As economist and historian respectively, Theresa and Edward McMahon responded to the rise of a labor movement, as well as the expansion of monopoly capitalism and industry—both fueled by a tide of immigration, and by the employment of women and children as workers. Only a handful of academics at the University of Washington took the side of labor during a time when the expansion of the university depended on the support, if not the largesse, of business interests within the state, committed to the use of a cheap labor market for the expansion of industry and the exploitation of resources, especially lumber. All through the twenties and into the thirties, university reports by the administrators of the department of which Theresa McMahon was a part cited numerous contributions of the faculty to the business interests of the state. Theresa

McMahon's "My Story" testifies to the tensions between "liberal" or "radical" faculty and the more "conservative" administration, responsible for serving the financial needs of the institution. She can be sympathetic to the dilemma of the president, torn between his own idealism and the budget of the university. But she is very hard on those who ignore the questions of the day entirely, or those who seem to be without the integrity she values.

For academics who have inherited the modern university formed during the first half of this century, the McMahons and their friends also contributed to the battle for academic freedom, a concept years in the making, and a struggle that "My Story" provides striking glimpses of. One of these instances, the "witch-hunting" period for German-Americans during the first world war, also illustrates Theresa McMahon's practical bent. For in this instance, rather than argue about her loyalty, she took the year off and did research in New York City.

The question of Theresa McMahon's feminism, or at least her views on women, and her contribution to the long revolution on behalf of women's rights have been left for last. These concerns are made difficult by the paradox right from the start of a woman silent on the subject in "My Story," yet not at all shy about claiming responsibility for legislation that gained the eight-hour day and a minimum wage for working women in the state of Washington. The question of feminism is difficult too because in addition to no sign of deep relationships with women, or with women mentors, in the one direct mention of women students, McMahon tells us that she never "helped to finance a girl student to do graduate work." In "My Story," she goes on to explain the traditional difference between male and female students who marry:

> The very fact that [male students] were engaged to be married or were married meant that they had to make unusual effort in order to provide for a family. The girl, in getting married, assumed and received economic security; it was the husband who was responsible not only for her economic well-being, but for her social well-being as well.

Was that true in her own life?

We have only the evidence the outline of her life provides: Edward went to work teaching and she went on with graduate study; then they both studied; he returned to teaching, as, eventually, did she. She also tells an anecdote, in another typescript (and more briefly in "My Story") about being offered a fellowship at the University of Wisconsin. When she noted her surprise, she was told, "You have been married a number of years and you haven't any children, so you probably will stay in a profession and will be a credit to the University of Wisconsin." Was the childlessness a natural circumstance or a conscious choice? We will never know, but in another typescript, she wrestles a bit more with the question of women and childbearing:

> That woman is now a prof. emeritus and she fulfilled her prophesy but she never had children to divert her attention from her major intellectual interests. The continued quest for profits has deprived the household of most of its formally considered arduous tasks so that with the assistance of a modern school system the mother of even five or six children finds ample time to spend 8 hrs a day 5 days a week in her chosen line of work.[13]

It is fascinating that, though she quotes Charlotte Perkins Gilman earlier, she does not credit women or the women's movement with any of the shifts in what she calls "cons[cious] beh[avior] as well as cons[cious] philosophy" responsible for the changes in women's lives by the end of the 1950s.

On the other hand, in her own life, she was deeply conscious of the views of university men about intellectual women. Twice in "My Story" she comments on the "question of recognizing women on the intellectual level with men." These are virtually the only spots of bitterness in the document. Twenty years earlier, shortly after her retirement, however, she was more openly angry about the status of women at the university. In the year before she retired, the university moved to limit the presence of married couples on the payroll, an action repeated not only by many campuses across the country, but also in government at all levels. In the first instance, this ruling was not to be applied retroactively, but in 1938, a year after Theresa McMahon retired, the ruling was applied retroactively, and a storm of protest—nationwide—followed but did not change the university's ruling.[14] In the midst of the furor, Theresa McMahon fearlessly and angrily spoke her piece. "About two years ago," she said,

> President Sieg had Mr. McMahon in his office and told him how the governor was bringing pressure to bear to remove one member of the family if two were on the payroll. He reassured Mr. McMahon that the ruling would not be retroactive but he made it clear that my resignation would be welcome.
>
> I have always been discriminated against in my salary. Whether it was because I was a progressive or because both of us were working, I do not know. If it is because I am a progressive my academic freedom has been worth whatever financial price I have had to pay.[15]

The anger is low key, and it is tempered by the reality, the practicality of her vision. For her, at sixty, living her intellectual life as she saw fit had been worth the price she had to pay for being a woman.[16]

Without further documentation, Theresa McMahon's feminist vision cannot be characterized. From her own and other's accounts, we know that she supported junior faculty in their efforts to gain both status and salary increases. She herself had to wait longer than most male faculty for promotion to associate professor and then full professor. From students' accounts, she was apparently not seen as an iconoclast, nor as a feminist, but there is a softer, more complex mixture of the two. Perhaps the best account of her as professor and professor's wife comes from the pen of a student, signed "MUM," published in a column called "Behind the Scenes," in the University of Washington *Daily,* on April 27, 1920, about midway through her twenty-five years as a faculty member:

> You all know Mrs. McMahon—she's the darner of Professor McMahon's socks. But she's not a darner by profession. The stocking bag to woman symbolizes the obligation of matrimony. Mrs. McMahon darns the professor's socks because she loves him.
>
> Her affection, directly proportional to the rise and fall of the stocking bag, may appear a trifle uncomplimentary to her husband, but then, you see, Mrs. McMahon's business is economics—Mr. McMahon is her recreation. . . .
>
> Younger students slip into her classes because she is known to have a big heart and give a square deal. Older students seek her out because she's an inspiration. They regard with a kind of fierce hope, her healthy, sparkling face. Into the pocket of economics she puts a heart, a soul. Her brain is keen and her lips are tender.
>
> To us students, Mrs. McMahon stands splendidly defiant—an advocate of justice and individualism. She is burdened with more grey matter than most humans, but her humor is democratic. She is very practical, but her eyes are kind. Her classes are hotbeds of crisscross opinions. They are vital, enthusiastic gatherings brought down to earth, discussions of the very wolf at the door. There isn't that feeling of the Instructor surprising the rear flank.
>
> Mrs. McMahon has no hobby lately. She's driven the car three years— it's Mr. McMahon's turn now. We may put by present experience that one driver at a time is the advisable thing.[17]

The freshness and the clarity of Theresa McMahon's vision in "My Story" and in other pieces of her prose are matched by her modesty and good humor; this is all the more remarkable given her age and the state of her health at the time she dictated the document.[18] One is left only with some regrets that she is not clearer about the subject of women, nor more revealing about her own female colleagues. And one is haunted by the question: Did she ever consider applying to women and women's movements the characteristic practical vision she could apply tersely to the labor movement?:

> The history of the labor movements constantly repeats itself. Men learn only by experience that lasting victory presupposes intelligent action on the part of the well organized, trained to accept as their aim for all times, the collective interests of the group.[19]

Notes

1. In 1974, with the support of a Ford Fellowship on Women and Society, I traveled to eight university archives in search of the history of women's studies in the nineteenth century. Mainly, when I got to a campus, I read a hundred years of catalogs. At the University of Washington, I found Theresa McMahon's courses on women and work, and then went in search of her papers. Among them, I found the typescript of the document we print here called "My Story." I found other materials as well, some untitled and undated typescripts that seem to have been drafts of what finally became "My Story," and some untitled and undated typescripts that may have been written earlier. Unfortunately, I have not been able to get back to the University of Washington's archives to supplement my earlier research. I am grateful for the kind assistance both of the archivist in charge in 1974, and the present university archivist, Kerry S. Bartels.

2. "McMahon, Once Head of History Department Dies," undated newspaper clipping cut so that only this much of its source is clear: *University Dis.,* Theresa McMahon Papers, University of Washington Archives, University of Washington Libraries.

3. From the manuscript, "My Story." References to this document should be apparent throughout this essay. Quotations from other sources will be footnoted.

4. For the detailed dates of Theresa McMahon's life, I am particularly indebted to Erika Gottfried's painstaking research in the university's archives and elsewhere to produce a valuable documented chronology of Theresa McMahon's life.

5. All references to the University of Washington's catalogues come from those documents, published annually. These courses and the description of the new department appear in *Catalogue for 1898–1899 and Announcements for*

1899–1900 of the University of Washington, Olympia, 1899, pp. 107–8. University of Washington Archives, University of Washington Libraries.

6. Ibid., 1916, pp. 193, 197.

7. Ibid., 1917, pp. 132–35.

8. Ibid., 1918, pp. 110–15.

9. After 1931, she no longer taught Women in Industry. Without further review of the archives, it is impossible to say whether the material in this course was simply integrated into her other courses.

10. Three and a half pages of typescript, labeled "University"—though the word itself is struck out, and in handwriting beneath, "Student 'E' " appears. The page begins in mid-sentence, "came to my office, he was writing his doctor's thesis on the subject of . . . ." The final paragraph on the final half-page has the word "Manchester" written above it. The pages I quote from are filled with details about the Seattle General Strike, which Theresa McMahon published an essay on in *The Survey,* 8 March 1919, but the published piece contains no mention of teaching methods or students. McMahon Papers.

11. Eight pages of typescript, the first four pages of which are labeled "University," in typescript, and then in handwriting, "Teacher student relationship/ Teaching Method," and "Book II/as/Teacher," McMahon Papers. In these pages, there is some handwriting over the typing, and some additional handwriting beyond the typing on the fourth page, which is not quite a full page. Page five begins a new anecdote, "Had repeated to his father a statement that had been made by my student assistant while conducting a quiz class." This is the start of a complex story of a parent's political influence on the university, not told in "My Story." I do not repeat this story, but I do quote her on "understanding," as well as on "intellectual integrity," two of the conclusions to these pages.

12. Ewan Clague to "Dear Mrs. Mac," 25 February 1957, and in response to her "delightful letter," which apparently contained what Commissioner Clague calls a "soliloquy on old age" that "deserves to rank with Cicero's De Senectute," McMahon Papers. He praises the "wisdom" with which she seems able to "gauge accurately [her] declining powers," and adds: "You yourself surely have made one of the most successful intellectual adjustments, probably because your inherent modesty has prevented you from ever overrating yourself; in fact, as I said before, I think you probably tend to underrate yourself in most circumstances." This letter supports my own view of the quite remarkable ability of Theresa McMahon—given her age and her state of health—to write "My Story" as she did.

13. Four pages of typescript, triple spaced, and with no heading at all. The first sentence begins, "Before the days of Darwin and Hucksley *[sic]* it was generally accepted that the will of God determined soc class lines." McMahon Papers.

14. While the ruling at the University of Washington never dictated which member of the husband-wife team would have to resign, the circumstances of its first application included the termination of a woman who had been em-

ployed by the university, and who, during the summer of 1937, had married another faculty member. The protest, therefore, focused on the termination of wives simply for being wives. There was a general review in 1944 that simply verified the original ruling.

15. "Instructor Hurls Unfair Charge at U." is the general headline on this *Seattle Post-Intelligencer* story of 7 January 1938, but there is also a photograph of Theresa McMahon and a headline over her picture, "Attacks U. Policy/Ex-Professor Speaks Her Mind in Controversy," McMahon Papers.

16. As a woman she was not alone on the faculty, though until 1926 she was the only female assistant professor in a social science or science department. Other women professors of that rank had been appointed chiefly in home economics, physical education, music, and English. In 1926, when Theresa McMahon was promoted to associate professor, Shirley Jay Coon, a new Ph.D. that very year from the University of Chicago was brought in as full professor. See "Alphabetical List of the University Faculty 1930–31," in the university catalogue, which lists degrees and titles of appointments, and the catalogue for 1926–27 for the presence and rank of Professor Coon and Associate Professor McMahon, University of Washington Archives, University of Washington Libraries. Coon was brought in, apparently, to teach theoretical courses; in "My Story," McMahon says she was never interested in being a theorist.

17. "Behind the Scenes," and the subhead, "Mrs. McMahon," *University of Washington Daily,* 27 April 1920, McMahon Papers.

18. McMahon to Mr. Brovig, 8 February 1959, typed by "zg." The subject is the allowance by the Internal Revenue Service for nursing services: "I claim the entire allowance for blindness: arthritis has destroyed my sight."

From a letter in the McMahon Papers dated 30 October 1958 to "Dear Bertha":

I thoroughly enjoy your cheerful letters, but not until lately has it been possible for me to answer them. When I lived at the University manor, the two women who took care of me, either didn't know how to write, or simply wouldn't write for me. They probably considered their duties were limited to nursing and housework. Now having a dictaphone and also a part-time secretary, life would be complete if I had a little more physical strength. After about two hours work I am exhausted, and exhaustion means sleeplessness and a hypodermic.

I am now living in a home established by the Norwegians and financed largely by the federal government—it is called the Norse Home. I am necessarily in the infirmary for I cannot stand on my feet. I have got to be dressed and undressed and treated very much as a baby. I am as blind as ever, but that is partly compensated for by Dr. Griswold's wife who reads to me occasionally. I have a portable radio at my side constantly, so that I really get all the news and some times more news than you get in reading magazines and newspapers.

19. Typescript, "The Longshoreman's Strike on the Pacific Coast," pp. 1–20. The sentences quoted appear on p. 4. Date probably 1916. McMahon Papers.

"MY STORY"

Theresa McMahon dictated this autobiography in 1958 at eighty years of age. It is published here in its entirety for the first time.

Introduction

A former student of mine, now a cherished friend, challenged my use of the word "liberals." In his college days we were considered radicals. In the course of time, ideas and words take on a different meaning. Radicalism now implies Communism. We were far from being Communists; perhaps a better descriptive word is Protestant, with the emphasis on the second syllable. We hated those self-seeking men who, in their pursuit of riches, trampled under foot men too weak to fight back. They seemed devoid of conscience. They became convinced, as they grew older, that the establishment of public libraries and universities would win them a passport into Heaven. Perhaps they were right, and the good they accomplished with their libraries and universities may have been greater than the harm they did at an earlier date to their fellow men. We so-called "radicals" never affiliated with any political party, but voted for the man we felt was most competent to perform the duties the office implied.

The following pages may be subjected to further criticism, for referring to Professor J. Allen Smith as "Smith." He was Smith not only to many of his best students but also to the faculty, and Edward McMahon was simply "Mac." These were terms of familiarity and endearment. Smith was also addressed as Doctor Smith, rather than Professor Smith. I don't know why, because "Professor" was a much higher title than "Doctor." Many businessmen and people employed in government service, as well as a considerable number of women who spent the major part of their later lives in caring for a family, had received a doctor's degree. Men expecting to devote their life to an academic career began at the foot of the academic ladder, as instructors, and it took a good many years before they attained the rank of full professors. To many of us, the title "Doctor," applied to Professor Smith, seemed of a higher social import than the term "Professor."

If the following pages had been written with the idea of publication, the story would have been told with more scholastic dignity, but, being blind and having hands which are of little use, I have told the story to the dictaphone in very much the same way as if it were told to a friend sitting by my side.

It is well to remember that the period of time this manuscript seeks to cover was a muckraking period in American history, when the crusade was being carried on against the great financial interests who were the exploiters in American industrial history. When these men grew old, they frequently endowed institutions of learning, as if in so doing they gained a passport to Heaven. Perhaps they made the Pearly Gates, as did the prodigal son of Biblical times. Who knows?

University Liberals as I Knew Them

Dr. Henry Schmitz, President of the University of Washington, on two different occasions has asked me to write the history of my connections with the University as a student and later as a teacher. I know that two other people, also members of the faculty, have performed this task, and yet I also know that if I comply with his request my history of the University will have so little in common with the histories already written that, except for dates and names, you wouldn't know that the three authors were discussing the same institution.

All such histories are really biographies of the writer. My experience with the University, though of many years duration, was limited to a small segment of the institution. I knew nothing about the sciences, the department of education, or the languages, and I am afraid I cared less. I was associated with the professors who were teaching in the field of social sciences. This is like looking at a tree from different angles. From one side it is one kind of a tree, and from the other, another kind of a tree. Perhaps Dr. Schmitz had the idea that if I wrote of my experiences there might be written a real history of the University. I am not sure, because I think every history is largely a biography of the writer.

My background, my environmental surrounding, my hereditary traits, all these are reflected in my interpretation of my surroundings. An individual situated similarly would put a different interpretation on the situation. For instance: I entered the University when I was sixteen; I came from an ungraded school on Mercer Island; I had few, if any, companions of my own age; I rode bareback through the woods; I sailed a boat on the rough lake; I knew very little about society in general. As I look back, I believe that about the only outstanding characteristic I really possessed, and it was one that remained with me all the rest of my life, was an absence of fear—people having interpreted it as courage. I didn't have courage; I simply didn't know what fear was. I wasn't afraid of the lake; I wasn't afraid to ride bareback through the woods on cowtrails. Fear is what retards a great many people from giving expression to their wishes, or, we might say their potential abilities.

I had three life-long friends who entered the University when I did: Edward McMahon, Walter Griswold, and Warner Karschner. They entered as freshmen and I, not having had any high school training and being five years younger than any of them, entered the sub-freshman class. They had what was comparable to a high school education. They had read rather widely, and their point of view or method of approach to problems was similar to my own. We were classed as liberals; we were critical of society—not that I knew anything about society, but I was very much influenced by these three bright young men who were outstanding students at the time.

Since Dr. Schmitz requested me to write my interpretations, I conferred with the two of them who are still living, Edward McMahon having passed away about eight years ago. We didn't agree on the interpretation of events as they occurred in the University when it was located downtown, on what we now call the Metropolitan Tract. This was natural, they were older and had had a wider range of experience than I.

All I remember about this early experience was that the University consisted of what was to me a very attractive colonial building with white pillars in front. The building stood on a hill and overlooked the business district, which consisted of First and Second Avenues. There was a building to the north end of the main structure which they called North Hall. I don't know what its original purpose was, but I do know that the poor boys lived there rent free, cooked their own meals, and talked over a good many of the problems that they came in contact with every day.

I remember only a few experiences; they had to do with my contact with teachers and reflect more upon my character than upon the teachers themselves. I was taking freshman Latin; we sat on long benches, I think about ten on each bench, with our notebooks on our knees—if we used notebooks—and we stood up and recited as we did when we were in the grades. The teacher had translated for us an idiomatic Latin expression which none of us seemed to be able to untangle. We thought that ended that episode, but the next day he came back at us and asked us to translate it. No one could translate until he came to me. I stood up, and stumbled; I was unable to make progress. His temper got the best of him and I got a good scolding; at least I took it personally. Now I realize it was meant for the whole class. Remember I was only sixteen, with braids down my back, green as it is possible for a freshman to be, or a sub-freshman. I went to his office after the class and I said, "Now look here, Professor Bailey, you can't talk to me that way in front of the other students; if you've got anything to say to me of a critical nature you call me to your office and say it! I couldn't translate that paragraph. I should have been able to, but I will not tolerate being humiliated!" He leaned back in his chair and he just roared. I can see now how amused he must have been to have that slip of a girl come up and tell him where to get off. From then on we were friends. He said to me, "Don't pay any attention to me; I am only an old bear, Miss Schmid."

On another occasion the English teacher ordered us to write a composition of a descriptive nature. I took as my subject "The Perrywinkle." Now I don't know what a perrywinkle was or is, but I do know that it is some sort of a little shell worm encased in a shell made of very tiny pebbles, and that it clung to the rocks on the shores of Lake Washington. They always intrigued me. I described this in my composition. When the next Monday came around and he took up the subject composition he picked mine as being the best of the lot. I'll never forget him as long as I live. It taught me one lesson that helped me in my later teaching career, and this was that what the students need—dumb student as I was—is faith and belief in one's ability. From then on I felt that I really would be able to realize my ambition after hard work.

Another such occasion occurred when I was a freshman in the new University; my teacher was ex-president Gatch. He had been demoted from the presidency when they moved into the new buildings, and he was a teacher of political economics and all the social sciences. In those days the professor's office was his classroom, there was plenty of room at that time, so that a teacher assigned to a room kept it all day long and no one interfered with him. I was sitting in the back of the room when a girl came in and said, "Professor Gatch, would you please tell me who are the students in your class? I'm thinking of joining it." He took out his notebook and he went down the list and he came to the name of Theresa Schmid. "There," he said, "is a good student."

Now I wasn't a good student: I really didn't know the meaning of words of more than two syllables. How I struggled to get those lessons,

with a dictionary on one side of me and a text book on the other side.
Very often I put in a whole hour in trying to decipher one page. My
difficulty was not in mental understanding, it was the lack of knowledge
of the meaning of words. I felt as if I wanted to run up and kiss his
bald head. He did wonders for me and I'll never forget him as long as
I live. It was a belief in me, although I was not a bright student. I had
a poor memory, but I was a hard worker and, although I didn't realize
it then, later on I was told I had a philosophical mind. I could see things
as other students couldn't see them, see them as a whole. Later on one
of the professors told me, when I said that one of my misfortunes was
not being able to go through high school, "That is good fortune for
you; it would have destroyed a good deal of your individuality. High
school means discipline, and you've never been disciplined." There is
more truth in that than poetry.

The reason I tell this is that these three boy friends of mine had a
different idea of Professor Gatch, and of some of the other teachers
who had been transferred from the old University to the new. They
thought that these men were not University material. Perhaps they were
not, but they were not so far ahead of me that they were beyond my
mental reach, so to speak. I have found in my teaching career that very
often a student teacher is accepted as a better teacher than the full
professor with his Ph.D. and his rather envious scholastic record. These
student assistants are not so far ahead of the freshman and sophomore
that the sophomore loses sight of what the teacher is trying to present.

I remember two instances which threw a good deal of light on
Gatch's character. We who knew him loved him dearly and resented it
very much when he was deposed from the presidency as material not
desirable, academically speaking, for the new University. When still in
the old building, Walter Griswold had to remove his furniture from
North Hall to the dock in order to ship it to his home on Vashon Island.
He and McMahon borrowed the president's wheelbarrow without so
much as "By your leave," filled it full of Griswold's belongings and
pushed the barrow down to the dock. When they returned Gatch met
them at the entrance of the building. "Where have you boys been?" he
asked. They explained the nature of their mission. "You cut class!"
"Yes, we had to do so in order to make the boat." He pulled out his
notebook, scowling vigorously, which as he was crosseyed, he could
do very well, and he looked crosser than he really was. "I've got to
punish you boys. Now, Edward McMahon, your average grade is 98.
I'm going to cut it down to 97. And you, Walter Griswold, your average
grade is 96 and I'm going to cut it down to 95!" He slammed his note-

book shut, put it in his pocket and walked off. They loved him for that bit of discipline.

There was another incident concerning Gatch which happened when we were in the new building. There was a trail from what is now University Way to the University grounds. We'd get off the street car at what is now 40th and make our way up through the grounds over logs to the new hall. The road from University Way, which was then called 14th, to the edge of the University grounds was muddy, so we hugged the side of the fence in order to keep our shoes from being all splattered. Gatch lived in the Denny Furman Addition at that time and he was one of those who had to wade through the mud to the main building. He hired men to put down planks and then he notified the students that all those students who used the planks should pay ten cents toward the cost. He didn't get one ten cent piece. It wasn't that we didn't think that he had a right to charge us ten cents, but ten cents at that time was worth about two or three of today's dollars. We were all poor and we would rather have waded through the mud than pay the ten cents. So he tore up the planks and we all trudged through the mud, he with the rest of us. Was it because he was stingy? Not at all. He was a very generous sort of man, but he was trying to teach us the important lesson of paying our way as we went along. I don't think that any student of Gatch's ever became a grafter.

I do not remember how long Gatch taught in the new building; I have an idea it was about two years. In the second year of President Edwards' administration he decided to clean house. I think there were three of the old teachers slated to go, and Gatch was one of them. At that time Edward McMahon was the editor of "The Pacific Wave," the student daily, and also at that time there was freedom of speech that has never been equalled even to the present time. He came out in his editorial upholding Edwards' plan of bringing new men on to the campus, men with a desirable scholastic background. In his editorial he was critical of the old regime, and the faculty was divided on the issue of the editor who had the nerve to bawl out, so to speak, teachers of long academic service. A faculty meeting was called and someone moved that Edward McMahon be discharged from the University. Now in those days faculty meetings had to be terminated by five o'clock so the men could get home in time for dinner, since none of them lived near the campus. They argued back and forth until five o'clock, and there wasn't a second to the motion. The question didn't come up again, and Edward McMahon sailed along in this aggressive sort of manner until the end of his school days.

I don't remember how many students there were in the University at the time, but I doubt if there were more than three or four hundred. I know that I graduated in the first large class. There were fifty of us; the year before there had been about a dozen, and less than that the year before that. The reason for the large graduation class was due to the fact that the regents had decreed that there would be an abolition of the sub-freshman year; no one could enter the University without a high school diploma thereafter. That made a heavy enrollment, and it was this that was responsible for the fifty graduates, in, I think, about 1898.

Two outstanding scholarly men were brought in from the outside. One was J. Allen Smith and the other was Dr. Bechdolt. Smith got his degree in political science, or rather you might say social science, since political science, economics and sociology were all in one department at Ann Arbor, even at that early date. Bechdolt was a graduate of one of the outstanding German universities. It was customary in those days to send students to German universities for their graduate work if financial means were available. A third man who stands out in my memory—I think he was from the old University—was Dr. Hill. I'm not sure if he had a Ph.D. degree or not, but he was a very able scientist. He was eased out for one reason or another and I think later became an instructor in a northwestern university.

J. Allen Smith was a handsome man, an excellent lecturer and an outstanding teacher. He revolutionized my educational career as he did that of Edward McMahon. I had majored up to that time in English literature; in fact I took my master's degree in the field of English literature. But from the time that Smith came on the campus I devoted my time to economics, political science and sociology. He lectured on all three subjects. I learned a fundamental lesson which has remained with me all during my teaching career: that those three subjects should never have been separated into three different departments.

Men are not economic men alone, they are social men and their political activities are influenced largely by their institutional backgrounds. I remember that Smith picked out as a text one by the most conservative economist in the country, and when we recited on the text he'd pound the table with his fist and tear the conclusions to shreds. He was what you'd call an iconoclast. He didn't have a constructive program. Or maybe he did have and I didn't recognize it; he was always for liberal legislation. In sociology we read Herbert Spencer, and in political science, Bryce's *American Commonwealth;* these two books were philosophical in their approach. I don't think that I had any special inclination or leaning toward economics or political science, but I

did towards sociology. I think it was my admiration for the man himself; this was true of a good many students. I have known students who
changed their method of approach towards social problems through
Smith's influence. The influence of a teacher, his personality, his method
of approach, very often determine the intellectual future of the student.
I used to spend my noon hour sitting in Dr. Smith's class room while
he ate his lunch. In those early days nearly everybody brought his lunch;
and while we ate, he would explain to me the law of marginal utility.
He went over it painstakingly and he thought that I must be bright to
show such an interest in the subject. I had no economic background, I
knew nothing about industry. I came from a rural community where
there was no political or social organization of any kind; there were no
churches, and the little social life that did occur centered around the
school house.

I worked with J. Allen Smith for two years and at the end of that
time I not only understood monopolies but I hated them. I hated the
injustice that occurred in the industrial field: the exploitation of common resources by the few and the exploitation of the workers, many
of whom were ignorant foreigners too helpless to remedy their lot. It
was a foregone conclusion that the men of wealth accepted their financial status as due wholly to their ability, with perhaps a little assistance
from the Almighty. This was the philosophy, not of recent origin, but
characteristic of ancient and medieval times.

This was a period when Darwin's theory of evolution became somewhat widespread among the intellectuals. I accepted it not so much
because of J. Allen Smith's teachings as because of the influence exercised over me by Edward McMahon and the philosopher Herbert Spencer. Edward McMahon had been raised a Catholic, and when he had
reached adult years his inquisitive mind had raised questions as to the
historical accuracy of some of the teachings he had been subjected to
by the Church. When he asked for enlightenment, the priest, probably
not knowing that there was another answer, discouraged him from pry-
ing into questions that were primarily the teachings of the Church, so
he left the Church.

I suspect that President Edwards had a good deal of influence on
Edward McMahon's theory of evolution. Edwards, I think, lasted about
two years as president. He objected not only to the scarcity of books
in the library, but to the quality of the books, and when he put in an
order for a goodly number of books to be purchased by the regents for
the University, they insisted that they be able to examine each book to
determine whether it was the kind of a book that should go into the
University library. I don't think one of the regents had a university

education. They did have a great deal of confidence in their knowledge, as most ignorant people do.

President Edwards was an evolutionist. The churches, all fundamentalistic at that time, began to make war on him. One of the outstanding ministers who fought him the hardest was named Matthews and was perhaps the most popular minister in Seattle. At the end of his second year's term, I think, Edwards was discharged.

Before we leave the subject of evolution, I'd like to call attention to what happened to one of the ministers of the community. He was the Congregationalist minister and a fundamentalist. He decided to start a student class, the purpose of which was to make a study of the Bible. Edward McMahon, Walter Griswold and Warner Karschner decided to join the class. They had gotten copies of Herbert Spencer's book on the principles of philosophy and they underscored paragraph after paragraph which challenged the Biblical statements. When Rev. Wiswold learned that they were going to enter the class he gave up the intention.

I was already engaged to Edward McMahon, and the Rev. Wiswold was reported to have said, "That Schmid girl is a pretty nice girl if she didn't come under the influence of that iconoclast Edward McMahon." I brought this up because it wasn't long before Rev. Wiswold became a little too progressive in his congregation and he stepped down. I think he sold typewriters for a while and later became a farmer in Eastern Washington. But before doing so he and Edward McMahon became the very best of friends. At that time many of the ministers who had the liberal ideas possessed by practically all of the enlightened ministers of the present day had no chance with congregations that were far from being open-minded.

Edwards was followed by a Dr. Herrington; I think he was a physicist, a very scholarly man, who came from some eastern university. He lasted only the year and I heard later he had resigned because of poor health; he apparently was becoming mentally confused. Herrington was followed by Graves and Graves by Kane. I think that while I was an undergraduate the University had five or six presidents. I am not quite sure of dates nor length of time in office, and I have no way of finding out, since my vision is gone. I graduated under Kane, taught school for a year or two and was married. Most of my graduate work was done in the University of Wisconsin. This is important because it will throw light on my teaching career of a later date.

Chapter II

At that time Wisconsin was the outstanding liberal university of the country. Robert LaFollette, who was, I think, then governor, was a patron saint of the University. Liberals were brought in to teach, men who had been discharged from other universities because of their liberalism. There was freedom of speech if there ever was freedom of speech in the University.

I remember that while I was a student in Wisconsin, Emma Goldman, the anarchist leader of the country, was invited to speak on the campus. She was given the armory in which to speak, and it was crowded. Later on some of the teachers, among them E. A. Ross and John R. Commons, invited her to speak to their classes. I am sure she didn't make a single convert. The University of Wisconsin taught students to think: not to accept things, but to examine them to see if they were logical, plausible. She was an ignorant woman, and when the students asked her questions she got so confused and was so contradictory that she was amusing. I really believe that it is a good idea to allow people of, let us say, unorthodox views to speak to the students with the understanding that the students will have a right to ask questions. I think they learn more about the "isms" by listening to the advocates and being allowed to ask questions.

John R. Commons, whose field was labor and economic theory, believed in educating the public as well as the employers to demand better working conditions for the employees. He was instrumental in establishing a bureau of labor in Wisconsin; he was also father of the Legislative Reference Library. He believed in unemployment insurance and had worked hard in establishing employers' liability laws. He didn't do so by fighting, but by converting the employers to his point of view.

Wisconsin was an agricultural state; Milwaukee was under the political control of the socialists. I remember distinctly Victor Berger. He was mayor of Milwaukee and would be classified now, perhaps, as a Democrat if not a progressive Republican. A good deal of the legislation he advocated is now taken for granted.

Commons was a kindly, sweet, gentle sort of man, a man you just loved; he possessed a most attractive smile, was soft-spoken, and looked as if he suffered from chronic ill-health. You never criticized or fought with him, you might say. I don't believe the man ever had an enemy. Before he quit teaching one of the big industrialists in Chicago paid his secretary so that he had the services of a secretary at his command. It was he who believed that Emma Goldman should have her say, as well as any other radical who came to the campus. It was during this time that Mrs. Russel Sage died and left more than a million dollars to be used for bettering the conditions of life for the masses. It was used for the purpose of promoting welfare; the money, as some might well remember, was gained on the stock market.

On leaving the University of Wisconsin I accepted a position with Jane Addams at Hull House. My work was to gather statistics on causes of the prevailingly high infantile mortality among the children of Chicago under three years of age. There were a number of recreational parks in Illinois financed by different organizations, among them the Church, and, in the case of Algunquin, one of the leading newspapers of Chicago. These recreational centers provided a two weeks vacation for women of the slums and their children. The Northwestern Railway gave us one car a week, with one provision, and that was that a social worker had to accompany the people to their destination. It was my task to take these women to the camps and stay with them until I had questioned them on the number of children they had lost and what was the cause of their early deaths, in the mother's opinion. Later on I was appointed statistician of The Associated Charities of Chicago. It fell to my lot to tabulate the material that had been gleaned from the various investigations made on the question of infant mortality.

My Chicago experience was my first introduction to the slums; I had read about poverty and about the miserable living conditions of the poor, but I had never experienced them. Hull House had been established by Miss Jane Addams and Miss Ellen Gates Starr in the heart of the slum district on Halstead Street. The poverty, the unsanitary conditions of the streets, the poor housing facilities, the high rents, and the ruthlessness of the landlords, all these were shocking to me. Jane Addams made it a point to visit the various homes in the vicinity of Hull House with the idea of trying to alleviate their lot. Hull House was inhabited by people who were dedicated to general welfare. There were doctors, lawyers, editors of magazines and newspapers, people representing their various professions who were putting in their spare time in offering their services gratis for helping out the poor. This was the beginning of free legal services; it was also the beginning of many other projects later taken over by the cities. Jane Addams established in Hull House a good many industrial projects, transplanting from Europe the skills that these immigrant people possessed—handicrafts, if you please—like spinning and weaving. They were taught ceramics; there was even a class for training the young people in theatrical performances. When I was there, the leader was an outstanding actress who had been in a railway wreck and was so crippled that her work was at an end as a theatrical producer. I doubt if she had any money and I suspect Hull House was carrying her, but she did a splendid piece of work.

What did I think of Jane Addams? She reminded me of John R. Commons in many ways. She had a sad face—a sadness that comes not from personal afflictions but from grief, from the sorrows and the sufferings she saw in the world; it was a kindly face, a gentle face. She, like Professor Commons, assumed that there was good in the worst of us and she always reached out for the good. This was rather difficult for me to understand as I was still young. I was about thirty-one years of age; I believed in swatting the exploiters. She believed in winning them over to her cause, and so did John R. Commons.

One of the worst employers in Chicago was Sears Roebuck Corporation. The girls were paid a miserable wage; they could not live on it unless they lived at home. Sears Roebuck contributed to the expenses of Hull House and to all other forms of charity; this was characteristic of most corporate businesses. I always considered it a cover-up for their unsocial and inhumanitarian activities. She befriended the manager of Sears Roebuck, and she askęd him, "What becomes of your employees when they get old? Their wages are not sufficient for savings." She won him over to her idea and he asked her to make out a plan. She promptly got the help of an attorney who lived in the house. It is alleged that Sears Roebuck adopted the plan and was the first corporation to establish old age pensions. How true this is I don't know; my information comes from an official employee of Sears Roebuck, a man who had, in his early days, been a student of mine in the University of Washington and had been employed by Sears Roebuck Company for many years and was retired.

The state of Wisconsin was outstanding, as most people know, as a pioneer in labor legislation. John R. Commons was the father of much of this legislation. He put it over in his kindly persuasive sort of way; he didn't condemn people for the bad, but he made them believe in the possibility of good.

One must not lose sight of the fact that at this time, when I was working in Chicago, Milwaukee had a socialist mayor, Victor Berger. The socialism of that day was German socialism, which would compare favorably with the progressivism of the present time, let us say the progressive wing of the Republican party. They advocated evolutionary methods, not revolutionary methods, a program that has been followed by many countries of Western Europe and that we are also following. Although we shout to the heavens that this is a free enterprise system, we are accused by many of heading straight for socialism. I go a step further and say that we are adopting gradually a form of communism, not the Russian variety, but the old variety that was characteristic of this country when colonies were established; self-helped colonies, co-operative colonies, which had as their motto, "Divide according to needs, produce according to ability."

The summer I spent at Hull House was a very hot one. The women in the slum district sat out on the sidewalk on boxes suckling their babies while the children played in the streets. There were no play-grounds in those days; the apartments were hot and the street seemed a relief. I used to stand on the corner and watch those people; there was something so primitive, even wholesome, about their attitude towards life. To us with our higher standard of living and a higher standard of comfort, theirs seemed distressingly low.

The most impressive lesson I learned while in Chicago I learned as statistician of the Associated Charities. When not busy with figures I went out into the field to investigate the needs of the poor. In one case a workman had been struck with a plank that had fallen from an upper floor. I don't know whether he was killed or not; he was not dead as yet, and the Associated Charities was called upon to come to the relief of the family. There were eight children.

I'm afraid that I frequently bluff, and this was one of the occasions. I said to the contractor, "There is a law in this state that orders you, or contractors, to put in temporary flooring so that nothing could fall through and hit a workman working in the lower stories." We had discussed such a law in our classes in the University of Wisconsin but I didn't know if Illinois had such a law. Evidently I hit on a sore spot, for when I got back to the office I was told, "You have been asking for a vacation to go home and visit your people; you can go right away!"

When I returned, I asked what had happened in that case, but it had been hushed up. The people who were building that building and the contractors were heavy donors to our charity fund. If you are here long enough you will find that people who contribute liberally to the charity fund are never challenged with the law.

On one occasion I visited an attic home where the woman was put-ting the finishing touches on a pair of coveralls. There she sat in the attic, very lonely, a half-clad child at her side and just one small win-dow. She said she made thirty-five cents a day. In another case I found the woman sewing fur on expensive garments; it was a poor dilapi-dated, dirty, home, only one room that I could see, with the children hovering around her half-naked. She was getting a mere pittance. Many of these workers were very recent immigrants from Italy or south Eu-rope.

People were rather indifferent to these conditions. What hit people hard was the discovery that many of the garments were sold to wealthy women who were accustomed to buying expensive garments trimmed with furs and braid, not knowing that these garments, allegedly claimed to be custom made, were sent to the homes of people in the slums who sewed on the braid and the fur because of the fact that they possessed a great deal of meted skill, as was true of the Italians. When these garments were found to be carriers of tuberculosis, immediately people became interested in putting a stop to this unsanitary practice.

At this time Florence Kelly saw an opportunity to establish a *Consumers' League*. The members of the *Consumers' League's* agreed not to buy any garment that did not have the consumers' label on it; this label indicated that the garment was fashioned and completed under sanitary conditions. This was the same Florence Kelly who in later years was responsible for my appointment on the minimum wage commission in the State of Washington.

Chicago made a great impression on me. It taught me to hate the exploiting employer, to hate people whose only value in life seemed to be monetary value, irrespective of how the money was procured. I am giving this chapter in my life as a means of throwing light on my career as a teacher; this experience stood me in good stead when it came to interpreting the labor problems of the country. This was my chosen field in my teaching career.

I hated Chicago! Chicago has always meant and still means to me slums, racketeering, all the unsocial elements that one can think of. In later years I was offered a position in the economics department of the University of Chicago. I couldn't imagine any conditions or any salary that would tempt me were I free to do so, to leave the University of Washington, where the salaries were low and the opportunities for advancement not great, in order to become a member of the economics staff of the University of Chicago. Our prejudices are very often unwarranted and deep.

Chapter III

At the end of my year with the Associated Charities I was offered a position by J. Allen Smith in the economics department of the University of Washington. I did not get the appointment that year, because instead of me a man named Beach, Walter Beach, was brought in to teach sociology. Beach was a teacher in Marionette College in Ohio when Smith was teaching there and they were the best of friends. Beach was a very able man, and I have an idea that President Kane suggested that they bring Beach in instead of bringing me in, knowing that there would be some opposition to my appointment just because I was a liberal, and secondly, or perhaps primarily, because I was a woman. Women at that time were not appointed to positions in the economics department; they still are rarely found there. Our universities are the most conservative institutions in the country when it comes to the question of recognizing women on the intellectual level with men. There are exceptions, but as a rule women are not found in economics departments in the universities of the country.

I said earlier that I graduated under President Kane. That is a mistake; I meant to say that I had graduated under President Graves. I entered the University as a teacher when Kane was president. Kane was a mild man, not an outstanding intellectual man. I don't think he had great intellectual interest. He was kindly, he was conscientious, and rather timid, but he admired J. Allen Smith very much. Smith did not admire him for his intellectual ability, bur rather for his kindliness. When I was recommended the second time, Kane called me into his office and told me that he would like to bring about segregation in the University. Would I help him? I said, "No! I promise you I'll fight you every inch of the way!" I'm surprised that I got in. I certainly wasn't playing politics; I meant exactly what I said. I wasn't going to compromise!

At first my classes consisted wholly of students registered in elementary economics. Later I added labor history in the United States, labor history in western Europe, and labor legislation. The classes were small; a class of fifteen was a good-sized class. There were comparatively few students in the University; I doubt if there were five-hundred. The faculty was close knit socially; they didn't associate with the outside business world. The salaries were too small, and I'm not sure we had a great deal in common. The business people thought we were socially exclusive, and I guess we were; it was a sort of consciousness of kind that we still see predominating throughout the world.

My work was very pleasant. Some of my former students come to see me occasionally; they are now grandfathers. What was the outstanding thing about their University career? To my surprise, they say, "The Friday nights at the McMahon home." We held open house on Friday nights. The students sat on the floor around the fireplace. I prepared chocolate and cookies, and we talked about the current topics of the day.

This is held to be one of the conversations—I must have been in the kitchen: Mr. Blethen, of the *Seattle Times,* was about to give chimes to the University, and the students had decided to make a protest. Mr. McMahon was asked, "What will the faculty do if we raise a rumpus?"

The answer was, "Nothing." This was repeated to me lately by one of the members of the small group who initiated the plot, Mrs. McNealy, formerly Bertha Banks. She is now seventy years of age, and she still chuckles about it. It was a tragic event and yet funny. Blethen had a reputation, justly or not, I don't know, of having had an unsavory reputation when he lived in Minnesota, where he was in the newspaper business, I think. This reputation followed him to Seattle. He was a moneyed man. The Board of Regents had persuaded him that he would be erecting a life-long monument if he presented a set of chimes to the University. It was appealing to the good side of Blethen, and he thought it was a splendid idea. I've always heard that old man Blethen, and even his son, were kindly folk when it came to dealing with employees, but rather unethical in many other ways.

When the chimes were ready to be donated to the University, it was decided there should be a general assembly and that the chimes should be accepted by the Board of Regents in ceremonial fashion. When the people entered the hall the students distributed leaflets; all I can remember is the first two lines, "Clang, Clang, the Chimes and Glorify the *Times!*" As I remember it was a very clever piece of poetry, if you could call it poetry. I wondered who wrote it, but I have not found out to this present day. I've asked some of the perpetrators and they say, "It was a composition of all of us." It was very clever, but it broke Blethen's heart. It simply knocked the props out from under the meeting, and it is alleged that it killed Blethen, finally. Whether it did or not, it certainly took a great deal of joy out of his life. He thought that he was doing one good thing that would last long after his death.

But that wasn't the end of the chimes episode. One of the girls who was part of the group was called out on the carpet by Purser Condon. He said, "Bertha, did you have something to do with that episode of last night?" She spoke up and said, "Yes, and I am proud of it!" I think they have all been proud of it and are still proud of it even though they are grandfathers and grandmothers.

Two of the men, who are now outstanding men nationally, were, in their earlier careers, recommended as professors, one of political science and the other, at a later date, as professor of sociology. They were both turned down by President Suzzallo, not because of their lack of academic efficiency, for they had made a reputation in their respective fields, but because of the taboo placed on them by the *Seattle Times*. The taboo was being carried on by Blethen's son. I have asked both of the men in recent years if they ever regretted that episode and they laugh heartily, "Oh my no, it was such fun!"

I think it throws a good deal of light on the students' spirits. They were fearless, they thought they were doing the right thing. Tainted money was more or less a subject of conversation at that time, and they didn't want tainted money given to the University. When the students had met at our house shortly before, they had read a volume on tainted money, a book which said that money should not be taken for any social purpose if acquired in an unethical enterprise. The students felt very seriously on the subject, especially the liberals students, the idealistic students. Why take money from men such as John D. Rockefeller Sr. and Andrew Carnegie for the establishment of universities and libraries?

Dr. J. Allen Smith pounded monopolies, especially the street car monopoly and the gas monopoly, and I shouted for the labor unions and labor legislation. I was for collective bargaining. We were both undesirable teachers. Mr. McMahon had chosen as his field American History. In high school he had been challenged because of the fact that he tarnished the reputation of some of the historical idols of the people of that day, but when he was in the University very few people cared about American history. He could point out the crookedness that took place among the politicians in Congress, for there were no angels on his pedestal, excepting Abraham Lincoln. The criticism against him was that "McMahon wouldn't be a radical if it wasn't for that wife of his. She is a socialist. He just happened to be lucky in the choice of his field of work." He upheld me in my so-called radicalism, my trying to bring about legislation and better conditions.

I felt very deeply the need for an employer liability law. I went down to the legislature and lobbied, a very undignified thing for a professor to do. I think my rank was that of an instructor at the time. I also lobbied for the minimum wage and the eight hour law. I wasn't particular about my job, but I was very, very, anxious to put over the issue.

Kane was let out; the Regents were determined to get someone who would get rid of the objection[able] teachers. The McMahons and Smiths were the principle target. I think that Professor Hart of education was one. Lull, too, perhaps, came under criticism, but I'm not sure which other ones were included. There were more than three of us; there might have been six or seven.

They peddled the job around to prospective candidates, and I think that the most spectacular refusal was by Professor Mariam of the University of Chicago; I think he was professor of political science in Chicago. When they offered him the presidency, and told him what was expected of him, he answered them with one sentence: "You go to

Hell!'' As a matter of fact, he was an admirer, and I think a friend, of
J. Allen Smith.

There was another man on the Chicago staff who thought that he
could swing it; his name was Henry Suzzallo. Henry Suzzallo was no
conservative. In fact, he belonged to our group or crowd of thinkers.
He had been raised, I think, in the slums of New York. He told me
himself that he had pulled himself up by hard work. He was a brilliant
youngster and he was a brilliant man. In all my career as a student and
as a teacher I have never known a president who could equal him in
brains. He was a brainy man, but he was ambitious too. He wanted to
be president, but, like Faust, he thought he could out wit Mephistoph-
eles. He could not fire these people off hand, but he would edge them
out whenever he got the chance; they certainly would get no promotions or any favors from him! So Suzzallo was brought in with the ring-
ing of bells and the tooting of horns. Gossip travels fast. I think before
Suzzallo got on the campus Smith knew of the deal. At least we were
told of the deal. Whether the deal actually took place I don't know, but
I haven't any doubt but that it was true.

Hart was in our group, and while he taught education, he was very
much interested in the labor movement and in social legislation. He
was a good lecturer and was well known in the community. Professor
Lull was another of the professors in education. I don't know whether
he took any active part in these social legislative movements or not, I
don't think he did, but he and Hart represented a new school of educational thought. They felt that Bolton and his orthodox educational
methods were outmoded. I am not sure that Lull and Hart were not
followers of Dewey, but at any rate, the conflict became so bitter in
the department that it looked as if either Bolton, or Lull and Hart, would
have to go. Now I knew Lull and Hart, and the liberals agreed with
them, but we all felt that the quarrel was a departmental quarrel and
that it was evident that the two men could not get along with Bolton.
One or the other had to go. Professor Landis was acting president, and,
knowing that he was in temporarily, he let the problem go over to
Suzzallo's administration. Suzzallo said, ''Bolton, being the executive
officer, had a right to dismiss the men and the men were dismissed.''

I had an experience with acting President Landis which now strikes
me as amusing. I had gone down to Olympia to save the eight-hour law
for women. A bill had been introduced changing the eight-hour law to
a forty-eight hour week, which, of course, meant destroying the law
entirely, because a girl would have to be followed every day for a week
to know whether she worked more than forty-eight hours. There was

a special hearing on the part of a committee of Senate and House, and the public was invited. The representative of the YWCA and various social agencies pleaded for the girls. The chairman, who was representative of the lumber industries, the outstanding political influence at the time, was rather impertinent to these women. He doubted the honesty of their statement when they alleged that the girls called them up and asked them to save a law.

I had been sent for. After my work was done, I hurried to Olympia, and I was at the hearing. I rose to my feet and told them the truth of the matter. I had statistics, because I had been on the minimum wage board and I knew what the set-up was. Before I was half through the chairman jumped up and said, "Who are you?" "I am Theresa McMahon of the University of Washington!" You could have heard a pin drop. Finally the head of the National Laundryman's Organization— I think the laundrymen were at the head of the movement—jumped up and said, "I move we adjourn." Later he came up to me and said, "I knew you were an educated woman as soon as you opened your mouth."

That was the end of the fight over the eight-hour law. It never came up again, but I came up again! When I got back to the campus, acting President Landis called me to the office and said, "The Regents are going to meet this afternoon and ask me to fire you. What shall I do?" I answered him impertinently, "Tell them to do their damndest!" I smile now at my rudeness, but I knew what I said. They couldn't fire me. If they fired me without the president's recommendation, the president would be forced to resign. The only person who could dismiss me on a recommendation was J. Allen Smith, and he always said by his actions, "Go it Rosy, I'll hold your bonnet." So I felt very safe. I had been a freshman in Landis' class; I had been a friend of the Landis family for years. I wasn't sassing my superior officer; I was talking to a friend whose sympathies I knew, were with me. I don't think he wanted to be president permanently. He made a good president, however. He had sympathy for and understanding of the faculty, for he was one of them, and he never would take dictation from a Board of Regents.

Chapter III [sic] Wage Episode

I played a very important part in getting the minimum wage law passed. It was up to the governor to appoint a commission of three to determine what a minimum wage should be and to see that it was enforced. The labor unions brought pressure to bear on Governor Lister to appoint me. As for the lumber interests, the manufacturing interests and the Chamber of Commerce, I was the last person they wanted to see on that board.

A woman was appointed; I don't remember her name, but she was at the head of the WCTU. The second woman was a daughter of an outstanding lumberman. (I haven't proof of this, but I suspect it was the lumbermen who financed Lister's campaign.) She was a nice, sweet woman with a small baby; she wasn't educated, she didn't know anything about labor laws, she was just about as green as they make them. She decided from the very start she was going to follow me. The fourth member was the labor commissioner. He was a member of the trade union ranks, and he held his position by political influence. He was a timid soul. The only one who seemed to have courage—let's say no sense—was Theresa McMahon!

The employers didn't want me, but unfortunately they drew me. Lister decided to allow the president of the State Federation of Women's clubs to appoint the third member. She appealed to Florence Kelly, who was lecturing here at the time in behalf of the Consumers' League. She said, "There is only one person to put on that board and she is Mrs. McMahon." So Mrs. McMahon was recommended and she was given the three-months term.

I decided that I had better make hay while the sun shone. Shortly after that the employers came out with their proposition, which looked feasible, on the face of it, to the average individual. They were willing to accept a minimum wage of $9.00, provided that the individual worker served an apprenticeship. I think they asked an apprenticeship of about eight or nine months, possibly one year, but I think it was eight months. I put in my time, with the help of the students, in going over some of the payrolls to see how long the girl who was getting, say, $5.00, really stayed on the job: making out slips for each individual worker, doing the same for the next month, and so on down the line. Tabulating the material, I found that the girls who worked nine months in a laundry were getting about $9.00. Among those who were getting $5.00, the length of service was of short duration; they were probably incompetent or restless. In University terms we'd say that they were C or D grade, probably nearer D.

There are a large number of workers who are mediocre. That is true of University students as well, but they've got to eat and they've got to work. For instance, Mr. McDermott, who was manager of the Bon Marche, said, "If you make a ruling that all workers in department stores have to be paid at least $9.00, I'll let go a large number of my workers who are not worth more than $5.00. They sew on buttons, they do odd jobs, and if I have to pay a worker $9.00 I'll get more competent workers."

I knew there was a great deal of truth in his contention. Just as soon as wages went up to a higher level, as they did when the war broke out, University girls were available. A wage of $5.00 represented, more or less, a class wage. When the girl got $10.00, $12.00 and $15.00 a week it became a rather respectable job. The employers could draw on a higher tier of workers, and undoubtedly a good many of the low grade workers were let out. Mr. McDermott called my attention to the fact that all they could do would be to get married. I think perhaps that that is the goal of most mediocre workers. The work is a sort of make-shift until they can get married; they get tired of the job. I found the same girl working in a laundry for a while, then I'd find her in Sears Roebuck; later I'd find her in the ten cent store. She had what you'd call itching feet—or was she discharged? I wouldn't be a bit surprised to learn that both factors play a part.

Modern manufacturers or employers know that this is one question they have to contend with when hiring women workers. A government official from Washington, D. C., asked one of the managers of a large corporation why it was that very few women were near the top, per-forming more or less executive work. Is it because they are not bright or capable? "Oh no," he said. "On the whole the women are brighter than the men, and more promising, but when we get a girl to the point where she seems indispensable—she has ability, she fits in—she notifies us that she is sorry but she is getting married, and she's going to quit at the end of the month." It's a natural thing for women to do, getting married and building homes, but it is not a very good foundation on which to claim promotions on the part of the individual.

When I was in the University of Wisconsin, I was awarded a fellow-ship, though it was rather unusual to award a fellowship to a woman in economics. When I asked why they had deviated from the general rule, the answer was, "You have been married a number of years and you haven't any children, so you probably will stay in a profession and will be a credit to the University of Wisconsin." It wasn't sex prejudice as much as it was the lack of stability on the part of the good students. In my experience as a teacher I never helped to finance a girl student to do graduate work. Why? Whenever I encouraged her it wasn't long before she said, "I am sorry, Mrs. McMahon, but I am to be married." And that was that. It was different with the boys. The very fact that they were engaged to be married or were married meant that they had to make unusual effort in order to provide for a family. The girl, in getting married, assumed and received economic security; it was the husband who was responsible not only for her economic well-being, but for her social well-being as well.

It was always interesting that, in the meetings of the Minimum Wage Board, all communications were addressed to me; I was considered the important person on that Board, although I wasn't chairman. The chairman was the Commissioner of Labor, but I was the one the employers had to interview, or at least they felt so.

I fought hard against the proposed apprenticeship. The intention of the law was to give at least a minimum living wage to the girl who worked, so that she wouldn't have to supplement her wages with immoral practices, as was claimed to be the case by many social investigators. I met my waterloo in Everett, where the council was in a meeting. The Board was in session, and we had several girls testifying as to the conditions under which they worked, what wages they received, etc. After the meeting was dismissed, there were two men sitting in the back of the hall. I didn't pay any attention to them, and nobody else did. I think it was the head of the telephone company who remained with the Board, and we discussed general questions. I raised the question, "Do you have detectives following your girls to see if they are immoral?" I knew that was the case. When I was talking to Mr. McDermott of the Bon Marche, he showed me some of the application blanks and I noticed a peculiar mark at the bottom of one of the blanks. "What is this for?" "That means that her morals are in question." "How do you know?" Now I knew that the girl couldn't ever get a job in any of the department stores: she wouldn't get a job anywhere she had to give a reference, because her former employer had that mark against her. I said, "Do you have men employees followed by detectives?" "Oh no." "Well, I don't see that it is any of your business as far as the girl's morals are concerned, as long as you are indifferent to the men's morals." That was my mistake. That night the Everett paper came out with red headlines: "THERESA McMAHON SAYS THAT THE MORALS OF THE WORKING GIRLS ARE NONE OF THE EMPLOYER'S BUSINESS!"

The fight was on! The women's clubs took it up, the churches, and so on down the line. They didn't think a person of that type should be teaching in the University; nor did they want their children to come in contact with a person who believed in free love! The only group that came to my rescue were the students. There was a brilliant editorial, or at least it seemed brilliant at the time, stating that my career, my record, was spotless, that I really was a woman of high moral standards. I was called upon to speak on several occasions. I turned down every invitation but one, which was a large meeting in one of the downtown halls. I had charts with me, and I said, "I know why you people are here; you want me to justify what I said. I'm going to ask you to pay no attention to me. My term expires at the end of three months, I'll not be reappointed, my work is done." I knew I wouldn't be reappointed. "I want you to direct your attention to the apprenticeship clause. Watch it." Then I had my chart showing exactly what an apprenticeship clause would do to the girls who needed minimum wage protection.

We had a meeting in one of the northern cities, Bellingham, I think, but I am not sure. The girls who testified were working in a candy factory. According to the law, if any employer discharged a girl because she testified before the Board, he would be liable to a fine and punishment. These girls were fired a few weeks after they testified; they wrote to me and asked what the Board was going to do about it. I knew that we could do nothing. The employer would say that they were fired because of incompetence, perhaps coming late to work, and so on. There were forty different excuses for getting rid of a workman when the real reason might be, and often was, that they were dismissed because they were trade union organizers. I told the girls that never again would I be a party to asking girls to testify, because the only protection they could have would be through a labor union. Because I held to that conviction, I did not want to serve again on the Board. I knew it was a futile service. The war came on, wages responded to the laws of supply and demand, and the minimum wage was inoperative. Never again did wages fall to the old level.

A committee was appointed by President Wilson to investigate labor unrest on the Pacific Coast; I was called to testify before the committee on the labor conditions in the fish canneries. I reported the canneries that were really in an excellent condition and those that were deplorable, as far as sanitation and wages were concerned. I told of the pacesetters who received high wages and how one of them told me she could not work more than one or two days at that pace, but her wages were high enough to make it possible for her to rest the remainder of the week. From that time on the people interested in the fish canneries had it in for me. Mr. Sims, who owned a fish cannery at Port Townsend, was a leader in the House of Representatives. My testimony was one more count against the University when the Regents asked for an increased appropriation.

I won the enmity of the lumber industry when I won a scoop over the Associated Press in getting a story of the Centralia riots. Reporters had been effectively kept out of Centralia, even the reporter who represented the Associated Press. The fact that I got in there and reported the story for an eastern magazine put me on the lumbermen's black list

and called the *New York Times'* attention to me. I received a letter
from that paper shortly afterwards asking me if I would be their Northwest Labor Correspondent. I suppose they thought I would make a
good reporter. The truth of the matter is that when I got off the train
at Centralia I didn't have a briefcase with me and I looked just like an
ordinary "Butter and Egg Woman." I never was a dressy person. When
I got to the hotel I called up the head of the American Legion, who
happened to be a former student of mine. He was a fine boy. As an
officer of the American Legion he took over to prevent bloodshed. He
told me both sides were heavily armed. I received far more credit than
I deserved.

The fish cannery and the lumber interests were not the only two
business concerns after my scalp. All business concerns that employed
a large number of women were perhaps my worst enemies. I was fighting the $5.00 weekly wage of the girls and the unlimited hours of work.
I think that I, with the help of Alice Lord, the head of the waitress
union, had more to do with getting across the law and the minimum
wage for women than anybody else in the state.

I sat with the Central Labor Council every Wednesday night when
it met, because I felt it was my duty, as most of my University work
was concerned with labor and its problems. I was told recently by
James Duncan, who was secretary of the Labor Council for years and
served many more years, I think, on the Seattle School Board, that the
reason I wasn't fired was because of the support I received from the
Central Labor Council. He said that he and several of the labor officials
went up to President Suzzallo and said, "If you fire the McMahons or
J. Allen Smith you won't last long as president, nor will Hartley remain
very long as governor of the state." At that time I was really proud of
my enemies, and I think J. Allen Smith was proud of his. I think Edward
McMahon's radical record rested almost solely on the fact that he was
the husband of Theresa McMahon. Some people said that if it wasn't
for Theresa McMahon he wouldn't be a radical. Little did they know
that he had made a radical of me long before he married me. I'm bringing out these environmental conditions to show that the president, no
matter how able he is in the construction of a university, is handicapped
by political pressure of interests who wish to control the University. At
the time, Suzzallo was under this political pressure.

The Chamber of Commerce wanted Smith to put in some commercial courses, but he was what you might call a social political economist.
He didn't feel that business courses had any place in a University; they
should be taught in a commercial school. The University wasn't alone
in that; Wisconsin had a school of commerce, but it was in no way

connected with economics. It was in a different building, and the faculty didn't associate together. In fact it was looked upon as uneducational, as an essential field of work only because of the demand of the business people. The teachers seldom had the academic standing that a Ph. D. in social or institutional economics would have. Finally, Smith consented to bring in a man to teach accounting. His name was H. E. Smith. He was a good man and a good teacher, but beyond that he had no interest.

When the College of Economics and Business Administration was established by Suzzallo in compliance with the wishes of many of the businessmen of Seattle, it brought into the University a destructive force as far as the intellectual caliber of the teaching force was concerned. A friend of President Suzzallo, a man who had been an excellent scholar at Harvard in the field of foreign languages, was brought here to teach Chinese and German, and when the war broke out there were no students, so he was transferred to business administration. His name was Professor Skinner, and I wish to give him credit for the fact that he trained himself to be a very competent teacher in the field of foreign trade.

Another German teacher they brought in was a man by the name of Ernst. I doubt if these men had ever had more than an elementary course in economics. Dakan had taught in Seattle high schools and he had been secretary to the Seattle School Board for many years. He had a good mind but his credentials consisted only of a bachelor's degree from some middlewestern university.

Preston had a Ph.D., I think, from the University of Ohio. He told me he preferred working in the field of labor, but since it was a controversial field he had decided to teach money and banking. He never took sides in any controversy, and that was probably the reason he obtained the Deanship in the course of time.

I was a black sheep in the department, since I was a social economist, as I have already related, but the people in the College of Business Administration were treated by the rest of the faculty with a sort of mild contempt which conveyed the idea to their victims that they really did not belong. I don't think the business faculty members cared a great deal because not all of them were the intellectual type, while those who were were like the birds of a feather that flock together. They simply ignored the College of Economics and Business Administration.

It was said by an eastern teacher that there was only one economist in the college, and she wore skirts. That wasn't wholly true. The men worked hard and became efficient teachers in their chosen field of work. Take, for instance, Professor Berg; he took his doctor's degree in the

University of Wisconsin, in English. He came into the school to teach business-letter writing, then gradually slid over into advertising in the marketing field. I think he was quite competent to take over the work and I thought highly of him.

Let me repeat; the president of a state university is not free of the pressures brought to bear on him, so it is unfair to hold him alone responsible for his academic sins. It is only a privately endowed university that is free from all outside pressure, when the donors have gone to their eternal rest.

If J. Allen Smith felt beaten when Suzzallo removed him as head of the Political Science, Economics and Sociology Department, he didn't show it outwardly. I doubt if he even resented it inwardly, for he considered Suzzallo, I am quite sure, as too small a man in terms of integrity to make him feel a slap. I think Mr. McMahon and I would have known if he had resented the change, because we were associated with him socially very closely. The two families spent many week-ends together in outings in my model T ford; we spent a whole summer camping together on Bainbridge Island. He hadn't been teaching any economics for a long time; his classes were all in the field of political science. He didn't like jurisdictional work; in fact, I would say he was a poor executive. I don't think he ever made a suggestion to any one of us, and if he did it was to keep us out of each other's hair.

A graduate student named McClintock, who took as his subject for a doctor's thesis a biography of J. Allen Smith and his philosophies, came to me for information, as I was the only surviving member of the faculty closely associated with him in his work. He said that Mr. Stevens, who had been for years in the recorder's office, told him that when Smith was removed as head of Economics, Political Science and Sociology he requested that I be transferred from the economics department to political science, and that Suzzallo refused. There is not a word of truth in the assertion. I was no political scientist; I had only taken an elementary course under Smith when I was a junior. It never entered my head that Smith wanted me in his department, and it never entered my head that I wanted to be in the department. I wasn't trained for that field, and I wasn't interested in it, but I can understand how such a rumor would get started. We were intimate friends and closely associated in our work. While he taught courses in Political Science, I considered myself his disciple and looked upon him for advice when working in the field of labor legislation. I was not politically minded, except insofar as I was interested in labor legislation. I never belonged to a political party.

It was not Smith who made a so-called radical out of me, but the misery I saw among the unorganized workers when I was a settlement worker and a statistician of the Chicago Charity Organization that made me bitter. The inhumanity of man to man was more than I could tolerate. When I saw men who were the victims of industrial accidents due to unprotected machinery, and who received no compensation nor consideration from their employers, but instead were thrust upon the Associated Charities for the care of their families, it made me an enemy of all those employers who were only interested in profits gleaned from the output of underpaid workmen. If some labor groups are now victimizing their employers, who represent the second generation of these ruthless industrialists, I can't help but think that the sins of the fathers are being visited upon their children; the tables are turned, temporarily at least.

It was mild-mannered Professor Beach who hated Suzzallo for what Beach saw as a lack of intellectual integrity, and it was this that made him decide to accept a position at Stanford University. I think he resigned the year after the department had been split. He had worked with Smith—I think in Marietta College and Smith had brought him to the University of Washington. His regard for Smith was a somewhat worshipful nature.

I don't think J. Allen Smith hid his resentment at the splitting of the department; I don't think there was any. He knew that the Department of Economics under Suzzallo's jurisdiction would be an economics of business without any social significance, and he wanted none of it. If he felt sorry for anybody he was sorry for me because I was the one liberal in the department, but on the other hand, I am quite sure he felt confident that I could hold my own—and I did!

Before Smith died there seemed to have emerged a friendship between Suzzallo and him. I don't think there was the slightest doubt that Suzzallo admired Smith. They belonged to the same school of thought, but Smith stood in the way of the realization of Suzzallo's ambition, which was to be president of the University. I am quite sure Smith recognized Suzzallo's executive ability, an ability that he himself did not possess, nor was interested in; but I think in the end he felt sorry for Suzzallo as having chosen the wrong path, which ultimately led to his destruction as an academic person. The University had for many years been in need of a good executive.

This was in the spring of 1917. I took a year's leave of absence in the fall, for the reason that I had been raised in a German family, and this was a witch-hunting period. That was a favorite sport of a good many people. I didn't believe that the war was being fought for democracy, as many did; I could see an economic motive. In fact, I am always looking for an economic motive, no matter what war it is. I came from a German home, and I knew that the wisest thing for me to do was to take a year off, so I left the campus and went to New York, and did some research work while there.

Before I left the campus, President Suzzallo put into operation a long-cherished plan of establishing a College of Business Administration. When he came to the campus he established two departments, political science and sociology. There were only two men in each department, at the same time, Dr. Smith was appointed head of the graduate school, and his assistant instructor, Mr. Laube, and Professor Beach and his assistant. Professor Beach, with the assistance of a young instructor, constituted a department of sociology. All the other courses were included in the College of Economics and Business Administration. Smith was out of the economic field, but Mrs. McMahon was still in, and she was a problem. Smith talked and I acted, so I think I was the greater menace of the two.

Carlton Parker was appointed head of the College of Economics and Business Administration. When he came from California to look over the staff, he came into my room and said, "I know about your work, Mrs. McMahon. You and I are going to run this college together." That was a good deal of a shock to me. I knew nothing about him, had never even heard of him. He took over, but instead of using a conservative, orthodox text in economics, he chose one of Thorstein Veblen's, an iconoclastic book. Veblen was, to me, one of the most original thinkers of his time. He was very critical of the prevalent economic theories. I think Veblen's most objection[able] book, to conservatives, was his *Theory of the Leisure Class,* which offended most women who were interested in their social status. Following it was his book on business enterprise. I don't know what the students could get out of the books, or did get out of the books, because his writing was not very clear. In any case, it was perfectly apparent that neither Smith nor Carlton Parker had much use for the orthodox economics.

The government was in need of lumber, and there was a shortage of lumbermen, so soldiers in uniform were put into the woods. They complained bitterly about the conditions under which they worked, and, as a result, the government called upon Professor Parker to make an investigation of the working conditions in the lumber industry. This he did, and his report was a most scathing criticism of the lumber industry. He asserted that the food was poor and fly-blown, the beds were unsanitary, and there were no facilities for bathing. The report caused the lumber people to bring pressure on Hartley to see to it that Suzzallo removed Parker.

Parker wrote an article for *Harper's Magazine* describing the situation; I think he called it "The I.W.W.'s." These were men in the lumber camps, a group of unskilled workers who were bent on forming the lumber employees into an organization. They called themselves "I.W.W."—Industrial Workers of the World—but they were more or less comparable to our modern communistic movement. Parker told why these people were I.W.W.'s: they had no social connections, they belonged to no church, they belonged to no community, they didn't have a right to vote because they didn't stay long enough in the community to be able to exercise the use of the ballot.

Carlton Parker was an intimate friend of President Suzzallo; they had been associates in the University of California. Suzzallo knew that Parker was a liberal, a reformer, but he thought that he could put in a man to his liking and at the same time satisfy the Board of Regents, since he had made a drastic change in getting rid of J. Allen Smith and bringing me under the jurisdiction of a business college. Carlton Parker was no business administration teacher; he was a social scientist of a much deeper liberal hue than either Smith or myself. What did Suzzallo do? Carlton Parker had received an offer, I think from Yale University. His writing had attracted a good deal of attention; he delivered a paper before the National Economics Association at Christmas time. He had a charming personality, and it wasn't long before he was offered a number of good positions on the Eastern Coast. I think he would have accepted one of them, for he was a man who liked to work with an associate and with the people who were in the same field as he. There were no such people in the Northwest. When he said that we two would run the department together, it was a recognition of the fact that we had the same philosophy and the same scholastic background. Parker was a victim of the flu epidemic of that time, and before he died the witch hunters were after him. I do not think that the lumber people ever forgave Suzzallo for bringing Parker into the University. It was alleged that Governor Hartley's interests were closely associated with the lumber industry. From that time on Suzzallo's position was in jeopardy.

Parker's place was filled by a man named Stephen I. Miller. Miller was a charming man; he could talk about every subject under the sun, even though he knew nothing about the subject. He had the ability of holding the audience's attention. He made a common practice of calling upon us if he were to lecture in our field, saying, "Please make an outline of the main points that I am to cover." I know that I did that for him when he was to give the commencement address in the University of Vancouver, B.C. His subject was "Unemployment," and while he knew nothing about labor problems, I'm quite sure he did a much better job than I would have been able to do under the same circumstances. His academic background was very poor. He took his master's degree from the University of Michigan, and whether the story is true or not—I suspect it is—I was told that it happened like this: The faculty told him, when he came up for his examination for the master's degree, that they would give him his degree on condition that he agree not to do any more graduate work in the University. He agreed.

He brought men into the department who had no academic background in the field in which they were to teach. One man, who got his doctor's degree in English, was brought in to teach business correspondence and soon was offering courses in marketing. Another man was a Ph.D., and was an outstanding linguist. He probably had had an elementary course in economics when he was in college, but he was brought in to teach foreign trade. And so on down the line; the academic background was rather meager. An incident I recall fortifies the above statement. It was decided by the local chapter of Phi Beta Kappa that each department would give a public lecture relating what advancement had been made in that specific line of work. When it came to the College of Economics and Business Administration, there was no one eligible, since there wasn't a single Phi Beta Kappa who had taken his degree in economics. The task fell to me. I don't know what sort of a job I did. I got no help from the department, no encouragement. When I gave the lecture there were a goodly number of college professors attending, but not one from the College of Economics and Business Administration. Why? I suspect they weren't interested—not that they resented the fact that a woman was presenting the subject—but they simply weren't interested. I don't think they were intellectually interested in any social science. Some of them became efficient by hard work in their respective fields.

Smith told me with a great deal of amusement of an incident that occurred in President Suzzallo's office. He had said something in his class that was objectionable to members of the Chamber of Commerce or to his enemies on the outside. Suzzallo called him into the office and gave him to understand that there should be an end to his criticism of business. He answered, "President Suzzallo, I've been teaching under four or five different presidents, and I'll still be here when you've gone!" I really think that Suzzallo admired Smith. Their point of view was very much the same, but their codes of ethics were far afield from each other. Smith was not ambitious; his integrity was unquestioned. Suzzallo was an opportunist.

Suzzallo still had to solve the Theresa McMahon problem: what to do with her? First, Dean Miller went to Professor Woolston, the head of the sociology department. He knew Woolston was a friend of mine, and that he had repeatedly said to his major students, "Any course you take with Mrs. McMahon will be classified as sociology." He asked Woolston to take me into his department. "If she wants to come," said Woolston, "we'll welcome her with open arms, but if you are trying to get rid of her, my answer is no!" Woolston came to me and told me what had happened.

Then they tried a second scheme as a means of getting me out of the labor field. I was becoming increasingly interested in theories. I was using as a text in a graduate course Pigou's book, *Economics of Welfare;* it was orthodox to the nth degree, a very scholarly piece of work. Later I devoted a good deal of time to John R. Common's *Institutional Economics.* Both books were distinctly theoretical. They challenged my intelligence, and they were stimulating for graduate students. Why not put her over into the theory field, and bring somebody else less objectionable to the outside interest in to teach labor problems? I was asked if I would make the change. I said, "No, I don't feel competent to teach theory. I ought to have a reading knowledge of French and German; I can read both languages just enough to pass my Ph.D. examination, but not fluently. Besides, I am middle-aged and I'm not willing to begin over again." If I had been offered the field early in my career my decision might have been different. So that was that.

The next move was to bring a man in who would gradually push me out of the labor field. One day as I came down the hall Professor Dakan met me. He had a stranger with him, and he stopped me and said, "Mrs. McMahon, meet Professor Douglas." He shook hands and he said, "I noticed you have a paper in your hand. What is it?" I said, "It is a petition. We teachers haven't had an increase of pay since inflation began, and we want to organize an Instructors' Association. I have been delegated to get the signatures of the people in this college, but I won't ask you to sign." "Oh, I'll sign," said Douglas, "and if you join the American Federation of Labor, I'm with you." I was floored for the second time; I knew then that Paul Douglas was no conservative, and that he was in my camp. We worked together beautifully. We were the best of friends; in fact we conducted a seminar together. When the end of the year came, I said, "Now we had better divide up labor courses." "No," he said, "I'm leaving here. I simply can't stand this atmosphere any longer; I'm going back to the University of Chicago." And he did. Several years later Paul Douglas wrote me and asked me if I would accept a position in the economics department in the University of Chicago; I turned him down, of course.

I don't remember how many members of the school signed my petition for the organization of the Instructors' Association, but I do know that one of the professors refused to do so, saying, "I'll not sign unless Dean Miller signs." I said, "You are a coward!" He reported it to the Dean, and I was called on the carpet. Dean Miller told me that Professor Blank's first duty was to the Dean, and the Dean's first duty was to the President. "Look here," I said, "let us have an understanding. My first duty is to my conscience, and whether it is to your interest or not, I will always do as my conscience dictates. If I'm wrong, I will retract, but as long as I am convinced I'm right, I'll stand my ground!" He looked at me for a moment and said, "Mrs. McMahon, I'm afraid your code of ethics is higher than mine." That moment I appreciated that there was a side of Miller I did not understand. He too was an opportunist. I think he had a better reason for being one than Suzzallo, he didn't have the educational qualifications, and he didn't know just where he was going to turn if he should lose out as Dean. As a matter of fact, in another year or so he became education director of the National Bankers' Association. With his qualifications, he was a good grandstander. He was a good talker, and he had a personality that would win people, although he knew precious little about money and banking.

Our next Dean was a man named Lewis; he was a member of our school. He told me that he had been tentatively offered a position at the university in St. Louis. He was going back there for an interview, and if it became a bona fide offer he would come back and put it up to Suzzallo: he would accept the St. Louis offer unless Suzzallo promised him the Deanship when Miller left. We all knew that Miller had resigned and would leave at the end of the year.

I had no trouble with Lewis. I don't know what he thought of me; in fact, I think all of the members of the school—the men—felt that I didn't belong in their school of thought, and they were perfectly correct. I was a social scientist—probably came nearer being a sociologist than an economic theorist. I had been trained by J. Allen Smith and by the Wisconsin Department of Economics, which stressed social sciences; as a matter of fact, sociology was a part of the economics department. I was a strange cat in a strange garret. Besides, I was a woman. I think there are still some men who think they are intellectually superior to women working in the same field simply because they are men. This has always amused me, especially when I realize the mediocrity of many of the men; the more mediocre they were the more conceited they were about being males.

While Lewis was in office, Professor Ely, of the University of Wisconsin, came to Seattle. He was head of the department in Wisconsin and he had been hired to go down to Los Angeles and make a comparative study of government ownership and private ownership of public utilities. He brought with him Professor Glaser, who was an expert in the field. When he passed through here it was natural for me to take him in hand, since he knew me, and he became my guest for much of the time. After I took him in and introduced him to Lewis, he said, "Isn't he a Wisconsin man?" "Yes." "My, did we make a serious mistake when we gave him his master's degree on condition? We said, we'll give it to you on condition you do not try to do any more graduate work in the University of Wisconsin. Were we so far wrong?" I looked him square in the eye and said, "No." Later on, Lewis was called to the Harvard School of Business Administration. He worked hard, and I think that he did satisfactory work; he was working, naturally, with the business interest. He was not a theory man, nor was he ever a social scientist. I think he is still there.

Suzzallo was followed as president by a man named Sieg; I think he was a physicist and came from the University of Pennsylvania. He did not impress me as being a clever man or possessing a pleasing personality, nor was he a good speaker. I was prejudiced against him right from the start. Why? Because he didn't have any use for women teachers. It was all right for them to teach home economics, or perhaps music, or physical education, but they had no place in the other departments. These departments were exclusively for the superior sex. All during his administration I don't think a woman ever got a promotion outside of the home economics department.

There were a few of us women in the University who were the wives of men who were also teaching there. An order went out from the president's office that hereafter no two members of the same family should teach in the University; the present people would not be disturbed, but in the future, if any of the teachers should marry a member of the teaching staff, one of them would have to resign. This notice was sent around to the heads of the different departments. My husband, being head of the history department, received such a notice; he filed it away without giving it a second thought. The women said, "As long as Mrs. McMahon is on the teaching staff, we are safe."

But she wasn't on the teaching staff very much longer; when I was sixty I retired, for various reasons. I gave poor health, although one of the reasons was that the new Dean, Dean Coon, had less integrity than all the others put together, and I felt I couldn't take it any longer. There was another reason, probably: I had purchased three acres of land on the shores of Mercer Island. I had loved that spot ever since I was a child. There was a stream running down through the middle of it; I loved the woods; I wanted to retire and landscape the place. I believe perhaps if I dare to be honest that that was one of the main influences, although I was suffering from arthritis.

I think it was during my second year away from the campus that notice went out from the president's office, after the end of the year that, where there were two members of the same family on the payroll, one must resign. This aroused a good deal of consternation among married women who had been working in the University for several years. There were very few of them, but there were some.

There was a young instructor in the art department named Miss Pembroke, who went to Europe for the summer, and while there she was joined by Professor Miller of the science department. They were married, and when they returned to the campus she was notified, after a few weeks of teaching, that at the end of the quarter her services would no longer be wanted; her attention was called to the ruling. She said she didn't know of the ruling, and besides she had a written statement from the president that she was hired for the following year. She came to me for advice. I was serving on the council revising the social security law, and I made several trips back and forth to Washington, D. C. I told her that I would take up the subject with the head of the National Association of University Instructors, which I did.

When I related the incident, the head of the organization said, "Have her make a statement and we'll send men out there immediately to investigate the situation. I'd love to get my hands in Sieg's hair." What was the trouble? It seems that when Sieg was Dean in the University of Pennsylvania, a young teacher was dismissed, allegedly for poor teaching, but actually because he offended some of the financial interests in the community. He was also a disciple of Thorstein Veblen, and he had the poor taste to lecture to a group of society women of enviable financial standing. It was a humorous tirade against the silly social usages of the alleged upper social classes. These women demanded his dismissal; I suppose their husbands also chimed in. If he was an admirer of Thorstein Veblen he probably agreed with Veblen in his criticism of the economic set-up, monopoly controls and other abuses. He was dismissed; he appealed immediately to the National Association of University Professors. Investigators were sent to the premises, and Sieg was the main witness for the Association. He made the statement that the young man was an excellent teacher and that he was dismissed because of his liberalism. When the Association was ready to publish the results, which would have made a target of the University, so that no university professor would want to offer his services to such an institution, Sieg retracted his statement, and made a public statement to the effect that the man was dropped not because of his liberalism, but because he was a poor teacher. No wonder that the head of the Association wanted to get his hands in Sieg's hair! I wasn't surprised at the story; I thought Sieg was a small man, intellectually speaking.

The discharged art instructor was asked to make a statement, and after the statement was made a committee would be appointed to take up her case. But she was unwilling to do so, for she felt that her husband's position would be in jeopardy. Before the summer was out, he received an offer to teach in California, for a much higher salary and more prestige than the position he held here; his wife was assigned to a position in the University of California art department. It was too late to investigate the Sieg episode!

I am not sure that the presidential job is not an impossible one. When the University's funds come from the legislature, and the members of the Board of Regents are holding their positions because of appointment by a political governor, the fact that they belong to the political party which elected the governor is one of their chief assets. It is almost impossible to act in a disinterested manner as president of the University. He must kowtow, not only to the regents and to the legislature, but to all the influential people who could bring influence to bear on the governor or members of the legislature.

One interesting incident in connection with the situation arose. At the end of the report that Sieg had made to the effect that no longer would a woman teacher be retained if her husband was on the teaching staff, this statement was added: "Please don't give any publicity to this order." No publicity was given and few people, even on the campus knew of its existance. The editor of the *P.I.* was a bright young man of liberal tendencies, and he saw a chance for some further publicity. He asked if he could have the order to copy and I said, "No, I promised my husband I would not allow you to copy it, but I see no reason in the world why you can't memorize it." The next day a scathing article appeared condemning Sieg's action. Later, a Seattle *P.I.* reporter came out to my house for an interview. I sat in front of the library with a whole wall of books behind me so as to give it an academic setting. Then I was asked certain questions, including this one: "Do you think that you did not receive the salary comparable to salaries of people with the same experience and rank because you are a married woman?" I am not sure; it may have been because I was assumed to be a radical. If the latter is the case, the price I had to pay is small indeed!

On another occasion, when Miller was Dean—this was after the First World War—he went to Suzzallo and said, "We've got to promote that woman. The students have her on a pedestal; they say she's the only one who has the courage to say what she thinks, and all the others are kowtowing to authority. We've got to do something about this!'' Suzzallo was reported to me as saying, ''We'll wait until summer when nobody is paying any attention, and we'll promote her then.'' Before the summer was over he had appointed a committee of faculty people to pass on promotions so that the responsibility was out of Suzzallo's hands. It was then that I was appointed to a full professorship.

I know this report sounds as if I were washing the University's dirty linen, insofar as it concerned me. As a matter of fact, I do not expect this to be published. After the report is typewritten, (I am dictating to a dictaphone) it will afford a great deal of amusement to my former students, most of who are over sixty years of age, just as I am getting a lot of fun over reciting it to a dictaphone. I'm not bitter. I had a lot of fun; I wouldn't change the situation if I could. If you follow the beaten path, life becomes somewhat monotonous. I never was one to follow the beaten path, even as a child. My brother once said to me, ''You think So-and-So is a queer girl?'' ''Yes.'' ''Do you realize you are a freak?'' I *was* a freak. I was different from other women, but when you realize that I had none of the feminine background or training, that I just grew up like Topsy, it is easily understood why I was a rebel and still am.

Before leaving the subject of academic controls on the part of the Administration, I'd like to add just one more paragraph.

When Sieg issued the order to the effect that at the end of the year all married women would have to resign if their husbands were similarly employed, he didn't realize the possible complications. When Professor Wilson was appointed as a psychologist it was with the understanding, written into their contract, that his wife should also be employed, since the two of them had been teaching in one of the middle-western universities. She was in the music department, and he was an outstanding psychologist. When Sieg's order was given the women threatened to appeal to the Association of University Professors. President Sieg decided it would be wise to withdraw his order. He restated it as follows: ''Hereafter, two members of the same family will not be employed by the University.'' The married women employed at the time were safe from the danger of possible dismissal in the future.

Witch-hunting was a common pastime during the First World War and for some time after. There were some victims, including two from the University. Professor Meisnest, the head of the German Department, was of German parentage; he had been raised in Wisconsin and graduated from the University of Wisconsin. He is alleged to have tried to persuade a truck-driver who was delivering coal to his house not to

volunteer to join the army. I doubt very much the truth of this allega-
tion. He may have attempted to argue with the truck-driver as to the
cause of the war, and may have implied, as I was convinced, that the
economic questions involved were of primary importance rather than
the question of democracy. Pressure was brought to bear on President
Suzzallo and Professor Meisnest was dismissed. His academic career
seemed at an end. It must have been ten years later, if not more, before
he was re-instated.

The other victim was Kate Gregg. She had graduated from the University of Washington and was awarded a doctor's degree. I think she
put herself through the University by teaching elementary courses in
English composition. After she had received her degree she was appointed instructor. I heard repeatedly that she was an excellent teacher,
one of the best in the department. She was a liberal, but she had a lot
of company. I am not sure that some of the older men in the department were not responsible for her leaning toward liberalism. She hadn't
any knowledge of economic or political conditions of the country; these
were not her primary interests. I knew her fairly well, although she was
never a guest in my home, nor had I ever been with her under any
circumstances excepting for meeting her on the campus, and occasionally, having a friendly chat with her.

She became interested in the labor problem. I think her interest was
largely social. There was a group of liberals, I suppose you'd call them
"crackpots," who were not really in the trade union movement; they
didn't belong to any organization. Ed called them "Parlor Bolsheviki,"
because they just liked to talk. They often went on small excursions
together. They were professional people for the most part, and Miss
Gregg was one of them; so was a woman by the name of Anna Louise
Strong. Anna Louise Strong's educational background was somewhat
similar to Miss Gregg's; she took her doctor's degree in the field of
psychology. She may have had a course in elementary economics but
she knew practically nothing about political or economic conditions.

The I.W.W. movement intrigued Kate Gregg. I'm not sure that I'm
not partly to blame, I sat in the Central Labor Council every Wednesday
night, but on the main floor; I always occupied one of the chairs reserved for guests. She decided to sit in the gallery and come in contact
with the I.W.W.'s. That is where the radicals sat; they may not have
been Unionists, however. She told me the next day that she had had a
wonderful time. She said an I.W.W. had sat on either side of her; she
pretended she sympathized with them and she got a volume of information. She was quite delighted. But the two men who sat on either
side of her were detectives! They reported her sympathy with the

I.W.W. movement to their employers and they in turn contacted Suzzallo. Suzzallo called on the head of the department, Professor Padelford, to get rid of Miss Gregg. He suggested that she move to another position, since it was impossible for her to stay in the University any longer. She wasn't given a trial, as far as I know. If she had been I would have been called as a witness, because she distinctly told me that she pretended to sympathize with her two companions, not having the slightest idea that these two I.W.W.'s were detectives watching her largely because of her connection with this radical group, whose members didn't belong to any organization but were just having a talkfest time by themselves. She was given a position in a middle-western girl's college, and that's the last I heard of her until she came home a few years ago to die.

The University lost an excellent teacher simply because Suzzallo was giving way to the pressure of the outside. Would he have done the same to Mrs. McMahon or J. Allen Smith? No! Why not? Pressure was brought to bear on him, as I've already said, by James Duncan, who was secretary of the Labor Council, and, at that time, the outstanding leader of trade unionism. He came from a family of professional people in England, and he was an intelligent speaker. He said that he and a few of the officers of the council called on Suzzallo and said, "If you discharge the McMahons or Smith your job is at an end and so is Hartley's." Labor was pretty well organized politically; they co-operated with the Farmer's Grange in Eastern Washington, and thereby hangs another tale.

When I was in Olympia lobbying for a labor bill—I've forgotten which one—I met a group of representatives of the grange movement and the labor organizations. They wanted to put through the employers' liability law, I think, and the grange representative said, "If you will go down the line for road building in Eastern Washington, we will go down the line for the employer liability law, provided it does not include the farm workers." Farmers should be excluded in spite of the fact that a great many accidents occurred on farms! Eastern Washington needed roads and the representatives had to come home with the bacon. This was my first introduction to trading in legislative bills.

It was Hartley who asked for Suzzallo's resignation; I'm quite sure that the reason for it was the Carlton Parker episode. They suspected that Suzzallo was a liberal, and they had every reason to believe so, judging by the men he was bringing into the University. He was delivering the promised goods, as far as he could, but they were shoddy, not the genuine article. We were quite safe. When Suzzallo was dismissed, I think it was Professor Padelford who called a meeting of some of the members of the Instructors' Association and requested that some effort be made to retain him as president. The motion was made, but after a great deal of discussion there was no second. When Suzzallo heard of this episode, he said it hurt him a great deal more than his dismissal. He couldn't understand why he didn't have the support of his faculty. Conservatives, liberals—no one supported Suzzallo. Why? I think it was the general conviction that he did not possess integrity. He had double crossed too many of them, and gossip spreads quickly.

A short time later he was appointed head of the Carnegie Foundation. This position called for him to make a trip to the Orient. The boat on which he returned landed in Seattle, and he, being a very sick man, was taken to the hospital. While there, he was taken care of in part by an old friend of mine, who had been a nurse in the Suzzallo family while he was president of the University. She said that when the flowers came to him he would say, "Who sent them?" And when she told him the names of the senders, he'd say, "I don't see why they sent flowers to me. Take them out, and don't bring them back into the room again!" He still felt bitter over the fact that the people he had thought were his friends did not stand by him when he was under fire.

I'm afraid I have painted a rather unattractive picture of Henry Suzzallo. I want to repeat: I consider that he was one of the brightest men who occupied the presidential chair while I was teaching. He really thought he could make a real university out of the University of Washington, which was not recognized as such by scholars in the East. The instructors were carrying too heavy a teaching load to devote much time to research. They were on the whole not research people. Suzzallo was a liberal; if he wasn't why did he bring in Carlton Parker? Why did he bring Osburn into sociology? Why did he bring in Paul Douglas? Why did he bring Woolston into sociology? He was complying with his agreement to subordinate some objectionable faculty members, but he didn't agree to put in the place of these various people men of intellectual standing that would conform to the wishes of the politicians or the men who were influential in the industrial field. He made serious mistakes. If he had been content to be a professor in the University of Chicago, he probably would have established for himself an enviable reputation as a scholar, a reputation that would continue long after his death.

Hartley was not an admirable man; he was probably the poorest governor we ever had; at least he rated the lowest in the intelligence scale, according to the faculty opinion.

I knew very few liberals in the University; I think that even now there are comparatively few. The engineers, the scientists, those in the department of education, on the whole, didn't seem to care about politics or social welfare. I suspect they voted as their fathers had voted, either as Republicans or Democrats; and yet, in spite of their indifference to the current affairs they were frequently good friends of the Smiths and the McMahons. I often think of a remark Smith made frequently; he said that he thought churches were a great menace to progress, because they taught people to accept the status quo. Yet two of his dearest friends were Congregational ministers. They were liberals, they were fundamentalists, and they were charming men. They were fond of Smith and Smith was fond of them; their families were intimate.

Another inconsistent pair was Edward McMahon and Edward Meany. Meany always voted the Republican party; the status quo was all right as far as he was concerned. I don't think he had any sympathy for or interest in the working man. A successful industrialist challenged his admiration as well as a man of political power, and yet he brought Edward McMahon into his department. Edward McMahon, a liberal, considered by his critics as a radical, was a friend of Meany's as long as Meany lived. As head of the department, Meany presented every knotty problem to Edward McMahon, and was most often guided by his advice. Edward was close to the faculty, Meany was not. Meany was a poet, rather than a historian, but few appreciated him as a poet.

A university faculty is not markedly different from any professional group of people; they frequently are interested in politics only when their interests are in jeopardy or can be promoted by supporting a charity. Like the rank and file of people, they are not especially interested in politics or religion. I think the attitude of a trade union painter I knew very well is not very much different from that of any group. I asked him what he thought of Dave Beck. He said, "I don't think about Dave Beck. I know that since I became a member of the union my wage is considerably higher and my hours shorter. Why should I concern myself with Dave Beck and his like?"

I want it understood, now that I am bringing my narrative to a close, that I have not attempted to give a history of the University. I have not given many dates; I probably haven't given the events in chronological order. I am blind, and I have no way of verifying dates. I understand that Bolton, Condon and Stevens have each written a history of the University. I suspect that if this material ever comes to light it will merely show up one neglected segment of the history. I couldn't give the history of the University if I wanted to, nor do I think these three men have given an entirely accurate account. As I stated in the beginning, we are influenced very much by our environmental conditions and our hereditary traits; what seems right to one is wrong to the other.

For the last twenty years I have been out of touch with the University. I know that some of my friends would like to know what my attitude would have been if I had been a part of the University when the three men were tried for Communism. Would I have voted for expulsion? Absolutely not! I do not think there was the slightest evidence that any one of the three had ever been concerned with subversive activities. Probably they talked a good deal, but I believe in freedom of speech. I often think of what Professor Laski, who was an outstanding scholar and socialist, said. He admitted that he did not teach conservative orthodox economics in the University of London. His opinion was that the students would be subjected to the intellectual influence of both conservative and socialistic ideas. I believe in the policy of freedom of speech adopted by England and the Scandinavian countries. They let the Communists talk; if there is any protection afforded it is not against the Communists, but rather protection of the Communists from any interference when they are talking propaganda. They talk their subjects to death, and make a few converts. There is nothing like opposition to further a cause, and making martyrs of people means converting some to the martyrs' point of view.

Now that I have completed the story of my connections with the University as a student and a teacher, I realize that what I really have done is to write the history of liberalism in the University of Washington. Perhaps I should say it is the story of a few rebels who were credited with a great deal more liberalism than they deserved. There were very few of us, and none of us was a socialist. Perhaps it would be truer to describe us as "fearless rebels." J. Allen Smith was our unnamed leader and it would have been far easier to remove presidents or board of regents than to remove J. Allen Smith. During the twenty-five years of my teaching career, I have never known a teacher who made such an impression on the students as he did. A leading educator once said that a professor sitting on one end of the log and a student on the other end constituted a university. If this statement is half true, Smith must be credited with the liberalism of the University of his day. His was a liberalism that flourished in fertile soil.

The English department, which I think was the largest department in the liberal arts school, was about one-hundred percent liberal, but the subjects taught did not lend themselves to propaganda of a so-called socialistic variety. There were three outstanding liberals in the history department, Mr. McMahon and two of his former students, Eva Dahlin and Merril Jensen. In the economics department, before the First World War, there were three liberals, J. Allen Smith, Walter Beach, and Theresa McMahon, and they didn't make up fifty percent of the teaching staff. Van DeVeer Custis, a New Englander, never had a progressive idea; he taught the text book and never questioned any of the statements made. H. E. Smith taught accounting, and he was not interested in any controversial subject; he was the kind of a person who, when called upon to make a decision, ran for the woods. Bergland, a heavy Scandinavian and a very poor teacher, according to the students' opinion, probably voted a liberal ticket, but he was not made of propaganda stuff. Ackerman was also a conformist, at that time. And I suspect if it hadn't been for Theresa McMahon, Smith would not have been a bone of contention much of the time during his teaching career. I was the aggressive one, and he stood by me; as long as he refused to dismiss me, the president could do nothing about it, nor could the regents. As I said earlier in this narrative, he said, in effect, "Go it, Rosy, I'll hold your bonnet." In other words, he always encouraged me and enjoyed my escapades, just as I did.

I have said very little about an outstanding liberal, Edward McMahon. The public was not interested in American history. Mr. McMahon was a splendid lecturer, and I wasn't, yet I received twenty invitations to lecture outside the University to his one. I lectured to the socialists, to the Chamber of Commerce, and to the various women's clubs. Labor was an interesting topic, and I seemed to be about the only one who was first in knowledge of its historical and present day status. I am quite sure I am not prejudiced when I say that Edward McMahon's liberalism carried further than that of anyone in the economics department. For a number of years, students found it somewhat difficult to get a high school appointment to teach American history when they had done their major work with Edward McMahon. But it wasn't long before the superintendent, who was a poor friend of Mr. McMahon's, if a friend at all, retired, and the new administrator was more liberal.

Mr. McMahon undoubtedly had a great influence in this state in the teaching of American history. I remember one incident that he enjoyed very much. A student of his who lived outside of the city limits had a rather difficult time in making her early classes at the University and took the risk of running through the red lights. After she had accumulated a number of slips she showed up in court and the judge said, "And what is your alibi?" She answered. "I have none. Professor McMahon says that unless you have a very good one, you'd better not give any!" "You know that man?" "Yes, I have classes with him." "Well, he certainly knows American history; my nephew is in his class and he talks about him incessantly." So they talked awhile about Professor McMahon and finally she said, "I'll have to go or I'll be late for Professor McMahon's class. "What is my fine?" He said, "Oh, forget it!" The next fellow pushed up to the window and when the judge asked, "What is your alibi?" he answered, "I haven't any. I don't know Professor McMahon!"

I wish I had been called upon to write this story twenty-five years ago, when I would have had the co-operation of Mr. McMahon. He had a much better memory than I, and between the two of us I think we could have written a rather interesting story about liberalism in the University of Washington. Now all my colleagues, if not dead, have forgotten practically all they knew of those early days. I know the chronological history of the University has been well written, but that none of the three writers knew the University that I knew. They sat on one end of the log, while the liberals also sat on one end of the log, but it was a far different log, one that furnished a great deal more entertainment and downright fun than the log that possessed no knots! I'm quite sure that none of us liberals would have been willing to change places with our conservative predecessors, who were self-appointed custodians of the status quo.

Theresa McMahon Papers, University of Washington Archives, University of Washington Libraries. Reprinted with permission.

Moorland-Springarn Research Center, Howard University

Brickbats and Roses

LUCY DIGGS SLOWE
1883–1937

by Karen Anderson

By the 1910s, unprecedented numbers of American women were engaging in public-sphere activities, challenging male hegemony in politics, the economy, and American culture. Some based their activism on the values of a distinctive women's culture and in the institutions that emerged from it—women's clubs, women's colleges, and settlement houses. Others broke more systematically from the tradition of separate spheres, entering coeducational colleges, business, government agencies, and other integrated institutions. All claimed an enlarged public role for women; many also sought a transformation of American politics and society.

As Estelle Freedman and others have pointed out, those women who sought entrance to public institutions on a basis of equality with men risked the loss of group identity as women and a diminution of the powers created by separate female institutions. Their success predicated on the internalization of the values of professionalization in work and partisanship in politics, these women had to accept social institutions on their own terms and hope that women would be accepted as equals if they conformed. On the other hand, those who justified and institutionalized women's public role on the basis of a unique female nature and the need for gender-appropriate contributions created limitations on the kinds and level of social power women could exercise.[1]

Because black women were excluded from politics throughout the South and faced discrimination in education and work everywhere, opportunities for them to assume an enlarged public role occurred primarily in northern urban areas and black institutions. One of the most important of those institutions that experienced and promoted change by and for black women was the black college. Because the black community could not afford the luxury of a separate system of women's colleges, the vast majority of black women students, faculty, and administrators were located in coeducational black schools.[2]

Focusing on the career of one activist black woman, Lucy Diggs Slowe, is a mean of understanding some of the dynamics of change experienced and shaped by women of color in this period. An examination of her background and career as dean of women at Howard University informs our understanding of the importance of black culture, Progressive education, feminism, and women's culture for the values and activities of black women educators. Because her career as an educator spanned the period from 1908 to 1937, Slowe's life provides a fuller perspective on the generational relationships between those women who had come of age at the zenith of women's activism in the Progressive era and the younger women who embraced the new freedoms and constraints symbolized by the flapper.

Lucy Diggs Slowe was by all accounts an extraordinary woman—bright, articulate, outspoken, and innovative. The youngest of seven children, Slowe was orphaned at age six and thereafter raised by her paternal aunt, Martha Slowe Price, a former domestic servant then supported by her adult children. In an autobiographical short story, Slowe described her feeling that going to live with her aunt "who didn't believe in playing in the mud, or with boys, or running up and down the road was more than I could bear." Her aunt did believe in education, however. She spent much time tutoring Lucy and moved the family from Lexington, Virginia to Baltimore, Maryland so that the Slowe children could get a better education.[3]

After graduating second in her class at the Colored High School of Baltimore, Slowe decided that she wanted to go to college. When told that it was not customary for young women to work in order to pay their way at Howard University, Slowe declared, "Well, I'll be a pioneer." Aided by a scholarship and a job, Slowe entered the prestigious black college in 1904. While at Howard, she quickly established herself as an able scholar and student leader. Involved in all phases of student life, Slowe was one of the founders of Alpha Kappa Alpha, the first national Greek sorority for black women, an organization that has since served as an important professional and political network for educated black women. Her instructors, "who discerned in her promise of leadership and service," encouraged her scholarship, consulted her on matters of importance to students, and, in some instances, formed lifelong friendships with her.[4]

After she graduated in 1908, Slowe taught English at Baltimore Colored High School. She received an M.A. in English from Columbia University in 1915 and began teaching in a Washington, D.C. high school. In 1919 she became the principal of the first junior high school for blacks in Washington, D.C. While there, she instituted the first integrated in-training service extension course for junior high school teachers in the district. In 1922 she was appointed the first permanent dean of women at Howard University, a position she held until her death in 1937.[5]

In addition to her professional work, Slowe participated in a variety of women's organizations, some all black and some integrated. She was the first secretary of the National Council of Negro Women and the first president of the National Association of College Women, the black counterpart to the American Association of University Women, of which she was also a member. She was also active in the YWCA, the Women's International League for Peace and Freedom, and a variety of professional groups.[6]

As was true of many activist white women in this period, she relied extensively on a homosocial network of women activists and educators for emotional and political support. She worked primarily with and on behalf of women; her home served as a center for women students, activists, and friends as well as a refuge from the stresses of her job. For at least the last fifteen years of her life she shared it with Mary Burrill, a loving and loyal friend who gave Slowe much-needed emotional support. Burrill, who taught English and dramatics at Dunbar High School from 1907 to 1945, also shared Slowe's concerns and values as an educator.[7]

As dean of women, Slowe sought to wield power on behalf of women at Howard University in the uncongenial atmosphere of the 1920s and 1930s. Imbued with many of the values of women's culture and experienced in the strategies of separate female networks, Slowe tried to use her position as a means of encouraging independence and social responsibility among young women. As an educated black woman, Slowe was keenly aware of the double limitations faced by black women in a society that was both sexist and racist. Because she worked within a predominantly black institution run by men and because she was a product of the Progressive era women's movement, Slowe's largest political concern in her professional life involved gender issues. She was, in the words of one of her teachers, "instinctively a feminist."[8]

Slowe was, in fact, part of a larger tradition of black feminism that has not been fully investigated by historians. She and other black women brought to their feminism assumptions and goals rooted in their specific experiences as blacks and as women. From black culture, many developed an understanding of the pervasiveness and unfairness of all forms of prejudice and discrimination. From the middle-class women's culture, they derived a sense of the worth of domestic values and attributes, and a conviction that the public world required a much stronger ethical component if inequality and oppression were to be banished from it. Despite the undeniable racism found within the women's movement, many black women identified fully with the feminist goals of empowering women and eliminating gender inequality.[9]

Operating within a male-controlled institution, Lucy Slowe tried to adapt separatist strategies to the goals of gender integration. Her insistence that women needed representation within university councils and in regard to policies developed to meet their special needs was based less on a belief in women's distinctive attributes than on a conviction that such treatment was necessary to aid women as historic victims of discrimination. As did many of her counterparts at white institutions, Slowe tended to regard much of the heterosexist campus culture of the 1920s as detrimental to the best interests of women students and sought to fight it by fostering community among women students and encouraging them to continue serving as culture bearers, civic activists, and career women. Her struggle at Howard serves as an indication of the strengths and limitations of the political tactics developed by women in the Progressive era and as a measure of the power of the reaction against feminist activism in male-controlled institutions.[10]

From the beginning, Slowe defined her job as that of a specialist in the education of women. In that capacity, she was to regulate all facets of student life for women, including the social, political, and practical aspects of their experiences at Howard. This meant that she was to sit on all university-wide councils and to have paramount powers in such diverse areas as dormitory operations and some aspects of academic counseling for women students. According to Slowe, a dean of women could only be successful if she understood and advocated for the whole student. For Slowe, the well-being of women students became inextricably tied to her ability to safeguard her powers and prerogatives at Howard.[11]

When she was hired by President J. Stanley Durkee in 1922, Slowe sent him a letter indicating her understanding regarding her institutional roles and authority. Thereafter, she worked to insure that disciplinary matters regarding women students would be delegated to her. In January 1923, she wrote a letter to Durkee, asserting that women students with disciplinary problems should talk to her before they were referred to him. If he decided otherwise, she suggested, she would again "become a non-entity in the University." By May 1923, she was requesting that more dormitories be built for women students so that she could better supervise their activities. Those who lived off campus did not abide by the university's rules and Slowe claimed that their activities tended to bring the university into disrepute.[12]

Her enthusiasm for an elaborate set of regulations imposed on women students was never great, however. She generally criticized such systems as demeaning to women students and detrimental to the development of independence and leadership skills in women. In a public address, Slowe took note of the tendency of black school to regulate women students' conduct and pointed out that such practices inhibited women's opportunities "for making independent choices without which real freedom of action cannot be developed." She further observed that "when a college woman cannot be trusted to go shopping without a chaperone she is not likely to develop powers of leadership."[13]

Slowe preferred internalized systems of values to institutional rules as a means of shaping the conduct of women students. In a time when a largely male-defined peer group threatened to undermine both institutional and internalized control in the lives of women students, Slowe fought to recover a maternal form of authority over the activities of her women students. By organizing a variety of cultural and social events in the dormitories and in her own home, she tried to exercise an informal and personal power and to serve as an independent, capable, and strong role model for women students. Through the persuasive power of her example and the exposure to the ideas and values she embodied, Slowe hoped to counteract the subversive effects of the male-centered peer culture and to avert any efforts on the part of male administrators to constrain women's actions. Lucy Slowe believed that the salient peer group for a woman should be other women.[14]

For Slowe the traditional values and recent activities of women in the areas of politics and culture constituted an attractive alternative to Jazz Age prescriptions for women. Her successful effort to locate more women students in campus residences and to focus much of women's extracurricular activities on campus-based cultural events represented her counteroffensive against the attractions of urban college culture in the 1920s and 1930s. She regarded the off-campus theaters and dance halls frequented by Howard women as distractions from the serious purposes of womanhood and as the means to women's denigration.[15]

For their part, women students were not always enthusiastic about the activities encouraged by Slowe or comfortable with her authoritative role in their lives. Former student Margaret Grooms described how Slowe had to persuade students to buy tickets for the recital concert series or to participate in various cultural events, commenting that in the late 1920s "we were younger and sometimes thought it smarter to stay away." Grooms also noted how effective her disciplinary role was because "Dean Slowe might be seen anywhere in the city where Howard women might be tempted and at strange hours."[16]

At the same time, however, many experienced directly her enthusiasm for cultural activities, her generosity and hospitality, and her sympathetic concern for them as individuals. In a letter to the board of trustees protesting President Mordecai Johnson's attempt to force Slowe to live on campus, Howard alumnae noted "how wide that door [to her home] has always been to Howard students." Recognizing that some of her students came from poor families, she sent them home from her house with the abundant "left-overs" that always appeared after her social events.[17]

Slowe's Victorianism was also reflected in her concern about the need for a respectful demeanor toward women students by faculty. In January 1927, she received a complaint from the parent of a Howard student that Professor Clarence Mills had used "improper and vulgar" language in a class with women students. Slowe talked the matter over with Mills, who then sent her a letter attacking her character and stating that "you forget that you are merely the Dean of Women and not the custodian of morals of the male teachers at Howard University."[18]

The incident sparked the first major confrontation between Slowe and Mordecai Johnson, the new president of the university. Despite Slowe's insistence that Mills be fired, Johnson initially gave him a year's leave of absence at half pay, claiming that Mills was emotionally ill. At the end of his leave, Mills was fired. Opinionated and jealous of her prerogatives, Slowe clashed with Johnson over her professional status and goals at Howard University for the rest of her life.[19]

Slowe's concern with the classroom experiences of women students extended far beyond the issue of the conduct of male professors. She consistently lamented women's concentration in courses in education, home economics, and the liberal arts. According to Slowe, such a narrow, vocational approach to education did not serve even the occupational needs of women graduates and fell far short of meeting their needs as citizens or as potential leaders for a black community that desperately needed their skills. In order to change this, she instituted a series of lectures on work opportunities for freshmen women in order to encourage them to develop careers outside of teaching. She also made vocational literature available and organized conferences on women and work to encourage women to develop marketplace skills.[20]

Slowe's interest in curricular matters was a product of her belief that the university had a crucial role to play in compensating for past damage done to black women by racial discrimination and by sex-role socialization. According to Slowe, the exclusion of blacks from political and civic activities had hampered black women's ability to believe that they could shape events in their society. Moreover, their socialization for passivity as women had compounded the damage. Slowe particularly singled out fundamentalist religious teachings as harmful to women, citing the "antiquated philosophy of Saint Paul in reference to women's place in the scheme of things" to illustrate her contention.[21]

In response to the complacency that resulted from such teachings, Slowe believed that universities had to foster initiative and self-direction in women. To do so, they had to stress the social sciences as an essential dimension in the female curriculum. According to Slowe, disciplines such as political science, economics, and sociology provide an understanding of the dynamics of human society and the importance of human agency in shaping it that would enable women to jettison the feeling of powerlessness encouraged by earlier training. Moreover, Slowe thought it essential that instructors in such courses relate the content of their teaching directly to contemporary social problems. Assignments should involve students in community projects and the college should regard the community surrounding it as a laboratory where settlement houses could be founded and students "could be brought face to face with the real conditions of the race; where they might learn the joy and value of service."[22]

Slowe thus derived from the Progressive tradition a belief in the efficacy of education as a tool for social betterment and in the ability of informed people to shape their world. As a good Progressive woman, she also sought the empowerment of women for their own sake as well as for the sake of a society which would benefit from their talents. As a black woman, she believed that sexism had to be eliminated because racial advance depended on the full mobilization of black women in the service of social justice.[23]

Whether her efforts to implement these ideas affected Howard women is not clear. Her own statistics indicate that women students at Howard majored in education in very large numbers, indicating a very traditional vocational choice. Within two years of Slowe's death, the university had initiated an annual "charm week" for freshman women, an activity that would not have been a priority for Slowe. A study of black college graduates in the 1930s found that educated black women were less likely to vote or join political associations than were black men. Whether this also held true for Howard women cannot be documented.[24]

In her first several years as dean of women, Slowe accomplished many of her major goals. The university honored her request for a major expenditure to expand dormitory facilities so that more women students could live on campus. She initiated a Cultural Series in 1929, which presented musical, literary, and theatrical performances. Under President Durkee, she served on the board of deans and other policy-making councils. Durkee did not support her because of her conviction that the dean of women should be elevated in status and power, however. He did so because he was attempting to dilute and weaken the power of the deans by expanding their numbers and appointing several new and inexperienced people to such administrative posts.[25]

During the Johnson years, however, Slowe faced enormous difficulties in merely holding her own with regard to her power and status within the university. Johnson refused her regular requests for a pay increase and for an increase in her office budget, removed her from policy-making councils, moved her office into a building next to a dump, and tried unsuccessfully to force her to move to living quarters on the campus. Johnson's initial actions were a part of his plan to further augment presidential power at the expense of the deans, rather than a specific attack on Slowe. Slowe's resolute defense of her prerogatives exacerbated the conflict between them, and Johnson retaliated with a series of actions designed to diminish Slowe's authority or, preferably, force her removal or resignation from her position as dean. The conflict culminated when Slowe was terminally ill and Johnson ordered her to return to work or lose her job.[26]

The dispute over her living arrangements escalated into a particularly bitter confrontation between Slowe and Johnson. When he suggested that she live in the dorm, she responded that such an arrangement would be demeaning to the women students, who would then be more closely supervised, and to her. Her authority would be undermined if she was not allowed to live independently, as the dean of men could, and if her position was transformed into that of a "glorified matron."[27]

Johnson then suggested that she resign as dean and return to teaching. As she frequently did when opposed by Johnson or the trustees, Slowe mobilized the support of a network of Howard alumnae and other black women activists and community leaders. According to Mary Burrill, the political pressure generated by these women gave Slowe a "partial rest from persecution." In this case, the pressure also enabled her to remain in her job without giving up her home. In other cases, however, her tactic of going over the head of Johnson to the trustees or of going to the community against the university created considerable ill will and limited her effectiveness. It is doubtful, however, that a more accommodationist posture could have brought her the power and rewards she wanted.[28]

Slowe's unwillingness to live on campus derived as much from her desire to retain her home with Burrill as from a concern for her professional status. Whether Johnson and the trustees moved to break up the Slowe/Burrill household because such relationships had become suspect in the post-Freudian age is impossible to determine; the historical record leaves no evidence that this is the case. That Johnson was willing to force Slowe to choose between her domestic support system and her job indicates the considerable power that male-controlled institutions could wield against nonconformist women in the post-Progressive period.[29]

That she suffered such a fate at Howard University during this period is particularly ironic. As American universities generally were adopting the professional tenets of specialization and "objectivity," which functioned to obscure the political dimension of knowledge, fragment the intellectual tradition, and to isolate the academy from movements for social change, many Howard students, faculty, and administrators were challenging existing institutional practices on political grounds. The appointment of Mordecai Johnson as the first black president of Howard signified Howard's determination to establish itself as the main institutional source for an informed and independent black leadership capable of challenging America's racial caste system. Johnson himself furthered this goal when he successfully defended the Howard faculty against charges of radicalism and asserted their right to academic freedom.[30]

When Lucy Slowe tried to expand the institution's agenda so as to indicate an explicit commitment to the advance and empowerment of black women as women, she encountered strong resistance. Her career thus serves as a case study of the marginality of women in male institutions in the middle of the twentieth century. An outspoken and stubborn woman, Slowe probably mobilized support somewhat too often on behalf of her own privileges and prerogatives and too little on behalf of the policies she desired. For Slowe, however, the latter depended on the former. Her failures stemmed more from the hostility of the institution to feminist challenge than from the liabilities of her strategies. It is not surprising that she questioned whether "brickbats aren't commoner for men to give Deans of Women than Roses."[31]

Slowe's career contributes to our understanding of the pervasive institutional and cultural barriers to feminist change in the postsuffrage era. The problem for feminist activists and educators was not simply the conservative ideological legacy bequeathed by the Progressive generation or the abandonment of separate network strategies. It was that feminists were underrepresented, dispersed, and isolated in male-dominated institutions. They had to devise a new agenda for change that would enable elite women to achieve positions of power as insiders and still implement policies of direct benefit to other women—no mean task in any period.

As Lucy Slowe's career indicates, women in male-run institutions had to expend large amounts of energy and political capital in order to secure small gains or, in some instances, merely to survive. Despite this, she never wavered in her conviction or her optimism. Slowe's commitments to education and to ending all social inequalities were inextricably linked. For Slowe, schools at all levels were to be models of equality in practice and sources of ethical values that banished prejudice and pointed the way to social change. Her feminism, which derived from her experiences and goals as a black and as a woman, was deeply embedded in a female world of work, struggle, and sisterly support. Above all, she sought to make that world her legacy to Howard women.

Notes

1. Estelle Freedman, "Separatism as Strategy: Female Institution Building and American Feminism, 1870–1930," *Feminist Studies* 5 (Fall 1979): 512–29; Rosalind Rosenberg, *Beyond Separate Spheres: Intellectual Roots of Modern Feminism* (New Haven: Yale University Press, 1982).

2. Florence M. Read, "The Place of the Women's College in the Pattern of Negro Education," *Opportunity* (November 1937): 267–70.

3. Marion Thompson Wright, "Lucy Diggs Slowe," *Notable American Women, 1607–1950: A Biographical Dictionary* (Cambridge, Mass.: Harvard University Press, 1971), pp. 299–300; Rayford W. Logan, "Lucy Diggs Slowe," *Dictionary of American Negro Biography*, ed. Rayford W. Logan and Michael R. Winston (New York: W. W. Norton, 1982), pp. 559–60; Lucy Diggs Slowe, "The Evolution of Dora Cole," Lucy Diggs Slowe Papers, Moorland-Spingarn Research Center, Howard University, Washington, D.C.

4. Wright, "Lucy Diggs Slowe"; Logan, "Lucy Diggs Slowe"; Coralie Franklin Cook, "Lucy D. Slowe—Student"; Dwight O. W. Holmes, Eulogy for Lucy Diggs Slowe, 25 October 1937, Slowe Papers.

5. Wright, "Lucy Diggs Slowe"; Logan, "Lucy Diggs Slowe"; Logan,

Howard University: The First Hundred Years, 1867–1967 (New York: University Press, 1969).

6. Ibid.

7. Washington *Star,* 15 March 1946; Alumnae to Board of Trustees, Howard University, Slowe Papers.

8. Cook, "Lucy D. Slowe—Student," Slowe Papers.

9. Rosalyn Terborg-Penn, "Afro-Americans in the Struggle for Woman Suffrage" (Ph.D. diss., Howard University, 1977); Angela Davis, *Women, Race, and Class* (New York: Random House, 1981), pp. 99–148; Terborg-Penn, "Discrimination against Afro-American Women in the Woman's Movement, 1830–1920," in *The Afro-American Woman: Struggles and Images,* ed. Sharon Harley and Rosalyn Terborg-Penn (Port Washington, N.Y.: Kennikat Press, 1978), pp. 17–27.

10. Slowe to Prof. Ralph J. Bunche, 2 November 1931, Slowe Papers; Slowe, "The Colored Girl Enters College," *Opportunity,* November 1937, pp. 276–79; Slowe to J. Stanley Durkee, 23 May 1923, Slowe Papers.

11. Holmes, Eulogy; Slowe to Prof. Ralph J. Bunche, 2 November 1931; Slowe to Pres. Mordecai Johnson, 11 March 1933, Slowe Papers.

12. Slowe to J. Stanley Durkee, 23 May 1923; Slowe to Durkee, 22 January 1923, Slowe Papers.

13. Slowe, Address to the Faculty and Student Body at Howard University, Slowe Papers. Howard University was much less restrictive with its students than other black colleges because it was less dependent on churches and white philanthropists for support. Raymond Wolters, *The New Negro on Campus: Black College Rebellions of the 1920s* (Princeton: Princeton University Press, 1975), pp. 70–136. For restrictions on women on other black campuses, see Joe M. Richardson, *A History of Fisk University, 1865–1946* (University: University of Alabama Press, 1980), pp. 84–88, 107, and B. Baldwin Dansby, *A Brief History of Jackson College* (Jackson, Miss.: Jackson College, 1953), pp. 83–84. Langston Hughes, after visiting a large number of black college campuses in 1932, commented that it was "like going back to mid-Victorian England, or Massachusetts in the days of witch-burning Puritans." Richardson, p. 88.

14. "Dean Lucy D. Slowe," Slowe Papers; Slowe, "The Colored Girl"; Slowe, Address to the Faculty, Slowe Papers.

15. Slowe to Martha McAdoo, 13 January 1925; Slowe to J. Stanley Durkee, 23 May 1923, Slowe Papers. Mayme Foster, dean of women at Fisk University, agreed with her. Foster to Slowe, 17 February 1937, Slowe Papers.

16. Valarie Justiss and Hilda Davis, "Tribute," *The Journal of the College Alumnae Club,* January 1939, pp. 72–74; Margaret Jean Grooms, "Lucy Diggs Slowe," Slowe Papers.

17. Ibid.; Alumnae to Trustees, Slowe Papers.

18. Memorandum on the Mills Case; Clarence Harvey Mills to Slowe, 11 January 1927; Mills to Slowe, 13 January 1927; Mary Burrill note attached to Mills letter of 11 January 1927, 1939, Slowe Papers.

19. Burrill note attached to Mills letter of 11 January 1927, 1939; Slowe to Members of the Executive Committee of the Board of Trustees, Howard University, 24 March 1931, Slowe Papers; Logan, *Howard University,* pp. 292, 336–38.

20. Slowe, "The Colored Girl"; Slowe, Address to the Faculty; Slowe, The Administration of Personnel Work at Howard University; Slowe, "The College Woman and her Community," April 1934, Slowe Papers; Slowe, To the Women of the Freshman Class, 15 April 1937, Howard University Archives, Moorland-Spingarn Research Center, Howard University, Washington, D.C.

21. Slowe, "The Colored Girl"; Slowe, Address to the Faculty, Slowe Papers.

22. Ibid. In order to instill self-confidence in women students, she also invited Mary Beard to campus to talk on the role of women in history. Slowe to Mary Beard, 16 March 1936, Slowe Papers.

23. Slowe, "The Colored Girl"; Slowe, Address to the Faculty, Slowe Papers.

24. Ibid.; Charles S. Johnson, *The Negro College Graduate* (College Park, Md.: McGrath Publishing, 1938), pp. 349–50. Educated black women were also more likely to be active church members than educated black men. Johnson, p. 347.

25. Walter Dyson, *Howard University, The Capstone of Negro Education: A History: 1867–1940* (Washington, D.C.: Howard University, 1941), pp. 65–66; "Dean Lucy D. Slowe," Slowe Papers; Logan, "Lucy Diggs Slowe."

26. Logan, *Howard University,* pp. 292, 336–38; Regret Expressed that President and Trustees of Howard Did Not Appreciate Dean Slowe, 8 November 1937; Slowe to Executive Committee, 24 March 1931; Memo for Mrs. Marian Bannister, n.d.; Charlotte Atwood to the Board of Trustees, Howard University, 25 September 1933, Slowe Papers.

27. Logan, *Howard University,* pp. 169, 292, 336–38; Regret Expressed, 8 November 1937; Slowe to Mr. Crawford, 17 August 1933 (Document 5 of this chapter); Slowe to Executive Committee, 24 March 1931; Bannister memo; Atwood to the Trustees, 25 September 1933, Slowe Papers.

28. Bannister memo; Note attached to Bannister memo by Mary Burrill; Atwood to Trustees, 25 September 1933, Slowe Papers. Mary McLeod Bethune advised her to refrain from going to the newspapers in support of her position. Bethune to Slowe, 23 November 1933, Slowe Papers.

29. Slowe to Crawford, 17 August 1933; Bannister memo; Slowe to Mrs. Howard Thurman, 14 December 1935, Slowe Papers.

30. Dyson, *Howard University,* pp. 398–439; Wolters, *The New Negro,* pp. 70–136.

31. Slowe to Mrs. Howard Thurman, 14 Demember 1935, Slowe Papers.

1. "THERE ARE TOO MANY OF ME"

Lucy Diggs Slowe dedicated this poem, dated May 1919, to "my good friend M.P.B. whose sympathetic encouragement induced me to write these lines, I dedicate them with the hope that some day I may show my better self to the world.—L.D.S."

There are too many of
me for me to know each one;
and yet I feel each clamoring
for a hearing from the depths
within me. Which shall I listen
to, above all others?

One, an abrupt, frank, insistent self
Telling truth, though truth may not be wise?
Or one a vigorous self, following life
To the great outdoors, in hunting, golfing
Tennis, hikes and all the like?
Or one, demure, lonely, loving solitude,
The evening stars, the sunset glow?
Or one, a mother self; a self
Which feels life's eternal pulses
beat wildly sometimes; mildly ever?
All these are me; pray tell me
Which shall become articulate?
which shall lift its voice above all others?
which shall be the voice triumphant
Guiding me on to full expression
Of that best and noblest self—,
That portrait of God divine?

Lucy Diggs Slowe Papers, Moorland-Spingarn Research Center, Howard University, Washington, D.C. Reproduced by permission.

2. LUCY D. SLOWE TO DR. J. STANLEY DURKEE

At the time of her hiring by President Durkee of Howard University, Slowe sent this unequivocal statement regarding the terms of her employment.

PUBLIC SCHOOLS OF THE DISTRICT OF COLUMBIA
M Street Junior High School
Washington, D.C.

Lucy D. Slowe   May 31, 1922
Principal

Dr. J. Stanley Durkee
Howard University
Washington, D. C.

My dear Dr. Durkee:

I have been going over in my own mind the various points brought
out in the conference which I had with you on May 12th. In order that
I may be sure that my understanding is correct, I am setting down the
several agreements covered for your verification and endorsement:

1. It is agreed that I be appointed to the position of Professor of
English in the School of Education with the administrative duties of
Dean of Women.

2. It is agreed that the salary for the two positions shall be not less
than $3200.

3. It is agreed that I be permitted to name a confidential Clerk whose
entire time will be spent in my office.

4. It is agreed that the suite of rooms now used by the Acting Dean
of Women be placed at my disposal, but that I shall not be required to
live on the campus.

5. It is agreed that all women in charge of girls in the University shall
be directly responsible to me in all matters affecting the girls in their
care.

6. It is agreed that all policies pertaining to the women in the University shall emanate from my office with the approval of the President.

Under such conditions as these, I shall be happy to work with you
in building up a fine morale among the women in the University.

Very sincerely yours,
(Signed) Lucy D. Slowe

Lucy Diggs Slowe Papers, Moorland-Spingarn Research Center, Howard University,
Washington, D.C. Reproduced by permission.

3. EXCERPTS FROM "THE EDUCATION OF NEGRO COLLEGE WOMEN FOR SOCIAL RESPONSIBILITY"

Slowe's lifelong concerns with the essential connection between the community and the academy and the importance of women's education for leadership roles are evident in these excerpts from a March 11, 1931 speech she made at Teachers College, Columbia University.

And this brings me to the most important consideration, the task of the college for training leaders of the masses. In the first place most college administrators must change their philosophy of education in reference to their women students. They must realize that whether they like it or not, the life that women are leading today is different from that which was led by their grandmothers. For this present day life demands that women must be ready to make their contribution not only to the home but also to the economic, political, and civic life of the communities. Therefore, to train the Negro women for these fields should be one of the important tasks of the college. . . .

Negro College Women have a most challenging opportunity for leadership of their people in education and in civic service if their communities and their schools are joined together for the purpose of developing the inate [*sic*] power which so many of them possess.

It is my earnest hope that Negro college women will accept their great opportunity for leadership of their people and that they shall obtain from their colleges and from their communities the sort of education "which fits one to perform justly, skillfully and magnanimously all the offices" which he is called upon to fill.

Lucy Diggs Slowe, Moorland-Spingarn Research Center, Howard University, Washington D.C. Reproduced by permission.

4. LUCY DIGGS SLOWE TO DR. MORDECAI W. JOHNSON

Her own life presented for students as a model of "culture and refinement," Slowe fought constantly against the leveling effect she saw in the university's encroachment in the areas of her purview—the women's dining halls and dormitories.

March 11 1933

My dear President Johnson:

I received on February 16, your letter enclosing a copy of the letter from Mr. V. D. Johnson, Treasurer of the University, in reference to his taking over the management of the Women's Dormitories.

This letter came as a complete surprise to me, since I did not know until its receipt that there was any legislation of the Board of Trustees giving the Treasurer control of the Women's Dormitories. The legislation quoted by Mr. Johnston, found in ARTICLE III, Section 5, of the By-Laws of the Board of Trustees, cannot possibly mean that the Treasurer shall control the personnel of the women's dormitories since it would be contrary to all accepted practice for a man to be in charge of the people who supervise women students.

It is reasonable to suppose that the By-Law refers to financial management, but it is most unreasonable to believe that the Trustees contemplated taking away from me the control of the staff which I have assembled and trained to direct the life of the women who live in the dormitories. I have entered into no financial agreements of any kind without the written consent of the Secretary-Treasurer of the University. All contracts for food have been signed by him, and charges of any kind against students have come through him from the Trustees. This is as it should be. However, when the new Treasurer suggests that he extend his relations in the women's dormitories to the control of the people who have direct contact with the women students, he is going into a field which is not properly his.

When the dormitories were being constructed, I made an exhaustive study of dormitory management, not only by reading the latest literature on the subject, but also by conferring with experts in institutional management. Those who make a business of operating dormitories for women in a co-educational school believe that women's dormitories should be under the control of the Dean of Women or under some woman who takes her place. . . .

After working our plans for the operation of the Women's Dormitories, I took my organization scheme to the Institutional Management Department of Columbia University for criticism and counsel. The experts in the department went over it with me and approved the present set-up. We discussed at length the system of dual control of personnel and reached the conclusion that it was bad for several reasons, hence we deliberately avoided it at Howard University.

Even if I had not been advised against dual control of personnel by people who ought to know its defects, I would not have recommended it for our new dormitories. You will recall that when the women ate in the old dining room, I had no control over the personnel. The women who ran the dining hall were responsible to the Secretary-Treasurer. There was constant complaint from the President's office down to the students about the general conduct of the dining hall. I could do nothing but confer on matters that caused the complaints and request the women in charge to take them up. There was constant misunderstanding and sometimes friction because my ideals for the dining hall were not always their ideals. I had the responsibility for the students, but not the authority needed to discharge my responsibility.

I discussed this situation with you time after time when complaints were made by you and to you about the lack of culture and refinement in the dining hall. I also discussed with you the necessity of my having complete control over the personnel which dealt with women students when we moved into the new dormitories. You, at that time, saw the necessity for this and agreed with my plans for putting this policy into practice.

In order that you and the Trustees might see the entire organization graphically represented, Mr. Cassell and I submitted to you, under date of March 5, 1931, a large chart containing the complete personnel needed for operating the three dormitories. In addition to the chart, I sent you under date of March 20, 1931, a letter in which I discussed the philosophy of sound dormitory management.

On July 10, 1931, the Executive Committee of the Board of Trustees upon your recommendation approved the plans which I submitted with only such modifications as limited finances demanded. They gave me the authority to recommend and assemble the needed personnel and to operate the dormitories under the unified control of my office. The matter of collecting money for room and board and of entering financial agreements with dealers was left in the hands of the business office where it belongs.

No word of mine is needed to show how wise the decision of the Trustees was. The dormitories have been operated with success from every standpoint. The students are well behaved, there are no complaints of any consequence about food and best of all there has been no deficit in the dining department. The staff is working well and is deeply interested in making the dormitories places of refinement and comfort for the students.

Since there is not a single good reason for placing the personnel of the dining hall under Mr. Johnston, and many reasons for not doing this, I sincerely hope that the Board of Trustees will not reverse its vote of July 10, 1931, and revert to the evils of the old system which we are so happily rid of now.

You can readily see what complications would arise in having two different people supervising personnel in the same building. A student would be under one jurisdiction on the first floor and under another on the second floor. Surely Mr. Johnson would not expect to come into a woman's building to supervise the people in charge of any phase of the student's life.

Up to this point, I have confined my discussion chiefly to the dining department, but Mr. Johnson even wishes to control the Assistant Director of the dormitory whose business it is to inspect students' bedrooms and to train students in neatness and care of their rooms. She must hold conferences with students and supervise many of their activities if the director is absent. Surely Mr. Johnston will see the impropriety of his supervising the work of a woman who has such intimate relations with women students.

I visit the dormitories every day to check up on the staff. Is he going to perform these duties? I hold weekly staff meetings for the purpose of unifying the various activities of the individuals who work in the dormitories. Up to the present moment, the finest sort of spirit prevails among my staff, and I believe that the organization should be let alone.

To return to the By-Law under which Mr. Johnston claims a right to take over almost entire control of the Women's Dormitories. These By-Laws must have been formulated when there was no Dean of Women or when the dining department was separate and distinct from the home-life of the women students. The situation in the University so far as women are concerned is quite different now, therefore, the By-Law should be changed to meet modern conditions.

The Treasurer should certainly receive financial reports regularly from the dormitories as he now does; he should sanction all financial commitments as he now does; but under no circumstances should he have any control over the people who work there. Even the janitors who are paid by the Maintenance Department should be directly responsible to the Director of the dormitory for she is always on the premises and knows what work should be done and when it should be done. In other words, there should be unified control of the personnel of the Women's Dormitories in the interest of economy of effort and efficiency of operation.

I believe that the intent of the By-Law under question is to give financial control of the dormitories to the Treasurer, but I do not believe that the Trustees mean to give him the right to select and control personnel in a woman's building. I am surprised that Mr. Johnston wishes to do this.

In conclusion, I recommend that since the Trustees definitely placed the Women's Dormitories under the control of the Dean of Women, that since they are being operated successfully and with no deficit in the dining department; and that since the present plan is in keeping with sound practice and has the endorsement of experts in this field, that the dormitory management remain as it is.

I recommend further that Article 3, Section 5 be clarified so that the duties of the Treasurer shall be confined to the collection of fees for room and board and to the sanctioning of all financial commitments in connection with the women's dormitories.

Very truly yours,
Lucy D. Slowe
Dean of Women

Dr. Mordecai W. Johnson
President
Howard University

LDS:WW

5. LUCY D. SLOWE TO GEORGE A. CRAWFORD

President Johnson's power plays are thoroughly explored in this letter to a trustee during Slowe's eleventh year of tenure at the university.

Washington, D. C.
August 17, 1933

My dear Mr. Crawford:

Although you are not a member of the Executive Committee which has been given power to provide "quarters" for the Dean of Women at Howard University, I want you to know of a conference which I had with President Johnson on August 15. He called me in and told me the Committee was willing to give me another house, but that they would not allow me money for a housekeeper. I told him it was customary for the Dean to be allowed upkeep and something for services when she was required to live in a University house. He said Howard could not afford it. I told him that I could not afford to take $40 or $50 a month out of my salary to pay for a person to care for the house. He then said he would suggest that I move into the dormitory. I told him that a woman who had heavy administrative duties such as I had could not get the quiet and relaxation necessary for her work if she lived in a dormitory. I told him that a person of my age and experience should have a comfortable home and that I had always been used to one. However, he left the matter right here.

It seems as soon as I get over one hurdle, he sets up another. It now looks as if I will have to assume an expense of $500 or $600 a year for a housekeeper, or live in the dormitory in order not to disobey the instructions of the Board. It looks as if the President has created this dilemma for me to force me into the dormitory where he thinks a dean of women should be. He does not want the Dean of Women at Howard to have any administrative standing; he has always wanted her to be a matron. This is why he took me off the Board of Deans in spite of the fact that the nature of my work—as shown in my annual report—relates to every school in the University.

I do not want the Trustees to think I am a nuisance, but in order to defend myself and to defend the interests of the women students I have had to take matters to the Executive Committee. The President has resented this so vigorously that I fear if I go to the Committee with the 'new' dilemma, they will not receive the matter sympathetically.

I asked the President to put in writing just what the Executive Committee proposed to do about the house, but he refused to do this. He said it was sufficient for me to have an understanding with him. I WANT NO MORE UNDERSTANDINGS WITH PRESIDENTS, FOR MY PRESENT TROUBLE IS DUE TO MY HAVING AN UNDERSTANDING WITH DR. DURKEE.

Before I leave my own home I want to know just what the University agrees to do. I cannot depend on any verbal agreements.

It is obvious to me and to many people in the University that the President is seeking a way to humiliate or inconvenience me so that in desperation I will give up the Deanship. He showed this very plainly when he placed me next to the University dump. He suggested to me, on Tuesday the 15th, that I devote myself to teaching and then I could stay home. It means nothing to him that I am one of the few trained and experienced Deans in the country.

He knows that all my money has gone into this home that I am buying with a friend; that last October I spent $2,500 in improvements; that all the expense here is shared 50 per cent by my friend; but he did not give the Trustees this information when he had them vote to move me to the campus.

He knows, too, that I have two able assistants who are members of the faculty who are head of each dormitory and directly supervise the women in them; he knows that I am in my office from 9 in the morning until 5 in the afternoon, and that I see dozens of students during the course of the day and return in the evening to University and student functions; he knows that my home is used by both students and faculty constantly. But he is determined to put up such conditions as will take from me all joy in the work and force me to give it up. THAT IS HIS AIM.

Howard women graduates all over the country are writing me about the matter, for they see in it not the 'mere change of residence for the Dean' but a change in the status of the position. They also resent the implied reflection on the women that they need me to watch them. They feel that Howard University ought to continue her example of having the Dean of Women an administrative officer for women and not a glorified matron.

Maybe I have no right to say these things to you, but I must trust somebody and I don't know whom to turn to. There is not a single man in my own family to confer with, and no woman can cope with this situation alone. If Dr. Slowe—my brother—were living, things would have been very different.

With deep appreciation for your interest, I am

> Very sincerely,
> Lucy D. Slowe
> Dean of Women

Lucy Diggs Slowe Papers, Moorland-Spingarn Research Center, Howard University, Washington, D.C. Reproduced by permission.

6. MARY BURRILL TO T.L. HUNGATE

Slowe received a postmortem hearing in this letter from her friend and companion to the trustees.

Washington D. C.
October 30, 1937

Mr. T. L. Hungate
Chairman, Howard University Board of Trustees
Office: Auditor, Teachers College
Columbia University, New York, N. Y.

Dear Sir:

I wish to acknowledge your letter of October 25 expressing to me your sympathy in the passing of Dean Lucy D. Slowe. We who loved Dean Slowe wish so much that the fine tributes paid her in the telegrams, letters and Resolutions from the Trustees of Howard University on the occasion of her death had found expression in deeds before her passing.

Howard University, under the leadership of Dean Slowe, with her nation-wide influence, might have become a great experimental ground for the education of Negro women had not the President and Trustees of the University handicapped her by allotting her the meager budget of $200 per year for the development of her social program for almost one thousand women.

Furthermore, in Howard University as unfortunately in many of our colleges, the measure of appreciation is the salary paid the members of its faculty. This being true, Howard never gave to Dean Slowe the measure of appreciation that the words of Trustees indicate she had. May I quote to you a letter written by Dean Slowe May 27, 1937 to a member of the Trustee Board:

You will recall that you mentioned to me at the time of the April meeting that I had been recommended for an increase in salary.

Up to the present time nothing has been said to me about my getting an increase, but several of my associates have been told that increases for them have been approved. I am wondering what happened to mine. You know (1) that I left a $4,000 salary to come to Howard University; (2) that I am a full professor, yet have never received a full professor's salary of $4,000; (3) that my present salary is the same as that of the Dean of Girls in the high schools here; (4) that in fifteen years I have received a total increase of $500.

Before all the money is allocated will you please see to it that justice is done me?

This, the Board of Trustees did not do.

Again, Ladies and Gentlemen, I give you my profound gratitude for your expressions of sympathy, for one who loses a friend of twenty-five years standing is in sore need of such words; but in accepting your sympathy may I at the same time extend to you my sympathy in that Howard University had in its midst in the person of Lucy D. Slowe a great woman but its President and Board of Trustees could not see it.

Very truly yours,
Mary Burrill.

Copies sent to all
Howard University Trustees.

Lucy Diggs Slowe Papers, Moorland-Spingarn Research Center, Howard University, Washington, D.C. Reproduced by permission.

7. EXCERPT FROM "THE DEAN OF WOMEN IN A MODERN UNIVERSITY"

Published in the Journal of the College Alumnae Club *in the year after her death, Slowe makes clear her conviction that women must be educated for leadership roles in the community and her vision of a university's dean of women as the facilitator of such an education.*

One of the most important tasks of the Dean of Women at Howard University is to advise the administration, the faculty, and the women students themselves on those aspects of education peculiar to women, if they are to be prepared to take their places in the social order as it exists today. Whether women are going to be wives and mothers, or whether they are going to follow careers outside the home, they need to emphasize in their college courses those subjects which will prepare them to be intelligent citizens and which will enable them to participate in the activities which all good citizens engage in. College women in general, and Negro college women in particular, need training in the science of government, of economics and community organization especially as they affect the lives of children who, after all, are women's particular interest.

College women need guidance in their choice of vocations in the light of the realities which they will face after they leave college, and it is the business of the Dean of Women to see that such guidance is furnished. Since vocational information is directly related to courses of study, the Dean of Women should be in close touch with the academic policies of the college and should be in position to advise the administration on curriculum matters of especial interest to women. President Harper of the University of Chicago must have had some such service to the University as this in mind when he appointed Alice Freeman Palmer as first Dean of Women in America.

Aside from her duties as educational adviser on women's interests, the Dean of Women has several other specific pieces of work to do for students. These lie outside of the classroom but are closely related to the students' success in the classroom. These activities come under the following general heads:

1. Housing of students in well appointed and well conducted homes.

2. Seeking and supervising part-time employment for those who must pay their own way.

3. Assisting students in organizing and executing some form of self-government in order that they may be educated in the art of self-control.

4. Planning activities which will connect students definitely with community life in order that they may realize their social responsibility.

A word or two on each of these divisions of the work of the Dean of Women may indicate to our alumni how important to students each is.

Proper housing is one of the most potent influences in the education of college students. Dormitories designed and furnished in accordance with decent standards of living, and presides over by members of the faculty trained in their supervision can be and should be valuable adjuncts to the academic life of the student. Because this is so, administrators in first-class colleges have sought to provide their students with houses which are in good taste and which are administered by persons of culture and learning. No longer are dormitories places in which students only sleep; they are centers of cultural activities, for rest and relaxation in association with one's fellows.

The new dormitories at Howard University were designed as complete homes for women of refinement. Each one is presided over by a member of the faculty who has a lighter teaching program than other members of the faculty and who has had definite training in dormitory management. The heads of these dormitories are the educational mentors of the students outside the classroom, and plan systematic programs of cultural activities in cooperation with the students in their buildings. These activities not only develop the individuality and initiative of the students, but they reduce to a minimum opportunities for unsocial behavior which frequently results in disciplinary action. In other words, the dormitory director assists students in finding useful ways of using information learned in the classroom.

In a University like Howard there are always students in financial need. With very limited sums of money for scholarships, University officials attempt to provide or to secure outside the institution part-time employment for its students. It is the business of the Dean of Women to make investigations to determine the needs of the women students and to secure work for as many as she possibly can. This phase of the work of the Dean of Women if properly done, consumes a great deal of time for not only must the student applying for work be investigated, but also the place where she is to work. In an urban university, many calls come for students to work after school hours but unless the Dean of Women has some way of being reasonably sure that the student is to work under proper conditions, she is not justified in sending a woman to a given place. Placing a student in a job means checking on the student as to health, as to scholarship, as to character, and checking on the employer as to working conditions. All of these checks consume a great deal of time but they must be done in the interest of the student.

Much complaint has come from community leaders in various sections of the country that college graduates do not take sufficient interest in community activities. At Howard University the Dean of Women has arranged for women students to become intimately acquainted with some of the projects of the community that have to do with making life happier and more wholesome. Many women students, for instance, do volunteer work with the Associate Charities, with the Juvenile Protective Association, with the Young Women's Christian Association, with the Southwest and the Southeast Community Houses. Others pay visits to the Juvenile Court and survey the needs of under-privileged children and youths in the neighborhood of the University. Whatever principles have been learned in the classes in Sociology, Political Science, and Economics can be tested in their practical applications by students working in these several community activities. Work of this sort is supervised by the Dean of Women or some one whom she interests in the activities. No greater service can be rendered students than directing their attention in practical ways to community needs.

Lucy Diggs Slowe Papers, Moorland-Spingarn Research Center, Howard University, Washington, D.C. Reproduced by permission.

Contributors

Karen Anderson is an associate professor of history at the University of Arizona. A specialist in women's history, her work focuses primarily on issues relating to women, work, and family. She is the author of *Wartime Women: Sex Roles, Family Relations, and the Status of Women during World War II* and numerous articles on women in recent U.S. history. She is currently completing *Changing Woman: A History of Racial Ethnic Women in Modern America*, a study of American Indian, black, and Mexican-origin women in the twentieth century.

Geraldine Jonçich Clifford teaches in the Graduate School of Education, University of California at Berkeley and in the Women's Studies Program and the social science field major. In 1988 and 1989 she directed the Education Abroad Program of the University of California for Australia and New Zealand. Her books include *Edward L. Thorndike: The Sane Positivist* (1968, 1984), *The Shape of American Education* (1976), and *Ed School: A Brief for Professional Education* (1988). The first woman to receive a Guggenheim Fellowship for research in education, she is currently working on a social history of women in teaching: *Those Good Gertrudes: The Woman Teacher in America*.

Ellen Fitzpatrick is visiting assistant professor at Massachusetts Institute of Technology on the history faculty. Her book *Endless Crusade:*

Women, Social Scientists, and Progressive Reform is forthcoming from Oxford University Press.

Margaret Gillett, Ed.D., LL.D., is Macdonald Professor of Education at McGill University, Montreal, Canada and founding director of the Mc-Gill Centre for Research and Teaching on Women. For more than twenty years she has been active in women's affairs on campus, teaching women's studies, helping to initiate a survey on women, contributing to the establishment of the Senate Committee on Women, and writing the first history of women at any Canadian university. This work, *We Walked Very Warily: A History of Women at McGill* (1981) has been supplemented by *A Fair Shake: Autobiographical Essays by McGill Women* (1984), which she co-edited with Kay Sibbald. The most recent of Gillett's eight books is *Dear Grace: A Romance of History* (1986), based on letters to Grace Ritchie, a pioneer woman student at McGill (B.A. 1888) and close friend of Dr. Maude Abbott, whose portrait Gillett presents here.

Elizabeth Griego is director of planning and research at Mills College. Her chapter on Clelia Mosher is drawn from her dissertation, *A Part and Yet Apart: Clelia Duel Mosher and Professional Women at the Turn of the Century*, which was awarded the Outstanding Dissertation Prize from the Graduate School of Education, University of California, Berkeley in 1983.

Florence Howe is director of The Feminist Press at The City University of New York and professor of English at City College/CUNY. The essay on Theresa McMahon grew out of her work in a dozen college and university archives in 1974, while holding a Ford Fellowship for Women in Society. Several other essays on the history of women and higher education have been published in *Myths of Coeducation: Selected Essays, 1964–1983*. She is the author of more than a hundred essays, several books, and the editor of six volumes in literature, history, and women's studies. Currently, she is planning a new and revised edition of *No More Masks! An Anthology of Poetry by American Women* and writing autobiographical essays.

Virginia Scharff is working on a book on American women and the automobile in the early car culture. She has written about women and technology, and about the history of women in the American West. Scharff has directed and participated in a number of public humanities programs, including spending several summers touring with Chautauqua troupes. She lives in Albuquerque and teaches history at the University of New Mexico.

The Feminist Press at The City University of New York offers alternatives in education and in literature. Founded in 1970, this nonprofit, tax-exempt educational and publishing organization works to eliminate sexual stereotypes in books and schools and to provide literature with a broad vision of human potential. The publishing program includes reprints of important works by women, feminist biographies of women, and nonsexist children's books. Curricular materials, bibliographies, directories, and a quarterly journal provide information and support for students and teachers of women's studies. Through publications and projects, The Feminist Press contributes to the rediscovery of the history of women and the emergence of a more humane society.

New and Forthcoming Books

Always a Sister: The Feminism of Lillian D. Wald, a biography by Doris Groshen Daniels. $24.95 cloth.

Bamboo Shoots after the Rain: Contemporary Stories by Women Writers of Taiwan, 1945–1985, edited by Anne C. Carver and Sung-sheng Yvonne Chang. $29.95 cloth, $12.95 paper.

A Brighter Coming Day: A Frances Ellen Watkins Harper Reader, edited by Frances Smith Foster. $29.95 cloth, $13.95 paper.

The Daughters of Danaus, a novel by Mona Caird. Afterword by Margaret Morganroth Gullette. $29.95 cloth, $11.95 paper.

The End of This Day's Business, a novel by Katharine Burdekin. Afterword by Daphne Patai. $8.95 paper.

Families in Flux (formerly *Household and Kin),* by Amy Swerdlow, Renate Bridenthal, Joan Kelly, and Phyllis Vine. $9.95 paper.

How I Wrote Jubilee *and Other Essays on Life and Literature,* by Margaret Walker. Edited by Maryemma Graham. $29.95 cloth, $9.95 paper.

Lillian D. Wald: Progressive Activist, a sourcebook edited by Clare Coss. $7.95 paper.

Not So Quiet: Stepdaughters of War, a novel by Helen Zenna Smith. Afterword by Jane Marcus. $26.95 cloth, $9.95 paper.

Seeds: Supporting Women's Work in the Third World, edited by Ann Leonard. Introduction by Adrienne Germain. Afterwords by Marguerite Berger, Vina Mazumdar, Kathleen Staudt, and Aminita Traore.

Sister Gin, a novel by June Arnold. Afterword by Jane Marcus. $8.95 paper.

These Modern Women: Autobiographical Essays from the Twenties, edited and with a revised introduction by Elaine Showalter. $8.95 paper.

Truth Tales: Contemporary Stories by Women Writers of India, selected by Kali for Women. Introduction by Meena Alexander. $22.95 cloth, $8.95 paper.

We That Were Young, a novel by Irene Rathbone. Introduction by Lynn Knight. Afterword by Jane Marcus. $29.95 cloth, $10.95 paper.

What Did Miss Darrington See? An Anthology of Feminist Supernatural Fiction, edited by Jessica Amanda Salmonson. Introduction by Rosemary Jackson. $29.95 cloth, $10.95 paper.

Women Composers: The Lost Tradition Found, by Diane Peacock Jezic. $29.95 cloth, $12.95 paper.

For a free, complete backlist catalog, write to The Feminist Press at The City University of New York, 311 East 94 Street, New York, NY 10128. Send book orders to The Talman Company, Inc., 150 Fifth Avenue, New York, NY 10011. Please include $1.75 postage and handling for one book, $.75 for each additional.